the Unofficial Guide® to New Orleans

1st Edition

U^{the}nofficial Guide® to New Orleans

1st
Edition

Eve Zibart

with Bob Sehlinger

Macmillan • USA

Every effort has been made to ensure the accuracy of information throughout this book. Bear in mind, however, that prices, schedules, etc., are constantly changing. Readers should always verify information before making final plans.

Macmillan Travel
A Simon & Schuster Macmillan Company
1633 Broadway
New York, New York 10019-6785

Produced by Menasha Ridge Press
Design by Barbara E. Williams

MACMILLAN is a registered trademark of Macmillan, Inc.
UNOFFICIAL GUIDE is a registered trademark of Simon & Schuster, Inc.
ISBN 0-02-862246-4
ISSN 1096-5211
Manufactured in the United States of America
10 9 8 7 6 5 4 3 2 1

First edition

CONTENTS

List of Illustrations

ACKNOWLEDGMENTS

Scores of New Orleanians were gracious enough to talk about their city, both on and off the record, and I thank them all, especially Lea Sinclair and Diane Genre.

Everybody needs a place to hang out: Thanks to Jeanine, Julie and Kim (say hello to Tiffany), Michael, Mark, and Viva.

Very special thanks to tour guide and amateur historian Noah Robert for more good stories than I could fit in (and to Kith & Kin for lending him to me) and also to Billy Murphy; to Grace Rogers for taking on the chauffeuring duty; and to Chris Rose and Lynne Bachleda for their contributions.

As always, thanks to Bob, Molly, Clay, Grace, Holly, Patt, Erin Willder, Carolyn Hassett, and Nicki Florence for pushing forward and reading behind.

—*Eve Zibart*

The Unofficial Guide® to
New Orleans

1st
Edition

Let the Good Times Roll

A fine spring evening in Jackson Square. As the sun gradually lowers, the shadows of St. Louis Cathedral and the Cabildo stretch across the flagstones, brushing the tables of the tarot readers; young couples with souvenir hurricane cups stand around a man playing saxophone, its case open in front of him.

And there it is, the mystique of New Orleans in a single vignette: empire, religion, music, voodoo, and alcohol. *Laissez les bons temps rouler* — let the good times roll.

And yet there are some who say that what passes for "good times" is rolling too long and too strong these days. There is a battle raging for the soul of New Orleans, most visibly in and around the French Quarter; and while it is not a contest between good and evil, at least not in the classical sense, it will in the next few years determine whether the character of this unique city is lost, restored, or permanently altered.

That the character of the Vieux Carré has already changed is clear from a few hours' acquaintance. An odd confluence of factors — renovation of some older houses into upscale condominiums and the gradual decline of others; a much-publicized increase in street crime and heavy investment by outside commercial interests into redevelopment, frequently uprooting smaller local firms — has reduced the number of the French Quarter's permanent residents from about 15,000 only a few years ago to an estimated 4,000 today.

A high tide of cheap souvenir and T-shirt shops has swamped Bourbon Street, and glossy, private club–style strip clubs, several bankrolled from out of town, are squeezing out the older, more authentic burlesque houses. At the same time, the number of bars offering heavily amplified rock and blues music, their doors open and competing for volume dominance, makes the retreat of jazz and Dixieland more obvious. Sit-down bars that specialized in classic New Orleans cocktails such as hurricanes and Sazeracs, touristy though they may have seemed before, now appear almost quaintly sophisticated in the face of carryout frozen margarita and daiquiri counters with their crayon-colored mixes spinning in laundromat-like rows.

Yes, souvenir shops are brighter than bars, but they certainly have less character. Sure, live blues is great, but it's more Texan than Louisianan.

Mardi Gras, once the most elegant and elaborate of festivities, has become the world's largest frat party, its traditions degraded, its legends distorted, and its principal actors, the Grand Krewes, overshadowed by the mobs of drinking and disrobing "spectators." Several of the oldest and most prestigious Krewes have withdrawn from the celebration, and travel agents say as many residents flee New Orleans during Carnival as tourists come in.

Altogether, New Orleans is in danger of becoming a parody of itself, a mini-Epcot or Busch Gardens' Old Country simulacrum. The posters and prints feature wrought-iron fences, but the real courtyards are gated and locked tight. Steamboats play recorded music intentionally out of tune—"old-fashioned" in the hokiest sense. Self-appointed tour guides mix all their legends together: The statue in St. Anthony's Garden behind St. Louis Cathedral, memorializing French sailors who volunteered as nurses during a yellow fever epidemic, has even been explained as "the Mardi Gras Jesus" because his outstretched hands are supposedly reaching for throws!

And yet for all the tawdriness and commercialization, one cannot help falling under the city's spell. It is a foreign country within American borders, not merely a multilingual hodgepodge like Miami or New York but a true Creole society blended through centuries. It is Old South in style, New South in ambition. It has a natural beauty that refutes even the most frivolous of franchised structures, a tradition of craftsmanship and even luxury that demands aesthetic scrutiny and surrender, and a flair for almost exquisite silliness—like those Jackson Square psychics with their Pier 1 Imports turbans—that keeps all New Orleanians young. Fine arts and fashionable cuisine center; voodoo, vampires, and Mardi Gras. It's all muddled up, sometimes enchanting, sometimes infuriating.

We hope to help you find the real New Orleans, the old and gracious one, that is just now in the shadow of the Big Too-Easy. We want to open your heart, not your wallet. We think you should leave Bourbon Street behind and visit City Park, one of the finest and most wide-ranging public facilities in the United States. We want you to see Longue Vue House as well as St. Louis Cemetery. We hope you'll walk Chartres Street in the evening shade, watch the mighty Mississippi churn contemptuously past the man-made barriers, and smell the chicory, whiskey, and pungent swamp water all mixed together the way Andy Jackson and Jean Lafitte might have the night before the great battle.

So get ready, get set, go. *Laissez les bons temps rouler!*

About This Guide

■ How Come "Unofficial"? ■

Most guides to New Orleans tout the well-known sights, promote the local restaurants and hotels indiscriminately, and leave out a lot of good stuff. This one is different.

Instead of pandering to the tourist industry, we'll tell you if the food is bad at a well-known restaurant, we'll complain loudly about high prices, and we'll guide you away from the crowds and traffic for a break now and then.

Visiting New Orleans requires wily strategies not unlike those used in the sacking of Troy. We've sent in a team of evaluators who toured each site, ate in the city's best restaurants, performed critical evaluations of its hotels, and visited New Orleans' wide variety of nightclubs. If a museum is boring, or standing in line for two hours to view a famous attraction is a waste of time, we say so — and, in the process, hopefully make your visit more fun, efficient, and economical.

■ Creating a Guidebook ■

We got into the guidebook business because we were unhappy with the way travel guides make the reader work to get any usable information. Wouldn't it be nice, we thought, if we were to make guides that are easy to use?

Most guidebooks are compilations of lists. This is true regardless of whether the information is presented in list form or artfully distributed through pages of prose. There is insufficient detail in a list, and prose can present tedious helpings of nonessential or marginally useful information. Not enough wheat, so to speak, for nourishment in one instance, and too much chaff in the other. Either way, these types of guides provide little more than departure points from which readers initiate their own quests.

Many guides are readable and well researched, but they tend to be difficult to use. To select a hotel, for example, a reader must study several pages of descriptions with only the boldface hotel names breaking up large blocks of text. Because each description essentially deals with the same variables, it is difficult to recall what was said concerning a particular hotel. Readers generally must work through all the write-ups before beginning to narrow their choices. The presentation of restaurants, nightclubs, and attractions is similar except that even more reading is usually required. To use such a guide is to undertake an exhaustive research process that requires examining nearly as many options and possibilities as starting from scratch. Recommendations, if any, lack depth and conviction. These guides compound rather than solve problems by failing to narrow travelers' choices down to a thoughtfully considered, well-distilled, and manageable few.

■ How Unofficial Guides Are Different ■

Readers care about the authors' opinions. The authors, after all, are supposed to know what they are talking about. This, coupled with the fact that the traveler wants quick answers (as opposed to endless alternatives), dictates that authors should be explicit, prescriptive, and above all, direct. The authors of the *Unofficial Guide* try to do just that. They spell out alternatives and recommend specific courses of action. They simplify complicated destinations and attractions and allow the traveler to feel in control in the most unfamiliar environments. The objective of the *Unofficial Guide* authors is not to give the most information or all of the information, but to offer the most accessible, useful information.

An *Unofficial Guide* is a critical reference work; it focuses on a travel destination that appears to be especially complex. Our authors and research team are completely independent from the attractions, restaurants, and hotels we describe. *The Unofficial Guide to New Orleans* is designed for individuals and families traveling for the fun of it, as well as for business travelers and conventioneers, especially those visiting the Crescent City for the first time. The guide is directed at value-conscious, consumer-oriented adults who seek a cost-effective, though not Spartan, travel style.

■ Special Features ■

The *Unofficial Guide* offers the following special features:

- Friendly introductions to New Orleans' most fascinating neighborhoods.

- "Best of" listings giving our well-qualified opinions on things ranging from raw oysters to blackened snapper, 4-star hotels to 12-story views.

- Listings that are keyed to your interests, so you can pick and choose.

- Advice to sight-seers on how to avoid the worst of the crowds; advice to business travelers on how to avoid traffic and excessive costs.

- Recommendations for lesser-known sights that are away from the French Quarter, but are no less worthwhile.

- A zone system and maps to make it easy to find places you want to go to and avoid places you don't.

- Expert advice on avoiding New Orleans' notorious street crime.

- A hotel chart that helps you narrow down your choices fast, according to your needs.

- Shorter listings that include only those restaurants, clubs, and hotels we think are worth considering.

- A table of contents and detailed index to help you find things fast.

- Insider advice on the French Quarter, Mardi Gras, Jazz Fest, best times of day (or night) to go places, and our secret weapon, New Orleans' streetcar system.

What you won't get:

- Long, useless lists where everything looks the same.

- Information that gets you to your destination at the worst possible time.

- Information without advice on how to use it.

■ How This Guide Was Researched and Written ■

Although many guidebooks have been written about New Orleans, very few have been evaluative. Some guides come close to regurgitating the hotels' and tourist office's own promotional material. In preparing this work, nothing was taken for granted. Each hotel, restaurant, shop, and attraction was visited by a team of trained observers who conducted detailed evaluations and rated each according to formal criteria. Team members conducted interviews with tourists of all ages to determine what they enjoyed most and least during their New Orleans visit.

While our observers are independent and impartial, they did not claim to have special expertise. Like you, they visited New Orleans as tourists or business travelers, noting their satisfaction or dissatisfaction.

The primary difference between the average tourist and the trained evaluator is the evaluator's skills in organization, preparation, and observation. The trained evaluator is responsible for much more than simply observing and cataloging. Observer teams use detailed checklists to analyze hotel rooms, restaurants, nightclubs, and attractions. Finally, evaluator ratings and observations are integrated with tourist reactions and the opinions of patrons for a comprehensive quality profile of each feature and service.

In compiling this guide, we recognize that a tourist's age, background, and interests will strongly influence his or her taste in New Orleans' wide array of attractions and will account for a preference for one sight or museum over another. Our sole objective is to provide the reader with sufficient description, critical evaluation, and pertinent data to make knowledgeable decisions according to individual tastes.

■ Letters, Comments, and Questions from Readers ■

We expect to learn from our mistakes, as well as from the input of our readers, and to improve with each new book and edition. Many of those who use the *Unofficial Guides* write to us asking questions, making comments, or sharing their own discoveries or lessons learned in New Orleans. We appreciate all such input, both positive and critical, and encourage our readers to continue writing. Readers' comments and observations will be frequently incorporated in revised editions of the *Unofficial Guide,* and will contribute immeasurably to its improvement.

How to Write the Authors:

Eve and Bob
The Unofficial Guide to New Orleans
P.O. Box 43059
Birmingham, AL 35243

When you write, be sure to put your return address on your letter as well as on the envelope—sometimes envelopes and letters get separated. And remember, our work takes us out of the office for long periods of time, so forgive us if our response is delayed.

Reader Survey

At the back of the guide you will find a short questionnaire that you can use to express opinions about your New Orleans visit. Clip the questionnaire out along the dotted line and mail it to the above address.

"Inside" New Orleans
for Outsiders

It's a funny thing about New Orleans travel guides: Most of them tell you too much, and a few tell you too little. It's because it's such a complex city, so ornate and enveloping and layered with history and happenstance, that it's hard to stop acquiring good stories and passing them on.

But the fact is, statistics show that the majority of visitors to New Orleans stay only three or four days—and frequently that even includes spending part of the time in seminars or conventions. How much can you squeeze into a long weekend? How much do you want to see? Walking tours of the French Quarter and Garden District often point to buildings with obscure claims to fame and with only partial facades to their name (and no admission offered in any case). Walking tours of the farther reaches are often redundant; even the keenest architecture critic will probably lose heart trying to cover the third or fourth neighborhood in 48 hours. Some tour books either stint on shopping or endorse every dealer in town; some forget any fine arts or theater productions at all, as if Bourbon Street bars were the sole form of nightlife available in the city. Some are too uncritical, some too "insider." Some have all the right stuff, but are poorly organized; some are easy to read, but boring.

So, hard as it is to limit this book, we have—sort of. We have tried to make the do-it-yourself walking tours short enough that they won't exhaust you, but full enough of sights and stories to give you the city's true flavor. (And if you want to do more, we'll tell you how.) We've tried to take things easy, but we don't forgive exploitation or boost unworthy distractions. If it isn't fun, informative, or accurate, we don't want you to go. If there's a better alternative, we want you to know. We don't make purely philosophical judgments—some people believe in the supernatural, some don't—but we do try to evaluate what you get for your money in a dispassionate fashion. We hope to keep the quality of your visit high, and the irritation quotient low.

We've also divided the attractions up in various ways, often overlapping, so you can pick out the ones you'd most enjoy: In "Planning Your Visit," we suggested attractions by type—family style, musical, festive, spooky, and so on. The neighborhood profiles in Part One are more strictly geographical descriptions to help you get your bearings and focus your interests, while the zone maps are designed to help you with the logistics of arranging accommodations and sight-seeing. More elaborate walking tours are laid out for you in "Sight-Seeing and Tours," and particular museums and exhibits in each zone are explored in more detail and rated for interest by age group in the chapter entitled "New Orleans' Attractions."

For those who don't wish to do-it-themselves at all, we have listed a number of commercial and customized tours tailored to almost any interest, also in "Sight-Seeing and Tours."

In addition, even granting that your time will be tight, we have included a list of opportunities to exercise or play. That's partly because we at the *Unofficial Guides* try to keep up with our workouts when we're on the road, and also because you may be visiting old friends, old teammates, and tennis players. Beyond that, although you may not think you'll want to make time for a run or ride, experience has taught us that sight-seeing and shopping can be exhausting, make you stiff, make you long for the outdoors— and New Orleans has some of the prettiest outdoors you'll ever see.

Finally, for visitors lucky enough to have more than a couple of days to spend, or who are returning for a second or third go-round, we have sketched out a few excursions outside the city.

Please do remember that prices and hours change constantly. We have listed the most up-to-date information we can get, but it never hurts to double-check times in particular (if prices of attractions change, it is generally not by much). And although usually a day or so is all the advance notice you need to get into any attraction in New Orleans, if your party is large, you might try calling ahead.

■ How Information Is Organized: By Subject and ■ by Geographic Zones

In order to give you fast access to information about the best of New Orleans, we've organized material in several formats.

Hotels   Since most people visiting New Orleans stay in one hotel for the duration of their trip, we have summarized our coverage of hotels in charts, maps, ratings, and rankings that allow you to quickly focus your decision-making process. We do not go on, page after page, describing lobbies and rooms which, in the final analysis, sound much the same. Instead, we concentrate on the specific variables that differentiate one hotel from another: location, size, room quality, services, amenities, and cost.

Entertainment and Nightlife   Visitors frequently try several different clubs or nightspots during their stay. Since clubs and nightspots, like restaurants, are usually selected spontaneously after arriving in New Orleans, we believe detailed descriptions are warranted. The best nightspots and lounges in New Orleans are profiled by category under nightlife (see pages 144–172).

Restaurants We provide plenty of detail when it comes to restaurants. Since you will probably eat a dozen or more restaurant meals during your stay, and since not even you can predict what you might be in the mood for on Saturday night, we provide detailed profiles of the best restaurants in and around New Orleans.

Geographic Zones Once you've decided where you're going, getting there becomes the issue. To help you do that, we have divided the city into geographic zones:

Zone 1   French Quarter

Zone 2   Central Business District

Zone 3   Uptown below Napoleon

Zone 4   Uptown above Napoleon

Zone 5   Downtown/St. Bernard

Zone 6   Mid-City/Gentilly

Zone 7   Lakeview/West End/Bucktown

Zone 8   New Orleans East

Zone 9   Metairie below Causeway

Zone 10   Metairie above Causeway/Kenner/Jefferson Highway

Zone 11   West Bank

Zone 12   North Shore

All profiles of hotels, restaurants, and nightspots include zone numbers. If you are staying at the Royal Orleans, for example, and are interested in Creole restaurants within walking distance, scanning the restaurant profiles for restaurants in Zone 1 (the French Quarter) will provide you with the best choices.

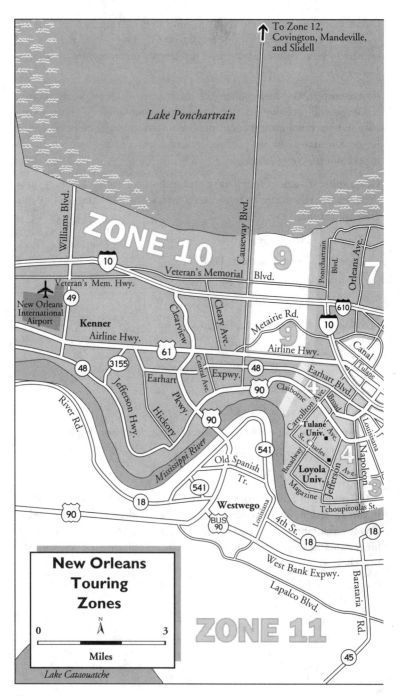

To Zone 12,
Covington, Mandeville,
and Slidell

Lake Ponchartrain

ZONE 10

Williams Blvd.

10

Veteran's Memorial Blvd.

Causeway Blvd.

Veteran's Mem. Hwy.

New Orleans
International
Airport

49

Kenner

Airline Hwy.

61

48

3155

Clearview

Cleary Ave.

Metairie Rd.

Airline Hwy.

9

9

7

Ponchartrain Blvd.

Orleans Ave.

610

10

Canal

Tulane

Earhart

Central Ave.

Expwy.

48

90

Earhart Blvd.

Claiborne

4

Broad

Carrollton Ave.

Louisiana

Jefferson Hwy.

Pkwy.

Hickory

90

**Tulane
Univ.**

St. Charles Ave.

Napoleon

4

River Rd.

Mississippi River

541

Old Spanish
Tr.

Broadway

**Loyola
Univ.**

Magazine

Jefferson Ave.

3

541

18

Westwego

BUS
90

Louisiana

4th St.

Tchoupitoulas St.

18

18

90

West Bank Expwy.

Lapalco Blvd.

Barataria Rd.

ZONE 11

45

**New Orleans
Touring
Zones**

N

0   3

Miles

Lake Cataouatche

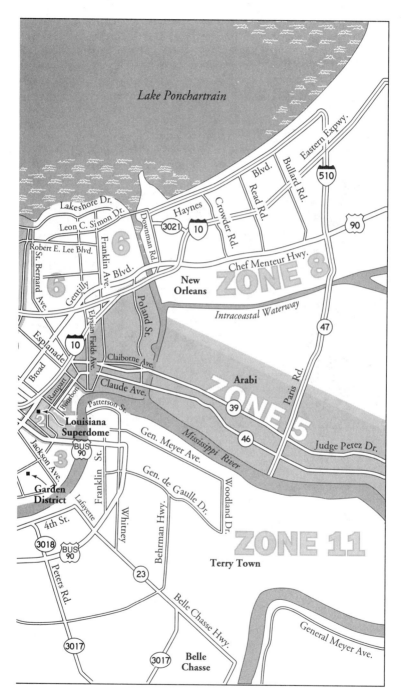

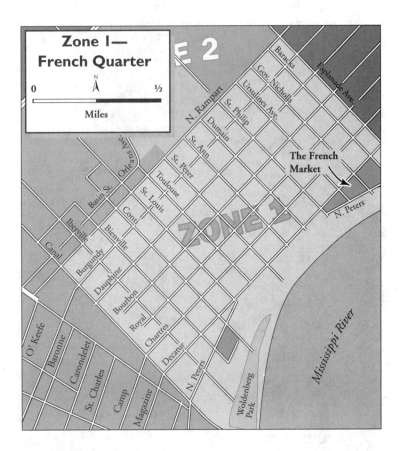

Zone 1—
French Quarter

0   N   ½

Miles

The French Market

Esplanade Ave.

Baracks

Gov. Nicholls

Ursulines Ave.

St. Philip

N. Rampart

Dumain

St. Ann

St. Peter

Toulouse

St. Louis

Conti

Bienville

Iberville

Canal

Burgundy

Dauphine

Bourbon

Royal

Chartres

Decatur

N. Peters

Basin St.

Orleans Ave.

O' Keefe

Baronne

Carondelet

St. Charles

Camp

Magazine

Woldenberg Park

Mississippi River

ZONE 2

ZONE 1

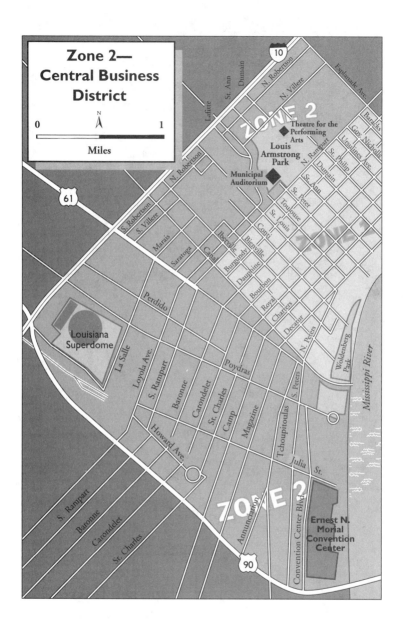

Zone 2—
Central Business
District

0 ᴺ⬆ 1

Miles

Theatre for the Performing Arts

Louis Armstrong Park

Municipal Auditorium

ZONE 2

ZONE 1

Louisiana Superdome

Perdido

Poydras

Ernest N. Morial Convention Center

ZONE 2

Mississippi River

Woldenberg Park

Esplanade Ave.

Barracks

Gov. Nicholls

Ursulines Ave.

St. Philip

Dumaine

St. Ann

St. Peter

Toulouse

St. Louis

Conti

Bienville

Iberville

Canal

Marais

Saratoga

Burgundy

Dauphine

Bourbon

Royal

Chartres

Decatur

N. Peters

N. Robertson

N. Villere

N. Rampart

St. Ann

Dumain

St. Ann

Lafitte

S. Robertson

S. Villere

La Salle

Loyola Ave.

S. Rampart

Baronne

Carondelet

St. Charles

Camp

Magazine

Tchoupitoulas

S. Peters

Howard Ave.

Julia St.

Annunciation

Convention Center Blvd.

S. Rampart

Baronne

Carondelet

St. Charles

10

61

90

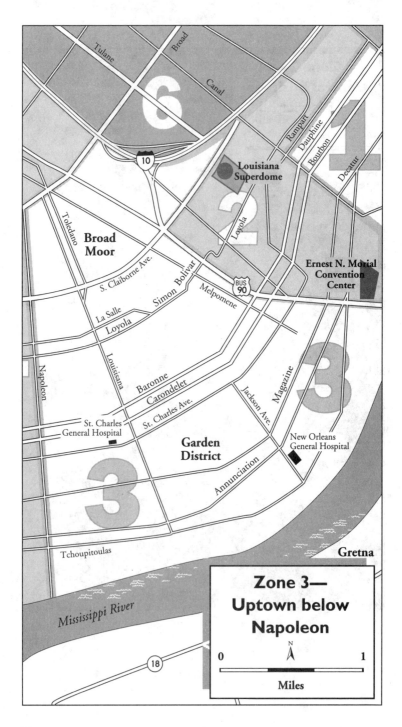

Zone 3—
Uptown below
Napoleon

0   1

Miles

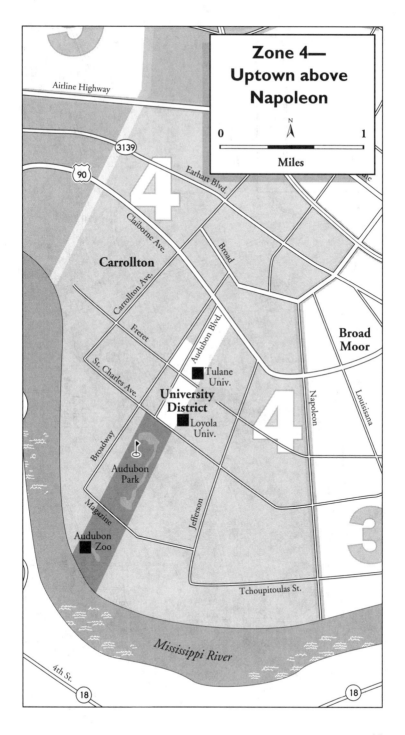

Zone 4—
Uptown above
Napoleon

N

0 1

Miles

Airline Highway

3139

90

Earhart Blvd.

Claiborne Ave.

Broad

Carrollton

Carrollton Ave.

Freret

Audubon Blvd.

Broad
Moor

St. Charles Ave.

Tulane
Univ.

University
District

Napoleon

Louisiana

Loyola
Univ.

Broadway

Audubon
Park

Magazine

Jefferson

Audubon
Zoo

Tchoupitoulas St.

Mississippi River

4th St.

18

18

15

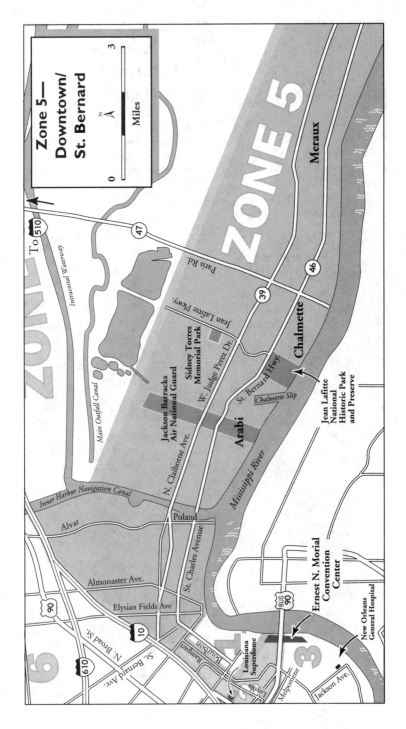

Zone 5—
Downtown/
St. Bernard

Miles

0   3

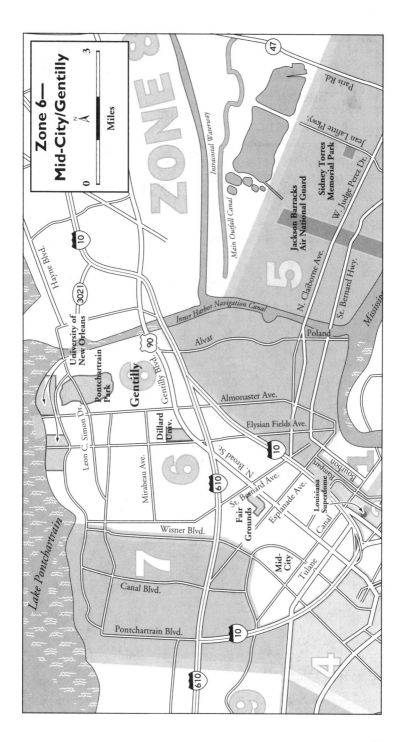

17

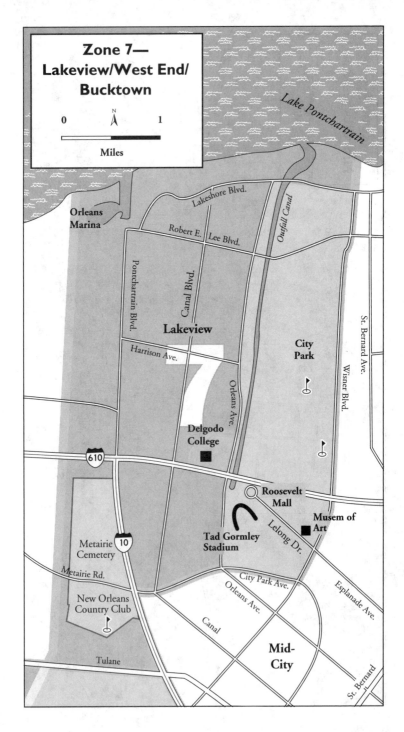

Zone 7—
Lakeview/West End/
Bucktown

0   N   1

Miles

Lake Pontchartrain

Orleans
Marina

Lakeshore Blvd.

Robert E. Lee Blvd.

Outfall Canal

Pontchartrain Blvd.

Canal Blvd.

Lakeview

Harrison Ave.

City
Park

St. Bernard Ave.

Orleans Ave.

Wisner Blvd.

**Delgodo
College**

610

Roosevelt
Mall

**Musem of
Art**

Lelong Dr.

10

Metairie
Cemetery

**Tad Gormley
Stadium**

Metairie Rd.

City Park Ave.

Esplanade Ave.

New Orleans
Country Club

Orleans Ave.

Canal

**Mid-
City**

Tulane

St. Bernard

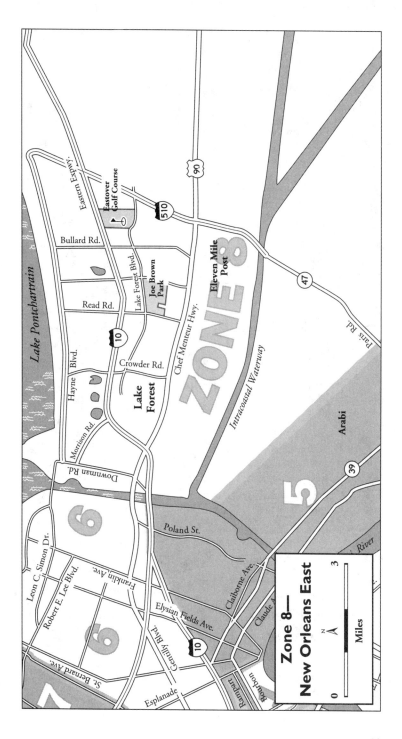

Zone 8—
New Orleans East

N
Miles
0   3

19

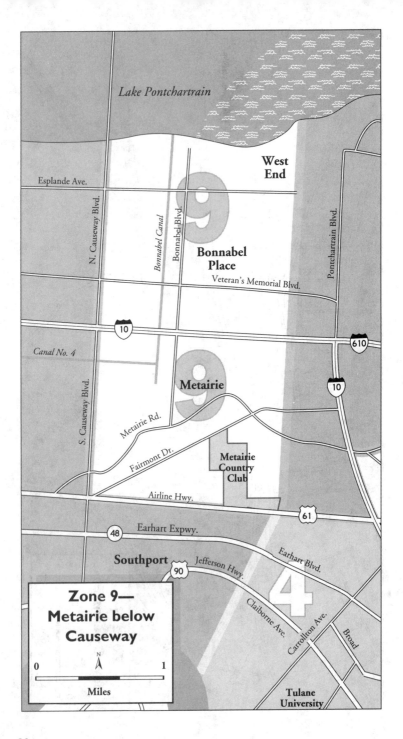

Lake Pontchartrain

West End

Esplande Ave.

Bonnabel Place

Veteran's Memorial Blvd.

N. Causeway Blvd.

Bonnabel Canal

Bonnabel Blvd.

Pontchartrain Blvd.

9

10

610

Canal No. 4

S. Causeway Blvd.

9

Metairie

10

Metairie Rd.

Fairmont Dr.

Metairie Country Club

Airline Hwy.

61

48

Earhart Expwy.

Southport

90

Jefferson Hwy.

Earhart Blvd.

4

Claiborne Ave.

Carrollton Ave.

Broad

Zone 9—
Metairie below
Causeway

N

0   1
Miles

Tulane
University

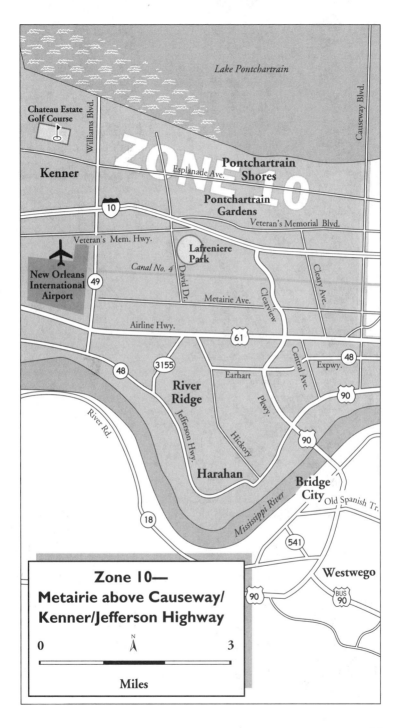

Lake Pontchartrain

Chateau Estate
Golf Course

Williams Blvd.

Causeway Blvd.

Kenner

ZONE 10

Esplanade Ave.

**Pontchartrain
Shores**

**Pontchartrain
Gardens**

Veteran's Memorial Blvd.

10

Veteran's Mem. Hwy.

**Lafreniere
Park**

Canal No. 4

**New Orleans
International
Airport**

49

David Dr.

Metairie Ave.

Clearview

Cleary Ave.

Airline Hwy.

61

48

3155

Earhart

Central Ave.

Expwy.

48

90

**River
Ridge**

River Rd.

Jefferson Hwy.

Hickory

Pkwy.

90

90

Harahan

Mississippi River

**Bridge
City**

Old Spanish Tr.

18

541

Westwego

BUS
90

90

Zone 10—
Metairie above Causeway/
Kenner/Jefferson Highway

0

N

3

Miles

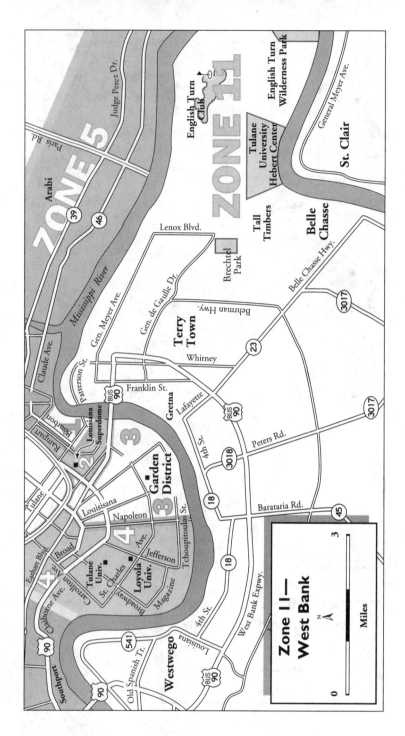

Zone 11—
West Bank

N

Miles

0   3

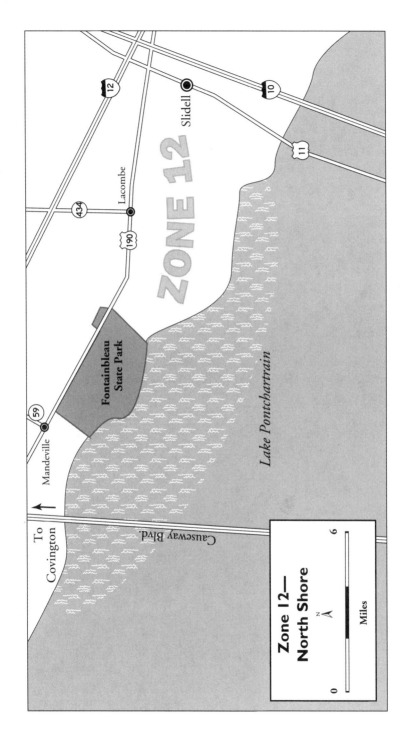

Zone 12—
North Shore

Miles

0   6

Understanding the City

A Too-Short History of a Fascinating Place

New Orleans exercises a strange fascination over the rest of the country, and for good reasons. It's foreign territory at heart. It has flown three national flags—four if you count the Confederate States of America—and changed hands a couple more times than that. Like several other Southern cities, it was "occupied" by then-hostile Union forces, had to repulse periodic Indian raids, and might briefly have flown a British flag as well if the Battle of Chalmette had turned out differently. (And legend aside, it might easily have done so.)

New Orleans lives an unnatural, enchanted life, an island dug out of the swamp some yards lower than the river that embraces it, tethered to the world by bridges, ferries, and causeways. Its proximity to the swamps exposed it to almost yearly epidemics of yellow fever and malaria; it was flattened by hurricanes and nearly erased by floods—and yet, with all that water around it, it was destroyed twice by fire, catastrophes that wiped out almost the entire first century of construction.

It has been identified with both the most sophisticated Creole culture and good ol' boy corruption, and produced a rich ethnic melting pot and the most virulent racism. Oil drillers rescued it in the first half of the twentieth century, and international petroleum prices nearly strangled it in the second half. When it threw a World's Fair to celebrate itself, it nearly went bankrupt.

Somehow, as low as New Orleans gets—as much as ten feet below sea level in some places—it never quite goes under. Like that Ol' Man River that surrounds it, like those famous good times, it just keeps rollin' along.

■ The French Flag ■

Louisiana stood at the center of imperial rivalries right from the beginning. Columbus had claimed the New World for Spain, but the other seagoing nations pursued colonial territory and (as they believed) Asian trade as well. In 1534, Cartier sailed down the St. Lawrence waterways from Canada into the northeast. Only a few years later, Hernando de Soto established settlements along the southeastern coast and actually reached the Mississippi River, but the Spanish attention was distracted by the conquest of Mexico, and the expansion into the American Southwest and northern South America.

In the 1670s, while the British were planting Union Jacks up and down the Atlantic Coast from Maine to the Carolinas, Rene Cavelier, Sieur de la Salle, set out from Canada with the intention of following the Illinois River all the way to the mouth of the Mississippi River in the Gulf of Mexico and, in 1682, claimed for France all the land drained by that great river. He named it all Louisiana in honor of his sovereign lord King Louis XIV, the Sun King. Spain launched a huge manhunt in an attempt to intercept him (when they finally reached his settlement, mutineers had already murdered him), but by the turn of the century, other Frenchmen had established settlements all over Louisiana and what is now Mississippi.

In 1699, the Sieur de Bienville planted a huge cross at the bend of the Mississippi River, and 20 years later his brother, the Sieur d'Iberville, stood looking out over the Mississippi where it connected to Lake Pontchartrain through Bayou St. John and ordered the construction of his "city." He named it La Nouvelle Orleans in honor of the then-Regent of France, Phillipe, Duc d'Orleans.

Marshy, mosquito-infested, and oppressively hot, New Orleans became the subject of a real estate scam that might have inspired the Florida land boom of the 1920s. Posters and supposed "eyewitness" tales of the gold-rich territories—most promulgated by an unscrupulous Scottish crony of the regent's with the ironic name of John Law—lured thousands of French optimists and opportunists to the crude settlement, where they had little choice but to build the city they had been told already existed. Life in the settlement was so meager that in 1727, 88 women convicts were released from prison on the condition they accompany the Ursuline nuns to New Orleans as mail-order brides.

Nor were they the only unaristocratic imports: In fact, there were probably far more exiles, common soldiers, petty thieves, intractable slaves, and indentured servants than blue-bloods, and fewer "casket girls"—the respectable but impoverished girls who also came out as wards of the Ursuline Sisters with their few belongings packed in small trunks—than street women. (It should be remembered, however, that life in Paris was very hard, and that many young girls fell or were sold into prostitution as a last resort, so that their records should perhaps not be held against them. They worked pitifully hard for their "freedom" in New Orleans, in any case.)

The city was laid out with the streets in a grid around a central square that faced the river: the Place d'Armes, now Jackson Square. "Vieux Carré" means Old Square, and it almost was square. It extended from the Mississippi River to Rampart Street, which was once literally a rampart or wall, and from Esplanade Avenue to Iberville. (It's generally said to extend to Canal Street, but that was originally intended to be just that, a canal, dividing the French Quarter from the American sector in what is now the Central Business District.) Gradually the settlement grew, and merchants, traders, and practical farmers, as well as more restless aristocrats, came to Louisiana to stay. With them came the beginnings of a caste system—aristocrats, merchants, farmers, and servants—that became a hallmark of Creole society.

■ The Spanish Flag ■

In the 1760s, two other groups arrived, one in extremity and one in force. The first were the Acadians—the Cajuns—whom the British forced to leave their homes in Nova Scotia, and who settled in the bayou country west of New Orleans. Though most New Orleanians looked down on the Acadians, whom they considered countrified (to say the least) and speaking an "uncultured" dialect, the Cajuns were French nationals, driven into exile by France's enemy, Britain, and so they were accepted.

The other new arrivals were anything but welcome: the Spanish. To their dismay, the ethnically proud New Orleanians discovered that King Louis XV had secretly surrendered the Louisiana Territory to his Spanish cousin Charles III (some writers say it was used to pay off huge gambling debts). The residents violently resisted the Spanish takeover, and succeeded in routing the first commissioner sent from Madrid. But in 1769, a more determined mercenary with the intriguing name of Don Alexander O'Reilly, or "Bloody Reilly," arrived with an armada of 24 warships and 2,000 soldiers, executed several of the most prominent rebels, and made swift work of the insurrection. The Arsenal and Cabildo were erected on the square ("cabildo" is actually the term for governor of the colony), and the French and Spanish aristocrats began inviting each other to dinner.

By the time the American colonies declared independence from Britain, New Orleans was an important Spanish outpost, which made the entrance of the Spanish on either side potentially decisive. Finally, Oliver Pollack, a New Orleans native who had become a member of the Continental Congress, persuaded the then-governor of New Orleans, Bernardo de Galvez, to send a convoy of 20 supply ships to New York to aid the American revolutionaries. Great Britain then declared war on Spain, and de Galvez proceeded to roll over the British colonies along the Gulf of Mexico. Consequently, although Lafayette and the French are usually remembered as the key European allies of the American forces, the Spanish also played an essential role.

■ Three Flags in Forty Years ■

Unsettled as New Orleans' first 60 years had been, the next 40 or so were just as dramatic.

The city was devastated by two great fires, the first in 1788 and the second, which came even before the community had really rebuilt, in 1794. Only a couple of buildings remain from before that time: the Old Ursuline Convent, whose age is undisputed; and Madame John's Legacy, which is the subject of some debate. Determined to prevent a third disaster, the Spanish promulgated new building codes: All roofs had to be tiled, houses were to be made of brick or plaster rather than wood, high walls had to separate gardens so one fire wouldn't spread from house to house, and alleys were eliminated to prevent a bellows effect that might feed a blaze. So what is considered classical French Quarter architecture, including arches, rear courtyards, and the famous ornamental wrought iron of the balconies and fences, is actually Spanish.

Meanwhile, the city's merchants and shippers continued to prosper. It was not only a major exchange point between the eastern and midwest markets, it controlled much of the European-American import and export trade. New Orleans' strategic position, both for trade and defense, made it highly attractive to the new government of the United States, and a source of great regret to the French government as well. The city remained solidly French at heart, with a royalist cast of mind—another wave of French aristocrats had fled the Revolution in 1789 —and so when Napoleon set out to establish his own French Empire, New Orleans became a spoil of war. In 1800, by yet another secret treaty, Spain ceded the Louisiana Territory back to France.

But when things began to turn sour for Napoleon, he decided to cash in the American colonies to finance his European campaigns. When President

Thomas Jefferson offered to buy the port of New Orleans, Napoleon surprised him by offering to sell the entire Louisiana Territory for the sum of $15 million. The sale was officially transacted in the Cabildo on December 20, 1803. Louisiana became a U.S. territory, and in 1812, it was granted statehood, a fact commemorated in the arrival of the first steamboat, the *New Orleans.*

The purchase of Louisiana by the United States inspired thousands of Americans—and not-yet-Americans, recent immigrants still looking to make their home there—to ride, raft, barge, stage, and even walk to the thriving port. In the first 7 years, the population of New Orleans more than tripled, from 8,000 to 25,000. A huge non-Creole community sprang up just upriver of the Vieux Carré, near the older sugar plantations and sometimes on top of them, and out into what is now the Garden District. The new arrivals were not exactly welcomed by the more-civilized-than-thou New Orleanians. The Scotch-Irish, who had already settled along the Carolina and Virginia mountains, were a new and particularly rough presence among the old Creole families; they took the word "riffing," Gaelic for "rowing," and contemptuously referred to all the laboring men and hardscrabble farmers who poled their way down the Mississippi as "riff raff."

A huge drainage canal emptying into the river was marked out along the upriver edge of the French Quarter, ostensibly as part of the construction of the booming city, but also to serve as an emotional if not actual barrier between the French Quarter, now also known as the First Municipality, and the American quadrant, officially the Second Municipality. In response to this subtle but elegant slight, the Americans laid out their sector, called Faubourg Ste. Marie, as a sort of mirror image of the Vieux Carré, with Lafayette Square (a seemingly polite tribute, but subtly claiming the marquis for the Americans) as a Place d'Armes; St. Patrick's as a rival to St. Louis Cathedral; and Gallier Hall, which was the official City Hall until the 1950s, in place of the old Cabildo. Each had its own mayor and council, each its own regulations. The city was not officially united until 1852.

As it happened, the canal was never built; and for a time, although it was referred to as the "neutral ground," the swath was the site of repeated brawls between Creole residents and brash, aggrandizing newcomers. Eventually a grand boulevard, divided by a great median, was paved through the strip instead, and was dubbed Canal Street. Even so, it remained the acknowledged border between the two communities, and ever since, the New Orleans term for a median strip is the neutral ground.

■ "The Whites of Their Eyes" ■

The winning of the Battle of New Orleans has become such a touch-stone of American pride that it has inspired hit songs (Johnny Horton's "Battle of New Orleans") and Hollywood epics (*The Buccaneer*, with Charleton Heston as Andrew Jackson and Yul Brynner as Jean Lafitte). The legend is glorious and shining—overnight excavations, secret meetings, Redcoats coming ghostlike through the fog to the banshee wailing of bag-pipes and Jackson shouting, "Don't shoot until you see the whites of their eyes!"

As is frequently the case with warfare, the truth is a little muddier. It is true, however, that the ruthless and lucky Jackson lost only 13 men while killing 2,000 British Army. It's probably true that without the combined efforts of 5,000 American, Creole, black, and Indian volunteers—not to mention the heavy arms and ammunition donated by Lafitte from his store of plunder—Jackson's Tennessee soldiers would have had a much harder time. And considering how intensely most Native Americans hated Jackson, who had commanded many brutal campaigns against the Creek and Choctaw tribes, their participation was even more remarkable.

The great irony is, the war was already over. The Treaty of Ghent had been signed a fortnight earlier. However, the campaign and victory served to unite the previously rancorous Creole and American communities, and to establish New Orleans, distinctive as it might be, as an all-American city.

■ Free Blacks, Slaves, and Mulattos ■

The presence of African and Caribbean blacks, both free and slave, in New Orleans can be documented as far back as the early clearing of the French Quarter neighborhood. In 1721, only a couple of years after the city's founding, there were 300 slaves for only 470 Europeans, and a "code noir" was enacted in 1724 as a way of regulating the slave trade.

Free blacks, people "of color" (meaning of mixed blood in almost any proportion), and slaves made up a substantial proportion of the popula-tion—the free blacks of New Orleans outnumbering those of any other Southern city. In fact by 1803, there were exactly as many blacks and mixed-blood residents as whites: 4,000 of each, with 1,300 (40%) of the blacks being free. By the beginning of the Civil War, there were an esti-mated 30,000 free blacks in New Orleans.

An elaborate caste system emerged in which the mulattos assumed social rank according to the amount of white (Creole) blood in their veins. Mulattos were half black, half white. Quadroons were one-quarter white (meaning one white grandparent), and octaroons were one-eighth white. Women of mixed blood were considered exceedingly handsome, and though the Creole aristocrats would never have dreamed of marrying a black woman, it was considered a mark of wealth and good taste — another bit of conspicuous consumption — to have a well-spoken, elegantly dressed black or mixed-blood mistress. Many of these women became heads of the Creoles' city homes, running second establishments, in effect, and if they were really lucky, might be freed at their master's death. If not, at least their children might be recognized as illegitimate offspring and left some money.

It was so widely recognized a custom that the Creoles might formally court these women, making their mothers (or owners) semi-official offers that included property settlements, allowances, etc. So the annual Quadroon Balls became notorious tableaux of young "available" beauties, something between an auction and a debutante ball. Many of them were held in the Orleans Ballroom, a grandiose hall built in 1817 and now a special events site within the Bourbon Orleans Hotel.

As time went on, the *gens de couleur libre* — literally "free men of color" — developed their own quite sophisticated culture; the sons of Creole aristocrats were often given first-class educations befitting their (fathers') status, and some were even sent to Europe, where such colonial cross-breeding was commonplace. Alexandre Dumas, the author and playwright, was mulatto, and by some accounts Napoleon's Josephine, from the island of Martinique, had some mixed-blood ancestors as well. Both free and slave blacks were allowed to congregate in Congo Square, near North Rampart and Orleans Streets in what is now Louis Armstrong Park; as many as 2,000 gathered in this onetime Choctaw meeting place on Sundays to sing, dance, trade, eat, fight, and perhaps practice a little voodoo until the curfew, a cannon in the Place d'Armes, sounded. (In tribute, the first New Orleans Jazz and Heritage Festival in 1969 was held in Congo Square.)

In the years just before the Civil War, New Orleans was the largest slave market in the nation. Blacks, even well-to-do mulattos and freemen, remained mere residents rather than citizens; blacks were not granted the vote until 1868, during Reconstruction and despite a campaign of terror by the Ku Klux Klan. They were effectively disenfranchised again in 1898 through a legislative maneuver requiring stringent proof of literacy. The vote was returned only in 1965, and although African-Americans make up more than half the city's population, the first black mayor, Ernest Morial, was not elected until 1978. (His son Marc also became mayor, in 1994.) Carnival krewes were not integrated until 1991, and some krewes boycotted or even withdrew from Mardi Gras.

■ The War Between the States ■
and Reconstruction

The port of New Orleans practically floated on money in the decades after the Treaty of Ghent. Steamboats were in their prime; at the peak, there were some 11,000 plying the waters of the Mississippi, and some of the luxury paddle wheelers, the "show boats," had capacities of 600 and served 500 for dinner. It was, so to speak, the beginning of New Orleans' tourism industry. Cotton, tobacco, and the slave trade fueled the economy, and by 1840, New Orleans was the second-busiest port in the nation, after New York, and had a population of more than 100,000. The Irish Famine of 1841 sparked another flood of immigrants who settled northwest of the American sector in what gradually became known as the Irish Channel, and a large number of Germans also moved in. Unfortunately, their arrivals were offset by the yellow fever epidemic of 1853, which killed 11,000 people and incapacitated another 40,000, making it the most deadly epidemic in the nation's history.

But in 1861, with the secession of the Confederate States, Louisiana changed flags for the fifth time—and with the taking of New Orleans by Union forces under Admiral David Farragut in 1862, a sixth.

The Union occupation (as New Orleanians saw it, although officially it ceased to be an "occupation" after 1865) lasted 15 years. It fell so early that its three-year occupation by "enemy troops" is the longest unfriendly occupation of any city in the country, and amnesty was not granted Confederate officers until 1872. Reconstruction was a period of tremendous unrest in the entire region.

In the final two decades of the nineteenth century, as the reviving port began to bring new industry and pleasure-seekers into the city, what might be called the Bourbon Street culture made its first bow. There were almost 800 saloons operating in New Orleans by 1880, along with about 80 gambling parlors and even more bordellos which, though officially banned, had never been prosecuted or even regulated. New Orleans was starting to develop a reputation as a party town, a reputation that many people resisted and resented.

So in 1897, an alderman named Sidney Story proposed that all these activities be restricted to a red-light district along Basin Street adjoining the French Quarter. The business of vice prospered almost virtuously in what was quickly dubbed "Storyville." The fanciest bordellos boasted not only elegant decor, sophisticated refreshments, and fine entertainment (these "sporting palaces" were where many of the great jazz improvisors got their start), but well-dressed and willing ladies whose names, addresses, and race mix were listed in "blue books" that parodied social registers. (One of the few surviving blue books is in the Old U.S. Mint Museum, along with several beautiful stained-glass windows from a bordello.)

■ The Twentieth Century ■

The new century began promisingly: Oil was discovered in Louisiana, and the new dredging and refining industry pumped new money into the regional economy (and pollutants into the water). But a second potential industry, jazz, which had struck its first ragtime notes just before the turn of the century, was turned out: The Storyville neighborhood, the bordello area and center of the burgeoning "jass" movement, was closed and virtually bulldozed off the face of the earth. "King" Oliver, Jelly Roll Morton, and other prominent musicians moved north to New York and Chicago, launching successful careers and a nationwide craze.

Some New Orleanians might have felt that the Great War was being fought at home. A massive hurricane struck the city in 1915, devastating the economy and widening the division between the well-to-do and the subsistence farmers; and although a cure for the dreaded yellow fever had been discovered in the early years of the century, the great influenza epidemic of 1918 killed at least 35,000 residents. One of the worst floods in history flattened the city in 1927, ushering the Depression into the state even before it struck the rest of the nation. (Such natural disasters continue to harass Louisiana. Hurricanes Betsy in 1965 and Camille in 1969 caused billions of dollars' worth of damage, and periodic floods have done millions more.)

Louisiana would have remained a virtual feudal society had it not been for the anti-establishment revolution of Huey Long, the "Kingfish," a populist, demagogue, and drunk who became governor in 1828 and bullied, bludgeoned, and blackmailed the state legislature into expanding public education, roads, and hospitals. Within a year he had been indicted on bribery charges, but was not convicted and instead was elected U.S. Senator. He began as a vocal New Deal supporter, but soon developed a populism, bordering on socialism, that alarmed even the most liberal of Washingtonians. In 1935, on a trip home, he was assassinated, but the Long arm of their family law stretched on: His brother Earl was a two-time governor, and his son Russell served in the U.S. Senate from 1948 until 1986.

The growth of industry, particularly oil and natural gas, has been a boon to the state economy, if not the ecology. By 1980, there were more than 40 countries maintaining consular offices in New Orleans, an indication of the power of a trade port that accommodated more than 5,000 international vessels every year. But in 1984, the massive World's Fair Exposition, set up along three wharves with an eye toward the rejuvenation of the Warehouse District, ran heavily into debt and, combined with the collapse in world oil prices, came perilously close to bankrupting the city. What resulted was symbolic: The harder industries turned to the softer tourism industry for partnership. The wharf areas that were renovated for the World's Fair are now the site of the Riverwalk Marketplace and the vast and expanding Convention Center, which brings in more than a million people a year by itself. The luxury hotels and burgeoning Warehouse/Arts District owe their existence primarily to the facelift connected to the fair. And the legalization of gambling has brought in some money to the state (although the on-again, off-again construction of the massive Harrah's casino near the foot of Canal Street has bankrupted many smaller subcontractors).

Nowadays the Mississippi riverfront is a microcosm of the city's spirit (for good or ill), combining franchised entertainment, name-brand boutiques and music clubs, huge international tankers and simulated steamboats, "real" Civil War coffee with chicory and reinvented Cajun cuisine, eighteenth-century voodoo, and twentieth-century vampires. They *laissez les bons temps rouler,* all right; they just make sure it's your money roll that's good-timing.

Parishes, Neighborhoods, and Districts

It would surprise those who think that "old" New Orleans is limited to the Vieux Carré and the Garden District, but metropolitan New Orleans actually has more than a dozen historical neighborhoods, including Treme and Faubourg Marigny (for pronunciation tips, see the section, "Talking the Talk," page 115) as well as the Garden District and the often-denigrated Ninth Ward.

These are all within Orleans Parish, the central portion of greater New Orleans. If you look at the map, it is roughly defined by the U-shaped bowl of the Mississippi River—the eponymous "crescent"—and lines running more or less north to Lake Pontchartrain. Many of these neighborhoods were originally laid out along fairly regular street grids, easily negotiated by newcomers, but because of the snaking of the Mississippi, the overall pattern of the center city now resembles a spider's web: Sets of parallel streets occasionally are "pieced out" or head off at wider angles, and a few great, long, curving avenues, such as St. Charles, Claiborne, and Magazine, follow the curve of the river. It takes a little getting used to.

New Orleans also incorporates Jefferson Parish, to the west beyond Audubon Park, and St. Bernard Parish, downriver to the east. ("Parish" is no longer a religious jurisdiction, but the equivalent of a county.)

Only a few of New Orleans' neighborhoods are of real interest to tourists, but a quick overview of them, and how we have arranged them into zones, may help you plan your trip. These are the same zones we have used to cluster special attractions, restaurants, nightlife entertainment, and hotels.

■ The French Quarter (Zone 1) ■

Although Vieux Carré literally means "Old Square," the French Quarter is, of course, not perfectly square, since it rides a hump of Mississippi sidesaddle. And since it's tilted with its corners at 12, 3, and 9, it's actually closer to a diamond. (Oddly, it's a fair mirror image of Washington, D.C., only in miniature.) Nevertheless, it's the easiest neighborhood to grasp logistically, because the streets do proceed in a perpendicular grid, most of them one-way in alternating directions.

The boundaries are Canal Street to the southwest, or from 6 to 9 o'clock; North Rampart Street to the northwest, or 9 to 12; Esplanade Avenue on the northeast, from 12 to 3; and the concave line of the Mississippi from 3 to 6. (The legal border on the southwest is Iberville Street, but we have used Canal Street as the border throughout this book.) If you look at the neighborhood square-on, with Rampart running across the top of the grid, Jackson Square and Artillery Park are in the center at the bottom, like a stem.

This is tourist central, the neighborhood of Bourbon Street and all-night beignets and St. Louis Cathedral and Preservation Hall and Pat O'Brien's hurricanes. It includes the oldest architectural examples in the city, the most inexhaustible souvenir vendors, and the finest antique shops, plus a handful of franchised star-power hangouts a la Planet Hollywood. The French Quarter is something of a year-round party, justly famous for strip joints and street drinking. It has also developed a second kind of "street life" in recent years, with some of the longtime street musicians giving way to groups of punk-styled teenagers and young adults, panhandlers, and vagrants; so you may want to be less freestyle with your partying. There are still fulltime residents here, but in general they have withdrawn to the quieter edges of the neighborhood.

For a full description, see the walking tour of the French Quarter in "Sight-Seeing and Tours."

■ Central Business District (Zone 2) ■

The Central Business District, generally shortened to the CBD, is a cleaver-shaped area adjoining the French Quarter on the southwest side of Canal Street and also bordering it on the northwest side of North Rampart. Zone 2 also includes two historic neighborhoods, the Warehouse/Arts District, which is sort of the lower half of the "blade," and the historic Treme neighborhood, which forms the handle. So on the map, the zone is defined by South Claiborne Avenue/Interstate 10 on the northwest side, Business 90/Pontchartrain Expressway on the southwest, and the Mississippi on the east, with a jag from Canal Street across Rampart to Esplanade. This is also the beginning of "uptown" New Orleans, that is, upriver from Canal Street, as opposed to "downtown."

The CBD includes most of the commercial area, including the Ernest N. Morial Convention Center, the Louisiana Superdome, Riverwalk Marketplace, the World Trade Center, and City Hall. In the beginning, this neighborhood was known as Faubourg Ste. Marie, and was the site of some early sugar plantations. However, when the Americans flooded in after the Louisiana Purchase, they chopped up the old plantations and began settling on the "other" side of Canal Street. Though it was begun long after unification, the U.S. Customs House on Canal Street sits as a sort of "hinge" between the two neighborhoods. The heart of the CBD is Lafayette Square, the Americans' answer to Jackson Square just as St. Patrick's Cathedral was their version of St. Louis.

Treme is one of the old Creole neighborhoods, part of the Claude Treme plantation that was bought by the city for residential development in the early nineteenth century. (The same Claude Treme was somewhat elevated when St. Claude Avenue was named after him.) Treme is where the famous Storyville red light district was established, now the site of a disgracefully decrepit housing project. Treme is also the area where you'll find Louis Armstrong Park, the Theatre for the Performing Arts, and the famous Congo Square, home of jazz; St. Louis Cemetery (Nos. 1 *and* 2); and Our Lady of Guadalupe Chapel.

The Warehouse/Arts District, on the other hand, is a fairly recent concept. The huge old storehouses, light industrial hangers, and factories, in the streets south of Lafayette Square and west of the Convention Center, originally had easy access to the docks. Many had been abandoned or allowed to fall into disrepair in the '60s and '70s, and the neighborhood was ripe for redevelopment, but when plans were made to transform the dock area for the World's Fair, artists and performers began moving in, turning them into lofts, studios, and display galleries. Now it's a trendy area, with several hot restaurants and museums and more coming in around Lee Circle, and a strong campaign is being mounted to preserve and restore the buildings rather than raze them.

And in a peculiar turnabout, the trendiness of the Warehouse/Arts District is one of the factors that has encouraged the revitalization of Canal Street not merely as a shopping strip but as a haven for high-profile hotels, including the Hotel Meridien, the Orient Express–owned Windsor Court, and the Ritz-Carlton. Even the old streetcar rails are being restored down the middle of Canal Street. (Unfortunately, much of the most elaborate development near the foot of Canal has been halted because of the ongoing financial travails of the huge Harrah's Casino that was under construction there.)

For more information, see the walking tours of both the CBD and Warehouse/Arts District in "Sight-Seeing and Tours."

■ Uptown below Napoleon (Zone 3) ■

This is the area of the Garden District, New Orleans' second most famous neighborhood, the upper-class residential portion of the old "American sector," and visually as well as historically a world away from the French Quarter. Originally there were some Creole plantation homes here, but after the turn of the nineteenth century, as Americans moved in above Canal Street, this became incorporated as the City of Lafayette (hence Lafayette Cemetery at its heart). It was annexed into the city in 1852. Although real estate promoters and area residents constantly "stretch" the description, the true Garden District is generally considered to fall between St. Charles Avenue and Magazine Street, Jackson Avenue on the northeast and Louisiana Avenue on the west.

However, for our purposes, Zone 3 is a somewhat larger, skirt-shaped wedge stretching from the Pontchartrain Expressway on the northeast, South Claiborne/Route 90 on the northwest, Napoleon Avenue to the west, and the river curving along the east and south.

Although the area's streets occasionally "shift" a little as the Mississippi curves back up, like the skirt's pleats, the Garden District is fairly gridlike within its borders and a fine residential neighborhood for exploring (see the walking tour of this area as well). Although it had become somewhat run-down, the ongoing revitalization of Magazine Street has made it a popular shopping area (see the "Shopping" chapter for more information).

■ Uptown above Napoleon (Zone 4) ■

This area, along with the Garden District, is most often what is meant by the general phrase "uptown"; at its northwest border, Monticello Avenue, which strikes off from the rim of the river's "cup," it marks the line between Orleans and Jefferson Parishes, so in one sense it is the far end of the Crescent City. (Some residents of the Metairie and Kenner suburbs would say that New Orleans' older families seem to think so, too.)

It is also called University, sort of shorthand for the "university neighborhood," because of the adjoining campuses of Loyola and Tulane Universities; and is split virtually down the middle by the St. Charles Avenue streetcar, which makes it, like the Garden District, easily accessible from the French Quarter or hotel district. Its most famous landmark is Audubon Park, which stretches from the universities right to the spot where the Mississippi River turns back north, with a fine view of both banks.

At the northwest edge of the area is the neighborhood called Riverbend, which is sort of uptown's own counter–French Quarter, with boutiques and art galleries, bookstores, and a booming restaurant scene. See the "Shopping" chapter for more information.

For the purposes of this book, Zone 4 is defined by Napoleon Avenue on the east, the Mississippi River on the south and west, Monticello up to Highway 61 (Old Airline Highway) on the north, and I-10 to the north and northeast.

■ Downtown/St. Bernard (Zone 5) ■

This area, which adjoins the French Quarter's east side, has suffered a great deal more than the French Quarter from the vicissitudes of time and industrial development, but it contains many fine old houses; the eccentric St. Roch Cemetery, Chalmette Battlefield, and Jackson Barracks; and the Old U.S. Mint Museum. Zone 5 is defined by Esplanade Avenue on the west, I-10 to the Industrial Canal on the north, the Back Levee and Florida Avenue on the east, and, of course, the river on the south.

It actually includes parts of two parishes, since the neighborhood of Faubourg Marigny, which faces the French Quarter across Esplanade Avenue, is part of Orleans Parish; the rest is St. Bernard Parish. In fact, St. Claude Avenue becomes St. Bernard Highway at the parish line, and leads down along the Mississippi to the city of St. Bernard, where you can visit the Isleño Center and the Ducros Museum. This is also, you should note, the Ninth Ward, which is the way locals refer to it in terms of crime (see the section on "How to Avoid Crime" in "Arriving and Getting Oriented").

But it has great beauty, still: Blanche DuBois's famous directions, "They told me to take a streetcar named Desire, transfer to one called Cemeteries, ride six blocks and get off at Elysian Fields," owes most of its charm to streets in Faubourg Marigny, although to be truthful, the routes wouldn't intersect. Faubourg Marigny is named for one of the greatest charmers and also greatest wastrels in New Orleans lore, Bernard Xavier Phillipe de Marigny de Mandeville, who gambled away an immense fortune and gradually sold off his vast holdings to developers. He subdivided his own plantation ("faubourg" means something like suburb or cluster development), and it was he who named Elysian Fields Avenue. (He also gave the name Rue d'Amour, the Street of Love, to what is now the far more truculent Rampart Street.) These days, the western part of Faubourg Marigny, from the edge of the French Quarter past Washington Square to Elysian Fields, is a mixed but lively neighborhood of artists, gays and hip straights, musicians, and young couples working to renovate the rambling old homes, something like the downtown Riverbend, but funkier and dicier.

■ Mid-City/Gentilly (Zone 6) ■

This is a fat-topped Santa's boot of a zone. Its cuff along the lakefront, which runs from the inner harbor canal on the east to I-10, follows the interstate southeast along the calf until it makes a sharp right at the heel of the boot and runs back up the sole toward the northwest; the toe is at City Park Avenue, and the shin goes up Wisner Boulevard to Lake Pontchartrain. Within this zone are the Fairgrounds, where the Jazz and Heritage Fest is held; the University of New Orleans and Kiefer Lakefront Arena; and Bayou St. John, the original passage the French took moving in from Lake Pontchartrain toward the Mississippi (and a Native American route long before that). And the stretch of Esplanade Avenue near the Fairgrounds and bayou, known as Esplanade Ridge, makes for a nice mini–walking tour.

■ Lakeview/West End/Bucktown (Zone 7) ■

This zone is a sort of bridge between Mid-City and Metairie, borrowing a little from each. From Lake Pontchartrain, it follows Wisner Boulevard down to City Park on the east; takes City Park Avenue west to I-10 and zigs down to Highway 61; and turns back up along the Jefferson Parish line, the 17th Street Canal, and Chicasaw Street to the lake.

Within this zone are lovely City Park (which includes the New Orleans Museum of Art, Botanical Gardens, etc.), Longue Vue House, and Gardens and Lake Lawn Metairie Cemetery. At the edge of Pontchartrain, along Lakeshore Drive, what is now developed was mostly fishing camps and speakeasies, gambling dens and partyhouses. Now it's a much fancier version, with fine yacht clubs, the West End Park, and Lakeshore Drive Park, a five-mile-long promenade (stretching into Zone 8) that includes the New Canal Lighthouse (a Coast Guard rescue center not open to the public) and the Mardi Gras Fountain.

■ New Orleans East (Zone 8) ■

This runs west from the Inner Harbor Canal to the St. Bernard Parish line, above the Back Levee and Florida Avenue on the south. It's dominated by bayous, lakes, and marshland, and includes New Orleans Lakefront Airport and the Louisiana Nature and Science Center.

■ Metairie below Causeway (Zone 9) ■

If this sounds like a strange location, remember that in New Orleans, "below" and "above" are derived from the flow of the Mississippi, and that Causeway is local shorthand for Causeway Boulevard, not the Pontchartrain Causeway it runs off; so to be below Causeway in this case means on the east side of the highway, not beneath a bridge. Zone 9 is a rectangular section bordered by Causeway on the west, Highway 61/Old Airport Highway on the south, the Jefferson/Orleans parish line, the Metairie Outfall Canal and Chicasaw on the east, and the lake on the north.

Both Zone 9 and Zone 10 are suburbs with multi-ethnic populations, so there are lots of up-and-coming or locals-only restaurants here, though it's best to go with friends from town if possible.

■ Metairie above Causeway/Kenner/Jefferson ■ Highway (Zone 10)

This booming suburban area lies just beyond the university neighborhood, bounded by Causeway Boulevard and a zigzag of Highway 61 and the Jefferson Parish line on the east, the Mississippi on the south, the Jefferson/Orleans parish line on the west, and Lake Pontchartrain on the north. Within Zone 10 are New Orleans International Airport (and so quite a number of less expensive hotels) and the Rivertown museum complex.

■ West Bank (Zone 11) ■

The apparently contradictory name—from most of New Orleans, this appears to be the *East* Bank, not to mention south!—comes from the fact that the Mississippi makes another of its huge loops east of the city, and these towns all lie west of that portion of the river. Among these are Algiers, Gretna, Harvey, Terrytown, and Marerro. Although Algiers is slowly being regentrified, and there are walking tours of the area designed to raise its profile, it is still not an area that offers much to the tourist, with the exception of the Canal Street Ferry landing and Blaine Kern's Mardi Gras World (see "Attractions").

Golf fans may also find themselves on the west bank, since several of the golf courses are across the river (see "Exercise and Recreation"). If you go down to English Turn Wilderness Park, or to English Turn country club, where the PGA tournament is held, you can see two other huge curves of the Mississippi River.

■ North Shore (Zone 12) ■

This is literally the north shore of Lake Pontchartrain, a zone that includes Slidell, Mandeville, Covington, Folsom, and other areas. Few tourists will get to this side of the lake unless they are looking for the Joyce Wildlife Management Area and Global Wildlife Center (see the "Swamp Tours" section of "Sight-Seeing and Tours" on page 198), or perhaps are lured by some of the restaurants there. The Joyce area is actually crossed by Interstate 55 and Highway 51, if you happen to be able to drive into New Orleans using that route. However, if you are part of a packaged tour, you may wind up at the factory outlet stores in Slidell. This is Tammany Parish, a pretty and mostly quiet area.

The Fictional City

There are many wonderful histories and cultural studies of New Orleans, but for some reason, fiction alway seems to convey more of the atmosphere, and is more fun to take along on a vacation. Some of my personal favorites (not all currently in print, but widely available in second-hand stores and libraries) include:

Anne Rice's books about the Vampire Lestat, the Mayfair Witches, and Lasher, etc., all have New Orleans settings, of course; but far more gripping is her historical novel, *The Feast of All Saints,* about the free people of color and their culture in the years leading up to the Civil War. And if you enjoy the old-fashioned style of murder mysteries, John Dickson Carr's *Papa La-Bas,* set amid the era of Marie Laveau and the Quadroon Balls, is as good as a voodoo tour of the French Quarter.

The posthumously-published black-humor masterpiece *A Confederacy of Dunces,* by John Kennedy Toole, contains some of the best dialect and Bourbon Street camp of all time. Ellen Gilchrist's interrelated short stories of Garden District life of "In the Land of Dreamy Dreams" and "Victory over Japan," and the contemporary crime novels of James Lee Burke and his Cajun hero Dave Robichaux, are all quite different, but all first-rate.

If you can find the books of George Washington Cable, you will love his late nineteenth-century stories of Creole romance and adventure. (One of his stories inspired the name of Madame John's Legacy, a historic house in the French Quarter.) The same is true of the novels of Frances Parkinson Keyes, notably *Dinner at Antoine's, Steamboat Gothic* (set at San Francisco Plantation), and *Madame Castel's Lodger,* about the house she and Beauregard both lived in.

Walker Percy might be the city's foremost "serious" novelist, edging out William Faulkner by dint of long residence (Faulkner only stayed a few years); and he had an almost unequaled sense of the minute degrees of social distinction, coming as he did from one of New Orleans' most prominent clans. Most of his novels, among them *The Moviegoer* and *Love among the Ruins,* are set in the New Orleans area. Faulkner's novel *Pylon* and several of his short stories have New Orleans backgrounds. So do Tennessee Williams' *A Streetcar Named Desire,* of course, *The Rose Tattoo,* and *Suddenly Last Summer,* among others.

William Sidney Porter, better known as O. Henry, lived in New Orleans for a little while before the turn of the century, and some of his stories, including "Cherchez la Femme," are set in the city. The city also makes several cameo appearances in Mark Twain's "Life on the Mississippi," the sketches he wrote about piloting a steamboat.

PART TWO

Planning Your Visit to New Orleans

When to Go

■ Pick Your Party ■

New Orleans always had a climate, of course, but most residents considered that it really had only two seasons: summer, a sticky, sweltering Southern classic prone to afternoon showers and dramatic sunsets that lasted roughly from May 1 to October 1; and a long, cool, and almost identically damp fall-into-spring that rarely dipped to the freezing point.

Meteorologically speaking, that's still the case.

But in terms of tourism, New Orleans has gradually developed four major holiday "seasons": Carnival (or, as most people think of it, Mardi Gras), which falls somewhere between February 3 and March 9; the New Orleans Jazz and Heritage Festival, from the last weekend of April through the first weekend of May; Halloween, which is booming in the Anne Rice era; and Creole Christmas, a lower-key but increasingly popular group of events spread throughout December and lasting through New Year's Eve and the Sugar Bowl. And that doesn't even count the occasional Super Bowl or the dozens of other festivals and celebrations around the city.

If you plan to come during the four big holidays, there are a few things you ought to consider. First, the fun is only nominally free. Don't be surprised if you have to pay premium rates for hotels and airfare, especially around Mardi Gras and Jazz Fest, *if* you can get them. That's another thing to know:

You'd better get a hotel reservation immediately, because most of the events are sold-out well in advance, and some people make reservations for Mardi Gras more than a year ahead. (Mardi Gras falls on February 24 in 1998, February 16 in 1999, and March 7 in 2000; it moves because it is fixed 46 days before Easter, which is itself fixed by the lunar schedule, falling on the first Sunday after the first full moon after the solstice.) You might seriously consider staying in the suburbs to avoid the almost 24-hour noise; or at least try to get something in the Garden District, where you can enjoy the traditional decorations without the full French Quarter free-for-all.

A third factor is that the sheer size of the crowd may begin to sour you after a while. Many restaurants and bars simply pack up the tables during Mardi Gras and settle for making money on the itinerant drinkers; restaurants that maintain their poise may refuse to make reservations or require you to leave a deposit or credit card number in case you fail to show up. (And realize again that with such a crowd, getting around town is really tricky.) Rest rooms quickly overload, and overloaded drinkers may settle for the street.

If you're coming in a Super Bowl year, you'll have the same problem with overcrowding: Even footballs fans without game tickets flock to the city, either in hopes of scalping seats or just to enjoy the televised hoopla. But if you can't resist these most famous events, read the special information on each in "New Orleans' Major Festivals," which starts on page 58.

If you have more general interests or want to take the family, pick a less frenetic time to go: Between Easter and the Jazz Fest, usually in early May, is very quiet (and you can enjoy the French Quarter Festival, a miniature and more local Jazz and Heritage Festival not yet too crowded for pleasure); and September and early October are warm and usually fine. The astonishing, high-spirited Tennessee Williams Festival in March is an underestimated attraction. Even winter can be nice if you like a brisk walk, and there are certainly no crowds in the museums. (If you're traveling on business, of course, you may not have much of a choice, although no convention is apt to coincide with Carnival unless it's the association of paper goods and party favors.)

The good news is that except during the big festivals, you will rarely have to stand in line, except perhaps for a table. There are so many distractions in New Orleans that only a couple of attractions (the ticket booth at the Aquarium of the Americas and IMAX theater, perhaps) collect much of a queue. And you can usually avoid that by going early or buying tickets a day in advance.

■ Weather or Not . . . ■

If you aren't used to Southern summers, you may find it a sticky experience. (You'll see T-shirts all over the French Quarter that read, "It's not the heat, it's the stupidity," which gives you some idea how tired the natives are of hearing tourists complain.) Thunderstorms are almost a daily occurrence in June, July, and August, but provide only temporary relief. The epidemics of yellow fever, malaria, and cholera that used to strike from the swamp are a thing of the past, but the social and performance calendars still tend to duck the extremes of summer, and so should you, when the sun is highest. If you skim the calendar of special events, you'll see they drop off in summertime, because even in early May, during the Jazz & Heritage Festival, temperatures can hit 100°.

On the other hand, compared to most places, the climate is pretty mild. Snow is a rare and festive occurrence, and the average low temperature, even in January, is 43. (The average high is 69, which should also give you an idea of how much the mercury can swing from midnight to mid-afternoon.) So you can easily consider an off-peak vacation.

There is one more fact to remember about summer: hurricanes. These are of course extremely rare, and generally there is plenty of warning from local authorities. However, just in case you have to deal with some temporary disaccommodation because of bad weather, it's a good idea to have any essential medication on hand, and perhaps to pack a small flashlight. If

New Orleans' Average Temperatures and Precipitation			
	Average High	Average Low	Average Rainfall
January	69	43	4.97"
February	65	45	5.23"
March	71	52	4.73"
April	79	59	4.50"
May	85	65	5.07"
June	90	71	4.63"
July	91	74	6.73"
August	90	73	6.02"
September	87	70	5.87"
October	79	59	2.66"
November	70	50	4.06"
December	64	45	5.27"

you're going to sign up for one of those haunting expeditions, you'll want it anyway.

■ What to Pack ■

Perhaps a little sadly, this once most elegant of societies has become extremely informal. You probably won't see a black tie or tuxedo outside of a wedding party unless you are fortunate enough to be invited to a serious social event. Even an old, established restaurant such as Galatoire's requires only a jacket (after 5 p.m. and all day Sunday) but not a tie, and most others only "recommend" a jacket.

Shorts and polo shirts are everywhere, night or day, and a sundress or reasonably neat pair of khakis will make you look downright respectable. A rainproof top of some sort, a lightweight jacket, and a sweater, even a sweatshirt, may be all you'll need in the summer, and remember that you will probably be going in and out of air conditioning as well as rain. Something along the lines of a trenchcoat with zip-in lining or wool walking coat with a sweater will usually do in winter. (Fur coats are not a moral issue in New Orleans, but the constant bustle of people carrying glasses and food around on the streets might make it a risk unless you plan to spend most of the time in nicer hotels and restaurants.)

Frankly, the two most important things to consider when packing are comfortable shoes (this is a culture of asphalt, concrete, and flagstone streets) and skirts or pants with expandable waistlines. Even if you don't think you're going to eat much, the scent of food constantly fills the air, and the Café du Monde by Jackson Square is still making those beignets—fried doughnuts dusted with powdered sugar, 3 for a buck—24 hours a day. Second, there is no other city in which the food is so rich (and full of fat, cholesterol, and calories) as this, and even if you don't eat more than usual, you may temporarily feel the effects. (Make that three things to pack—Alka Seltzer.) If you don't want to pack "fat day" clothes, you'd better pack your running shoes.

And finally, this city has developed a crime problem (see "How to Avoid Crime" on page 120), so there is no good reason to walk around flashing expensive jewelry. Leave it at home and stick to the Mardi Gras beads.

■ Gathering Information ■

Brochures, historical background, and up-to-date schedules are available from the New Orleans Metropolitan Convention and Visitors Bureau (1520 Sugar Bowl Drive, New Orleans, LA 70112-1259 or 566-5011). For information targeted to African-American visitors, contact the Greater New Orleans Black Tourism Network (523-5652). Incidentally, the area code for the New Orleans metro area is 504; that should be assumed for all phone numbers in this guide unless otherwise noted.

New Orleans also has a couple of Internet sites: http://www.neworleans. com and http://www.nawlins.com.

■ Playing Host ■

If you are coming in with a family or business group, and are in charge of arranging some sort of party or reception, there are plenty of restaurants, music clubs (check out the Voodoo Garden at House of Blues or the private room at Lucky Cheng's), steamboats, and hotels with private rooms. But there are also a few less ordinary places to throw a party, if you really want to make an impression. Within City Park, for example, the New Orleans Botanical Garden has the 9,000-square-foot Pavilion of the Two Sisters (483-9386), and Storyland and Carousel Gardens (483-9381) can be reserved after hours, and the carousel provides on-site catering as well. The Contemporary Arts Center (523-1216) and the Louisiana Children's Museum (523-1357), both within easy walking distance of the Convention Center, have spaces for rent. Blaine Kern's Mardi Gras World in Algiers lets guests try on the parade masks (361-7821). And out in Rivertown near the airport, the Mardi Gras Museum (468-7258) is also available for parties. The restored third-floor "Appartement de l'Empereur" at the Napoleon House can be reserved as well, and even though Bonaparte himself never came here, the atmosphere is quite imperial.

Special Considerations

Of course, New Orleans is most famous as a sort of adults' playground, but if you're considering a family vacation here, don't worry: For all the round-the-clock bars and burlesque houses, New Orleans is full of family-style attractions, both inside and outside the French Quarter. And since these are year-round, you can avoid the special-event crowds altogether. Just remember that warnings about dehydration go double for small children.

Within the Vieux Carré is the entire **French Market, Jackson Square** with all its balloon-twisters and clowns, and the mule-drawn carriages which, while somewhat undependable as far as historic detail is concerned, are high on entertainment values. The **Musée Conti Wax Museum** is a perennial favorite, as is the free **Canal Street ferry** ride across the Missis-sippi. There are several doll and toy museum-stores that may attract some children, as well as **Le Petit Soldier** store and, for some, the **Pharmacy Museum.** Kids who play dress-up will love the Carnival exhibit at the **U.S. Mint,** with its Aladdin's cave of crowns and pins. (And you should check the schedule of **Le Petit Théâtre du Vieux Carré,** which sometimes has children's productions.)

The state-of-the-art **Louisiana Children's Museum** is in the Warehouse/ Arts District nearby. At the edge of the riverwalk area is the **Aquarium of the Americas,** from which you can take a boat directly to **Audubon Zoo** in the Garden District. (The Zoo is also accessible from the St. Charles street-car, which is another family possibility.)

City Park in Mid-City has an antique carousel, miniature rideable trains, a toy museum, and the Storyland playground designed around Mother Goose characters, plus botanical gardens and a riding stable. Be-yond that in eastern New Orleans is the **Louisiana Nature and Science Center,** which has a planetarium, hands-on exhibits, and trails though 86 acres of forest.

East of the city on the way to **Chalmette National Battlefield,** site of the Battle of New Orleans of glorious memory, is a remarkable military museum at the **Jackson Barracks,** that will almost certainly transfix any normally bloody-minded kid. The **Confederate Museum,** while more spe-cific and semi-hagiographic, is close to the Louisiana Children's Museum.

Near the airport is a treasure trove for families, a complex of attractions called **Rivertown** that includes an observatory and planetarium, Mardi Gras and toy train museums, the New Orleans Saints Hall of Fame, a Native American living museum within the Louisiana Wildlife Museum, and the Children's Castle, where puppet shows and magic shows are put on. There is also a repertory theater there.

And if you're interested in swamp and bayou life, you can either sign up for one of the several swamp tours or cruises or take a short drive to the **Barataria Preserve,** Jean Lafitte's old stronghold and now a 20,000-acre park with a Park Service visitors center, trails, and boardwalks that wind among the cypress swamps and freshwater branches. Even wilder, spend the night at the **Global Wildlife Center** near Folsom and go nose-to-nose with a giraffe (see "Sight-Seeing and Tours").

If you do bring the kids, but would like to have a little adults-only or work time, contact Accents on Arrangements (524-1227) to hook up with children's tours; or the day care/field trip–oriented Conference Child Care Service (241-7321), which is a member of the Greater New Orleans Black Tourism Network.

■ Tips for International Travelers ■

Visitors from Western Europe, the United Kingdom, Japan, or New Zealand who stay in the United States fewer than 90 days only need a valid passport, not a visa, and a round-trip or return ticket. Canadian citizens can get by with only proof of residence. Citizens of other countries must have a passport (good for at least six months beyond the projected end of the visit) and a tourist visa as well, available from any U.S. consulate. Contact consular officials for application forms; some airlines and travel agents may also have forms available.

If you are taking prescription drugs containing narcotics or requiring injection by syringe, be sure to get a doctor's signed prescription and instructions. Also check with the local consulate to see whether travelers from your country are currently required to have any inoculations; there are no set requirements to enter the United States, but if there has been any sort of epidemic in your homeland, there may be temporary restrictions.

If you arrive by air, be prepared to spend as much as two hours entering the United States and getting through U.S. Customs. Canadians and Mexicans crossing the borders either by car or by train will find a much quicker and easier system. Every adult traveler may bring in, duty-free, up to 1 liter of wine or hard liquor; 200 cigarettes, 100 non-Cuban cigars, or 3 pounds of loose tobacco; and $100 worth of gifts, as well as up to $10,000 in U.S.

currency or its equivalent in foreign currency. No food or plants may be brought in. For information on sales tax refunds, see the chapter on "Shopping in New Orleans."

Credit cards are by far the most common form of payment in New Orleans, especially American Express, Visa (also known as BarclayCard in Britain) and MasterCard (Access in Britain, Eurocard in Western Europe, or Chargex in Canada). Other popular cards include Diners Club, Discover, and Carte Blanche. Travelers checks will be accepted at most hotels and restaurants if they are in American dollars; other currencies should be taken to a bank or foreign exchange (the Mutual of Omaha office offers this service and wires funds in or out) and turned into dollar figures.

The dollar is the basic unit of monetary exchange, and the entire system is decimal. The smaller sums are represented by coins. One hundred "cents" (or pennies, as the 1-cent coin is known) equal one dollar; 5 cents is a nickel (20 nickels to a dollar); 10 cents is called a dime (10 dimes to a dollar); and the 25-cent coin is called a quarter (4 to a dollar). Beginning with one dollar, money is in currency bills (although there are some one-dollar coins around as well). Bills come in $1, $2 (rare), $5, $10, $20, $50, $100, $500, and so on, although you are unlikely to want to carry $1,000 or more. Stick to $20s for taxicabs and such; drivers rarely can make change for anything larger.

If you need additional assistance, there is a Foreign Language Assistance office in the airport (586-8191) and an Immigration Service desk (467-1713).

And throughout the United States, if you have a medical, police, or fire emergency, dial 911, even on a pay telephone, and an ambulance or police cruiser will be dispatched to help you.

■ Tips for the Disabled ■

Visitors who use walking aids should be warned: Only the larger museums and the newer shopping areas can be counted on to be wheelchair accessible. Many individual stores and smaller collections are housed in what were once private homes with stairs, and even those at sidewalk level are unlikely to have wider aisles or specially equipped bathrooms. The restaurants that we profile later in the book all have a disabled access rating, but you need to call any other eatery or any store in advance. (In fact, you might check with some restaurants that were listed as not accessible at press time, as it's possible they've renovated their facilities since.) Similarly, you need to call any stores you're particularly interested in. Antique stores in particular tend to be tightly packed and with shelving at all levels.

■ For the Nose That Knows ■

If you are smoke- or allergy-sensitive, watch out for spring. As for smoking, it is prohibited in any public building, on the streetcars, and in taxis. Restaurants with more than 50 seats have to have a nonsmoking section, but that's not practical in a smaller restaurant, and all bars welcome smokers.

■ A Calendar of Special Events ■

These are the major celebrations and their approximate dates (specific ones where possible). Remember, if the event requires tickets, it's best to try to arrange them before leaving home; otherwise you may find yourself paying extra or being locked out entirely. Please note that many festivals, especially in the summer, move around from year to year, and that some close down or are replaced by others; so if you are interested, contact organizers as soon as possible.

In addition to the contacts listed below, TicketMaster (522-5555) may be able to supply tickets to particular events, although there will be an additional handling charge.

January

Sugar Bowl   One of the three major collegiate alliance bowls, held New Year's Day. For information on tickets and festivities, contact organizers at 1500 Sugar Bowl Drive, New Orleans, LA 70112, or call 525-8573. Associated with the football classic are other sporting events, including flag football, tennis, races, and basketball.

Super Bowl (not held again in New Orleans until 1998)   Apart from the football showdown itself, events include a celebrity golf tournament, a huge public meet-the-players party, and a "theme park" of football games at the convention center. Contact the Convention and Visitors Bureau, 1520 Sugar Bowl Drive, New Orleans, LA 70112, or call 566-5005.

Twelfth Night   January 6, or the Feast of Epiphany, when the Three Wise Men are supposed to have reached Bethlehem, also marks the beginning of Carnival season in New Orleans; contact the Convention and Visitors Bureau.

The Anniversary of the Battle of New Orleans   Early January. The actual date is January 8, and the special mass is held on that day (see the profile of St. Ursuline's Convent in "New Orleans Attractions"). However, the reenactment of the battle, with Redcoats, cannons, and encampment demonstrations, varies slightly around that. Call 589-4428.

February

Louisiana Black Heritage Festival   Early March. A two-day celebration, with exhibits and concerts set up along Riverwalk, Audubon Park, and the Louisiana State Museum buildings. Contact the festival at 6500 Magazine Street, New Orleans, LA 70118, or 861-2537.

Mardi Gras   February 24 in 1998, February 16 in 1999, and March 7 in the year 2000. Contact the Convention and Visitors Bureau and ask for the latest schedules. The day before, now called Lundi Gras or "Fat Monday," is also an organized event; contact Riverwalk, 1 Poydras Street, New Orleans, LA 70130, or call 522-1555.

NCAA Baseball   For tickets and times contact the Superdome Ticket Office, P.O. Box 50488, New Orleans, LA 70150, or call 587-3663.

March

St. Patrick's Day   Mid-March. The actual date is March 17, but the parade dates vary. For information on the French Quarter celebration, contact Molly's Pub at the Market, 1107 Decatur Street, New Orleans, LA 70116, or call 525-5169. For information on the parade through the Irish Channel, contact Ron Burke, 565-7080.

St. Joseph's Day   Mid-March. The Italian equivalent of St. Patrick's Day salutes Jesus's adopted father and officially falls on March 19. But like St. Paddy's, the celebrations spread out a little. The gift of the feast is fava beans, which the saint is believed to have showered upon the starving of Sicily.

Spring Fiesta   Mid-March. A five-day celebration, dating back to the 1930s, featuring tours of historic homes, courtyard receptions, and plantation tours, and culminating in a grand parade down River Road with costumed figures from history riding in horse-drawn carriages. Arias pour out over the French Quarter in honor of such past stars as Adelina Patti and Jenny Lind. Tickets are $15 for city tours, $45 for the plantation tours. Contact organizers at 826 St. Ann Street, New Orleans, LA 70112, or call 581-1367.

Tennessee Williams New Orleans Literary Festival   Third week of March to early April. This three-day event feature seminars, dramatic readings (often featuring Hollywood and Broadway celebrities), theatrical productions, walking tours of the French Quarter, and the popular Stella & Stanley Shouting

Competition in Jackson Square. Contact the University of New Orleans, ED122, New Orleans, LA 70148, or call 280-6680.

Crescent City Classic Late March. An international field runs this scenic 10K race from Jackson Square to Audubon Park. Contact organizers at 8200 Hampson Street, Suite 217, New Orleans, LA 70118, or 861-8686.

Freeport McDermott PGA Classic Late March–early April. A million-dollar purse at English Turn Golf & Country Club in Metairie. Contact Beth Garon, 110 Veteran's Blvd. #170, New Orleans, LA 70148, or call 831-4653.

April

French Quarter Festival Mid-April. This is something of an apology to area residents, and performers, for the fact that the Jazz and Heritage Festival has gotten so large and so national. Throughout the Quarter, 500 local musicians perform free concerts, and there are patio tours, fireworks, and second-lining brass parades. On Sunday, the whole of Jackson Square becomes a huge jazz brunch, thanks to the efforts of several dozen Cajun and Creole restaurants. Contact the French Quarter Festival office at 100 Conti Street, New Orleans, LA 70130, or call 522-5730.

New Orleans Jazz & Heritage Festival Last weekend in April through the first weekend in May. See details above, or contact Jazz Fest, P.O. Box 53407, New Orleans, LA 70153, or call 522-4786.

May

Greek Festival Late May. All those streets around Lee Circle didn't get to be named for the Muses for no reason. Enjoy folk dancing, Greek food, music, and crafts. Contact festival organizers at Holy Trinity Cathedral, 1200 Robert E. Lee Boulevard, New Orleans, LA 70122, or call 282-0259.

June

The Great French Market Tomato Festival Around the first of June. Cooking demonstrations, tastings, and music along the French Market promenade. Contact organizers at P.O. Box 51749, New Orleans, LA 70151, or call 522-2621.

Reggae Riddums Festival Mid-June. City Park hosts a weekend of international performers of reggae, calypso, and soca, surrounded by booths selling food and African-American crafts. Contact Ernest Kelly, P.O. Box 6156, New Orleans, LA 70174, or call (800) 367-1317 or (504) 367-1313.

New Orleans Food & Wine Experience Late June. The premier taste-of-the-town event distributes goodies from more than 40 restaurants and 150 wineries. Contact organizers at P.O. Box 70514, New Orleans, LA 70172, or call 529-WINE.

July

Go Fourth on the River July 4. Independence Day celebrations include street performances, shopping specials, discounts to riverfront attractions, and fireworks. Contact the French Quarter Festival office.

August

African Heritage Festival Black arts, crafts, storytelling, and children's activities. Contact the African Heritage Foundation, 1683 North Claiborne Avenue, New Orleans, LA 70116, or 949-5610.

October

Jazz Awareness Month Throughout October. Concerts, many of them free, lectures, and family events. Contact the Louisiana Jazz Federation at 522-3154.

Octoberfest Weekends throughout the month. Venues and restaurants around town set out German food and drink; watch for polka lessons. Call 522-8014.

Art for Art's Sake The new season kicks off with gallery openings up and down Julia, Magazine, and Royal Streets. Contact the Contemporary Arts Center, 900 Camp Street, New Orleans, LA 70130, or call 523-1216.

Swamp Festival Early to mid-October. Sponsored by the Audubon Institute and held at the zoo over two weekends, this offers close encounters with indigenous animals, a taste of Cajun food, and music and crafts. Contact the Audubon Institute, 6500 Magazine Street, New Orleans, LA 70118, or call 861-2537.

New Orleans Film & Video Festival Mid-October. Regional and world premieres of films and screenings of award-winners; the main screenings are at Canal Street Cinemas. Call 523-3818.

Jeff Fest Mid-October. This onetime family picnic is now an annual community event with 30 bands and plenty of food in Metairie's Lafreniere Park. Contact organizers at 3816 Haring Road, Metairie, LA 70006, or call 888-2900.

Boo at the Zoo   End of October. Annual Halloween extravaganza at Audubon Zoo with special children's entertainment, a "ghost train," and a haunted house. Contact the Audubon Institute, 6500 Magazine Street, New Orleans, LA 70118, or call 861-2537.

November

Racing Season at the Fairgrounds   Late November to early January. The country's third-oldest racetrack still hosts thoroughbred races Thursday through Monday during the holiday season. For reservations call (800) 262-7893 or (504) 944-5515.

Celebration in the Oaks   Late November to early January. City Park kicks off the holiday season with a display of 750,000 lights, music, seasonal foods, and special events. Contact Friends of City Park, #1 Dreyfous, New Orleans, LA 70122, or call 483-9415.

Bayou Classic   Late November. One of collegiate football's long-standing rivalries. Grambling and Southern University wind up the season at the Superdome, P.O. Box 50488, New Orleans, LA 70150, or call 587-3663.

December

New Orleans Christmas   Throughout the month. See "Creole Christmas" on page 64, for details.

New Year's Eve   December 31. Jackson Square may not be as big as Times Square, but it holds a heck of a street party, complete with countdown and, yes, a lighted ball that drops from the top of Jax Brewery. Contact the Convention and Visitors Bureau, 1520 Sugar Bowl Drive, New Orleans, LA 70112, or call 566-5005.

PART THREE

New Orleans' Major Festivals

Hot Times in the Big Easy

■ Mardi Gras Mania ■

You could write a book about **Mardi Gras,** and several people probably have. The big picture, you already know: It's a loud, public, and highly indulgent series of parades, "second-line" dancing (that refers to the parasol-wielding high-steppers who traditionally formed a second line behind the brass band), costume-donning (and doffing), and balls. There's partying in the streets, in the bars, in the restaurants, in the courtyards, in the parks, in the alleys—no wonder most French Quarter residents rent their homes out for the week. There's little sleep to be had, with an estimated million visitors packed elbow to armpit and mug to go-cup. Tourism officials estimate that Mardi Gras generates over three-quarters of a billion dollars every year.

But in recent years, the ever-increasing incidents of public inebriation, nudity, petty (and occasionally greater) crime, and general vagrancy have for many people irretrievably tarnished the event; some of the oldest and most respected societies have pulled out entirely. Locals tend to avoid Bourbon Street and enjoy smaller parties in the suburbs.

Tarnished or not, no city, except perhaps for Rio de Janeiro, is so closely associated with Mardi Gras as New Orleans. In fact, it almost seems as if the city's destiny was to be the biggest Mardi Gras party town in the world: On March 3, 1699, when the Sieur d'Iberville (brother of the Sieur de Bienville) camped on the Mississippi River, the day *was* Mardi Gras, and that was what he named the site—Mardi Gras Point.

Mardi Gras, for those who may think it means "bottoms up," actually translates as "Fat Tuesday"; it's so called because it's the last day before Lent, when observant Catholics were supposed to give up meat-eating (and ideally various other fleshly pleasures). The weeks leading up to Lent are called Carnival, from the Latin for "farewell to meat," although the festival season certainly involves plenty of feasting—stocking up, so to speak. (Although most people refer to the entire Carnival season as Mardi Gras, that title rightfully applies to only that one day, and using the term wrong is one way to brand yourself a really green outsider.)

The day after "Fat Tuesday" is Ash Wednesday, the beginning of the sober Lenten season, which continues until Easter; so in other words, Tuesday is your last day to enjoy yourself for about six weeks. Carnival season in New Orleans traditionally begins with the Krewe of Twelfth Night ball held on Twelfth Night or Epiphany (January 6). Mardi Gras is also a legal holiday in Louisiana, so get your banking done on Monday.

Mardi Gras has had a checkered history in New Orleans. The French colonists celebrated Mardi Gras for some 50 years, but when the city was turned over to the Spanish empire, which adhered to a much more rigorous and ascetic form of Catholicism, the governor banned the festivities—and the anti-Catholic Americans who took over after the Louisiana Purchase weren't favorably inclined toward such Papist displays, either. However, by 1823 the balls were legal again, and within a few years the street parties took hold.

The first secret Krewe, the Mystick Krewe of Comus, was formed in 1856 to give the mayhem some form, and it was Comus that designed the first theme parties and parades. The Twelfth Night club first threw trinkets right after the Civil War; the Krewe of Rex designed the first "doubloons" in 1884. Nowadays, yelling, "Throw me somethin', mister" may get you beads, candy, bikini pants, or almost anything—if you can wrest it away from the next guy, or the girl on his shoulders. (The familiar purple, green, and gold colors represent justice, faith, and power, and you may need all three to survive.) Each parade has dozens of floats, and may require the talents of 2,000 or 3,000 people. And just to give you an idea of the number of throws required, Mardi Gras expert Arthur Hardy has calculated that between them, the 2,300 members of the parades of Endymion and Bacchus, which are held the Saturday and Sunday before Mardi Gras, toss more than 1.5 million plastic cups, 2.5 million doubloons, and around 25 million beads.

Most of the krewes have names and themes taken from classical mythology: Aphrodite, Pegasus, and Hermes all have their own krewes. One of the newest is Orpheus, named after the musician so eloquent [1] persuaded Pluto to release his dead wife (although she slipped away again); the Krewe of Orpheus was founded by Harry Connick, Jr. Although the strict secrecy has eased a little, some krewes still keep parade themes and rules quiet until the last minute. (The captain is permanent, but the king and queen change from year to year.) The theme song, the rather sappy "If Ever I Cease to Love," was a signature song of New York vaudeville star Lydia Thompson, who was performing in New Orleans in 1872. The lovesick Grand Duke Alexis of Russia followed her south, and in his honor every Krewe played the number in its parade.

In its heyday, and even up until fairly recently, Creole Carnival season was a much more elegant affair, with fancy dress and masquerade balls, elaborate trinkets, and *lagniappes* (pronounced lan-yaps), a word meaning something like "a little extra," and applied to any small gift or token, even a nibble or free drink. The most traditional dances and floats are sponsored by old-line Krewes (the correct spelling for parade "crews"), and their parties are still by closely guarded invitation only, many of them doubling as the debutante balls of their members' daughters. Even if somehow you do get invited, remember that you are not a member and can only sit in the spectator seats and enjoy the show. The last year's court will be presented, the costumes displayed in tableaux, etc. (The only exception is a woman guest issued a "call-out card"; she will sit with the other called women until the dancing begins and her escort calls her out.)

However, there are many newer and more liberal Krewes which throw more public "supper dances," and you may be able to get tickets to some of those. Get a copy of Arthur Hardy's *Mardi Gras Guide* magazine for more information. Various routes go uptown, downtown, or into the suburbs, and some guidebooks have maps and information. The *Times-Picayune* also publishes a daily list of routes and times during Carnival. (For ideas on renting or buying costumes, see the section on "Mardi Gras and Music" on page 201 or look in the chapter on shopping.)

The last ten days or so of Carnival is high parade season, when at almost any moment police sirens announce the imminent arrival of a marching band, motorcycle drill team or horseback troupe, stilt-walking clowns, acrobats, balloon-twisters, and professional and amateur dancing girls. And since that whole last weekend is pretty much lost, a more recent celebration has been instituted, called "Lundi Gras," or Fat Monday, offering a free public masquerade ball, fireworks, and music on the Spanish Plaza near the Aquarium of the Americas.

Mardi Gras more or less officially kicks off with one of the real highlights, the Zulu Social Aid and Pleasure Club parade. The Zulu parade dates from early in this century, when a black resident named William

Storey parodied the elaborately crowned King Rex by strutting behind his float wearing an old lard can on his head and calling himself "King Zulu." Nowadays the Zulu's gilded coconut shells are among the most coveted "throws," and it is an honor, especially for a white resident, to be invited to participate (in blackface and grass skirt). Their parade begins at the Canal Street landing at 8 a.m. (theoretically).

Meanwhile the "walking clubs" are promenading along Canal and St. Charles Streets (legendary jazz clarinetist Pete Fountain leads the Half Fast Walking Club), and the fantastically beaded and befeathered black "Indians," such as the revered Wild Tchoupitoulas tribe, whose chiefs are required to sew their costumes themselves, are indulging in great competitions of face, style, and song. The highly competitive gay costume competition, around the intersection of St. Ann and Burgundy Streets outside the Rawhide Bar, warms up about midday, and less formal processions form all over town.

The greatest float, the crown-shaped vessel of Rex, King of Carnival, arrives at Gallier Hall in the early afternoon, preceded by a cohort of gold-helmeted lieutenants and white horses. Among his followers is a papier mâché fatted ox, or "boeuf gras," reminding you of that meatless future. At Gallier Hall, the mayor makes a toast, the king makes a little speech, his debutante queen gets her flowers, and the parade—and the party—takes off.

The parade route goes across St. Charles Avenue over as far as Napoleon Street, so if you can find a place along St. Charles—maybe take a very early streetcar ride—you can see everything without being swamped by the Bourbon Street brawlers. There are limited bleachers put up, but the tickets generally go on sale right after Christmas; contact the Metropolitan Visitors Bureau. (The Hotel Inter-Continental at 444 St. Charles sets up grandstand seats and sells them in a package with buffet meals; call 525-5566.) But remember, "Fat Tuesday" ends on Ash Wednesday, and like Cinderella's coach, it turns into a pumpkin exactly at midnight. This is the one instance "time" is definitely called in New Orleans, so be prepared.

In the meantime, try to pace yourself. Consider the paucity of restrooms (and don't expect bars or restaurants to welcome you if you don't plan to purchase anything). There will be some porta-potties set up along the routes, but they will quickly get overloaded (and unfortunately, since a lot of people will lose either patience or control, be careful where you walk after a while, much less sit). Plastic containers only are allowed, no glass or metal. Don't carry a lot of cash, and put it someplace other than your pocket. Leave your car well out of the neighborhood if possible; many streets are closed off, and parking regulations are vigorously enforced. If you inadvertently drive into a parade route, it can cost you a cool $100. And if you get the little doll in your slice of the tricolor King Cake, you have to throw the next party.

If you want to come to Mardi Gras and bring your kids, there are a few activities for them in addition to those mentioned earlier in "New Orleans for Families." Several of the hotels provide "kids' carnivals" or parties, and the Louisiana Children's Museum offers special in-house parades, mask-making classes, and so on. There is a rather different but fascinating **"Cajun Mardi Gras"** celebration in Lafayette, Louisiana, about three hours from the city; see "Cajun Country Festivals" at the end of this chapter.

■ Jazz and Heritage Fest ■

The **New Orleans Jazz & Heritage Festival** spans a ten-day period in late April and early May. It's usually called Jazz Fest for short, and in fact the first festival, organized over a quarter-century ago by the same folks who brought you the Newport Jazz Festival, featured such stars as Duke Ellington, Mahalia Jackson, and Al Hirt. Now, however, the folk, gumbo, zydeco, Latin, R&B, swamp rock, brass, bounce (brass crossed with rap), ragtime-revival, bluegrass, gospel, and even klezmer performers far outnumber the jazz traditionalists; it's estimated that close to 5,000 musicians show up.

Long a favorite of lower-key visitors, it has in recent years come to rival Carnival in its crowds and extravagance (although not yet in its sheer overindulgence). The main stages, a dozen of them, are erected at the Fairgrounds, with the biggest performance stage right in the racetrack infield and tents all around the 25-acre site. The music is big-time but wide-ranging: Veterans include the Neville Brothers, the Marsalis brothers (and sometimes patriarch Ellis as well), Irma Thomas, Gladys Knight, Wilson Pickett, the Indigo Girls, the Dave Matthews Band, the Radiators, Buckwheat Zydeco, Joan Baez, and Van Morrison. You just wander around until something grabs your fancy. And there are related concerts at clubs and venues all around the city, some even on the water, and the streets are full.

Meanwhile, parts of the Fairgrounds are spread out with scores of food concessions—not the usual fast-food junk, but gumbo, fried alligator, red beans and rice, jambalaya, crabs, oysters, poorboys, and even roast pig. Jewelry, hand-crafted furniture and even finer hand-crafted instruments, decoys, beadwork, and baskets make for some of the most worthwhile souvenirs the city has to offer.

The Fairgrounds are in a constant state of ferment from 11 A.M. to 7 P.M.; tickets are $10 in advance or $15 at the gate (kids $1.50 in advance,

$2 at the gate). Nighttime concerts, with tickets ranging up to $30, are held at various locations, although if you cock an ear toward the nicer hotel lounges and jazz clubs, you may pick up a free jam or two.

If you have a choice, go for the second part of the festival: On Sunday morning, New Orleans' most famous falsetto, Aaron Neville, usually steps up with the famous Zion Harmonizers at the gospel show.

Note that this frequently falls during one of the first real heat waves, so be sure to pack sunglasses, sunblock, water, and a hat or at least a bandana. And forget driving over; either take public transportation or a cab.

For more information, contact the Jazz & Heritage Festival office at P.O. Box 53407, New Orleans, LA 70153, or call (504) 522-4786. The festival also has a World Wide Web site: www.nojazzfest.com. You can also buy advance tickets through TicketMaster: (800) 488-5252 or (504) 522-5555.

■ Halloween ■

Real Anne Rice fans probably already know about the **Memnoch Ball,** a.k.a. the Vampire Lestat Extravaganza, which is held in the former chapel at St. Elizabeth's Orphanage, which figures heavily in *Memnoch the Devil* and which she bought and renovated as her company's offices. The ball is one of the few chances for visitors to see the orphanage and Rice's hundreds of antique dolls, odd antiques (Nipper the RCA dog, for example) and Hollywood monster characters, and the coffin she sometimes uses for grand entrances. Otherwise, the orphanage is used only for special events, and there are fantasy-setting guest bedrooms—such as the gold lamé and animal-print "Sunset Boulevard" suite—and a health club for employees in the upper levels as well as some private apartments for older family members.

To find out how you can get a ticket to the Memnoch Ball, contact the Vampire Lestat Fan Club at Box 58277, New Orleans, LA 70158-8277; or go more directly to the source: Kith and Kin, the family-run tour company (call (504) 529-0560 or (888) SEE-RICE). More recently, Rice has purchased the Happy Hour Theatre, a former cinema at the corner of Magazine and St. Andrew's Streets, which she is considering turning into a Cafe Lestat restaurant with elaborate black statuary and effects; it is possible that the Memnoch Ball will be held there, instead. You can actually hear Rice give news updates on her own semi-private answering machine and even leave a 60-second message (522-8634) or surf her Internet site (www. annerice.com). See "Sight-Seeing and Tours" for lots more Rice information, or call (888) SEE-RICE for tour information.

But you don't have to be invited to the coven ball to enjoy Halloween in New Orleans; there are costume parties all over the French Quarter, a huge one at the Convention Center, a midnight "Witches' Run" (not so much to offset all that trick-or-treating as an excuse to run in costume), and for kids, the Boo at the Zoo festival (see calendar on page 53). Contact the Convention and Visitors Bureau, 1520 Sugar Bowl Drive, New Orleans, LA 70112, or call 566-5005.

Also, you can make up a Halloween holiday of your own; see "The Great Hereafter" in "Sight-Seeing and Tours."

■ Creole Christmas ■

This is the sort of tourism-industry creation that still seems a little packaged—in fact, some brochures refer to it as "New Orleans Christmas" because, although old Creole society supplied the inspiration for many of the events, visitors tend to lump Cajun and Creole together. (If you're confused yourself, see "A Too-Short History of a Fascinating Place.") Gradually, however, it has developed some fine moments: City Park's old live oaks are hung with lights, and you can ride the miniature trains or hire a carriage. Many fine older homes are decorated in the old style and lit up at night. Many events are free—special walking tours and concerts, parades, museum exhibits, cooking exhibitions, and candlelight caroling in Jackson Square—and perfect for a family vacation. Many hotels, both chain and independent, offer special low "Papa Noel" or "Creole Christmas" rates, while restaurants of the quality of Arnaud's and Alex Patout's set out "Reveillon" menus adapted from old Creole celebrations which usually include champagne or eggnog and perhaps a little *lagniappe*.

At 7 p.m. on Christmas Eve, huge bonfires are set up and down the Mississippi around the plantations, and the homes themselves are all decked out, which makes this a really good time to plan your plantation tour. For more information about "New Orleans Christmas" contact the French Quarter Festivals: 100 Conti Street, New Orleans, LA 70130, or call (800) 673-5725.

Of course, major party town that it is, New Orleans doesn't really surrender the Christmas season until New Year's Eve, which is another wild, woolly, loud, and lively night on the town, culminating with a giant crowd singing "Auld Lange Syne" in Jackson Square. It also coincides with the collegiate football championship Sugar Bowl, held in the Superdome. Just as for Mardi Gras, you need to make your hotel reservations early; however, you may be able to sneak in a good airfare by waiting to come until, say, December 27 or 28 and staying over until after New Year's Day.

Or you could stay through until Twelfth Night on January 6, when the first Carnival Krewe kicks off the pre–Mardi Gras season . . . or even January 8, for the annual celebration of Jackson's victory at the Battle of New Orleans. . .

■ Cajun Country Festivals ■

There is more and more interest in Cajun culture—just notice what sort of music all those souvenir shops are blaring out onto Bourbon Street these days—and what's called "Cajun Mardi Gras" in Lafayette, Louisiana, about three hours west of New Orleans, is a much more family-style festival than the Bourbon Street blowout. There the festival's sovereigns are King Gabriel and Queen Evangeline, from Longfellow's epic story of the Cajun diaspora (see "A Too-Short History of a Fascinating Place"), and several of the events are geared specifically to children. And unlike the Rex ball, the final party is open to the public (though you should still tie that black tie). You can also participate in some even older, country-style events, such as house-to-house partying. For information contact the Lafayette Parish Convention and Visitors Commission, P.O. Box 52066, Lafayette, LA 70505, or call (800) 346-1958 or (318) 232-3808.

Around the third week of September, Lafayette is the site of a multi-theme celebration, the Festivals Acadiens, spotlighting Cajun traditions and history. The best-known part is the Festival de Musique Acadienne, now more than 20 years old and drawing 50,000 fans of two-step, zydeco, and traditional Cajun-French music. Set up alongside the music stages is the Bayou Food Festival, a mouthwatering abundance of smothered quail, oysters en brochette, boudin sausages, and other Cajun specialties, prepared by area restaurants. The Louisiana Native Crafts Festival spotlights traditional methods and native materials: duck decoy carving, caning, basket weaving, quilting, pottery-making, jewelry, and even alligator skinning. Artists over 60 have their own "seniors circuit," so to speak, the RSVP (Retired Senior Volunteer Program) Fair, where you get the tall tales along with the traditional crafts.

You can find Cajun tradition (and likely, some smaller festival or other) any time you visit Lafayette.

PART FOUR

New Orleans Lodging

Deciding Where to Stay

New Orleans, you must understand, has an almost palpable feel. History here is cumulative, and from the French to the Spanish to the Confederacy to the present, every sailor, gambler, barmaid, and merchant has left something for you to savor. When you are in New Orleans you know without being told that you are someplace very different. In fact, it's not so much a place to be as a place to know. Even as a first-time tourist, your heart aches to know this city intimately, to be part of its exotic rhythms and steaminess. The city never, never leaves your consciousness. You wear it and breathe it at the same time, all of it, and hundreds of years of blues in the night, chicory coffee, and sweat on the docks become part of your reality.

This reality is sustained by the river, the humidity, the narrow streets, and even by the city's grittiness and poverty. And it is reflected by its small, quirky hotels and inns. Some of the most delightful, interesting, and intimate hotels in America can be found in New Orleans. Ditto for guest houses and B&B's. Zoning and historic preservation ordinances, particularly in the French Quarter, have limited the construction of modern highrise hotels and stimulated the evolution of an eclectic mix of medium- and small-sized properties, many of which are proprietorships. In an age of standardization and cookie-cutter chain hotels, these smaller hotels, distinguished by cozy courtyards, shuttered windows, balconies, and wrought-iron trim, offer guests a truly unique lodging experience.

Hotels in New Orleans are concentrated in the French Quarter and along Canal Street between Claiborne Avenue and the river. Most of the larger, modern chain hotels are situated near the convention center at the river end of Canal Street. Smaller hotels, inns, and guest houses are sprinkled liberally around the French Quarter and along St. Charles Avenue west of Lee Circle. Historically, there have been relatively few hotels located in other parts of town. Although today there are some hotels near the airport and along I-10 east of the city, hotels outside of the downtown/French Quarter area are relatively scarce.

Because New Orleans thrives on tourism, weekday hotel rates are often lower than weekend rates (the opposite of most cities where business travel rules). If you would like to visit during Mardi Gras (late February to early March), the New Orleans Jazz and Heritage Festival (late April to early May), or during the week of Christmas to New Year's, make your reservations six months or more in advance.

While we would not dissuade you from experiencing Mardi Gras, be advised that the city is pretty much turned upside-down. Hotels are jammed, prices are jacked up, parking is impossible, and the streets are full of staggering drunks. In the French Quarter many bars and restaurants dispatch their furniture and fixtures to warehouses to make room for the throng of wall-to-wall people. While Mardi Gras is a hell of a good party, it essentially deprives visitors of experiencing "the real" New Orleans.

If you happen to be attending one of the big conventions, book early and use some of the tips listed below to get a discounted room rate. To assist in timing your visit, we have included a convention and trade show calendar in the chapter "Visiting New Orleans on Business."

■ Some Considerations ■

1. When choosing your New Orleans lodging, make sure your hotel is situated in a location convenient to your recreation or business needs, and that it is in a safe and comfortable area.

2. New Orleans hotels generally offer lower-quality rooms than those in most cities profiled by the *Unofficial Guides*. A meager 17% of the hotels in New Orleans merit a quality rating of four stars or higher. Compare this with Atlanta, where 23% of the hotels are rated four stars and higher, Chicago, where 29% of the hotels are four stars or higher, and Washington, D.C., which boasts 38% of its hotels being four- and five-star properties. As a consequence of the generally lower quality standard, newer chain hotels have not had to invest in superior rooms in order to be competitive.

Surprisingly, New Orleans is not home to a single five-star hotel. The two nicest hotels in New Orleans, the Windsor Court and the Omni Royal Crescent, are older properties that have found ways to cram insane amounts of luxurious amenities into shoebox-sized rooms. These hotels rely as much on their dignified reputations as on their guest room quality to attract guests. Although extremely nice, their rooms lack the square footage to be called "luxurious by any standard."

New Orleans is full of old hotels, some well maintained, some not. Many are situated in ancient buildings, with guest rooms in varying states of renovation and dilapidation. Lobbies of the nicer hotels are characteristically decorated in gaudy antique gilt, with Old World sculptures and crystal chandeliers. Along similar lines, you are likely to find more antique and antique-replica furniture in New Orleans hotel rooms than in most any other U.S. tourist destination. Four-poster rice beds are a particular favorite.

And it's gonna cost you. In general, New Orleans hotels are pricey. But good deals can still be found, and upon inspection, a pattern emerges. With a handful of exceptions, the hotels which offer the best values are found outside the French Quarter. And within the French Quarter, those hotels found on or within one block of Bourbon Street are often outrageously expensive. So, as is often the case with urban hotels, the address of the hotel is the deciding factor in the room price.

A good example of this phenomenon can be found when comparing New Orleans' two Omni properties. The Omni Royal Crescent is located downtown, while the Omni Royal Orleans stands in the heart of the French Quarter. Although the Royal Crescent has a quality rating which is five points higher than the Royal Orleans, a room at the former costs $54 less than the same type of room at the latter at the height of the tourist season.

Similarly, the most expensive hotel in New Orleans, the Best Western Inn on Bourbon, is located right in the middle of the Bourbon Street action. Although the Best Western Inn on Bourbon offers only a three-star room, it is continually booked due to location.

Before making any reservations, find out when the guest rooms in your prospective hotel were last renovated. Request that the hotel send you its promotional brochure. Ask if brochure photos of guest rooms are accurate and current.

3. If you plan to take a car, inquire about the parking situation. Some hotels offer no parking at all, some charge dearly for parking, and some offer free parking.

4. If you are not a city dweller, or perhaps are a light sleeper, try to book a hotel on a quieter side street. In the French Quarter, avoid hotels on Bourbon Street. If you book a Central Business District or Canal Street hotel, ask for a room off the street and high up.

5. When you plan your budget, remember that New Orleans' hotel tax is 11%.

6. The ratings and rankings in this chapter are based solely on room quality and value. To determine if a particular hotel has room service, a pool, or other services and amenities, see the alphabetical hotel charts beginning on page 85.

Getting a Good Deal on a Room

■ Value Season ■

New Orleans' value season generally starts the first weekend in July (it seems New Orleans is not a hot Fourth destination) and ends on the first weekend in September.

■ Special Weekday Rates ■

Although well-located New Orleans hotels are tough for the budget-conscious, it's not impossible to get a good deal, at least relatively speaking. For starters, many French Quarter hotels that cater to tourists offer special weekday discount rates that range from 5% to 25% below weekend rates. You can find out about weekday specials by calling individual hotels or by consulting your travel agent.

■ Getting Corporate Rates ■

Many hotels offer discounted corporate rates (5–20% off rack). Usually you do not need to work for a large company or have a special relationship with the hotel to obtain these rates. Simply call the hotel of your choice and ask for their corporate rates. Many hotels will guarantee you the discounted rate on the phone when you make your reservation. Others may make the rate conditional on your providing some sort of bona fides, for instance a fax on your company's letterhead requesting the rate, or a

Seasonal Rate Changes in New Orleans			
Hotel	Late August	Late September	Mardi Gras and Jazz Fest
Omni Royal Orleans	$109	$239	$279
Best Western (Bourbon)	$149	$255	$345
Ramada Plaza Hotel	$99	$99	$179
Holiday Inn Metairie	$80	$112	$145
Westin Canal Place	$129	$220	$259

company credit card or business card on check-in. Generally, the screening is not rigorous.

■ Half-Price Programs ■

The larger discounts on rooms (35–60%), in New Orleans or anywhere else, are available through half-price hotel programs, often called travel clubs. Program operators contract with an individual hotel to provide rooms at deep discounts, usually 50% off rack rate, on a "space available" basis. Space available in practice generally means that you can reserve a room at the discounted rate whenever the hotel expects to be at less than 80% occupancy. A little calendar sleuthing to help you avoid Mardi Gras, Jazz Fest, special events, and city-wide conventions will increase your chances of choosing a time when the discounts are available.

Most half-price programs charge an annual membership fee or directory subscription charge of $25 to $125. Once enrolled, you are mailed a membership card and a directory listing participating hotels. Examining the directory, you will notice immediately that there are many restrictions and exceptions. Some hotels, for instance, "black out" certain dates or times of year. Others may only offer the discount on certain days of the week, or require you to stay a certain number of nights. Still others may offer a much smaller discount than 50% off the rack rate.

Programs specialize in domestic travel, international travel, or both. More established operators offer members between 1,000 and 4,000 hotels to choose from in the United States. All of the programs have a heavy concentration of hotels in California and Florida, and most have a very limited selection of participating properties in New York City or Boston. Offerings in other cities and regions of the United States vary considerably. The programs with the largest selections of New Orleans hotels are Encore, ITC-50, Great American Traveler, and Entertainment Publications. Each of these programs lists between 9 and 30 hotels in the greater New Orleans area.

Encore	(800) 444-9800
Entertainment Publications	(800) 445-4137
ITC-50	(800) 987-6216
Great American Traveler	(800) 548-2812

One problem with half-price programs is that not all hotels offer a full 50% discount. Another slippery problem is the base rate against which the discount is applied. Some hotels figure the discount on an exaggerated rack rate that nobody would ever have to pay. A few participating hotels may deduct the discount from a supposed "superior" or "upgraded" room rate, even though the room you get is the hotel's standard accommodation. Though hard to pin down, the majority of participating properties base discounts on the published rate in the *Hotel & Travel Index* (a quarterly reference work used by travel agents) and work within the spirit of their agreement with the program operator. As a rule, if you travel several times a year, your room rate savings will easily compensate you for program membership fees.

A noteworthy addendum: Deeply discounted rooms through half-price programs are not commissionable to travel agents. In practical terms this means that you must ordinarily make your own inquiry calls and reservations. If you travel frequently, however, and run a lot of business through your travel agent, he or she will probably do your legwork, lack of commission notwithstanding.

■ Preferred Rates ■

If you cannot book the hotel of your choice through a half-price program, you and your travel agent may have to search for a lesser discount, often called a preferred rate. A preferred rate could be a discount made available to travel agents to stimulate their booking activity, or a discount initiated to attract a certain class of traveler. Most preferred rates are promoted through travel industry publications and are often accessible only through an agent.

We recommend sounding out your travel agent about possible deals. Be aware, however, that the rates shown on travel agents' computerized reservations systems are not always the lowest rates obtainable. Zero in on a couple of hotels that fill your needs in terms of location and quality of accommodations, and then have your travel agent call the hotel for the latest rates and specials. Hotel reps are almost always more responsive to travel agents because travel agents represent a source of additional business. There are certain specials that hotel reps will disclose only to travel agents. Travel agents also come in handy when the hotel you want is supposedly booked. A personal appeal from your agent to the hotel's director of sales and marketing will get you a room more than 50% of the time.

■ Wholesalers, Consolidators, and ■ Reservation Services

If you do not want to join a program or buy a discount directory, you can take advantage of the services of a wholesaler or consolidator. Wholesalers and consolidators buy rooms, or options on rooms (room blocks), from hotels at a low, negotiated rate. They then resell the rooms at a profit through travel agents or tour operators, or directly to the public. Most wholesalers and consolidators have a provision for returning unsold rooms to participating hotels, but are not inclined to do so. The wholesaler's or consolidator's relationship with any hotel is predicated on volume. If they return rooms unsold, the hotel may not make as many rooms available to them the next time around. Thus wholesalers and consolidators often offer rooms at bargain rates, anywhere from 15–50% off rack, occasionally sacrificing their profit margins in the process, to avoid returning the rooms to the hotel unsold.

When wholesalers and consolidators deal directly with the public, they frequently represent themselves as "reservation services." When you call, you can ask for a rate quote for a particular hotel or, alternatively, ask for their best available deal in the area you prefer to stay. If there is a maximum amount you are willing to pay, say so. Chances are the service will find something that will work for you, even if they have to shave a dollar or two off their own profit. Following is a list of several services that sell rooms in New Orleans:

Hotel Reservations Network	(800) 964-6835
Room Finders USA (Headquartered in New Orleans)	(800) 473-7829
RMC Travel	(800) 245-5738
Accommodations Express	(800) 444-7666

The discount available (if any) from a reservation service depends on whether the service functions as a consolidator or a wholesaler. Consolidators are strictly sales agents who do not own or control the room inventory they are trying to sell. Discounts offered by consolidators are determined by the hotels with rooms to fill. Consolidator discounts vary enormously depending on how desperate the hotel is to unload the rooms. When you deal with a room reservation service that operates as a consolidator, you pay for your room as usual when you check out of the hotel.

Wholesalers have longstanding contracts with hotels that allow the wholesaler to purchase rooms at an established deep discount. Some wholesalers hold purchase options on blocks of rooms, while others actually pay for rooms and own the inventory. Because a wholesaler controls the room inventory, it can offer whatever discount it pleases, consistent with current demand. In practice, most wholesaler reservation service discounts fall in the 10–40% range. When you reserve a room with a reservation service that operates as a wholesaler, you must usually pay for your entire stay in advance with your credit card. The service then sends you a written confirmation and usually a voucher (indicating prepayment) for you to present at the hotel.

Our experience has been that the reservation services are more useful in finding rooms when availability is scarce than in obtaining deep discounts. Calling the hotels ourselves, we were often able to beat the reservation services' rates when rooms were generally available. When the city was booked, however, and we could not find a room by calling the hotels ourselves, the reservation services could almost always get us a room at a fair price.

■ How to Evaluate a Travel Package ■

Hundreds of New Orleans package vacations are offered to the public each year. Packages should be a win/win proposition for both the buyer and the seller. The buyer only has to make one phone call and deal with a single salesperson to set up the whole vacation: transportation, rental car, lodging, meals, attraction admissions, and even golf and tennis. The seller, likewise, only has to deal with the buyer once, eliminating the need for separate sales, confirmations, and billing. In addition to streamlining sales, processing, and administration, some packagers also buy airfares in bulk on contract like a broker playing the commodities market. Buying a large number of airfares in advance allows the packager to buy them at a significant savings from posted fares. The same practice is also applied to hotel rooms. Because selling vacation packages is an efficient way of doing business, and because the packager can often buy individual package components (airfare, lodging, etc.) in bulk at discount, savings in operating expenses realized by the seller are sometimes passed on to the buyer so that, in addition to convenience, the package is also an exceptional value. In any event, that is the way it is supposed to work.

All too often, in practice, the seller cashes in on discounts and passes none on to the buyer. In some instances, packages are loaded with extras that cost the packager next to nothing, but inflate the retail price sky-high. As you may expect, the savings to be passed along to customers do not materialize.

When considering a package, choose one that includes features you are sure to use; whether you use all the features or not, you will most certainly pay for them. Second, if cost is of greater concern than convenience, make a few phone calls and see what the package would cost if you booked its individual components (airfare, rental car, lodging, etc.) on your own. If the package price is less than the a la carte cost, the package is a good deal. If the costs are about the same, the package is probably worth buying just for the convenience.

If your package includes a choice of rental car or airport transfers (transportation to and from the airport), take the transfers if you plan to spend most of your time in the French Quarter or the Central Business District. If you want to run around town or go on excursions outside the city, take the car. If you take the car, be sure to ask if the package includes free parking at your hotel.

The following tour operators specialize in vacation packages to New Orleans. Book directly or through your travel agent.

Destination Management	(800) 366-8882
Tours by Andrea	(800) 535-2732
Travel New Orleans	(800) 535-8747

Tour operators, of course, prefer to sell you a whole vacation package. When business is slow, however, they will often agree to sell you just the lodging component of the package, usually at a nicely discounted rate.

Hotel-Sponsored Packages

In addition to tour operators, packages are frequently offered by hotels. Usually "land only" (i.e., no airfare included), the hotel packages are some-times exceptional deals. Many packages are specialized, offering plantation tours, jazz tours, or the like, while others are only offered at certain times of the year, such as "Papa Noel" deals during the December holiday season. Promotion of hotel specials tends to be limited to the hotel's primary markets, which for most properties is Louisiana, Texas, Alabama, Florida, Mississippi, Georgia, Arkansas, and Tennessee. If you live in other parts of the country, you can take advantage of the packages but probably will not see them advertised in your local newspaper. An important point regarding hotel specials is that the hotel reservationists do not usually inform you of existing specials or offer them to you. In other words, *you have to ask.*

■ Helping Your Travel Agent Help You ■

When you call your travel agent, ask if he or she has been to New Orleans. If the answer is no, be prepared to give your travel agent some direction. Do not accept any recommendations at face value. Check out the location and rates of any suggested hotel and make certain that the hotel is suited to your itinerary.

Because some travel agents are unfamiliar with New Orleans, your agent may try to plug you into a tour operator's preset package. This essentially allows the travel agent to set up your whole trip with a single phone call and still collect an 8–10% commission. The problem with this scenario is that most agents will place 90% of their New Orleans business with only one or two wholesalers or tour operators. In other words, it's the line of least resistance for them, and not much choice for you.

Travel agents will often use wholesalers who run packages in conjunction with airlines, like Delta's Dream Vacations or American's Fly-Away Vacations. Because of the wholesaler's exclusive relationship with the carrier, these trips are very easy for travel agents to book. However, they will probably be more expensive than a package offered by a high-volume wholesaler who works with a number of airlines in a primary New Orleans market.

To help your travel agent get you the best possible deal, do the following:

1. Determine where you want to stay in New Orleans, and if possible choose a specific hotel. This can be accomplished by reviewing the hotel information provided in this guide, and by writing or calling hotels that interest you.

2. Check out the hotel deals and package vacations advertised in the Sunday travel sections of the *Atlanta Journal-Constitution, New Orleans Times-Picayune,* or *Dallas Morning News* newspapers. Often you will be able to find deals that beat the socks off anything offered in your local paper. See if you can find specials that fit your plans and include a hotel you like.

3. Call the hotels or tour operators whose ads you have collected. Ask any questions you have concerning their packages, but do not book your trip with them directly.

4. Tell your travel agent about the deals you find and ask if he or she can get you something better. The deals in the paper will serve as a benchmark against which to compare alternatives proposed by your travel agent.

5. Choose from the options that you and your travel agent uncover. No matter which option you select, have your travel agent book it. Even if you go with one of the packages in the newspaper, it will probably be commissionable (at no additional cost to you) and will provide the agent some return on the time invested on your behalf. Also, as a travel professional, your agent should be able to verify the quality and integrity of the deal.

■ If You Make Your Own Reservation ■

As you poke around trying to find a good deal, there are several things you should know. First, always call the specific hotel rather than the hotel chain's national 800 number. Quite often, the reservationists at the national 800 number are unaware of local specials. Always ask about specials before you inquire about corporate rates. Do not be reluctant to bargain. If you are buying a hotel's weekday package, for example, and want to extend your stay into the following weekend, you can often obtain at least the corporate rate for the extra days. Do your bargaining, however, before you check in, preferably when you make your reservations.

Hotel/Motel Toll-Free Chain 800 Numbers	
Best Western	(800) 528-1234 U.S. & Canada, (800) 528-2222 TDD
Comfort Inn	(800) 228-5150 U.S.
Courtyard by Marriott	(800) 321-2211 U.S.
Days Inn	(800) 325-2525 U.S.
DoubleTree Hotels	(800) 222-8733 U.S. & Canada
Econo Lodge	(800) 424-4777 U.S.
Embassy Suites	(800) 362-2779 U.S. & Canada
Fairfield Inn by Marriott	(800) 228-2800 U.S.
Hampton Inn	(800) 426-7866 U.S. & Canada
Hilton	(800) 445-8667 U.S. (800) 368-1133 TDD
Holiday Inn	(800) 465-4329 U.S. & Canada
Howard Johnson	(800) 654-2000 U.S. & Canada, (800) 654-8442 TDD
Hyatt	(800) 233-1234 U.S. & Canada
Loew's	(800) 223-0888 U.S. & Canada

Hotel/Motel Toll-Free Chain 800 Numbers (continued)	
Marriott	(800) 228-9290 U.S. & Canada,
	(800) 228-7014 TDD
Quality Inn	(800) 228-5151 U.S. & Canada
Radisson	(800) 333-3333 U.S. & Canada
Ramada Inn	(800) 228-3838 U.S.
	(800) 228-3232 TDD
Renaissance Hotels and Resorts	(800) 468-3571 U.S. & Canada
Residence Inn by Marriott	(800) 331-3131 U.S.
Ritz-Carlton	(800) 241-3333 U.S.
Sheraton	(800) 325-3535 U.S. & Canada
Wyndham	(800) 822-4200 U.S.

Hotels and Motels:
Rated and Ranked

■ What's in a Room? ■

Except for cleanliness, state of repair, and decor, most travelers do not pay much attention to hotel rooms. There is, of course, a discernible standard of quality and luxury that differentiates Motel 6 from Holiday Inn, Holiday Inn from Marriott, and so on. In general, however, hotel guests fail to appreciate the fact that some rooms are better engineered than others.

Contrary to what you might suppose, designing a hotel room is (or should be) much more complex than picking a bedspread to match the carpet and drapes. Making the room usable to its occupants is an art, a planning discipline that combines both form and function.

Decor and taste are important, certainly. No one wants to spend several days in a room whose decor is dated, garish, or even ugly. But beyond the decor, several variables determine how "livable" a hotel room is. In New Orleans, for example, we have seen some beautifully appointed rooms that are simply not well designed for human habitation. The next time you stay in a hotel, pay attention to the details and design elements of your room. Even more than decor, these will make you feel comfortable and at home.

It takes the *Unofficial Guide* researchers quite a while to inspect a hotel room. Here are a few of the things we check that you may want to start paying attention to:

Room Size   While some smaller rooms are cozy and well designed, a large and uncluttered room is generally preferable, especially for a stay of more than three days.

Temperature Control, Ventilation, and Odor   The guest should be able to control the temperature of the room. The best system, because it's so quiet, is central heating and air conditioning, controlled by the room's own thermostat. The next best system is a room module heater and air conditioner, preferably controlled by an automatic thermostat, but usually by manually operated button controls. The worst system is central heating and air without any sort of room thermostat or guest control.

The vast majority of hotel rooms have windows or balcony doors that have been permanently sealed. Though there are some legitimate safety and liability issues involved, we prefer windows and balcony doors that can be opened to admit fresh air. Hotel rooms should be odor and smoke free, and not feel stuffy or damp.

Room Security   Better rooms have locks that require a plastic card instead of the traditional lock and key. Card and slot systems allow the hotel, essentially, to change the combination or entry code of the lock with each new guest. A burglar who has somehow acquired a conventional room key can afford to wait until the situation is right before using the key to gain access. Not so with a card and slot system. Though larger hotels and hotel chains with lock and key systems usually rotate their locks once each year, they remain vulnerable to hotel thieves much of the time. Many smaller or independent properties rarely rotate their locks.

In addition to the entry lock system, the door should have a deadbolt, and preferably a chain that can be locked from the inside. A chain by itself is not sufficient. Doors should also have a peephole. Windows and balcony doors, if any, should have secure locks.

Safety   Every room should have a fire or smoke alarm, clear fire instructions, and preferably a sprinkler system. Bathtubs should have a nonskid surface, and shower stalls should have doors that either open outward or slide side-to-side. Bathroom electrical outlets should be high on the wall and not too close to the sink. Balconies should have sturdy, high rails.

Noise   Most travelers have been kept awake by the television, partying, or amorous activities of people in the next room, or by traffic on the street outside. Better hotels are designed with noise control in mind. Wall and ceiling construction are substantial, effectively screening routine noise. Carpets and drapes, in addition to being decorative, also absorb and muffle sounds. Mattresses mounted on stable platforms or sturdy bed frames do not squeak, even when challenged by the most acrobatic lovers. Televisions enclosed in cabinets, and with volume governors, rarely disturb guests in adjacent rooms.

In better hotels, the air conditioning and heating system is well maintained and operates without noise or vibration. Likewise, plumbing is quiet and positioned away from the sleeping area. Doors to the hall, and to adjoining rooms, are thick and well fitted to better block out noise.

If you are easily disturbed by noise, ask for a room on a higher floor, off main thoroughfares, and away from elevators and ice and vending machines.

Darkness Control   Ever been in a hotel room where the curtains would not quite meet in the middle? Thick, lined curtains that close completely in the center and extend beyond the edges of the window or door frame are required. In a well-planned room, the curtains, shades, or blinds should almost totally block light at any time of day.

Lighting   Poor lighting is an extremely common problem in American hotel rooms. The lighting is usually adequate for dressing, relaxing, or watching television, but not for reading or working. Lighting needs to be bright over tables and desks, and beside couches or easy chairs. Since so many people read in bed, there should be a separate light for each person. A room with two queen beds should have individual lights for four people. Better bedside reading lights illuminate a small area, so if one person wants to sleep and another to read, the sleeper will not be bothered by the light. The worst situation by far is a single lamp on a table between beds. In each bed, only the person next to the lamp will have sufficient light to read. This deficiency is often compounded by weak light bulbs.

In addition, closet areas should be well-lit, and there should be a switch near the door that turns on room lights when you enter. A seldom seen, but desirable, feature is a bedside console that allows a guest to control all or most lights in the room from bed.

Furnishings   At bare minimum, the bed(s) must be firm. Pillows should be made with nonallergic fillers and, in addition to the sheets and spread, a blanket should be provided. Bedclothes should be laundered with fabric softener and changed daily. Better hotels usually provide extra blankets and pillows in the room or on request, and sometimes use a second topsheet between the blanket and spread.

There should be a dresser large enough to hold clothes for two people during a five-day stay. A small table with two chairs, or a desk with a chair, should be provided. The room should be equipped with a luggage rack and a three-quarter- to full-length mirror.

The television should be color and cable-connected; ideally, it should have a volume governor and remote control. It should be mounted on a swivel base, and preferably enclosed in a cabinet. Local channels should be posted on the set and a local TV program guide should be supplied. The telephone should be touchtone, conveniently situated for bedside use, and should have, on or near it, easy-to-understand dialing instructions and a rate card. Local white and yellow pages should be provided. Better hotels install phones in the bathroom and equip room phones with long cords.

Well-designed hotel rooms usually have a plush armchair or a sleeper sofa for lounging and reading. Better headboards are padded for comfortable reading in bed, and there should be a nightstand or table on each side of the bed(s). Nice extras in any hotel room include a small refrigerator, a digital alarm clock, and a coffeemaker.

Bathroom   Two sinks are better than one, and you cannot have too much counter space. A sink outside the bath is a great convenience when one person bathes as another dresses. Sinks should have drains with stoppers.

Better bathrooms have both a tub and shower with a nonslip bottom. Tub and shower controls should be easy to operate. Adjustable shower heads are preferred. The bath needs to be well lit and should have an exhaust fan and a guest-controlled bathroom heater. Towels and washcloths should be large, soft, and fluffy, and generously supplied. There should be an electrical outlet for each sink, conveniently and safely placed.

Complimentary shampoo, conditioner, and lotion are a plus, as are robes and bathmats. Better hotels supply bathrooms with tissues and extra toilet paper. Luxurious baths feature a phone, a hair dryer, sometimes a small television, or even a jacuzzi.

Vending   Complimentary ice and a drink machine should be located on each floor. Welcome additions include a snack machine and a sundries (combs, toothpaste) machine. The latter are seldom found in large hotels that have restaurants and shops.

■ Room Ratings ■

To distinguish properties according to relative quality, tastefulness, state of repair, cleanliness, and size of standard rooms, we have grouped the hotels and motels into classifications denoted by stars. Star ratings in this guide apply to New Orleans area properties only, and do not necessarily correspond to ratings awarded by Mobil, AAA, or other travel critics. Because stars carry little weight when awarded in the absence of commonly recognized standards of comparison, we have linked our ratings to expected levels of quality established by specific American hotel corporations.

Star ratings apply to room quality only, and describe the property's standard accommodations. For most hotels and motels a "standard accommodation" is a hotel room with either one king bed or two queen beds. In an all-suite property, the standard accommodation is either a one- or two-room suite. In addition to standard accommodations, many hotels offer luxury rooms and special suites that are not rated in this guide. Star ratings for rooms are assigned without regard to whether a property has restaurant(s), recreational facilities, entertainment, or other extras.

In addition to stars (which delineate broad categories), we also employ a numerical rating system. Our rating scale is 0–100, with 100 as the best

Room Star Ratings		
★★★★★	Superior Rooms	Tasteful and luxurious by any standard
★★★★	Extremely Nice Rooms	What you would expect at a Hyatt Regency or Marriott
★★★	Nice Rooms	Holiday Inn or comparable quality
★★	Adequate Rooms	Clean, comfortable, and functional without frills (like a Motel 6)
★	Super Budget	

possible rating, and zero (0) as the worst. Numerical ratings are presented to show the difference we perceive between one property and another. Rooms at the Meridian Hotel New Orleans, Marriott New Orleans, and the Lafitte Guest House are all rated as three and a half stars (★★★½). In the supplemental numerical ratings, the Meridian Hotel is rated an 82, the Marriott is rated an 81, and the Lafitte Guest House is rated a 75. This means that within the three-and-a-half-star category, the Meridian and Marriott are comparable, and both have slightly nicer rooms than the Lafitte Guest House.

The location column identifies the New Orleans zone where you will find a particular property.

■ How the Hotels Compare ■

Cost estimates are based on the hotel's published rack rates for standard rooms. Each "$" represents $30. Thus a cost symbol of "$$$" means a room (or suite) at that hotel will cost about $90 a night.

Below is a hit parade of the nicest rooms in town. We've focused strictly on room quality, and excluded any consideration of location, services, recreation, or amenities. In some instances, a one- or two-room suite can be had for the same price or less than that of a hotel room.

If you use subsequent editions of this guide, you will notice that many of the ratings and rankings change. In addition to the inclusion of new properties, these changes also consider guest room renovations or improved maintenance and housekeeping. A failure to properly maintain guest rooms or a lapse in housekeeping standards can negatively affect the ratings.

Finally, before you begin to shop for a hotel, take a hard look at this letter we received from a couple in Hot Springs, Arkansas:

We cancelled our room reservations to follow the advice in your book [and reserved a hotel room highly ranked by the Unofficial Guide*]. We wanted inexpensive, but clean and cheerful. We got inexpensive, but [also] dirty, grim, and depressing. I really felt disappointed in your advice and the room. It was the pits. That was the one real piece of information I needed from your book! The room spoiled the holiday for me aside from our touring.*

Needless to say, this letter was as unsettling to us as the bad room was to our reader. Our integrity as travel journalists, after all, is based on the quality of the information we provide our readers. Even with the best of intentions and the most conscientious research, however, we cannot inspect every room in every hotel. What we do, in statistical terms, is take a sample: We check out several rooms selected at random in each hotel and base our ratings and rankings on those rooms. The inspections are conducted anonymously and without the knowledge of the management. Although unusual, it is certainly possible that the rooms we randomly inspect are not representative of the majority of rooms at a particular hotel. Another possibility is that the rooms we inspect in a given hotel are representative, but that by bad luck a reader is assigned a room that is inferior. When we rechecked the hotel our reader disliked, we discovered our rating was correctly representative, but that he and his wife had unfortunately been assigned to one of a small number of threadbare rooms scheduled for renovation.

The key to avoiding disappointment is to snoop around in advance. We recommend that you ask for a photo of a hotel's standard guest room before you book, or at least get a copy of the hotel's promotional brochure. Be forewarned, however, that some hotel chains use the same guest room photo in their promotional literature for all hotels in the chain; a specific guest room may not resemble the brochure photo. When you or your travel agent call, ask how old the property is and when your guest room was last renovated. If you arrive and are assigned a room inferior to that which you had been led to expect, demand to be moved to another room.

How the Hotels Compare

Hotel	Zone	Quality Rating	Star Rating	Price
Omni Royal Crescent Hotel	2	93	★★★★½	$$$$$$$–
Windsor Court	2	93	★★★★½	$$$$$$$$$$$–
The Westin Canal Place	1	92	★★★★½	$$$$$$$$–
Maison Dupuy Hotel	1	90	★★★★½	$$$$$$$$$$–
Royal Sonesta Hotel	1	90	★★★★½	$$$$$$$$$+
Bienville House	1	89	★★★★	$$$$$$$$+
Omni Royal Orleans Hotel	1	89	★★★★	$$$$$$$$$+
McKendrick-Breaux House	3	89	★★★★	$$$$$–
Wyndham Riverfront Hotel	2	87	★★★★	$$$$$$$+
Chateau Sonesta Hotel	1	86	★★★★	$$$$$$$$$$
Fairmont Hotel	2	86	★★★★	$$$$$$$$$$–
Le Pavillion Hotel	2	86	★★★★	$$$$$$$$–
Embassy Suites New Orleans	2	85	★★★★	$$$$$$$+
Hotel Ste. Helene	1	85	★★★★	$$$$$$+
Avenue Plaza Hotel	2	84	★★★★	$$$$$$–
Grenoble House	1	84	★★★★	$$$$$$$$$–
DoubleTree Hotel Lakeside New Orleans	9	83	★★★★	$$$$$–
Hotel de la Monnaie	1	83	★★★★	$$$$$$$$–
Hotel Inter-Continental New Orleans	2	83	★★★★	$$$$$$$$$–
Pontchartrain Hotel	3	83	★★★★	$$$$$$$$–
Hilton New Orleans Riverside	2	82	★★★½	$$$$$$$$$$–
Meridian Hotel New Orleans	1	82	★★★½	$$$$$$$$$$+
Queen and Crescent Hotel	2	82	★★★½	$$$$$$+
Sheraton New Orleans Hotel	1	82	★★★½	$$$$$$$$+
Holiday Inn Select	2	81	★★★½	$$$$$$–
Hotel St. Marie	1	81	★★★½	$$$$$$$
Hyatt Regency New Orleans at Superdome	2	81	★★★½	$$$$$$

How the Hotels Compare (continued)

Hotel	Zone	Quality Rating	Star Rating	Price
Lafayette Hotel	2	81	★★★½	$$$$$$$$–
Marriott New Orleans	1	81	★★★½	$$$$$$$$–
Prince Conti Hotel	1	81	★★★½	$$$$$$$–
Ambassador Hotel New Orleans	2	80	★★★½	$$$$$$$–
Dauphine Orleans	1	80	★★★½	$$$$$$+
Hilton, New Orleans Airport	10	80	★★★½	$$$$$+
Rathbone Inn	5	80	★★★½	$$$$$$$$–
The Cornstalk	1	80	★★★½	$$$$$$$$+
The Monteleone	1	80	★★★½	$$$$$$$$$–
DoubleTree Hotel New Orleans	1	79	★★★½	$$$$$$$$–
Hotel de la Poste	1	79	★★★½	$$$$$$$$$+
Maison de Ville	1	79	★★★½	$$$$$$$$$
The Soniat House	1	79	★★★½	$$$$$$$$+
Hampton Inn Downtown	2	78	★★★½	$$$$$$$–
Provincial Hotel	1	78	★★★½	$$$$$$$
The Pelham Hotel	2	78	★★★½	$$$$$$$–
Best Western Airport All Suite	10	77	★★★½	$$$+
Courtyard by Marriott	2	77	★★★½	$$$$$–
Crowne Plaza New Orleans	2	76	★★★½	$$$$$$$$+
Lafitte Guest House	1	75	★★★½	$$$$$$$$–
Le Richelieu in the French Quarter	1	74	★★★	$$$$$$$–
The Saint Louis	1	73	★★★	$$$$$$$$+
Bourbon Orleans Hotel	1	72	★★★	$$$$$$$$$–
Holiday Inn Downtown/ Superdome	2	72	★★★	$$$$$$+
Lamothe House	1	72	★★★	$$$$$$$$–
Comfort Suites	2	71	★★★	$$$$$$–
Ramada Plaza Hotel	3	71	★★★	$$$$$$–
St. Peter Guest House	1	71	★★★	$$$$$$
Chateau LeMoyne French Quarter Holiday Inn	1	70	★★★	$$$$$$$$$+

How the Hotels Compare (continued)

Hotel	Zone	Quality Rating	Star Rating	Price
Prytania Park Hotel	3	70	★★★	$$$$$$$+
Historic French Market Inn	1	69	★★★	$$$$$$$$$–
Holiday Inn New Orleans I-10	10	69	★★★	$$$$–
Best Western Inn Landmark Hotel	10	68	★★★	$$$$$–
Best Western Inn on Bourbon	1	68	★★★	$$$$$$$$$$$$–
Olivier House Hotel	1	68	★★★	$$$$$$$–
Best Western Patio Downtown	6	67	★★★	$$$$$$$–
Holiday Inn Airport	10	67	★★★	$$$$$–
Place D'Armes Hotel	1	67	★★★	$$$$$$$$–
Quality Inn Maison Hotel	3	67	★★★	$$+
Radisson Hotel New Orleans	5	67	★★★	$$$$$$+
The Columns	3	67	★★★	$$$$$$–
Holiday Inn French Quarter	1	66	★★★	$$$$$$$$+
New Orleans Guest House	5	66	★★★	$$$$$+
Saint Ann/Marie Anntoinette	1	66	★★★	$$$$$$$$–
French Quarter Suites	1	65	★★★	$$$$$$$$$$–
Hotel Villa Convento	1	65	★★★	$$$$$–
La Quinta Inn Williams Blvd.	10	65	★★★	$$$$
La Quinta Inn Veteran's Mem. Blvd.	10	65	★★★	$$$$$–
La Quinta Inn Bullard	8	65	★★★	$$$$
La Quinta Inn Causeway	9	65	★★★	$$$$$–
La Quinta Inn Crowder Road	10	65	★★★	$$$$+
Chateau Hotel	1	64	★★½	$$$$$$–
French Quarter Courtyard Hotel	1	64	★★½	$$$$$$$$–
Holiday Inn Metairie	10	64	★★½	$$$$$–

How the Hotels Compare (continued)

Hotel	Zone	Quality Rating	Star Rating	Price
La Quinta Inn West Bank	11	64	★★½	$$$$$–
Pallas Hotel	6	64	★★½	$$$$$
Radisson Inn Airport	10	64	★★½	$$$$
Rodeway Inn Airport	10	64	★★½	$$$–
Best Western Inn Airport	10	63	★★½	$$$$+
Holiday Inn New Orleans Westbank	11	63	★★½	$$$$$–
The Frenchmen	5	63	★★½	$$$$$+
Landmark French Quarter	1	61	★★½	$$$$$$$–
Quality Hotel and Conference Center	9	61	★★½	$$$+
Quality Inn Midtown	6	61	★★½	$$$$$+
Ramada Inn Highrise	8	60	★★½	$$$$–
Shoney's Inn	10	60	★★½	$$$$+
Days Inn	8	59	★★½	$$$$$–
Super 8 New Orleans	8	59	★★½	$$$$$–
Travelodge Hotel New Orleans	11	59	★★½	$$$$+
Comfort Inn Downtown/Superdome	2	58	★★½	$$$$$–
Ramada Limited Causeway	9	58	★★½	$$$$+
Days Inn Kenner Airport	10	57	★★½	$$+
Days Inn New Orleans/ Canal Street	6	57	★★½	$$$$$$+
Rue Royal Inn	1	57	★★½	$$$$$$+
St. Charles Inn	3	57	★★½	$$$$–
Econo Lodge	8	56	★★½	$$$$+
Orleans Courtyard Inn	10	56	★★½	$$$+
Quality Inn Westbank Harvey	11	56	★★½	$$$$–
Park Plaza Inn	10	55	★★	$$$+
Andrew Jackson	1	53	★★	$$$$$+
Hotel St. Pierre	1	53	★★	$$$$$$$$+
Travelodge	10	52	★★	$$$–
Lasalle Hotel	5	48	★★	$$$+
Rodeway Inn Downtown	6	48	★★	$$$$$–

How the Hotels Compare (continued)				
Hotel	Zone	Quality Rating	Star Rating	Price
Travelodge New Orleans Airport Hotel	10	47	★★	$$$+
Old World Inn	3	44	★½	$$$$
A Creole House	1	43	★½	$$$$$$–
Howard Johnson Westbank	11	42	★½	$$$$$–
Family Inns of America	8	30	★	$+
Friendly Inn	8	28	½	$$+
Hampton Inn and Suites	10	Inn 66 Sts. 68	★★★	$$$$$$–

■ The Top 30 Best Deals in New Orleans ■

Having listed the nicest rooms in town, let's reorder the list to rank the best combinations of quality and value in a room. As before, the rankings are made without consideration of location or the availability of restaurant(s), recreational facilities, entertainment, and/or amenities. Once again, each lodging property is awarded a value rating on a 0–100 scale. The higher the rating, the better the value.

A reader recently complained to us that he had booked one of our top-ranked rooms in terms of value and had been very disappointed in the room. We noticed that the room the reader occupied had a quality rating of ★★½. We would remind you that the value ratings are intended to give you some sense of value received for dollars spent. A ★★½ room at $30 may have the same value rating as a ★★★★ room at $85, but that does not mean the rooms will be of comparable quality. Regardless of whether it's a good deal or not, a ★★½ room is still a ★★½ room.

Listed below are the best room buys for the money, regardless of location or star classification, based on averaged rack rates. Note that sometimes a suite can cost less than a hotel room.

Top 30 Best Deals in New Orleans

Hotel	Zone	Quality Rating	Star Rating	Price
1. Quality Inn Maison Hotel	3	67	★★★	$$+
2. Best Western Airport All Suite	10	77	★★★½	$$$+
3. McKendrick-Breaux House	3	89	★★★★	$$$$$–
4. DoubleTree Hotel LakesideNew Orleans	9	83	★★★★	$$$$$–
5. Days Inn Kenner Airport	10	57	★★½	$$+
6. Rodeway Inn Airport	10	64	★★½	$$$–
7. Courtyard by Marriott	2	77	★★★½	$$$$$–
8. Omni Royal Crescent Hotel	2	93	★★★★½	$$$$$$$$–
9. Hotel Ste. Helene	1	85	★★★★	$$$$$$+
10. Avenue Plaza Hotel	2	84	★★★★	$$$$$$–
11. Hilton, New Orleans Airport	10	80	★★★½	$$$$$+
12. Holiday Inn New Orleans I-10	10	69	★★★	$$$$–
13. The Westin Canal Place	1	92	★★★★½	$$$$$$$$$–
14. Wyndham Riverfront Hotel	2	87	★★★★	$$$$$$$+
15. La Quinta Inn	10	65	★★★	$$$$
16. La Quinta Inn Crowder Road	10	65	★★★	$$$$+
17. Embassy Suites New Orleans	2	85	★★★★	$$$$$$$+
18. Queen and Crescent Hotel	2	82	★★★½	$$$$$$+
19. La Quinta Inn Bullard	8	65	★★★	$$$$
20. Le Pavillion Hotel	2	86	★★★★	$$$$$$$–
21. Hotel de la Monnaie	1	83	★★★★	$$$$$$$–
22. Pontchartrain Hotel	3	83	★★★★	$$$$$$$–
23. Dauphine Orleans	1	80	★★★½	$$$$$$+
24. Quality Hotel and Conference Center	9	61	★★½	$$$+
25. Royal Sonesta Hotel	1	90	★★★★½	$$$$$$$$$+

Top 30 Best Deals in New Orleans (continued)

Hotel	Zone	Quality Rating	Star Rating	Price
26. Bienville House	1	89	★★★★	$$$$$$$$+
27. Prince Conti Hotel	1	81	★★★½	$$$$$$$–
28. Ambassador Hotel New Orleans	2	80	★★★½	$$$$$$$–
29. La Quinta Inn	10	65	★★★	$$$$$–
30. La Quinta Inn Causeway	9	65	★★★	$$$$$–

PART FIVE

Visiting New Orleans on Business

New Orleans Lodging for Business Travelers

The primary hotel considerations for business travelers are affordability and proximity to the site or area where you will transact your business. Identify the zone(s) where your business will take you, and then use the hotel chart to cross-reference the hotels located in that area. Once you have developed a short list of possible hotels that are conveniently located, fit your budget, and offer the standard of accommodations you require, you (or your travel agent) can make use of the cost-saving suggestions discussed earlier to obtain the lowest rate.

■ Lodging Convenient to Morial ■ Convention Center

If you are attending a meeting or trade show at Morial Convention Center, the most convenient lodging is in the Central Business District or in the French Quarter. Closest to the convention center (but not to much of anything else) is the Embassy Suites at 315 Julia Street. Next in proximity are the hotels at the river end of Canal Street, the New Orleans Hilton Riverside on Poydras, and the hotels in the French Quarter. Two Vieux Carré shuttle bus routes combine with the Riverfront Streetcar to make commuting from the French Quarter to the convention center easy. It takes about 10–12 minutes to walk from the exhibit halls to the river end of Canal Street and about 5–12 minutes more to reach hotels in the upper Quarter (between St. Peter and Canal Streets). Parking is available at the convention center, but it is expensive and not all that convenient. We recommend that you leave your car at home and use shuttles, streetcars, or cabs.

Commuting to Morial Convention Center from the suburbs or the airports during rush hour should be avoided if possible. If you want a room near the convention center, book early—very early. If you screw up and need a room at the last minute, try a wholesaler or reservation service, or one of the strategies listed below.

■ Convention Rates: How They Work ■ and How to Do Better

If you are attending a major convention or trade show, the meeting's sponsoring organization probably has negotiated "convention rates" with a number of hotels. Under this arrangement, hotels agree to "block" a certain number of rooms at an agreed-upon price for conventioneers. Sometimes, as in the case of a small meeting, only one hotel is involved. In the event of a large convention at Morial Convention Center, however, a high percentage of Central Business District and larger French Quarter hotels will participate in the room block.

Because the convention sponsor brings a lot of business to the city and reserves a large number of rooms, it usually can negotiate a volume discount on the room rate, a rate that should be substantially below rack rate. The bottom line, however, is that some conventions and trade shows have more bargaining clout and negotiating skill than others. Hence, your convention sponsor may or may not be able to obtain the lowest possible rate.

Once a convention or trade show sponsor has completed negotiations with participating hotels, it will send its attendees a housing list that includes all the hotels serving the convention, along with the special convention rate for each. When you receive the housing list, you can compare the convention rates with the rates obtainable using the strategies listed below. If the negotiated convention rate doesn't sound like a good deal, you can try to reserve a room using a half-price club, a consolidator, a reservations service, or a tour operator. Remember, however, that many of the deep discounts are available only when the hotel expects to be at less than 80% occupancy, a condition that rarely prevails when a big convention comes to town.

Strategies for Beating Convention Rates

There are several tactics for getting around convention rates:

1. Reserve early. Most big conventions and trade shows announce meeting sites one to three years in advance. Get your reservation booked as far in advance as possible using a half-price club. If you book well ahead of the time the convention sponsor sends out the housing list, chances are good that the hotel will accept your reservation.

2. Compare your convention's housing list with the list of hotels presented in this guide. You may be able to find a suitable hotel that is not on the housing list.

3. Use a local reservations service, a wholesaler, or a consolidator. This is also a good strategy to employ if, for some reason, you need to make reservations at the last minute. Local reservations services, wholesalers, and consolidators almost always control some rooms, even in the midst of a huge convention or trade show.

■ The Ernest N. Morial Convention Center ■

The Morial Convention Center is located at 900 Convention Center Boulevard, New Orleans, LA 70130. The phone number is 582-3023, and the fax is 582-3088.

The New Orleans Convention Center will include 1.1 million square feet of contiguous exhibit space under one roof after its Phase III expansion is complete in early 1999. All this muscle backs up to and stretches out along the bank of the Mississippi. The front of the Center runs along South Front Street, also called Convention Center Boulevard, reached easily from Interstate 10 by the Tchoupitoulas/St. Peter exit. For pedestrians attending an event at the Convention Center, the battle is won after you've found the front door. For many attendees coming from the Canal Street major hotels and the French Quarter lodgings, the way in is simply not clear from a distance, nor is it strongly marked once you come to it. The primary entrance is on Convention Center Boulevard, but the doors are actually perpendicular to the street, not parallel to the facade. The entrance is not marked by a plaza, flags, sculpture, or a fountain—nothing really shouts, "Enter Here!"

This only poses a problem on that first critical day of registration when many people still feel disoriented. The best advice is to head for the Riverwalk Marketplace shopping center, which is highly visible on the Mississippi at Canal, Poydras, and Julia Streets. As you face it (and the River), go to your right and have faith that the door will appear. It is a low-key ramp leading to a series of glass doors. Once you're inside, the facility is very well marked. The exhibit halls are alphabetically labeled, with "A" nearest the main entrance.

If the original architect missed the downbeat, the Convention Center administration does its best to set the right tempo. Clear, handsome promotional literature is readily available by calling the marketing and sales department office. The publication details the floor plans of the facility, including the capacities of the various spaces. There are 55 spaces for highway vans and 13 freight drive-in entrances. This same brochure specifies the dimensions of these entrances, the floor load capacity (350 lbs./sq. ft.) and a host of other details needed by exhibitors. The facility is non-union.

Another handy piece to help you get around is "Walking Tours of the Warehouse District & Lafayette Square: Art, History & Architecture," produced by the Downtown Development District in cooperation with the Warehouse District Arts Association. (Ask the Convention Center or the Chamber of Commerce for it. You can also find it in hotel lobby racks.) The Center borders this district, and this brochure lists museums and institutions, galleries, landmarks, hotels, cafes and restaurants, and the St. Charles streetcar route, all within walking distance of the Center.

Getting Food

The food in the Center is definitely above average, and the promo literature makes much of their prize-winning chef, Leon West, who can supervise the production of two kitchens, each of which can produce 20,000 meals in a 24-hour period. In the 400-seat Atrium/Restaurant Lounge you can order Cajun and Creole favorites. There are "conventional" concession/refreshment areas located off each exhibit hall floor. Prices are not as high as they could be for hostages of conventions, but no bargains can be found either.

If you can break free, there are several good restaurants within a 10- to 15-minute walk. A terrific, delicious value is at Taqueria Corona, 857 Fulton, where an outstanding Mexican lunch can be yours for about $5. They also serve dinner later in the day (they're closed in the mid-afternoon). True Brew Coffee, 200 Julia Street, can make the vegetarians happy; they also have a pastrami and pepper-cheese sandwich. Some sidewalk seating is available, and they have a bar. The Red Bike Cafe, 746 Tchoupitoulas, specializes in bakery goods and vegetarian delights. Ernst Cafe, 600 South Peters, offers plate lunches and sandwiches. Business people needing a quieter atmosphere

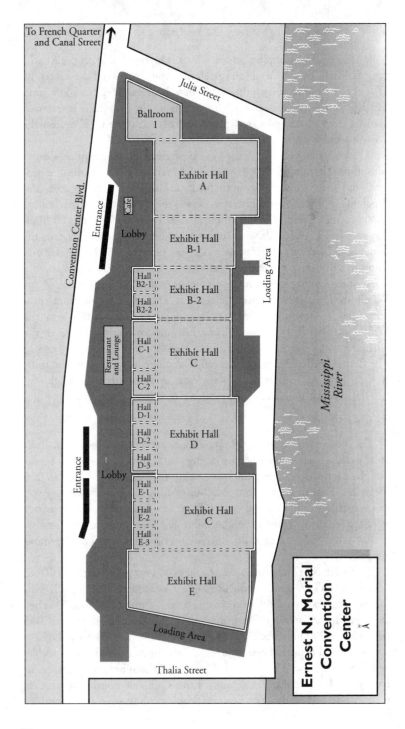

To French Quarter
and Canal Street

Julia Street

Ballroom
1

Exhibit Hall
A

Convention Center Blvd.

Entrance

Café

Lobby

Exhibit Hall
B-1

Loading Area

Hall
B2-1

Hall
B2-2

Exhibit Hall
B-2

Restaurant
and Lounge

Hall
C-1

Hall
C-2

Exhibit Hall
C

Hall
D-1

Hall
D-2

Hall
D-3

Exhibit Hall
D

Entrance

Hall
E-1

Hall
E-2

Hall
E-3

Exhibit Hall
C

Lobby

Exhibit Hall
E

Mississippi
River

Loading Area

Thalia Street

Ernest N. Morial
Convention
Center

N

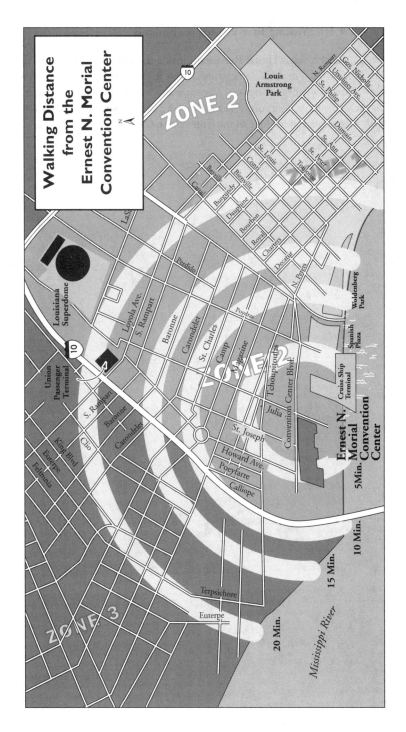

Walking Distance from the Ernest N. Morial Convention Center

ZONE 2

Louis Armstrong Park

N. Rampart
Gov. Nicholls
Ursulines Ave.
St. Philip
Dumain
St. Ann
St. Peter
Toulouse

Canal
Iberville
Bienville
Conti
St. Louis
Burgundy
Dauphine
Bourbon
Royal
Chartres
Decatur
N. Peters

Woldenberg Park

LaSa

Louisiana Superdome

Perdido

Loyola Ave.
S. Rampart
Baronne
Carondelet
St. Charles
Camp
Magazine

Poydras

ZONE 2

Spanish Plaza

Union Passenger Terminal

S. Rampart
Baronne
Carondelet

Clio

King Blvd
Euterpe
Felicuna

Tchoupitoulas

Convention Center Blvd.

Julia

St. Joseph

Howard Ave.

Poeyfarre

Calliope

Cruise Ship Terminal

Ernest N. Morial Convention Center

5 Min.

10 Min.

15 Min.

Terpsichore

Euterpe

20 Min.

ZONE 3

Mississippi River

can dine at the Sugar House Restaurant inside the Embassy Suite Hotel at 315 Julia Street. The muffuletta joints across the street from the Convention Center are another quick option. There are also many choices, some featuring local cuisine on short order, at the Bon Fête Food Court inside the Riverwalk Marketplace next door to the Convention Center.

Using the World Wide Web
for Travel Planning

The advent of the World Wide Web and its immense popularity have brought about many changes in the way we seek out everyday information. Travel information is one of the most popular and useful areas of publishing and access on the Web. In just a few short years we have gone from getting most of our travel information from printed books or magazines and our favorite travel agent to a time where we can book entire vacations online. But as wonderful as this sounds, there are pitfalls. It's no small task figuring out how to find the information you need and understanding the tricks that make navigating the Web easy. Finally, even as an accomplished Web user, you may be surprised to find that your most valuable travel resource is still your tried-and-true travel agent.

You may have heard that travel providers like to sell directly to consumers on the Web in order to avoid paying commissions to travel agents, and that the commission savings are passed along to the buyer. While there is some truth in this, discounts (online or anywhere else) have much more to do with time perishability of travel products than with commissions. An empty seat on an airliner, for example, cannot be sold once the plane has left the gate. As the point of perishability approaches, the travel provider (hotel, airline, cruise line, etc.) begins cutting deals to fill its rooms, cabins, and seats. Web sites provide a cheap, quick, and efficient way for travel sellers to make these deals known to the public. You should understand, however, that the same deals are usually also communicated to travel agents.

We like the Web as a method of window-shopping for travel, for scouting deals, and for obtaining information. We do not believe that the Web is necessarily the best or cheapest way of purchasing travel or that it can be substituted for the services of a good travel agent. The people who get the most out of the Web are those who work in cooperation with their travel agent, using it as a tool to help their agent help them. First, almost any deal you locate online can be purchased through a travel agent, and second, the more business you give your travel agent, the harder your agent will work for you. It's all about relationships.

It is a bit convoluted to write about the interactive travel experience on paper without the benefit of the very medium we are discussing. We urge you to use your computer or to find a friend with a computer and a Web connection in order to get the most out of these guidelines. We guarantee that you will discover some wonderful things along the way, many things in all likelihood that even we haven't seen. Each person's experience on the Web is unique, and you'll find many compelling distractions along the way. But bring your patience to the Web because it can take some time getting used to it, and it is not perfect. Once you know your way around even slightly you will save a lot of time, and occasionally, some money. When you find resources that you like, bookmark them in your browser. The more you use them the more efficient you will become.

■ New Orleans on the Web ■

Searching the World Wide Web for New Orleans information is like navigating an immense maze in search of a very small piece of cheese. There are quite a few New Orleans web pages which offer information, advertisements, and services. To be sure, there is a lot of information available on the internet, but if you do not use specific addresses, you may have to wade through list after list until you find the addresses you need. Once you have them, finding information can also be time-consuming.

Here are some addresses we found helpful:

- **www.neworleans.com** is maintained by the New Orleans Publishing Group, and contains advertisements, travel coupons, a hotel booking service, and articles on various subjects. Business people researching New Orleans will find useful articles on banking, industry, and trade.

- **www.neworleansonline.com** is a fun web page which is maintained by a group called the New Orleans Marketing Corporation. Subjects found on this page include music, history, people, and dining. On the practical side, you can search by amenity for a hotel room or check out the calendar of events.

- **www.nawlins.com** is an extensive web page maintained by the New Orleans Convention and Visitors Bureau. Although this page contains helpful information for leisure travelers, meeting and convention planners will find it particularly useful.

- **www.neworleans.net** is maintained by a group called Hospitality Enterprise, along with the New Orleans *Times-Picayune*. This page offers information on gambling, events, sights, and festivals. It also offers a five-day weather forecast and a chat forum.

■ Major Travel and Reservation Sites ■

The travel and booking sites are some of the most useful sites on the Web today. They allow you to designate your destinations and preferences and then immediately check on a variety of available flights, cruises, tours, hotels, and rental cars. If you see something you like you can purchase the ticket online. Each service has its own unique interface and design, and you may find one easier to use than another depending on the kind of travel you do.

You should fill out a travel profile in each site you try; it is what allows you to indicate your preferences, such as favorite airline, aisle seat, or cheapest fare. Most of these sites allow you to register to receive an e-mail notification when a great fare or special deal comes up for your favorite destinations. Web sites always have the latest information on any fare wars that might be happening. Just like any bargain, if you see a good price you should try to make a decision about it as soon as possible, because if you take too much time it could easily be gone when you come back.

Although there are great deals to be found on the Web, remember that each travel provider's site is nothing more than an electronic media billboard. Be prepared for all of the hype, purple prose, and exaggeration you would find in any other kind of advertisement. Also be aware that filling out a profile will potentially make you a target for all of the provider's promotional messages. If you like to receive a lot of e-mail, fine. Otherwise, be selective.

When a deal comes along that you like, do not assume that it is the best you can do. Check the web sites of direct competitors as well as deals in newspapers that target the travel provider's primary geographic market. Los Angeles, for example, is a primary market for most Las Vegas casinos, and you can often find deals in the Sunday travel section of the *Los Angeles Times* that equal or beat what you find on the Web. When you have narrowed your possibilities, bring your travel agent into the loop and give him or her an opportunity to improve on any deals you have found.

There's a fair amount of cross-pollination in web sites, with some companies sharing information and features. Some have travel content along with booking features (Travelocity and ITN), and others offer a variety of vacation packages along with the comprehensive booking information (www.previewvacations.com). But even if you just need a flight from San

Francisco to Los Angeles, with the cheapest fare, at the most convenient time, and don't need the other travel information, you can just bookmark the page of the site that allows you to set up an itinerary or go directly to it.

If you make a reservation online, remember that it's just like making reservations on the phone or through your travel agent. Make sure that you are aware of any restrictions or refund policies that the sites or the related companies have in place. If you make a reservation with an airline through a web site, you can generally assume that that airline's policies apply. If you are purchasing a vacation package or something else from one of the vacation sites, be sure to visit the policies or disclaimer sections of the site so you understand what will happen if you need to change or cancel your plans. Always check this before you submit your order.

You may have read some of the news stories about the security of doing transactions over the Web—of presenting your credit card online. Much progress has been made in this area in the past year, and you'll find most, if not all, of these sites allow you to enter through a "secure" server, which simply means that they are taking extra steps to protect your personal information. As the online transaction businesses grow, the technology will only get better. In reality, there have been very few problems with completing transactions online, but if you prefer, most sites will give you the option to call a toll-free number to make your purchase.

■ Some Reservation Sites to Check Out ■

Listed below are some sites we find particulary useful. We are not listing all the reservation sites with booking capabilities—just the main ones as of this writing. New sites are launched every month.

www.travelocity.com	www.sabre.com
www.itn.com	www.expedia.com
www.previewvacations.com	www.outtahere.com
www.reservations.com	www.the trip.com

The Airlines

Most of the airlines have sites these days, and they can be quite useful if you like to stick to one carrier. These sites will include flight schedules, information about their frequent flier clubs, policies, and specials. One of the best things about airline-specific sites is the information on fare specials and last-minute discounts. There are often excellent deals available. Sometimes the deals are so good you want to look for a reason to go.

If you just want the best fare or the most convenient itinerary, then looking only at one airline's schedule will not give the full picture. You should also be aware that there are certain airlines, generally those that offer extra-discounted fares most of the time, that are not part of the major reservation systems. So if you want to fly on these airlines you either have to call them directly, use your travel agent, or go to their web sites. At the time of this writing Southwest Airlines is one of the airlines not participating in the main reservations systems.

Hotels and Rental Cars

Most of the travel sites listed above also have connections to hotel and rental car booking services, and they work in much the same way as making airline reservations. On the airlines' sites you will find that they generally have a relationship with one or two car rental companies and will put you in touch with them for reservations. And like the airlines, the rental car companies have their own sites, but that means if you want to comparison shop you have to go to multiple sites.

■ The Travel and Local Information Resources ■

The most dynamic places to find all kinds of travel information are the unique travel web sites that present information in a totally new way. There are also many sites presented by some of the big players in the internet business that are designed to provide detailed information about particular cities—not just travel information but also information on the government, schools, movies, shopping, services, and transportation. These sites can be very useful as you prepare to leave for your destination or, if you are lucky enough to have a computer with you, after you arrive. One of the best all-around resources for finding information on just about any place in the world is Excite's City.Net (www.city.net or through www.excite.com). While they do present some information directly on their site, City.Net is primarily a resource of other travel providers on the Web. Almost all of these sites have direct links or partnerships with the reservations sites listed above.

At this point most major cities' newspapers have web sites, and they are often excellent sources of local information. You may also want to check with your regional AAA office to see if they have a web site. For example, AAA of Northern California, Nevada, and Utah has an excellent web site that contains information about the auto club's road services and their extensive travel planning services. It is a great resource.

Listed below are some of our favorite travel and local information resource sites:

www.city.net   www.sidewalk.com

www.gorp.com   www.digitalcity.com

www.citysearch.com

Newspapers

www.nytimes.com   www.latimes.com

www.washingtonpost.com   www.tribune.com

www.csaa.com (AAA of   www.sfgate.com
    Northern California,
    Nevada, and Utah)

■ Travel Book and Magazine Publishers' Sites ■

Many book and magazine publishers have sites that present some of their content online and give you an opportunity to order their publications. Some of these are very well done and worth checking out.

Condé Nast Traveler (www.cntraveler.com)

Fodor's (www.fodors.com)

Frommer's (www.frommers.com)—You can find *Unofficial Guide* info at this site!

Lonely Planet (www.lonelyplanet.com)

Moon Travel Handbooks (www.moon.com)

■ Search Engines and Directories ■

One of the best ways to make your time on the Web the most useful and fun is to learn how to use one or more search engines. The most popular, and arguably the best, include Yahoo! (www.yahoo.com), Excite (www. excite.com), Lycos (www.lycos.com), Infoseek (www.infoseek.com), and Alta Vista (www.altavista.com), which is also the search engine that is used in Yahoo! along with their directories. The "directories" in Yahoo! and the "channels" in Excite, for example, are lists of sites that are already organized into categories and can be very useful. But if you don't see what you want in these directories, read on.

If you can, we suggest that you take an hour or two and just experiment. Input the same search topic in each and compare the results. For example: Alaskan Cruises. You will get different results from each site (sometimes slightly different, sometimes totally different), but each should give you some useful sites. These are essential tools if you can describe what you are looking for but have no idea where to find it, or if you have looked in the better-known travel sites and have not seen the information you want. There is usually a tutorial or "help" area on the search engine site that will show you how to get the most out of that particular service. All of these services figure importantly in having a good Web experience. You will probably find a favorite service and use it frequently.

Before you take your trip you should take a few minutes and visit a few other sites. One is Amazon.com Books! It is called Earth's Biggest Bookstore (www.amazon.com), and it is just that. It contains millions of books that you can order, so if you want to know more about the history, culture, or sights in the region you will be visiting, Amazon is a terrific resource. When it comes time to pack, you can go to the Weather Channel online (www.weather.com) and see a forecast, precipitation map, the business travelers' forecast with airport delays, and much more. It is even better than their cable channel because you don't have to wait until your area comes on the air—you can just go directly to it.

All of these services will only get better with time and improved technology. While the amount spent on online booking of travel is only a tiny fraction of what is spent today, the predicted growth rate of these businesses is nothing short of phenomenal. So go online and try booking a trip today!

PART SIX

Arriving and Getting Oriented

Coming into the City

Nothing spoils a vacation quicker than a traffic jam, a missed connection, or a too-long walk with luggage—the sorts of misadventures that often are overlooked in the excitement of planning a trip. New Orleans happily abandons its claim to mystery when it comes to making tourists comfortable: It's well supplied with public transportation; the airport is new and efficient but not impersonal or intimidating; and once you sling a little lingo, you can get directions from anyone. Just take a few minutes to get organized before you cut loose.

■ By Plane ■

New Orleans Moisant International Airport (464-3547) is a slightly hooked rectangle, something like a squared-off smile, about ten miles west of New Orleans in Kenner. At four feet above sea level, it's a frequent source of jokes about "high-flying" airstrips and so on, but it is relatively high and dry, at least compared to the surrounding area—and if you fly in, watching the complex gradually take shape from the swampland around it, you'll see why that's important.

The airport is fully wheelchair accessible, and the telephone banks in each concourse have TDD phones as well. Ticket counters are in the center on the upper level, with the four concourses at the ends, and information counters, concessions, and gift stands scattered about. A full-service Whitney National Bank, 24-hour automated teller machines, and a post office are in the main central hall. There is a Traveler's Aid Booth (464-3522) in the east end of the lobby, and both east and west there are general information desks. The Mutual of Omaha Business Service Center (465-9647) office and an American Express traveler's check machine are in the west lobby. Transportation and baggage claim are downstairs, with additional ATMs; there are elevators at each end. The airport shuttle desk downstairs (522-3500) is staffed around the clock.

New Orleans is served by more than a dozen airlines. American, Northwest/KLM, USAirways, and USAir Express all use Concourse A. Some American Airlines flights also go into the larger Concourse B, along with Continental, Continental Express, Southwest, and TWA. Aeromexico, Aviateca, LACSA, TACA, and United Air Lines all use Concourse C, and Delta uses Concourse D.

Incidentally, the rest rooms in the airport are very nice. The toilets are automatically sanitized with each flush, and motorized seat covers slip over the seats at the push of a button. All faucets are touch-free as well, operated by electric eyes.

Getting to the City from the Airport

To get from the airport to the city, you may take the Airport Shuttle (522-3500) for $10 per person; the van will take you directly to the hotel. If you want to have the shuttle pick you up and take you back to the airport, call 24 hours in advance with your flight departure information, and they will schedule a pick-up.

Taxi fare from the airport is currently $21 for one or two passengers and $8 apiece for three or more. You can either pick one up off the line or contact United Cabs in advance (at (800) 323-3303 or (504) 522-9711) and arrange to have a driver waiting for no additional charge. A limo can be ordered from the airport shuttle service, or a luxury-class stretch limo can be hired from Olde Quarter Livery (595-5010): $50 for four or $65 for the full six-passenger model and uniformed chauffeur—great for honeymooners. Other limousine services include London Livery (831-0700), Carey Bonomolo (523-5466), and A Touch of Class (522-7565). *Hint:* If you want a showy chauffeur during any of the special events in town (i.e., Superbowl or Mardi Gras), better call in early.

A Louisiana Transit express bus to the Central Business District (737-7433) puts you within a few blocks' walking distance of many of the newer hotels along Canal Street; it costs only $1.10, which may be the best choice if you are not lugging tons of baggage. The bus leaves the airport every 15 minutes or so at rush hour (6–9 A.M. and 3–6 P.M.) and closer to every 25 minutes the rest of the time, but it is only available between 6 A.M. and 6:30 P.M. The terminus is on Tulane Avenue between Elks Place and South Saratoga Street.

There are also regular Regional Transit Authority buses that may serve your route; call RTA at 248-3900 for exact times. (For more on RTA passes, see the section on "Public Transportation" on page 129.)

As mentioned before, the rent-a-car counters are in the lower level of the airport: Hertz, (800) 654-3131; Avis, (800) 331-1212; Alamo, (800) 327-9633; Budget, (800) 527-0700; National, (800) 227-7368; and Dollar, (800) 800-4000 are all on-site and also have second offices downtown, if for some reason you don't want to return the car to the airport. Sears, (800) 527-0770 and Value, (504) 589-2668 have airport lots only. From the rental car lots, signs will direct you onto Interstate 10 to the city (be sure to read "By Car" below).

For Private Planes

There is a small private airstrip as well for those who fly or charter their own aircraft. New Orleans Lakefront Airport, on the south side of Lake Pontchartrain, also has some rentals; call 243-4010 for more information.

■ By Car ■

New Orleans is connected to the interstate highway system by I-10, which goes pretty much right through the city east and west, though with a few tricky spots. One thing to remember is that I-10 makes an unusual V-dip toward the French Quarter and Central Business District (CBD), while I-610 sails straight across the mid-city region and dumps you back out on I-10 at the east end of town; it won't get you where you want to go, and it is a rush-hour trap of the first order. The other thing to know is that there is no "French Quarter" exit off I-10; it's marked Vieux Carré, Exit 235A. (If your hotel is along Canal Street in the CBD, take the Poydras Street exit.) Signage is not particularly good here in any case, and turn signal indicators seem to be a lost art, so be careful.

If you are driving in from the east along Interstate 10, there is a Visitors Information Center at the Paris Road exit where you can pick up brochures, maps, discount coupons, and coffee, and make last-minute hotel reservations, if necessary.

East-west US 61 is Airline Highway, the older route from Kenner into the city, and becomes Tulane Avenue heading to the CBD near the French Quarter. US 90, also called the Old Spanish Trail, makes a squiggly circle around the river, curving around uptown and the West Bank before scooting back south and west toward New Iberia and Lafayette. (Highway 90 is the "scenic route" to Cajun country, but you can take I-10 nearly to Lafayette and on to Baton Rouge.)

I-12 runs east-west as well, but along the north shore of Lake Pontchartrain, as if putting a lid on the bowl of I-10. From I-12 you can take either I-59 or I-56 south, but the 24-mile-long Lake Pontchartrain Causeway (toll road) is the world's longest over-water bridge, and it's a beautiful drive; sometimes you can see nothing but sky and water, and sometimes glimpses of the skyline or sailboat fleets. The causeway comes straight south and joins I-10, US 61/Airline Highway, US 90/Claiborne Avenue, and so on. Interstate 59 (north-south) intersects I-10 east of the city; I-56 from Jackson, Mississippi, joins I-10 west of the city.

■ By Bus or Train ■

Greyhound Bus Lines coaches (call (800) 231-2222) roll into Union Terminal at Loyola and Howard Avenues at the edge of the Central Business District not far from the Superdome. Ticket counters are open 5:30 A.M.–11 P.M.

Union Terminal is also the Amtrak station (call (800) 872-7245 or (504) 524-7571), with connections to New York/Washington, Miami, Los Angeles, and Chicago. Ticket counters are open 5:50 A.M.–8:30 P.M. (check for senior citizen discounts and special fares). There is a taxi stop outside the terminal, of course.

■ Where to Find Tourist Information ■
in New Orleans

You can get an amazing amount of material and background from the New Orleans Metropolitan Convention and Visitors Bureau (1520 Sugar Bowl Drive, New Orleans, LA 70112-1259, or 566-5011), which also operates information centers within each terminal of the New Orleans International Airport. For specialized information, contact the Greater New Orleans Black Tourism Network (523-5652). In the French Quarter itself, there is a combined Louisiana state welcome office and NOMCVB info center right on Jackson Square in the Pontalba Apartments (529 St. Ann Street, 566-5011) that has hundreds of brochures on attractions and tours and street maps. And the visitors bureau also distributes these brochures on a motorized cart that stops during the day at such gathering spots as Union Terminal, Aquarium of the Americas, Spanish Plaza, the Louisiana Children's Museum, and the 600 block of Canal Street.

If you have trouble, contact the Traveler's Aid Society (525-8726) or stop by the booth in the east lobby of the airport.

Once you are in town, the main source of information on special events, sports, arts, and tours is the *Times-Picayune,* which has an entertainment calendar every day and a special pull-out section on Fridays, called "Lagniappe," devoted to recreation and family fun. Among the free magazines you'll see around town and in hotel and restaurant lobbies are *Offbeat,* which covers the local music and nightlife scene (you can peruse it in advance at www. nola.com), *Gambit, Arrive,* and *Where. Ambush* magazine (www.ambushmag. com) and *Impact Gulf South News* are gay and lesbian publications. Or check in bookstores for *New Orleans Magazine* and the black-oriented monthly *New Orleans Tribune.*

Getting Oriented

New Orleans geography is confusing (even for locals) because it conflicts with our notion of U.S. geography and our basic sense of north/south orientation. Louisiana is shaped like an **L**. New Orleans is at the bottom of the **L** on the east end and is sandwiched between Lake Pontchartrain to the north and the Mississippi River to the south. Most folks picture the Mississippi River as flowing due south and emptying into the Gulf of Mexico. While this is correct, generally speaking, the river happens to snake along in west-to-east fashion as it passes New Orleans, not veering south again until after Chalmette, where the battle of New Orleans was fought in the War of 1812. To the surprise of many, the mouth of the Mississippi River is actually more than five hours south of New Orleans by boat.

If you spend time in New Orleans, the presence of the lake and the river are inescapable. As you begin to explore, you will discover that much of the city is tucked into one long bend of the river and that many of the streets and highways follow the curve of that bend. The curve in question, when viewed in the customary north/south orientation, is shaped like the smile of a "happy face." Although suburbs and industrial areas parallel the river both east and west of the "smile" (and also across the river—south of the smile), the areas of the city most interesting to visitors are located within

The New Orleans Smile

Lake Pontchartrain

the curve. This curve, or smile as we put it, is why New Orleans is called "The Crescent City."

The oldest part of the city, the French Quarter or Vieux Carré, is situated at the right (east) corner of the smile, while the University District with Tulane and Loyola Universities is located at the left (west) corner. Moving from the right corner toward the bottom of the smile, you will leave the French Quarter, cross Canal Street, and enter the Warehouse/Arts and Central Business District. The Central Business District is New Orleans' *real* downtown. The warehouses line the river and serve the city's bustling port.

If you look at a map of downtown, you will notice that all the streets emanating from the French Quarter change names after they cross Canal Street. Royal Street in the French Quarter becomes St. Charles Avenue in the Business District and parallels the river like a mustache above the smile. On St. Charles, you can drive or take the St. Charles streetcar around the curve of the smile to visit some of New Orleans' most interesting neighborhoods. As you work down the smile to the bicuspids and incisors, you will encounter the Irish Channel, the Garden District, and finally, the University

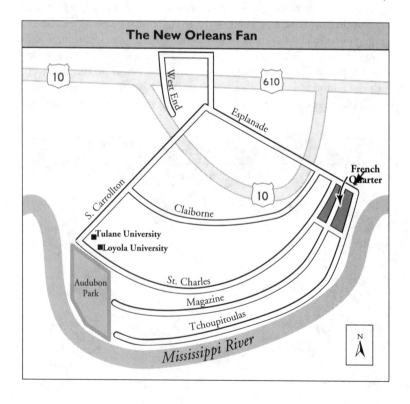
The New Orleans Fan

District, including Audubon Park (described in Part 11, "Sight-Seeing and Tours.")

If you are driving in New Orleans, picture holding a fan upside-down over the happy face. Position the fan so that the handle points north toward the lake and the curved spread of the fan aligns with the bend in the river (the smile). Tchoupitoulas Street runs at the edge of the fan along the river. A few blocks inland is St. Charles, paralleling both Tchoupitoulas and the river. Farther away from the river toward the handle is Claiborne Avenue, following the same crescent-shaped route. The sides of the fan angling up to the handle are Esplanade on the right (east) and Carrollton on the left (west). The handle of the fan extends to the lake and includes City Park. Tourists, convention-goers, and most business visitors spend the vast majority of their time within the area of the fan.

Just outside the fan to the west is Metairie, where you can access the Lake Pontchartrain Causeway. Farther west is Kenner and the New Orleans International Airport. To the northeast is Elysian Fields and Gentilly, where you will find Dillard and Southern Universities, the University of New Orleans, and Pontchartrain Park. To the southeast along the river is the Chalmette Battlefield, Jean Lafitte National Historic Park, and Pakenham Oaks.

■ Finding Your Way Around the French Quarter ■

While orientation in the greater New Orleans area tends to be confusing, finding your way around the French Quarter is a cinch. The French Quarter is rectangular and arranged in a grid like Midtown Manhattan. The long side of the rectangle is bordered by the river on one side and Rampart Street on the other. The short side of the rectangle is hemmed on one side by Canal Street, New Orleans' main downtown thoroughfare, and by Esplanade Avenue on the other end.

The longer streets, which parallel the river, are the French Quarter's primary commercial, traffic, and pedestrian arteries. Moving from the river inland, these streets are Decatur, Chartres, Royal, Bourbon, Dauphine, Burgundy, and finally, Rampart. The more commercially developed blocks toward Canal Street are traditionally known as the "Upper Quarter," while the quieter, more residential blocks toward Esplanade are called the "Lower Quarter."

As recently as 30 years ago, upper Decatur, next to the river, was the domain of visiting sailors and home of the fabled Jax Brewery. Lower Decatur then, as now, was home to the French Market. With the closing of the brewery and the advent of the Riverwalk promenade, Decatur was effectively sanitized and turned into a souvenir shopping mall and restaurant venue. St. Louis Cathedral and Jackson Square face Decatur, and most of the modern tourist development is between Jackson Square and Canal Street. Moving down Decatur toward Esplanade is a rejuvenated French Market, the timeless Café du Monde, and the Central Grocery, with its signature muffuletta Italian sandwich.

Heading away from the river, you'll come to Chartres, with its galleries, restaurants, cozy taverns, and small hotels. Chartres, perhaps more than any other French Quarter street, has maintained its historic identity. Commerce rules here, as elsewhere, but it's softer, less crass, and much more respectful of its heritage.

Royal, the next street over, has always been the patrician of the Quarter's main thoroughfares. Lined with antique and art galleries, as well as some of the city's most famous restaurants, hotels, and architecture, Royal Street is the prestige address of the Vieux Carré.

One block walking takes you from the grand and sophisticated to the carnal and crass: You have arrived on Bourbon Street. While Bourbon Street has always appealed to more primitive instincts, it did so within the worn, steamy context of its colorful past. But today, Bourbon Street is a parody of itself, a plastic corporate version of the honky-tonks, burlesque shows, and diners that molded its image. Between the T-shirt shops, trendy bars, and modern, upscale strip clubs, you can still find a few survivors from Bourbon Street's halcyon days, but they are an endangered species.

Burgundy and Dauphine, the two streets between Bourbon and the boundary of the French Quarter at Rampart Street, were once primarily residential. During the past two decades, however, homes have made way for small hotels, shops, and restaurants. Burgundy and Dauphine, while less architecturally compelling than Royal or Chartres, are nonetheless quite lovely. Quieter and less commercially developed than the streets between Bourbon and the river, Burgundy and Dauphine provide a glimpse of what the Quarter was like when it was still a thriving neighborhood.

Rampart Street, like Canal and Esplanade, is essentially a border street: broad, heavily trafficked, and very different from the streets within the French Quarter. Twelve streets run from Rampart to Decatur, intersecting the main commercial thoroughfares discussed above and completing the grid.

St. Peter and St. Ann Streets bisect the Vieux Carré halfway between Canal and Esplanade. St. Peter, especially the block between Bourbon and Royal, is regarded by many as the "heart of the Quarter." Most of the tourist and commercial activity in the French Quarter occurs toward Canal Street, and from Bourbon Street down to the river. Except for lower Decatur and the French Market, the Esplanade half of the Vieux Carré remains residential, albeit with an increasing number of proprietary hotels and guest houses.

Things the Natives Already Know

■ New Orleans Customs and Protocol ■

New Orleans is a city that prides itself on Southern hospitality, and most residents and business owners have learned to be very patient with tourists. They need to be. And so may you.

To be blunt about it, for all the mutterings about crime you will hear from locals (see "How to Avoid Crime and Keep Safe in Public Places," below), it's almost certain that the biggest problem you'll run into in New Orleans is other tourists, particularly on Bourbon Street. Women will have to be prepared for a few juvenile remarks from the inebriated and the eternally self-deluded (amazing how attractive some people seem to consider themselves). There is a vital gay community here, and gay and lesbian visitors are welcome, but as always, there may be a few ill-mannered heteros to ignore. And a few visitors may be taken aback by the number of extravagantly dressed punksters on the streets, with their Technicolor spiked hair and heavy leathers. Longtime locals seem to find them a little scary, but they don't seem particularly interested in bothering anyone as far as we could tell. And there are more panhandlers than there used to be, though most of them will spin you a tale rather than just accost you.

Otherwise, just go by what you might call the flip-side of the Golden Rule: Do nothing unto others that would be embarrassing if done unto you.

Incidentally, sections of the French Quarter, parts of Bourbon Street, Royal, and around Jackson Square are often closed to cars, encouraging pedestrian traffic. And many intersections have stop signs in both directions (these are one-way streets, remember). But don't let that lead you into dropping your guard on other streets. Just be aware of where you are, or you may find yourself stepping in front of a moving vehicle.

■ Talking the Talk ■

Ironically, for a city with so many obvious European influences, New Orleans talks with a very American accent. (So American, in fact, that a lot of "dese guys," especially the ones with roots in the Irish Channel and Metairie, sound as if they just disembarked from Brooklyn or New Jersey, because they come from the same river roustabout stock.)

What that means for outsiders is that local names can be wildly confusing—not to mention the name of the city itself. Much has been written about how to say it (and to be fair, there isn't an easy answer), but what it is *not,* is Nawlins, in two syllables, or Noo OrLEENS in three or New Or-Lee-Uns in four. It's something in between: Noo-AW-lins, with the first two syllables blending together, sort of two-and-a-half beats. Unfortunately, Orleans Street *is* pronounced Or-LEENS, and so is Orleans Parish.

Then comes the Vieux Carré (View Kah-RAY), the original name for the French Quarter; it's one of the few things around that still has a French accent aside from beignets (ben-yays), Arnaud's (Ar-KNOWS), and Treme and Faubourg Marigny (Truh-may and Foh-burg Mare-in-yee), the neighborhoods adjoining the Vieux Carré. Metairie is pronounced Met-uh-ree; Pontchartrain is PAWN-cha-train. And Marie Laveau (Mar-ee Lah-voh), Jean Lafitte (Zhawn Lah-feet), and Mardi Gras (Mar-dee Grah), of course.

Most confusing of all are the street names, which have in many cases been translated first from Spanish to French (memorialized on blue-and-white tile signs on the sides of buildings at intersections throughout the French Quarter), and from French to fractured French or Italianese, or occasionally English (for example, most people say Royal Street now, though you will still see Rue Royale on some business cards).

Burgundy is pronounced bur-GUN-dee; Conti is con-TIE; Chartres is CHAR-ters; Esplanade is es-pluh-NADE; Carondelet is kuh-ron-duh-LET; Milan is MY-lun; and Iberville is EYE-ber-ville.

Even worse is what happened to the classic Greek names of the Muses east of the Garden District: Terpsichore is TERP-si-core; Calliope is KAL-ee-ope; Clio is KLIE-oh; Melpomene is MEL-poe-mean; and so on.

The Indian Tchoupitoulas is easier than it looks, like an old tomahawk joke: chop-it-TOOL-us.

As for the city's various nicknames, "The Big Easy," "Crescent City," or the older "Paris of America" and "The City That Care Forgot," none is particularly popular, and you probably will never hear a resident use one.

Incidentally, although it works wonderfully in literary sense to speak of Desire, as in *A Streetcar Named Desire,* the line's destination was originally pronounced Desiré (dez-ih-RAY), a popular woman's name, and was like many other ladies' names applied to a wharf—just in case you wondered.

■ Dress ■

In a town as hot and humid as New Orleans, only bankers, lawyers, and maitres d' regularly wear suits. That's something of an exaggeration, but not much: What it really boils down to is, self-respecting New Orleanians dress, tourists don't. Decades of Southern culture still persuade many women to wear dresses and hose, and you'll notice the docents and information ladies usually do. The minimum "dress" for women is nice earrings and long pants rather than shorts, shoes rather than athletic wear or sandals for men. But again, this is a tourist town, and you're on vacation, so you can decide how much you care about sticking out or fitting in. Except for social occasions, you're not likely to be penalized for wearing shorts or sports clothes anywhere around town. It's just that those who do dress neatly may get better treatment or tables than a total slob.

Even at night, only a few restaurants ask men to wear a jacket, mostly the older standbys such as Antoine's and Arnaud's. But "dressy casual" is the style at most of the new celebrity spots such as Nola, Emeril's, and Mr. B's, and you may feel more comfortable in a jacket, even wearing it over a golf shirt or "nice" T-shirt—that is, unmarked and monotone, a la Don Johnson. The most famous exception is Galatoire's, which continues to demand jacket and tie at dinner and all day Sunday.

■ Eating in Restaurants ■

New Orleans fare may be famous, but it's not all that varied. Continental, Creole (which is very similar, but has kept more traditional rich cream sauces than modern Continental), and Cajun styles dominate, particularly in the areas tourists are most likely to visit. And to be honest, you may find several days of such food not only filling but a trifle too rich; go slow. Most other restaurants are either new-American or Italian (or franchised).

Compared to many cities, the number of restaurants in New Orleans that do not accept reservations is fairly high. (During Mardi Gras, you may not find anybody willing to take a reservation.) Standing in line at Galatoire's, where the host is amazingly deft at juggling parties in his head, and at K-Paul's Louisiana Kitchen, where you may share your table with another party, is the stuff of legend. (K-Paul's now takes reservations for its upstairs dining room.)

As a rule of thumb, the restaurants that require reservations tend to be the same ones that require jacket and tie. In the same way, however, many of those would be willing to seat you, perhaps at the bar, if you are dressed at least neatly.

(A tip for dining at Antoine's: If you can make a reservation with a particular waiter, you can enter through the unmarked door just to the left of the main entrance, go down the hallway, ask for said waiter, and be seated with a little more respect and speed than if you just arrive at the "tourist" entrance. This probably means, however, that you have a friend who is a regular there—in which case you should get him to take you, anyway—or you should become a repeat customer.)

It shouldn't require saying, but having seen too many slightly overexuberant tourists trying to slip into restaurants past the queue, we will say it: Please be considerate, and stay in place. Besides, these hosts are pros; they'll catch you.

■ Tipping (and Stripping) ■

New Orleans is a service-oriented economy, and you should expect to recognize that. The going tip rate for bartenders or waiters and taxi drivers is 15–20%, although if you use them as sources of local information—which is always a good bet—add a dollar for luck. In your hotel, you should leave the maids at least $1 per day of your stay, and it really should be $2. If there is a bellman, give him $1 per suitcase, and while it isn't quite rude not to slip the doorman a buck for getting you a taxi, it never hurts. After all, it might be a longer wait next time.

As for tipping strippers, it's usually $1 in one of the older, cheaper joints, or $5 for something special (you will probably be offered a "table dance," which offers a sort of up-close-and-personal view). In the really upscale places, such as Maiden Voyage or Rick's, the going rate may be a little higher, but it's up to you. Total nudity is prohibited, so there will also be some sort of G-string, skimpy bathing suit, or garter to tuck it into.

However, there are a few strip joint no-no's you should be aware of (all common sense, but as we've said, the behavior of some tourists will astound you): Absolutely no fondling or feeling up of the dancers is allowed, and you may find the dancers ready to retaliate if you try. If you visit a burlesque house (and to be fair, this reminder more often applies to women), behave yourself; don't make faces, denigrate the dancers, or pull on your escort to get away. If you are offended by the spectacle, don't go. Similarly, if you are a man whose companion wants to see a male dancer, don't play the chauvinist and get jealous: What's sauce for the goose . . .

■ New Orleans on the Air ■

Aside from the usual babble of format rock, talk, easy listening, and country music stations, New Orleans is home to a few stations that really stand out for high-quality broadcasting. Tune in to what hip locals are listening to.

New Orleans' Radio Stations		
Station	**Frequency**	**Format**
WWNO	89.9 FM	National Public Radio
WWOZ	90.7 FM	Lots of music with local history
WQUE	93.3 FM	Hip-hop, soul, R&B
WEZB	97.1 FM	Conventional and mainstream Top 40 radio
WNOE	101.1 FM	New Orleans' country music flagship
KKND	106.7 FM	Hottest alternative and modern rock
WODT	1280 AM	All-blues radio

How to Avoid Crime and Keep Safe in Public Places

■ Crime in New Orleans ■

From the news clips of Mardi Gras, New Orleans may seem like an X-rated Disney World, but this is real life—and it's real life in a city with big gaps in income levels and housing. Translation: Trouble. With a capital "T" and that rhymes with "P" and that stands for poor. And, as it happens, for police.

New Orleans is in an unfortunate contest with Washington, D.C., for that infamous title, Murder Capital of the Nation; its murder rate is five times that of New York City, and up until recently, only about a third of those were being solved. In 1994, homicides hit a record high of 421. New Orleans' poverty level is the third-worst in the country. Discomfittingly, it is legal in New Orleans to carry a concealed weapon. And since the '80s, crack cocaine has been big bad business here, fueling tensions and gang machismo.

While the overwhelming majority of violent crimes still occur in the poorest parts of town around the housing projects, you can no longer take for granted that you are safe even in the French Quarter. In fact, the crime rate within the Quarter itself has become a major concern. After all, that's where the rich, or at least "rich" by housing project standards only blocks away, are to be found.

Tourists are particularly easy marks; so are the dancers and waitstaff at bars, who earn much of their money in cash tips. During the 1996 Thanksgiving holidays, an advertising executive was raped and killed by a parking lot attendant near the Ursuline Convent, and three of four employees of the Louisiana Pizza Kitchen in the French Market died of gunshot wounds they received during a hold-up. And in May 1997, a Kentucky postal worker and father of three visiting New Orleans for a convention was shot and killed in a botched robbery as he and a companion walked through the Quarter to their hotel.

Worse, the New Orleans Police Department has a long history of notorious corruption: In recent years NOPD officers have been convicted of having witnesses beaten and even executed, of robbery and murder, and of institutional extortion. ("Institutional" in both senses of the word: With starting salaries of only $16,000 a year, even honest cops were almost forced to moonlight or otherwise pad their take-home pay to get by.)

Admittedly, such headlines make things sound pretty bad, and local authorities have finally begun to take them—and their effect on the city's reputation—seriously. The latest attempt to reform the police department began with the hiring of former D.C. deputy police chief Richard Pennington in 1994. Pennington in turn has launched a number of highly publicized police initiatives, firing or disciplining hundreds of officers, hiring hundreds more, and raising salaries and standards. A private coalition of New Orleans businesses and residents kicked in the money to hire consultants Jack Maple, former deputy commissioner of the New York Police Department, and John Linder to set up a computerized "map" of the city's highest crime spots of the type that is credited with having cut the New York murder rate in half since 1993.

Residents disagree on how effective such methods have been so far; in general, the perception of Pennington's success is directly proportionate to the distance people live from the French Quarter. Suburban commuters think things are much better, while French Quarter residents say they never see any police except those sitting in their cars around the Royal Street precinct station. Nevertheless, violent crime statistics are beginning to drop, and police officials promise that the campaign to educate officers and the public about crime prevention will make even more of a dent in the numbers.

In the meantime, you should be careful, as you would in any major city. The whole French Quarter is pretty safe during the day, but after dark you should stick to the more populated streets—Bourbon, Royal, Chartres, Decatur, Canal, and Dauphine, and Burgundy between Dumaine and Canal—and even then you should be wary of the outer blocks. Avoid walking alone outside the commercial areas, and be sure not to flash your personal belongings if you do. Jackson Square is a good bet at all hours, thanks to the round-the-clock crowd at the Café du Monde. Still, travel in a group or take a cab; if you aren't sure how safe an area is, ask one of the locals.

The cemeteries may seem pretty quiet, but they have become particularly dangerous to visitors wandering about; even in daylight, you should go only with a tour or at least several friends. Audubon Park and City Park are both fine and busy during the day, but again, you shouldn't be strolling through them after sunset, and you should probably avoid Armstrong Park altogether, at least until the city's elaborate plans to fix it up as a community music center and to secure it are complete. Although the

St. Charles Streetcar runs 24 hours a day, it's best to use it in the wee hours only if your destination is within sight of the stop, or perhaps if you just want to take a round trip to view the great houses of the Garden District lit up.

Don't leave a lot of money or traveler's checks in your hotel room; even though the employees are probably dependable, the older, smaller buildings are not exactly inaccessible. And if you buy any valuable antiques of the sort that can be easily pawned, such as silver or gems, ask the hotel to lock them in the safe.

Unless you actually drove into the city, you will find that you don't really want a car. Wait until you're headed into the country to rent one, or just take a cab. Parking can be tough and several days' parking quite expensive; traffic customs carry more weight than laws in some cases; tickets are stiff; and unless you're familiar with all the one-way roads and eccentric highway signage, you can make life harder on yourself. Besides, a parked car is another target for criminals and drunks.

The worst time, not surprisingly, is around Mardi Gras, when the throngs and lubrication invite pickpockets. In any case, if you are accosted by a thief, don't argue; try to stay calm, and hope he does, too.

■ Having a Plan ■

Random violence and street crime are facts of life in any large city. You've got to be cautious and alert, and plan ahead. When you are out and about you must work under the assumption that you must use caution because you are on your own; if you run into trouble, it's unlikely that police or anyone else will be able to come to your rescue. You must give some advance thought to the ugly scenarios that could occur, and consider both preventive measures and an escape plan just in case.

Not being a victim of street crime is sort of a survival-of-the-fittest thing. Just as a lion stalks the weakest member of the antelope herd, muggers and thieves target the easiest victim. Simply put, no matter where you are or what you are doing, you want potential felons to think of you as a bad risk.

On the Street   For starters, you always present less of an appealing target if you are with other people. Second, if you must be out alone, act alert, be alert, and always have at least one of your arms and hands free. Felons gravitate toward preoccupied folks, the kind found plodding along staring at the sidewalk, with both arms encumbered by briefcases or packages. Visible jewelry (on either men or women) attracts the wrong kind of attention. Men, keep your billfolds in your front trouser or coat pocket, or in a shoulder pouch. Women, keep your purses tucked tightly under your arm; if you're wearing a coat, put it on over your shoulder bag strap.

Here's another tip: Men can carry two wallets, including one inexpensive one, carried in your hip pocket, containing about $20 in cash and some expired credit cards. This is the one you hand over if you're accosted. Your real credit cards and the bulk of whatever cash you have should be in either a money clip or a second wallet hidden elsewhere on your person. Women can carry a fake wallet in their purse, and keep the real one in a pocket or money belt.

If You're Approached Police will tell you that a felon has the least amount of control over his intended victim during the few moments of his initial approach. A good strategy, therefore, is to short-circuit the crime scenario as quickly as possible. If a felon starts by demanding your money, for instance, quickly take out your billfold (preferably your fake one), and hurl it in one direction while you run shouting for help in the opposite direction. The odds are greatly in your favor that the felon will prefer to collect your silent billfold rather than pursue you. If you hand over your wallet and just stand there, the felon will likely ask for your watch and jewelry next. If you're a woman, the longer you hang around, the greater your vulnerability to personal injury or rape.

Secondary Crime Scenes Under no circumstance, police warn, should you ever allow yourself to be taken to another location—a "secondary crime scene" in police jargon. This move, they explain, provides the felon more privacy and consequently more control. A felon can rob you on the street very quickly and efficiently. If he tries to remove you to another location, whether by car or on foot, it is a certain indication that he has more in mind than robbery. Even if the felon has a gun or knife, your chances are infinitely better running away. If the felon grabs your purse, let him have it. If he grabs your coat, come out of the coat. Hanging onto your money or coat is not worth getting mugged, raped, or murdered.

Another maxim: Never believe anything a felon tells you, even if he's telling you something you desperately want to believe, for example, "I won't hurt you if you come with me." No matter how logical or benign he sounds, assume the worst. Always, always, break off contact as quickly as possible, even if that means running.

In Public Transport When riding a bus, always take a seat as close to the driver as you can; never ride in the back. Likewise, on the streeetcars, sit near the driver's or attendant's compartment. These people have a phone and can summon help in the event of trouble.

In Cabs   While it is possible to hail a cab on the street in New Orleans at night, it's best to go to one of the hotel stands or call a reliable cab company and stay inside while they dispatch a cab to your door. When your cab arrives, check the driver's certificate, which must, by law, be posted on the dashboard. Address the cabbie by his last name (Mr. Jones or whatever) or mention the number of his cab. This alerts the driver to the fact that you are going to remember him and/or his cab. Not only will this contribute to your safety, it will keep your cabbie from trying to run up the fare.

If you need to catch a cab at the train station or at the airport, always use the taxi queue. Taxis in the official queue are properly licensed and regulated. Never accept an offer for a cab or limo made by a stranger in the terminal or baggage claim. At best, you will be significantly overcharged for the ride. At worst, you may be abducted.

■ Personal Attitude ■

While some areas of every city are more dangerous than others, never assume that any area is completely safe. Never let down your guard. You can be the victim of a crime, and it can happen to you anywhere. If you go to a restaurant or nightspot, use valet parking or park in a well-lighted lot. Women leaving a restaurant or club alone should never be reluctant to ask to be escorted to their car.

Never let your pride or sense of righteousness and indignation imperil your survival. This is especially difficult for many men, particularly for men in the presence of women. It makes no difference whether you are approached by an aggressive drunk, an unbalanced street person, or an actual felon, the rule is the same: Forget your pride and break off contact as quickly as possible. Who cares whether the drunk insulted you, if everyone ends up back at the hotel safe and sound? When you wake up in the hospital with a concussion and your jaw sewn shut, it's too late to decide that the drunk's filthy remark wasn't really all that important.

Felons, druggies, some street people, and even some drunks play for keeps. They can attack with a bloodthirsty hostility and hellish abandon that is beyond the imagination of most people. Believe me, you are not in their league (nor do you want to be).

■ Self-Defense ■

In a situation where it is impossible to run, you'll need to be prepared to defend yourself. Most policemen insist that a gun or knife is not much use to the average person. More often than not, they say, the weapon will be turned against the victim. The best self-defense device for the average person is Mace. Not only is it legal in most states, it is nonlethal and easy to use.

When you shop for Mace, look for two things: It should be able to fire about eight feet, and it should have a protector cap so it won't go off by mistake in your purse or pocket. Carefully read the directions that come with your device, paying particular attention to how it should be carried and stored, and how long the active ingredients will remain potent. Wearing a rubber glove, test-fire your Mace, making sure that you fire downwind.

When you are out about town, make sure your Mace is someplace easily accessible, say, attached to your keychain. If you are a woman and you keep your Mace on a keychain, avoid the habit of dropping your keys (and the Mace) into the bowels of your purse when you leave your hotel room or your car. The Mace will not do you any good if you have to dig around in your purse for it. Keep your keys and your Mace in your hand until you have safely reached your destination.

■ Carjackings and Highway Robbery ■

With the recent surge in carjackings, drivers also need to take special precautions. "Keep alert when you're driving in traffic," one police official warns. "Keep your doors locked, with the windows rolled up and the air conditioning or heat on. In traffic, leave enough space in front of you so that you're not blocked in and can make a U-turn. That way, if someone approaches your car and starts beating on your windshield, you can drive off." Store your purse or briefcase under your knees when you are driving, rather than on the seat beside you.

Also be aware of other drivers bumping you from the rear or driving alongside you and gesturing that something is wrong with your car. In either case, do not stop or get out of your car. Continue on until you reach a very public and well-lighted place where you can check things out, and if necessary, get help.

■ **Ripoffs and Scams** ■

A lively street scene harboring hundreds of strolling tourists is a veritable incubator for ripoffs and scams. Although pickpockets, scam artists, and tricksters work the whole French Quarter, they are particularly active on Bourbon Street, Jackson Square, Decatur, and along the Riverwalk. While some of the scams, such as the cocky teen who bets $5 he can tell you where "you got your shoes," are relatively harmless ("You got them on your feet, sucker!"), others can be costly as well as dangerous.

Pickpockets work in teams, often involving children. One person creates a distraction such as dropping coins, spilling ice cream on you, or trying to sell you something, while a second person deftly picks your pocket. In most cases your stolen wallet is instantly passed to a third team member walking past. Even if you realize immediately that your wallet has been lifted, the pickpocket will have unburdened himself of the evidence.

Because pickpockets come in all shapes and sizes, be especially wary of any encounter with a stranger. Anyone, from a six-year-old child wobbling toward you on a bicycle to a man in a nice suit asking directions, could be creating a diversion for a pickpocket. Think twice before rendering assistance and be particularly cognizant of other people in your immediate area. Don't let children touch you or allow street peddlers to get too close. Be particularly wary of people whose hands are concealed by newspapers or other items. Oh yeah, one more thing: If somebody *does* spill ice cream on you, be wary of the Good Samaritan who suddenly appears to help you clean up.

Most travelers carry more cash, credit cards, and other stuff in their wallet than they need. If you plan to walk in a busy tourist area in New Orleans or anywhere else, transfer exactly what you will need to a very small, low-profile wallet or pouch. When the *Unofficial Guide* authors are on the street, they carry one American Express card, one VISA card, and a minimal amount of cash. Think about it: You don't need your gas credit cards if you are walking or those hometown, department-store credit cards if you are away from home.

Do not, under any circumstances, carry your wallet and valuables in a fanny pack. Thieves and pickpockets can easily snip the belt and disappear into the crowd with the entire fanny pack before you realize what's happened. As far as pockets are concerned, front pockets are safer than back or coat pockets, though, with a little extra effort, pickpockets can get at front pockets, too. The safest place to carry valuables is under your arm in a shoulder holster–style pouch. Lightweight, comfortable, and especially accessible when worn under a coat or vest, shoulder pouches are available from catalogs and at most good travel stores. Incidentally, avoid chest pouches that are suspended around your neck by a cord. Like the fanny pack, they can be removed easily by pickpockets.

■ More Things to Avoid ■

When you do go out, walk with a minimum of two people whenever possible. If you have to walk alone, stay in well-lighted areas that have plenty of people around. Be careful about whom you ask for directions. (When in doubt, shopkeepers are a good bet.) Don't count your money in public, and carry as little cash as possible. At public phones, if you must say your calling card number to make a long-distance call, don't say it loud enough for strangers around you to hear. And, with the exception of the Riverfront area near Jackson Square, avoid public parks after dark.

■ Help May Be Nearer Than You Think ■

While this litany of warnings and precautions may sound grim, it's really commonsense advice that applies to visitors in any large American city. Keep in mind that New Orleans' reputation for crime has been exaggerated by media attention. Finally, remember that millions of visitors a year still flock to New Orleans, making it one of the most-visited destinations in the United States. The overwhelming majority encounter no problems with crime during their New Orleans visit.

■ The Homeless ■

If you're not from a big city or haven't visited one in a while, you're in for a shock when you come to New Orleans, where there is a fairly substantial homeless population. Though most evident along the Riverwalk, Decatur Street, and Jackson Square, you are likely to bump into them any place that's frequented by tourists.

Who Are These People?   "Most are lifelong [city] residents who are poor," according to Joan Alker, assistant director of the National Coalition for the Homeless, an advocacy group headquartered in Washington. "The people you see on the streets are primarily single men and women. A disproportionate number of them are minorities and people with disabilities—they're either mentally ill, or substance abusers, or have physical disabilities."

Are They a Threat to Visitors?   "No," Ms. Alker says. "Studies done in Washington show that homeless men have lower rates of conviction for violent crimes than the population at large. We know that murders aren't being committed by the homeless. I can't make a blanket statement, but most homeless people you see are no more likely to commit a violent crime than other people."

Should You Give the Homeless Money?   "That's a personal decision," Ms. Alker says. "But if you can't, at least try to acknowledge their existence by looking them in the eye and saying, 'No, I can't.'" While there's no way to tell if the guy with the Styrofoam cup asking for a handout is really destitute or just a con artist, no one can dispute that most of these people are what they claim to be: homeless.

Ways to Help   It's really a matter for your own conscience. We confess to being both moved and annoyed by these unfortunate people: moved by their need and annoyed that we cannot enjoy the city without running a gauntlet of begging men and women. In the final analysis, we found that it is easier on the conscience and spirit to carry an overcoat or jacket pocket full of change at all times. The cost of giving those homeless who approach you a quarter really does not add up to all that much, and it is much better for the psyche to respond to their plight than to deny or ignore their presence.

There is a notion, perhaps valid in some instances, that money given to a homeless person generally goes toward the purchase of alcohol or drugs. If this bothers you excessively, carry granola bars for distribution, or, alternatively, buy some inexpensive gift coupons that can be redeemed at a McDonald's or other fast-food restaurant for coffee or a sandwich.

We have found that a little kindness regarding the homeless goes a long way, and that a few kind words delivered along with your quarter or granola bar brighten the day for both you and your friend in need. We are not suggesting a lengthy conversation or prolonged involvement, just something simple like, "Sure, I can help a little bit. Take care of yourself, fella."

Those moved to get more involved in the nationwide problem of homelessness can send inquiries—or a check—to the National Coalition for the Homeless, 1612 K Street, NW, Suite 1004, Washington, D.C. 20006.

Keep It Brief   Finally, don't play psychologist. All the people you encounter on the street are strangers. They may be harmless, or they may be dangerous. Either way, maintain distance and keep any contacts or encounters brief. Be prepared to handle street people in accordance with your principles, but mostly, just be prepared. If you have a druggie in your face wanting a handout, the last thing you want to do is pull out your wallet and thumb through the twenties looking for a one-dollar bill. As the sergeant on *Hill Street Blues* used to say, be careful out there.

PART SEVEN

Getting Around New Orleans

New Orleans is a very hands-on, hospitable city. And the main neighborhood attractions, especially for tourists, are accessible by public transportation, give or take a taxi or two. But you will probably be asking for directions and addresses, and those are two of the most peculiar things about this idiosyncratic city. Names can be unrecognizable, and maps can seem upside down. In fact, in at least one case, west really is east, as you'll see below.

■ Public Transportation ■

As we pointed out earlier, you probably don't need or want a car in the city. Most of the time, when you're in the French Quarter, or any other neighborhood, you'll be walking. If you do think you'll want a car, you should figure out exactly what excursions you want to take outside the city and only rent one for those days. Otherwise you'll have to worry about parking lots, parking tickets, and perhaps vandalism—not to mention being impounded. (If you are, call the Claiborne Auto Pound at 565-7450.) If you are staying at one of the larger hotels around Canal Street or in the suburbs, it may have parking (it may or may not be free). But most visitors will find the buses, streetcars, and taxis handy for anywhere they want to go.

By far the nicest way to get from one neighborhood to the other, or to rest your feet after a good promenade, is the streetcar. (Locals always used to call them "trolleys," but perhaps because of the heavy promotion the lines are getting these days, the word "streetcar" is gradually winning out. Still, you will sound less like a tourist if you want to refer to them as trolleys.)

There is one streetcar that runs the length of the Quarter, the Riverfront Streetcar, which originates near Esplanade Avenue and makes stops all the way to the Warehouse/Arts District near the Convention Center. Each trip costs $1.25. The Riverfront Streetcar operates from 6 A.M. to midnight weekdays and 8 A.M. to midnight on weekends.

The more famous St. Charles Avenue Streetcar originates at Canal Street and runs 24 hours a day through the Garden District past Audubon Park and Riverbend. Each one-way trip is $1. And, in a sort of historical about-face, the two lines are connected by track down the center of Canal Street.

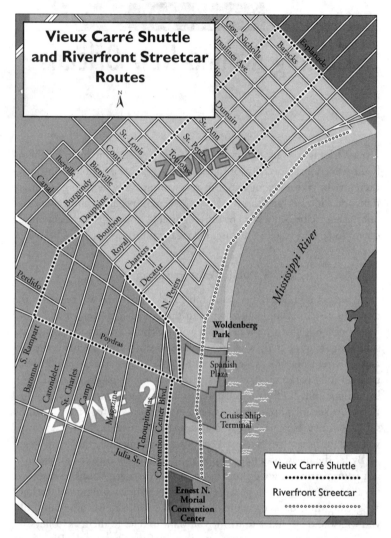

Unfortunately, since the city, in a previous facelift, had decided the street-car was dispensible, it had long since paved over the old Canal Street tracks, and the median had to be dug up for the tracks to be relaid.

City bus trips are also $1, transfers 10 cents (25 cents for express buses). But both the streetcars and the buses are operated by the Regional Transit Authority, and you can get one- or three-day VisiTour passes good for unlimited rides on any of them. A one-day pass is $4, and a three-day pass, which really saves you money, is only $8. Most hotels and information

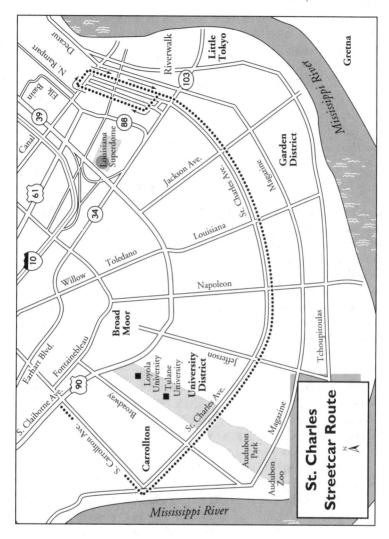

centers and many shops sell the RTA passes. For bus routes and times, call the 24-hour RTA RideLine at 248-3900.

Taxicabs are pretty easy to find in the French Quarter, especially around hotels, but if you're out somewhere without a lift, call White Fleet (948-6605), Yellow-Checker Cabs (943-2411), or United (524-9606). New Orleans cabs run on meters—base charge $2.10, plus 20 cents for each one-sixth of a mile or 40 seconds, and $1 per additional passenger—but if you come during a special event, such as Jazz and Heritage Fest, there may be a minimum $3 charge in effect. Taxis can also usually be hired for a flat rate if a group of several people want to tour a few attractions; call the dispatcher's office and see what sort of deal you can get. Or if you happen to be picked up by one of the really friendly ones, and New Orleans cabbies can be hilariously well informed, find out if he freelances.

You can also rent a bicycle and combine touring and exercise: Bicycle Michael's has a variety of mountain bikes, three-speeders, and even bicycles built for two (622 Frenchmen Street; 945-9505). French Quarter Bicycles stocks mostly mountain bikes (522 Dumaine Street; 529-3136).

■ Walking the Walk ■

Much of New Orleans can be covered on foot, and that's a good thing, because it means you can settle for pedestrian directions such as "turn right" and "go three blocks on." What you *don't* want to get into is traditional directions—north, south, etc.—because in New Orleans, it just isn't very helpful. Because of the Mississippi's snaking, the city somewhat resembles an open fan: Although various neighborhoods have right angles within themselves, including the Garden District and the French Quarter, just about the only intersection that aligns with the compass is Napoleon Avenue and Tchoupitoulas Street.

So directions in New Orleans are given according to the biggest landmarks around: the Mississippi River and Lake Pontchartrain. Locals speak of going "toward the river" or of something's being "riverside"; an address "toward the lake" might also be "lakeside." "Uptown" is above—that is, more or less west of—Canal Street, while "downtown" is said to be below, or on the French Quarter side, of Canal. That also helps tell you which is "upriver"—toward Uptown—vs. "downriver." Audubon Park is upriver, as are the River Road plantations, but the French Quarter is downriver from the Garden District. Got it?

Other apparently specific directions are merely relative. South Claiborne actually goes mostly northwest, and North Claiborne swings in a curve that runs mostly east and southeast. As for the West Bank . . . it's south and east of the city, somewhere between Algiers and Gretna. The East Bank, naturally, is to the west.

■ Public Accommodations ■

The *Unofficial Guides* are starting to get a reputation for worrying about rest rooms, or rather, about your being able to find them. This is a tribute to the relatively short staying power of our founder, Bob Sehlinger, and someday we'll stop teasing him about it. But he has a good point: Being uncomfortable doesn't help you enjoy a walking tour or a museum. And especially in summer, when New Orleans can be so hot, it's tempting to drink a lot. (When in New Orleans is it *not* tempting to drink a lot?)

The greatest concentration of rest rooms in the French Quarter is down near the water (no pun intended, surely): Riverwalk, Jax Brewery-Millhouse Complex, Canal Place, and World Trade Center all have good, clean bathrooms, as does the French Market (two sets, in the 900 and 1200 blocks). Across from Jackson Square, there are rest rooms in Waldenburg Park. City Park and the Audubon Park tennis courts also have public rest rooms. Museums and department stores are equipped as well. Some places have pay toilets, so it's a good idea to keep some emergency change around; and where there is an attendant, it's considered polite to leave a tip, though only a quarter or so—cheap by big-city standards.

The large hotel lobbies usually have rest rooms, although you should only take advantage of them in an emergency, and when you are reasonably well dressed. If you are really in a pinch, go to a bar and at least order a soda before you hit the john.

PART EIGHT

Entertainment and Nightlife

Performing Arts

$\mathbf{L}$et's be up-front about this: Few people head for New Orleans intending to spend a night at the theater. But that's not to say you shouldn't look around for something beyond the strip joints and jazz bars. There is no multistate performing arts center here like New York's Lincoln Center or Washington's Kennedy Center, but there are several venues, most in the Central Business District, that book touring companies of Broadway shows, concerts, etc. Most shows will be listed in the *Times-Picayune*.

The main theatrical venue to check into is the **Saenger Performing Arts Center** (524-2490) at Rampart and Canal, a gorgeously restored Renaissance-style cinema worth visiting just for its "living sky" ceiling of drifting clouds and constellations; it books national touring companies of Broadway productions and the occasional big-name pop star. The **State Palace Theater** (522-4435) at Rampart and Basin is another old venue whose boxes and chandeliers go rather strangely with some of its non-middle-of-the-road music acts. The grand-old-style **Mahalia Jackson Theatre of the Performing Arts** (565-7470), although in the somewhat questionable Louis Armstrong Park at the edge of the French Quarter, is home to the **New Orleans Opera Association** and the primarily imported productions of the **New Orleans Ballet Association.**

The **Louisiana Philharmonic Orchestra** (523-6530) performs, in a season that roughly matches the school year, at the ornately restored Beaux Arts **Orpheum Theatre**—part of the original Orpheum vaudeville circuit—on University Place just off Canal; Maxim Shostakovich, conductor of the LPO's predecessor, the bankrupt New Orleans Symphony, occasionally picks up the baton. The only Equity company in New Orleans, the **Southern Repertory Theater** (861-8163), has a small 150-seat house on the third floor of Canal Place. It's not the most professional of companies yet, perhaps, but the fact that so many of its productions have local connections — plays by Tennessee Williams, Lillian Hellman, and others — makes it interesting. **Le Petit Théâtre du Vieux Carré** (522-2081) has plenty of atmosphere, and a reputed phantom to boot, though its seasons aren't as ambitious as they once were.

The **Contemporary Arts Center** (523-1216) in the Warehouse/Arts District books more cutting-edge productions, which sometimes are merely artsy-for-art's-sake and more apt to draw local residents than tourists. (On the other hand, Edward Albee directed his own "Fragments" at CAC, using local actors.) It has two stages, so sometimes dance and theatrical performances are booked at the same time. Other very local small and avant theater productions are held in the **Theater Marigny** on Frenchman Street (944-2653).

In the Garden District, both **Loyola** and **Tulane** frequently offer classical or dramatic works; contact the Loyola ticket office (865-3492) or Tulane box office (865-5143).

Big-name rock and pop concerts are usually scheduled either for the **Louisiana Superdome** (call 587-3800 or TicketMaster) or the University of New Orleans' **Kiefer Lakefront Arena,** a 10,000-seat venue near Lake Pontchartrain at UNO's east campus (286-7222).

New Orleans Nightlife

■ The Quarter ■

New Orleans is indeed a nightlife town. For all the city fathers' efforts to portray the Big Easy as a family-oriented destination, there's little doubt that legions of folks come here to do what they can't or won't do back home—holler in the streets and drink all night. They've come to the right place, with its relaxed laws, lusty hideaways, and rich, sultry nights. There are hundreds of bars here to cater to every conceivable appetite and mood. And it all starts in one special place.

When most folks think of New Orleans nightlife, they think of the French Quarter. You think French Quarter and you think *Bourbon Street.*

And while the image of Bourbon Street—with its tawdry parlors, beer-soaked juke joints, strip clubs, and drunken college kids stumbling about with "go cups" full of super-potent hurricanes—has tarnished the street's reputation as the epicenter of improvisational jazz and blues, the fact is, it never really was.

Bourbon Street is and always has been a mishmash of nightlife styles: elegant, rowdy, punky, sleazy, gay—in all senses of the term—and, yes, at times, jazzy. This is not to condemn the entire street to a sea of cultural irrelevance, because quite the opposite is true.

The point is, much to the newcomer's surprise, many of the city's great hangouts and, in particular, the great venues for live music, are not on Bourbon Street. Its live music scene is largely relegated to a series of bad cover bands, karaoke clubs, and cheap trios playing to recorded drum machine accompaniment, with a few notable exceptions.

Fritzel's (733 Bourbon, 561-0432) offers traditional Dixieland jazz on weekends and has evolved into a hotbed for European jazz players looking for a place to sit in. **Chris Owen's Club** (500 Bourbon, 523-6400) is where trumpeter Al Hirt, the cantankerous Jumbo himself, hangs his hat these days, and where the club's namesake matriarch cranks out two high-energy dance shows a night, despite her rapidly approaching septuagenarianism.

Patout's Cajun Cabin (501 Bourbon, 529-4256) offers spirited and visitor-friendly Cajun music, long on familiar favorites but often wanting for a true roadhouse feel.

Oddly, the most popular and crowded spot on Bourbon is often the **Cat's Meow** (701 Bourbon, 523-2788), the city's flagship karaoke bar. The most romantic spot on Bourbon is undoubtedly **Lafitte's Blacksmith Shop** (941 Bourbon, 523-0066), which is dimly lit, heated by fire in the winter, and an ideal spot to disappear into a dark corner (by the piano bar in the back). Three of the city's major gay dance clubs are clustered on Bourbon: **The Bourbon Pub and Parade** (801 Bourbon, 529-2107), **Cafe Lafitte in Exile** (901 Bourbon, 522-8397), and the upstart **Oz** (800 Bourbon, 593-9491), a straight-friendly, anything-goes, dance-all-night kind of place.

There's a bunch of strip clubs on Bourbon Street, both elegant and sleazy. Two notables are the **Maiden Voyage** (225 Bourbon, 524-0010) and **Rick's Cabaret** (315 Bourbon, 524-4222), two of the city's premier "upscale" gentlemen's clubs.

Other hangouts where beer and jello shots outpace scintillating conversation are the **Funky Pirate** (727 Bourbon Street, 523-1960) and **Krazy Korner** (640 Bourbon Street, 524-3157), and any of the dozens of other locations where adult beverages are served. Scores of taverns have courtyard hideaways for intimacy or second-story balconies offering a visual feast on the sea of humanity below, those stumbling, bead-mongering party animals from across the globe. The truth is, just about every 20 feet down the street there's another bar beckoning you inside, and if you can't find a giggle or two on this most lively and entertaining stretch of American roadway, then we can't help you.

The rest of the French Quarter is also a mesh of varying styles and atmospheres, from the impressive and ornately decorated **House of Blues** (225 Decatur Street, 529-BLUE), where the biggest names in the music business congregate, to the affected elegance of the **Bombay Club** (830 Conti Street, 586-0972), where $9 martinis rule the roost, to the ultimate in barroom bizarro, the **Dungeon** (738 Toulouse Street, 523-5530), which opens at midnight and offers an experience not unlike the LSD sequence by Peter Fonda in *Easy Rider,* complete with blacklights, Gothic decor, and heavy-metal dance tapes.

Across the French Quarter spectrum, there's **Preservation Hall** (726 St. Peter Street, 523-8939), where tourists congregate in thick lines to hear some of the great old traditional jazzmen of the city play in a dusty and dim old-time listening hall. (The thirsty beware: There are no refreshments served.)

Next door is **Pat O'Brien's** (718 St. Peter, 525-4823), said to boast the largest alcohol sales of any bar in America, but New Orleans is full of stories like that. Check out the dueling pianos bar and the flaming water fountain in the courtyard.

Over on Rampart Street are **Donna's Bar and Grill** (800 N. Rampart, 596-6914) and the **Funky Butt at Congo Square** (714 N. Rampart, 558-0872), two venues featuring hot young brass bands from around the city, often till the wee hours.

Besides the House of Blues, there are several other celebrity-owned theme bars and restaurants including the **Hard Rock Cafe** (418 N. Peters Street, 529-5617), **Planet Hollywood** (620 Decatur Street, 522-7826), and the super-model wannabe hangout, **Fashion Cafe** (619–621 Decatur Street, 522-3181). These glitzy and impressive big-dollar layouts are long on tourists and souvenirs but absent any native ambiance.

O'Flaherty's (514 Toulouse Street, 529-1317) and **Kerry Irish Pub** (331 Decatur Street, 527-5954), the area's only Irish music clubs, feature live music and Guinness on tap.

Maxwell's Jazz Cabaret (615 Toulouse Street, 523-2407) and the **Palm Court Jazz Cafe** (1202 Decatur Street, 525-0200) are venues for traditional New Orleans jazz, and the **Crescent City Brewhouse** (527 Decatur Street, 522-0571) is the Quarter's only brewpub and a playground for some of the area's fresh-faced young jazz players.

The Fourth Quarter (309 Decatur Street, 525-7529) is the neighborhood's grand new pool hall and sports club, featuring more than a dozen full-sized pool tables, eight big TVs, and all the latest trendy vodkas and smokes.

You'll probably never run into the owner at **Jimmy Buffett's Margaritaville** (1104 Decatur Street, 592-2569), but the open-air windows along the sidewalk and the good-time music—pop, blues, piano bangers, and such—make for an atmosphere that would please the boss. Closer to Jimmy Buffett's musical style, the **Tropical Isle** (738 Toulouse Street, 525-1689) offers blue-eyed Caribbean music nightly. **The Hog's Breath Saloon** (339 Chartres Street, 522-1736) has local rock and country bands in a brass-accented saloon atmosphere. Another local and international favorite is the **Napoleon House**.

There's a load of neighborhood (yes, people live in the Quarter) hangouts for straight folks (notably, the 1100 block of Decatur Street) and gay, perhaps most notably the low-key **Good Friends** (740 Dauphine Street, 523-9938) and the campier **Mint** (504 Esplanade Avenue, 525-2000), a lively mixed-gender hangout featuring various drag, comedy, and burlesque shows.

There is more, so much more, in the Quarter. Literally dozens more juke joints, pool halls, daiquiri bars, meat markets both gay and straight, strip clubs of all varieties, video poker hangouts, sports bars, and something you won't see anywhere else in town: the speakeasy at **Lucky Cheng's** (720 St. Louis Street, 529-2045), a restaurant staffed entirely by Asian drag queens.

There are so many establishments of so many colors that, at times, it seems there are as many bars in the French Quarter as there are T-shirt shops. But this is only an illusion.

■ The Jazz Scene ■

Yes, jazz is everywhere. In many forms, variations, and presentations, from the cobblestones of Jackson Square to the overdressed cigar bars of the Warehouse District, someone, somewhere, is carrying on the traditions of the great masters of American improvisational music.

Preservation Hall, Palm Court Cafe, Fritzel's, Snug Harbor, The Showcase, Donna's, The Funky Butt, Après, Café Brasil, Maxwell's, The Columns, and the **Bombay Club** are all profiled in the following pages. They are some of the finer locations for jazz around town, but far from the whole catalog.

In the French Quarter alone, the strains of horn solos pour forth, it seems, from every street corner. It ranges from the sublime to the downright cheesy, but it's what people come to hear, and the city aims to please. For the most part, the term "jazz" in New Orleans refers to traditional Dixieland, the stuff of old Satchmo and Al Hirt records. On Bourbon Street, the **Famous Door Jazz Cafe** (411 Bourbon Street, 522-7623) offers Dixieland among its many afternoon and evening music shows. The **Richelieu Room** at Arnaud's restaurant (corner of Bienville and Bourbon Streets, 523-2847) and **The Court of Two Sisters** (613 Royal Street, with an entrance on Bourbon Street, 522-7261) offer jazz while you eat. The lobby bar of the Royal Sonesta Hotel (300 Bourbon Street, 586-0300) generally offers low-key combos in the evenings.

Elsewhere in the Quarter, the cafes, restaurants, and pubs where you can hear native music are nearly too plentiful to mention. Just walk about. A few places of note include **Andrew Jaeger's Seafood House** (622 Conti Street, 522-4964), where Dr. John's old recording pal, drummer Freddy Staehle, holds court with friends. **Cafe Sbisa** (1011 Decatur Street, 522-5565) serves up jazz with dinner on weekends. The many cafes and public kiosks of the French Market host jazz bands nightly on the sidewalks, free for the listening from nearby benches. A great moment to remember in the city is the night you danced arm-in-arm on the curbside while a mule buggy clopped by and a saxman serenaded you in the rain.

It happens all the time.

Outside the Quarter, several hotels offer jazz samplings in their lobby bars, including but not exclusive to the **Fairmont** (123 Baronne Street, 529-7111), the **Marriott New Orleans** (555 Canal Street, 581-1000), the **Hotel Inter-Continental** (444 St. Charles Avenue, 525-5566), and the **Hotel Meridien** (614 Canal Street, 525-6500), where Frenchman Gilles Marschall brings his mixed bag of cabaret and New Orleans piano history together five nights a week. In the **Hilton Hotel** (2 Poydras Street, 523-4374), Pete Fountain, America's first prince of the clarinet, plays to full houses in the club that bears his name. (Call ahead for reservations; he's very popular with the old Johnny Carson crowd.) Down in the city's Ninth Ward, one of the area's favorite jazz traditions unfolds Thursday nights, when Kermit Ruffins, the second coming of Louis Armstrong, cooks turkey neck stew for the patrons and plays trumpet at **Vaughan's Lounge** (4229 Dauphine Street, 947-5562). A little farther off the path are the **Steak Knife** restaurant (888 Harrison Avenue, 488-8981) in the Lakeview neighborhood, offering late-night weekend shows, and the **Sandbar** pub, located in the Cove student union building at the University of New Orleans, where university students, under the tutelage of jazz granddaddy and UNO instructor Ellis Marsalis, perform for intimate and undersized crowds on Wednesday nights during the school year.

And, finally, for those who really want to get away from the maddening crowd, the famed Dukes of Dixieland play weekend dinner shows on the **Steamboat Natchez** (at the Toulouse Street Wharf behind the Jax Brewery, 586-8777).

■ What Else Is There? ■

Indigenous Louisiana music forms other than jazz—primarily Cajun and zydeco—are among the state's great exports. In New Orleans, they are plentiful. **Mid City Lanes, Mulate's,** and **Tipitina's** are all profiled in the following section, but fiddles and accordions abound in lesser-known areas as well. **Patout's Cajun Cabin** (501 Bourbon Street, 529-4256) pulls crowds off the street for dancing and fun, lured by the crazy syncopated washboard rhythms. **Michaul's** (840 St. Charles Avenue, 522-5517) offers Cajun cuisine and two-stepping six nights a week in a roadhouse atmosphere.

The Four Columns (3711 Westbank Expressway, 340-4109) is a dance hall on the West Bank of the Mississippi River, in the Harvey suburb, where Cajun families gather for fais-do-dos on a frequent but irregular basis.

(Check listings in the *Times-Picayune,* or call ahead.) A little farther down the road, in Crown Point, the Bayou Barn (Route 1 at Highway 45, 689-2663) has Sunday afternoon barbecues and dances. For the real deal in Cajun and zydeco, you need to drive about two hours west, to the Acadiana Parishes of Louisiana—Cajun Country—but that's a whole different guidebook.

The blues is the stepchild of New Orleans musical tradition: every bit as vital and necessary to the development of the city's heritage, but often overlooked as a cultural staple.

The name notwithstanding, the **House of Blues** is not actually a blues club, per se, as much as a blues museum. Its actual live musical fare covers all spectrums, from Latin to punk to funk to fusion. **Tipitina's, The Maple Leaf,** and **The Showcase** are all profiled in the following section, but there are plenty of other spots around town where you can drown your sorrows in wailing guitar riffs. **Benny's** (938 Valence Street, 897-9690) is certainly a legend among them. Located on the block where the Neville Brothers grew up, Benny's is where they and their buddies played before big record labels and Linda Ronstadt came calling. It's a late-night place, starting up around 11 or later, and anyone from dicey-looking neighborhood characters to Dennis Quaid and Keith Richards may show up here. The music is almost always bluesy in some fashion, and very local, but don't expect any Nevilles to sit in—their come-lately and much-deserved financial rewards have afforded them better digs elsewhere in town. Benny's has a history of closing for weeks, sometimes months, without notice. Check newspaper listings or call ahead before going.

Pampy's Tight Squeeze (200 N. Broad Street, 949-7970) not only has the best name in town, but it's where New Orleans mayor Marc Morial and some of his cronies sit in tight quarters and bury their deficit blues.

The blues mix with rock and pop at a legion of other clubs around town. **Jimmy's** (8200 Willow Street, 861-8200) and the neighboring **Carrollton Station** (8140 Willow Street, 865-9190) both offer local and national acts in intimate Uptown surroundings. Sunday nights at Carrollton Station sometimes finds local rock guru Peter Holsapple—keyboard player for both R.E.M. and Hootie and the Blowfish—playing silly songs and inviting friends out of the audience to join him (among them, his wife, the silky-voiced Susan Cowsill of the '60s singing family). **The Dream Palace** (534 Frenchmen Street, 945-2040), **The Dragon's Den** (435 Esplanade Avenue, 949-1750), and **Checkpoint Charlie** (501 Esplanade Avenue, 947-0979) are three clubs on the outer fringe of the French Quarter that dabble in all forms of contemporary music, from jazz to funk to folk. Checkpoint Charlie's is especially curious; it also houses a laundromat and a paperback book exchange.

On the wilder side, **Monaco Bob's Touchdown Lounge** (1179 Annunciation Street, 586-1282) and **The Angel** (2441 Bayou Road, 940-0666) host all sorts of curious musical and performance events, anything from hardcore rock shows and amateur strip nights at the Touchdown, to Gothic and industrial dance parties and "fetish specials" at The Angel. Use your own judgment on this.

Le Bon Temps Roule (4801 Magazine Street, 895-8117) is a boozy neighborhood pool palace with live bands in the back room one or two nights a week.

The Acadian Brewing Company (201 N. Carrollton Avenue, 483-9003) is one of two New Orleans brewpubs, featuring homemade suds and occasional folk and rock music sets. (The other brewpub, **Crescent City,** is featured in the following section.)

For the nonalcoholic set, **Kaldi's** coffeehouse and museum (941 Decatur Street, 586-8989) is a bohemian French Quarter hangout with super-strong brews and occasional jazz and gospel performances. Uptown, the **Neutral Ground Coffee House** is the city's foremost folk and singer/songwriter showcase, with no cover charge.

Contrary to popular belief, not every bar in New Orleans is a jazz club, or even a music club, for that matter. Conversation and the art of flirting are alive and well on the bayou, and places abound to indulge. A favorite of artists and celebrities is the deliciously offbeat and out-of-the-way **Saturn Bar** (3067 St. Claude Avenue, 949-7532), where Alec Baldwin, Sam Shepard, Robbie Robertson, and Nicolas Cage are among the many notables who have dropped in to drop out of the local scene for a night. It's dark, quiet, and full of bad art and poets who smoke too much. **Dos Jefes Uptown Cigar Bar** (5535 Tchoupitoulas Street, 891-8500) and **Spanky's** (5243 Canal Boulevard, 488-0100) are two in-the-know trendy spots for 30- and 40-somethings who favor walk-in humidors and expensive martinis to Marlboros and draft beer. **Amberjack's** (7306 Lakeshore Drive, 282-6660) is a lively singles dance club on the north end of town with a great view of Lake Pontchartrain and a comedy showcase Wednesday nights. The only other steady comedy gig is at **Movie Pitchers** (3941 Bienville Street, 488-8881), a movie art house and comedy club on weekends.

The Balcony Bar (3201 Magazine Street, 895-1600) and the **Bulldog** (3236 Magazine Street, 891-1516) are anchors of the expanding yuppie nightlife scene in the arts and antiques district Uptown, both offering big beer selections and great people-watching venues.

In the Warehouse District, the **Ernst Cafe** (600 S. Peters Street, 525-

8544) is a popular happy hour hangout for upwardly mobiles, and is one of local hero John Goodman's many favorite hangouts. Finally, there is **My Father's Junkyard** (350 Douglas Road, 340-1117), across the Mississippi River in Marrero, where West Bank couples and singles gather in the most unusual of settings—a former junkyard. The automobiles suspended from the ceilings here are not pop memorabilia—a la Hard Rock Cafe's signature pink Cadillacs. No, the car parts here, alas, are left over from the former tenants.

■ A Note on Safety ■

New Orleans is a city with predictable danger zones and drug-peddling neighborhoods. Some deserving bars and nightclubs have been left out of this guide because the risks involved in going to them are not worth it. Most visitors are aware of the city's high murder and robbery rates, and you should always bear these unflattering statistics in mind. Fringe areas of the French Quarter are particularly vulnerable spots for robbery. Always be aware when walking the streets, and don't hesitate to cross a street or turn around to avoid coming face-to-face with what appears to be an unsavory character. The risk of offending said stranger is far outweighed by ensuring your personal safety. In short, the deal is this: In the highly commercial areas of the French Quarter, feel free and safe to walk about. In all other areas, we recommend you take a cab. They're cheap and efficient.

There is a common scam on Bourbon Street that goes like this: A stranger approaches you and says, "I bet I know where you got them shoes. I know the street and the city and the state where you got them shoes." Don't take the bet. He knows: You got them shoes on your feet on Bourbon Street, in New Orleans, Louisiana.

Get it? No matter. If you take the bet, be prepared to pay up or face a bad scene on the street. Never play games on other people's playing fields. That's it for the lecture. Now go ahead, have fun.

APRÈS

Speakeasy jazz bar and cigar club

Who Goes There: Lounge lizards, buppies, junior partners, post-debs

709 St. Charles Avenue
566-7000   Zone 2 Central Business District

Cover: None
Minimum: One drink per set
Mixed drinks: $4–8
Wine: $5–8
Beer: $3–4
Dress: For success

Specials: Happy hour 5–7 P.M.
weekdays, $1 off all drinks
Food available: A kitchen is currently
under construction
Disabled access: Yes

Hours: Tuesday–Friday, 5 P.M.–2 A.M.; Saturday, 9 P.M.–4 A.M.;
Sunday and Monday, closed.

What goes on: It took a few decades, but somebody finally figured out that local nightclubbers would pay a cover charge for a jazz trio, as long as you didn't call the place a jazz club. Après is more of an extended happy hour for the Warehouse District set, decidedly upward-mobiles whose Friday night thrills include a couple of $8 martinis. It's a back-slapping, power-mingling sort of place for the post-dining hours. The crowd, though generally inattentive to the music, is hearing some of the great 20-something jazz players in town, including trumpet supernova Jeremy Davenport and the marvelously funky and ever-grinning Marvin Williams.

Setting & atmosphere: Those newfangled tiny halogen lights suspended from the ceiling look great but don't illuminate much but the attitude. It's everything a '90s lounge should be, with angular artwork and a generally bloated post-modern decor. A couple of big comfy leather couches anchor the music listening area.

If you go: If you're easily bothered by smoke—cigars and cigarettes—don't waste your time here. There's plenty of both. Also, the music is an afterthought, not the main event, so it requires the delicate balance of respectful disinterest, clapping at the appropriate moments, and being sure never to tell your loudest story during a soft melody. Musicians hate that. If you actually pull a chair up to the stage area, the musicians will love and no doubt reward you with a well-grooved solo.

BOMBAY CLUB

Delightfully pretentious gin joint and armchair lounge

Who Goes There: 30–75, movers, shakers, pols, yuppies, buppies, second sceners, the courthouse crowd

830 Conti Street
586-0972   Zone 1 French Quarter

Cover: None
Minimum: None
Mixed drinks: $4.25–15
Wine: $5–7
Beer: $3–4.50
Dress: The sign says "Proper attire required." Let that be your guide. Jackets for men.

Specials: Wednesday night is "New Orleans Networking Night," and its attendance is enhanced by free drinks for women all night.
Food available: Appetizers along the lines of pâté, salmon plates, and cheese boards
Disabled access: Yes

Hours: Tuesday–Saturday, 4 P.M.–2 A.M.

What goes on: Networking, schmoozing, flirting, and general bedazzling, both physical and verbal. The Bombay is where monied but demure locals gather to chatter and booze to the soft piano strains of local and generally very talented ivory ticklers. The Bombay was the first of the city's upscale cigar and martini bars—by ten years—and still stands above the others.

Setting & atmosphere: Downright Churchillian, the Bombay has the trappings of a British men's club, which is what it was supposed to be when it opened. But there are not many Brits here, and it turns out women like it, too. It is darkly paneled with rich reds amid the decor, with a variety of bar stools, booths, sofas, or comfy living room settings. The subtle hints at old-line decadence, the hushed conversation emanating from the booths, and the background sound of tinkling glasses make for a convivial step back in time to an era when a slew of martinis after work was considered classy, not reprehensible.

If you go: Demure, please. Remember, everyone is putting on a show, but no one wants to look like it. Play the game. Overtip. Don't sing along to the piano. Don't ogle the enhanced cleavage, and there is plenty. Overdress —go ahead, get your stones out of the hotel safe for this one. Recommended refreshments: Clear liquors are the toast of the Bombay—all the great, new, triple-distilled, and overpriced gins and vodkas. Try one. Try two and take a cab. Please.

CAFÉ BRASIL

International watering hole and live music club

Who Goes There: Latins, Africans, rastas, punks, rockers, Liv Tyler, and New Yorkers who miss the Village

2100 Chartres Street
947-9386   Zone 5 Downtown/St. Bernard

Cover: Varies, from none to $10
Minimum: None
Mixed drinks: $3 and up
Wine: $3 and up
Beer: $2.50 and up

Dress: Turtlenecks, sandals, dreads,
  tie-dyes, leather, kenta cloth,
  Sex Pistols T-shirts
Food available: None
Disabled access: Yes

Hours: Varies. Generally, daily, 6 P.M.–3 A.M., but there is much left to the whimsy of club management.

What goes on: Situated just a block outside the French Quarter, in the trendy Faubourg Marigny section of town, Café Brasil led the revival of this funky and decidedly hip neighborhood, now full of bistros and music clubs. Brasil is an international town hall, with many complexions, dialects, and orientations at play. The music is mellow early, a place for young lions of jazz to show their chops, then more dance-oriented in the later evening, generally along the lines of funk, Latin, or reggae.

Setting & atmosphere: Wide open and neon, it looks more like New York —or perhaps Brazil—than New Orleans. The clientele spills onto the street and sidewalk nightly, creating a vibrant and colorful neighborhood atmosphere. Plenty of Harleys, tattoos, lounging dogs, and clove cigarettes to make for a funky, underground feel.

If you go: Relax and enjoy. No one here is in a hurry. Drink coffee or imported beer and soak up the international flair. So close to the French Market side of the Quarter, it's a safe walk. Also, check out the handful of other music clubs in the area—The Dragon's Den, The Dream Palace, Checkpoint Charlie's, and Snug Harbor—all listed elsewhere in this guide. These, and the smattering of bistros on Frenchmen Street, have made the Marigny an unofficial extension of the Vieux Carré, with a considerably more local and multicultural accent.

CAT'S MEOW

Bourbon Street karaoke

Who Goes There: 20–45, suburban singles, folks who wouldn't be caught dead in a place like this back home

701 Bourbon Street
    523-2788   Zone 1 French Quarter

Cover: None
Minimum: None
Mixed drinks: $4.50–5.75
Wine: $4
Beer: $3.50

Dress: Anything goes
Specials: Happy hour 4–8 P.M. weekdays, with three-for-one drinks
Food available: None
Disabled access: Yes

Hours: Monday–Friday, 4 P.M.–4 A.M.; Saturday and Sunday, 2 P.M.–sunrise

What goes on: For reasons no one seems able to explain, this is on many nights the most crowded and raucous club on a very crowded and raucous street. It is certainly the city's flagship karaoke club and has the best sound, the most selections, and a staff of professional host/singers to keep the night running with controlled chaos and provide at least an occasional listenable performance. If you want to participate, be prepared to wait—as you'll see, a lot of people think they belong on-stage in this world, and most of them wind up here.

Setting & atmosphere: We're talking dead-center, ground-zero Bourbon Street here. People are stacked shoulder to shoulder, so you never really see the decor, other than the bright stage lights and the pink-and-green neon backdrop. If the street level proves too crowded for your taste, walk up to the balcony; Mardi Gras plays out 365 days a year on the street below. Hooting, hollering, bartering for plastic beads, and flashing are part of the nightly ritual.

If you go: Be prepared to wear some beer on your clothes. It's hot and crowded, and jostling for space and movement is inevitable. Along with tourists, the place draws younger suburban folks looking for a good drink and a few laughs. This is no place for the uptight or the overdressed.

THE COLUMNS

Part sophisticated singles club, part debutante ball

Who Goes There: Debs, old frats, old money, Uptowners, porch potatoes

3811 St. Charles Avenue
   899-9308   Zone 3 Uptown below Napoleon

Cover: $5 for the jazz parlor, none
   for the barroom and porch
Minimum: One drink during happy
   hour
Mixed drinks: $3–6.50
Wine: $2–6.50
Beer: $2.50–3.50

Dress: Polo, Ralph, post-ballroom,
   $75 shorts
Specials: Weekdays, happy hour
   5–7 P.M., $2 house wines
Food available: Hot-plate munchies
   during happy hour only
Disabled access: Yes

Hours: Monday–Thursday, 3 P.M.–midnight; Friday, 2 P.M.–2 A.M.;
   Saturday, 11 A.M.–2 A.M.; Sunday 11 A.M.–midnight

What goes on: From the expansive Victorian front porch, watch the street-cars run up and down the oak-lined, placidly genteel avenue—New Orleans' most famous and beautiful. Inside the rich and lusty barroom, tell your best investment stories. On some Tuesday nights and most Wednesdays, the Tony Green trio plays gypsy jazz in the side parlor.

Setting & atmosphere: This old hotel was the setting for *Pretty Baby,* Brooke Shields' breakout film, but don't hold that against the place. It's old, musty, and a little lopsided, but full of the charm and mystery of old-line Uptown New Orleans, so eccentric, monied, and talkative. It is cozy, romantic, sultry, and on hot nights, sweaty—in the best sense. Take the time to soak in the architectural details of the parlors off the main bar, a trove of pilasters, cornices, chandeliers, gilded frames, and Victorian mirrors and furniture.

If you go: Make no plans after the Columns: You could get stuck here for hours, imprisoned by the absolute passivity and laissez-faire of the locals who congregate here to tell the stories of their gloried pasts. If this all sounds pretentious, it's not. In fact, consider this to be one of the city's communal living rooms, where family and friends gather in sloe gin comfort.

CRESCENT CITY BREWHOUSE

French Quarter brewpub and jazz joint

Who Goes There: 25–75, tourists, home brewers

527 Decatur Street
522-0571   Zone 1 French Quarter

Cover: None
Minimum: None
Mixed drinks: $4.50–6
Wine: $4–7
Beer: $2.75–5.25
Dress: Suits to sandals

Specials: Weekdays, happy hour from 5–7 P.M., two-for-one
Food available: Full menu of pastas, seafood, steaks, gumbo, and an oyster bar
Disabled access: Yes

Hours: Sunday–Thursday, 11 A.M.–10 P.M.; Friday and Saturday, 11 A.M.–midnight

What goes on: This is a spacious and lively brewpub pushed right up on one of the busiest sidewalks in the Quarter. Music is usually provided by trios of wannabe young lions, cutting jazz chops. Sometimes it's a Latin combo. Either way, the band is usually background to chatter and conversation, though Wynton Marsalis did show up one night when his little brother was playing, and that pretty much shut everybody up.

Setting & atmosphere: Before your very eyes are the huge copper vats in which Red Stallion and Black Forest ales are brewed, as well as Crescent City Pilsner and a rotating beer-of-the-month. Fine brews, all. Lots of exposed and shiny wood, very clean, very modern. Tons of seats. Plenty of light. Always a friendly and energetic crowd.

If you go: Check a stool at the bar; it gives you a look at the brewing process, the band, and the sidewalk, where an endless parade of buggies, buses, skateboarders, gutter punks, waiters, and Kansans loll by. If the band doesn't impress you and you long for grander vistas, go upstairs on the balcony overlooking Decatur, where you can see tourists hovering outside the Hard Rock Cafe and Planet Hollywood hoping for a glimpse of celebrities who don't go there. And, even better, the balcony affords a view across a parking lot to the Mississippi River traffic, with its tankers, steamers, barges, and paddle wheelers. (Don't worry—you're too far inland to get rammed by a runaway barge.)

DONNA'S

Live brass band jazz

Who Goes There: Euro jazzhounds, second-liners, old hats, thrill seekers

800 N. Rampart Street
596-6914   Zone I French Quarter

Cover: $5
Minimum: One drink per set
Mixed drinks: $3–5.50
Wine: $3
Beer: $2–3

Dress: Very casual, umbrellas optional
Food available: Southern barbecue,
   ribs, pulled pork sandwiches,
   étouffée, and burgers
Disabled access: Adequate

Hours: Wednesday–Monday, 8 P.M.–2 A.M.; Tuesday, closed.

What goes on: Donna Sims has built the headquarters for the city's hottest musical renaissance-brass band jazz, the swirling and frenetic interplay of horns and percussion. This is the place for nationally touring acts like Kermit Ruffins, the Rebirth Brass Band, the Treme Brass Band, and lesser-known yet more adventurous gangs like the Soul Rebels and Newbirth Brass bands who mix urban shades of hip-hop with the traditional brass.

Setting & atmosphere: The bar stools, beer lights, industrial carpet, and second-hand fast-food booths don't make much for aesthetics, but that's not why people come here. Be ready to dance and sashay or grab a space out of the way and against the wall. Locals will pull out hankies and umbrellas and act like their old Uncle Joe just died and this is his jazz funeral. Out of respect for old Uncle Joe, get off your duff and live a little. Do the funky chicken. Grab a stranger and dance. You may already have gotten this impression, but Donna's is loose on structure and form. What else can you say about a place where you have to part soloing trombonists to get to the rest rooms?

If you go: Beware: Rampart Street is the dark side of the Quarter, literally and figuratively. It is seedier and more dangerous than the spry and lively Bourbon and Decatur Streets. This doesn't mean don't go there. It means take a cab to the door. If you're already nearby in the Quarter and are with a group of three or more, feel safe to hoof it, but be on maximum alert in the street. After hours, scram. All this information becomes even more pertinent when you realize Donna's takes cash only—no credit cards.

F&M PATIO BAR

<u>Late-night party bar</u>

Who Goes There: Uptowners, debs, post-debs, lawyers, post-grads, cops, insomniacs, John Goodman

4841 Tchoupitoulas Street
895-6784   Zone 4 Uptown above Napoleon

Cover: None
Minimum: None
Mixed drinks: $3 and up
Wine: $3 and up
Beer: $2.50 and up
Dress: Parrothead chic, Saints jerseys, loose ties, food stains from dinner

Food available: New Orleans bar food: cheese fries, quesadillas, burgers, and poorboys
Disabled access: Adequate; however, the men's rest room is inaccessible.

Hours: Monday, 5 P.M.–4 A.M. or later; Tuesday–Friday, 1 P.M.–4 A.M. or later; Saturday and Sunday, 3 P.M.–sunrise

What goes on: This is the party after the party, the place where folks go after the Quarter, after the music, after the Carnival ball, and after their other favorite bars have closed. Nowhere do well-heeled Orleanians more consistently display the city's all-night colors more forcefully than here, shouting lyrics to Beatles tunes on the jukebox, dancing on pool tables, and cramming four-at-a-time into the bar's trademark photo booth. The scene plays out on many levels, from last-chance pick-up joint to a place to wind down the wee hours.

Setting & atmosphere: Fraternity house basement decor: bare cement floors, neon beer signs, pinball tables, etc. The jukebox is rich with pop classics, from Haley to Hootie. Sometimes the smell of beer is a little pungent.

If you go: It can be rowdy sometimes, and a little too collegiate for some tastes, but it's mostly a harmless place to catch up on the goings on of Uptown locals, many of whom have cell phones, children, and 401k plans and know better than to be here at this hour. It is a party until the last gasps of dawn have surrendered to the sun, so bring your sunglasses—it can be awfully harsh walking out into the sunny glare of the industrial Tchoupitoulas Street corridor.

FRITZEL'S

Bourbon Street Jazz

Who Goes There: Europeans, jazzheads, horn players, old-timers

733 Bourbon Street
561-0432   Zone 1 French Quarter

Cover: None
Minimum: One drink per set
Mixed drinks: $3 and up
Wine: $4
Beer: $2.50–4
Dress: This being Bourbon Street,
the expectations are low, but the quality of the music begs for something decent.
Food available: Popcorn, bags of chips
Disabled access: Yes

Hours: Performances at 9:30 on weekends, sometimes on weeknights (best to call ahead)

What goes on: This place is better known in European jazz circles than American, probably because few Americans believe there's any true Dixieland jazz left on Bourbon Street, and for the most part they're correct. Fritzel's is an exception. Jazz players from around the globe come here, many of them bearing their instruments, as the house bands here are unusually hospitable to guest sit-ins and jam sessions. On any given night there will be visiting bands and musicians from London, Munich, Sydney, or Tokyo. The weekend host and band leader, Jack Maheu, is one of the deserving but underrated masters of Dixieland clarinet.

Setting & atmosphere: It looks like two dozen other nineteenth-century Bourbon Street pubs: foreign currency and business cards haphazardly hung around the bar area, jazz posters, beer posters, whirling ceiling fans, and hardwood floors that haven't been polished since Eisenhower was president.

If you go: As explained above, if you're a player—a damn good one— bring your instrument along and realize that the mood of the evening dictates whether you'll be asked to join along. If you're not a musician, keep the conversation to a dull roar or go to any of the dozens of bars on the block where musical integrity is not the chief stock in trade. Also, be prepared for tight quarters. The place is small, and some nights the crowd is stacked all the way out the door.

FUNKY BUTT AT CONGO SQUARE

Jazz, blues, and jazzy blues in a Deco setting

Who Goes There: Lounge lizards, nighthawks, poets, bohos, jazzheads

714 N. Rampart Street
558-0872   Zone I French Quarter

Cover: None—$10
Minimum: One drink per set
Mixed drinks: $3—5
Wine: $3.50—7
Beer: $1—4
Dress: Anything goes; Gothic to black tie
Specials: Funky Buttjuice, a $6 concoction of secret ingredients, for the daring only
Food available: Gumbo, jambalaya, étouffée
Disabled access: Adequate; wheelchair access through kitchen; upper level is inaccessible.

Hours: Daily, 8 P.M.—3 A.M.

What goes on: When proprietor Richard Rochester isn't giving guided tours of French Quarter haunted properties (that's another story), he is here hosting one of the newest and hippest music clubs in town. Carved out of the classic and formerly exclusive Art Deco restaurant called Jonathan, the Funky Butt is now a lively mélange of conversation and dance, seven nights a week, with the likes of Kermit Ruffins and other world-class horn players holding court. The Funky Butt, by the way, was the name of a dance that accompanied the music of the pioneering Buddy Bolden, the city's first King of Jazz and a cornet player with chops so loud that legend tells of listeners enjoying his solos from half a mile away. We cannot document this.

Setting & atmosphere: Downstairs, the lounge retains many of the Deco treasures and details from the Jonathan era—black-lacquered woods, cut-glass fixtures, and Erte prints. The jukebox is one of the great archives of New Orleans music history. Upstairs in the live music club, it has a dark speakeasy feel, with a few hidden corners for discreet couples. One reviewer called the decor "a cross between a '30s jazz crib and a brothel," and we think the description fitting.

If you go: Like its neighbor Donna's (see profile), the Funky Butt hovers on the sketchy side of the Quarter. We suggest alertness when coming and going and a cab to do both.

HOUSE OF BLUES

National, regional, and local-circuit music club

Who Goes There: Dan Aykroyd and friends, out-of-towners,
locals because it's the only place left to see the Nevilles

225 Decatur Street
529-BLUE   Zone 1 French Quarter

Cover: Varies from $5 for good local acts to $30+ for the rare appearances of heavy hitters like Jackson Brown or Bob Dylan. The back bar—where you can watch the show on live TV—is free.
Minimum: None
Mixed drinks: $4 and up
Wine: $3.50 and up
Beer: $2.75 and up

Dress: To fit the show. For Trisha Yearwood, boots and buckles would suit; for the Nevilles, perhaps something in unity colors. For the Gospel Brunch, dare to be different: Dress nice.
Food available: Full menu of Louisiana, Cajun, and American cafe dishes.
Disabled access: Yes

Hours: Tuesday–Thursday, 11 A.M.–midnight, or whenever the show ends; Saturday and Sunday, 11 A.M.–4 A.M.; Monday, 11 A.M.–sunrise

What goes on: When the House of Blues opened in 1994, its New Age–friendly motto "Help Ever, Hurt Never" was tarnished by the club's cut-throat pursuit of every major player in the local rock, blues, and jazz circles, outbidding and nearly snuffing out several local and long-established music clubs. In the ensuing years, an easy equilibrium has settled over the local industry; it's a given now that the House gets the biggest names in the business, from Eric Clapton and Jackson Brown to Tito Puente and Herbie Hancock. And the biggest crowds.

Setting & atmosphere: This is a New York club in a small town; the goon-sized bouncers with headsets and ear phones, quite frankly, scare the hell out of some locals who prefer to hang out at a place where they can park within three or four blocks of the front door. On the positive side, HOB has amassed an awesome collection of Southern folk art, which hangs everywhere, including the rest rooms. Take the time to look at these colorful treasures from Louisiana, Mississippi, and Alabama.

If you go: First and foremost, never mess with the bouncers. There are stories. Second, be ready to pay the price—both monetarily and in comfort. There is not enough seating available, and what there is seems always reserved for visiting celebrities who hinted to management that they were coming but never showed up. This leaves the great seats empty on the most crowded nights and adds to the generally antagonistic relationship between the club and longtime local music fans who have lived by a first-come, first-served basis for decades. But these ill-wishing locals realize that the House of Blues will succeed, even thrive, on one-time customers or those who will put up with the club's icy treatment because it's the only place to catch the great national tours. And the Neville Brothers.

THE HOWLIN' WOLF

Live regional, alternative, progressive country, and folk music

Who Goes There: Rockers, cowpunks, musicians

828 S. Peters Street
523-2551   Zone 2 Central Business District

Cover: Varies with act, roughly
  $5–15
Minimum: None
Mixed drinks: $3.50 and up
Wine: $3.50 and up

Beer: $3 and up
Dress: Rock-club casual
Food available: None
Disabled access: Yes

Hours: 6 P.M. until the show ends (anywhere from midnight to 3 A.M.)

What goes on: The Wolf is the musicians' music club; half the house on any night may be the city's rock fraternity checking out the latest acts on the local alternative, rockabilly, or singer/songwriter circuit. The Wolf also draws an eclectic array of lesser-known but established national acts — anybody from country-crooning Iris Dement to jazz poet John Sinclair to surf-guitar guru Dick Dale. This is where up-and-coming bands play before the House of Blues gets wind of who they are and books them on the next tour.

Setting & atmosphere: A roomy two-level music hall decorated with old movie set signs, the Wolf is dimly lit but very clean. The clientele is respectful of the music, so don't be surprised to find the pool table light extinguished before the performance, and many acoustic acts will request your attention. It's a mix of listening and dancing crowds; feel free to do either. If you need to be off your feet for the evening, get there early, as available bar stools and raised tables are rare.

If you go: The Wolf operates on a time-honored rock tradition — the music begins when the music begins, and ends when it ends. The newspaper will no doubt list a performance at 10:00, and this raises a strategic riddle: Do you go on time and end up cooling your heels for an hour while band members drift in, or do you arrive late and risk missing the rare prompt performer? Our advice: Go on time, get a table, and if the show is late, chill out to the great sound system and a cold Abita draft.

LAFITTE'S BLACKSMITH SHOP

Romantic hideaway and piano lounge

Who Goes There: Couples, romantics, Quarter rats, pirates

941 Bourbon Street
   523-0066   Zone 1 French Quarter

Cover: None	Dress: Casual
Minimum: One drink	Food available: None
Mixed drinks: $3.50–4	Disabled access: Yes, but access to the
Wine: $3.50	rest rooms is hindered by a step;
Beer: $2.50–3.50	staff members are glad to help.

Hours: Daily, noon–3 A.M. or later

What goes on: One of the oldest buildings in the city, Lafitte's is said to be America's oldest bar, but you hear stories like that in New Orleans all the time. What we do know is that the building actually belonged to the famed privateer Jean Lafitte—or one of his colleagues—and was used for the storage of loot pilfered from ships in Barataria Bay and the Gulf of Mexico. Somewhere along the line, many years after Lafitte disappeared into the Confederate mist, the building became one of the city's most beloved bars.
Setting & atmosphere: Other than a single bulb behind the bar, the only light in here is provided by candles and, during cool seasons, the fireplace. It is dark, damp, and lusty inside, made of old brick, stone, crumbling mortar, and exposed beams. In the back cove, local piano bar aficionados gather around the keys and sing along to time-honored classics every night except Wednesday. There's an overgrown and musty courtyard on the side for those who truly want to disappear.
If you go: This is an ideal spot to get to know better that special someone you met at the planning seminar earlier in the day at the Marriott conference center. Lafitte's is a port of calm on Bourbon Street's sea of bedlam, so if the racket is getting to you but you still want to be a part of the night scene, pull in here for a couple of hours. The closed quarters and slow and easy pace of the staff and clientele beg for intimacy.

THE LION'S DEN

The place Irma Thomas calls home

Who Goes There: European youngsters and American oldies, the neighborhood, music historians

2655 Gravier Street
  822-4693   Zone 6 Mid-City/Gentilly

Cover: $15
Minimum: None
Mixed drinks: $3 and up
Wine: $3 and up
Beer: $3 and up

Dress: Old striped suits with open collars, fedoras, rhinestones, big earrings
Food available: Varies (see below)
Disabled access: Yes

Hours: Varies, call ahead.

What goes on: Irma Thomas, the Soul Queen of New Orleans, hit the Billboard charts in 1964 with "Wish Someone Would Care," followed by "It's Raining" and "Breakaway," putting her alongside Fats Domino, Ernie K-Doe, and Frogman Henry as the ambassadors of New Orleans R&B over the next two decades. She and her band, the Professionals, play here about one weekend a month and always during peak tourist events like Mardi Gras, Jazz Fest, and the Sugar and Super Bowls. It is a quintessential New Orleans music showcase, full of horns, heartache, love lost and found, and plenty of soul.

Setting & atmosphere: During a Jazz Fest gig in the late '80s, Thomas promised the festival crowd that if they came to see her husband's new nightclub that night, she would feed them. They filled the house; she filled their bellies. Now it's tradition. If her mood and schedule allow it, Thomas will brew up some gumbo, fish stew, or red beans for the audience on performance nights. The decor is urban lounge, very '70s.

If you go: Be advised: Thomas and the Professionals are the only live act at the Lion's Den. Since they tour internationally, their local gigs are irregularly scheduled. Call ahead or look in Friday's *Times-Picayune* entertainment section. And one caution: The Lion's Den is on an out-of-the-way side street in the Bail Bond district. We don't know what the Bail Bond district looks like in your hometown, but ours ain't pretty. Take a cab.

LUCY'S RETIRED SURFER'S BAR

Singles sidewalk hangout

Who Goes There: 25–45, suits, debs, hot shots, climbers, condo-dwellers

701 Tchoupitoulas Street
523-8995   Zone 2 Central Business District

Cover: None
Minimum: None
Mixed drinks: $3.50 and up
Wine: $3
Beer: $2.25 and up
Dress: Loose ties, Hawaii Five-O, Banana Republic

Specials: Wednesday night margaritas for $2.50
Food available: A full California/MexAmerican menu
Disabled access: Yes

Hours: Monday, happy hour, 4–8 P.M.; Tuesday–Saturday, 11 A.M.–2 A.M.; Sunday, closed.

What goes on: Big on happy hour and weekend nights, Lucy's fills to capacity with young banker- and lawyer-types from the neighboring Central Business District and with the rising number of yuppie Warehouse District inhabitants escaping from the confines of their nearby cubicle condos. Though everyone seems to know everyone else here, a well-timed compliment on a tie or nail color may open doors for strangers in the crowd.

Setting & atmosphere: Sidewalk chic; even in the heat of summer, the crowd at Lucy's flows into the street, making for a super-casual block party environment. The interior is exposed brick with hints of South Pacific blues and greens. Generally patrons stand three or four deep at the bar, but there are booths and a back room for stretching out.

If you go: The scene at Lucy's is somewhat interchangeable with a smaller, funkier, less hustling, and more intimate tavern across the street, Vic's Kangaroo Cafe, a Down Under joint serving up imported drafts, Aussie meat pies, and live blues bands on weekends. This is a late-night watering hole for the black-and-white–clad waiters and waitresses of the many chic bistros of the Warehouse District. Vic's also has the last and only Asteroids video game that we have found in the city, if that matters.

THE MAPLE LEAF

Live regional music

Who Goes There: Dancers, poets, chessmen, Uptowners, celebrities escaping the fuss

8316 Oak Street
866-9359   Zone 4 Uptown above Napoleon

Cover: Varies with act, generally $3–7

Minimum: None

Mixed drinks: $3.50 and up

Wine: $3 and up

Beer: $2.50 and up

Dress: Bowling shirts, sundresses, jeans, bandanas

Food available: None

Disabled access: Yes

Hours: Sunday–Thursday, 3 P.M.–2 A.M.; Friday and Saturday, 3 P.M.–3 A.M.

What goes on: Dancing and drinking nightly, with a broad range of local and regional musical offerings: brass on Tuesday nights, poetry Sunday afternoons, Cajun and zydeco Thursdays, and blends of the blues, Latin, and funk the rest of the week. Shows get rolling around 10:30.

Setting & atmosphere: One of the great old survivors of the local music scene, the Maple Leaf long ago ditched its courtyard laundromat—a local favorite—but retains all the other aspects of its funky Uptown charm: the pressed tin ceiling; the narrow, inviting dance floor; the overgrown and candle-lit patio; the reliable musical palette; and the loveable, unemployable intellectuals who plop on bar stools every afternoon and bet on Jeopardy games on TV—and always score better than anyone on the show.

If you go: Be ready for one of New Orleans' favorite contact sports, two-stepping. The Leaf's dance floor is famously narrow, and when the likes of the Iguanas, Wolfman Washington, or Jumpin' Johnny's Blues Party open the throttle, it gets a little bouncy. If you get bumped, get out of the way or bump back. No whining. Also, the Leaf is two short blocks off the streetcar line Uptown. Take the St. Charles line there, then take a cab home.

MAXWELL'S JAZZ CABARET

Traditional jazz and soft swing dinner theater

Who Goes There: 40+ couples and groups, families, assistant district attornies

615 Toulouse Street
523-4207   Zone 1 French Quarter

Cover: $15 for the show and one drink; $33 for dinner, show and drink
Minimum: One drink
Mixed drinks: $4 and up
Wine: $4 and up
Beer: $3 and up

Dress: Dinner-theater casual
Food available: The buffet includes the likes of étouffées and gumbos, spicy corn and potatoes, bread pudding
Disabled access: Building is accessible; rest rooms are not.

Hours: Buffet, 6:30–9:30; performance at 8 and 11 weeknights, 8 and midnight weekends

What goes on: This is sort of a timid approach to old-time New Orleans fare, a little less down and dirty—let's call it Dixieland Lite. The novelty and main draw here is Harry Connick, Sr., the New Orleans district attorney and the father of a very famous and wealthy musician. He croons golden swing tunes and such. It's a place that doesn't take itself too seriously and deserves its nickname: The Goodtime Music Hall.

Setting & atmosphere: The tiered seating arrangements and sparkling lamé stage curtains lend the proper kitschy ersatz Vegas touch. The room is cozy and intimate, seating no more than 100 or so. The front lobby opens wide onto the street, giving a great sidewalk view of the goings-on. If you like the show, the souvenir shop has all the artists on tape and disc.

If you go: Make reservations ahead of time, particularly during peak tourism and event seasons. Maxwell's does brisk tour group business and because of its size can fill up easily, especially the early shows.

THE MERMAID LOUNGE

Live performance art, lounge music, and the general rants and raves of music-minded if sometimes unsavory misfits

Who Goes There: 25–45, Gothics, rockers, the Paisley Parade, human tattoos, poseurs, the Lounge Nation

---

1100 Constance Avenue
524-4747   Zone 2 Central Business District

Cover: $2–10
Minimum: None
Mixed drinks: $3–4
Wine: $3
Beer: $3.50–4
Dress: Glitter, gloss, Elton John as Pinball Wizard, black tie, whatever. Go ahead, try to be noticed.

Specials: $1.50 Schaefer beers
Food available: The consortium of 30- and 40-something partners likes to host impromptu cookouts, buffets, and barbecues, but when it happens is up to whimsy.
Disabled access: Poor

Hours: 9 P.M. until

What goes on: When the Mermaid opened in 1994, it gave a nightclub presence to a varied and overlooked array of Louisiana artists: Glyn Styler, the local angst-ridden crooner and champion of lounge lizards; the Hackberry Ramblers, an octogenarian Cajun swing band; C.C. Adcock, a guitar-blazing swamp-pop incarnation; and Quintron, a local curiosity who locks himself in a room offstage and raises racket out of old electric organs. The Mermaid has become the epicenter of the alternative nightclub scene, wonderfully bizarre and calculatingly offbeat.

Setting & atmosphere: The bar hosts rotating art shows and could be hanging anything from neon art to ersatz porn on any given weekend. There is no describing how casual this place can be, so full of attitude and European cigarettes. The crowd generally spills out onto the sidewalk for impromptu street scenes among the Harleys and '72 Impalas parked outside. Its reclusive location and the costumed clientele often give it the feeling of being on the set of a Mad Max movie.

If you go: Take a cab, not because it's so dangerous, but because the Mermaid is the hardest club in the city to find, tucked away under an interstate ramp at the end of a one-way street. Just hope the cab driver can find it. In summer, very light clothes are advised; the Mermaid is not strong on modern cooling amenities.

MID CITY LANES

Rock 'n Bowl

Who Goes There: Bowlers, rockers, two-steppers, Zydecajuns, Tom Cruise, The Rolling Stones (just to watch, not play)

4133 S. Carrollton Avenue
482-3133   Zone 4 Uptown above Napoleon

Cover: $5–10
Minimum: None
Mixed drinks: $3.50–4.50
Wine: $3
Beer: $2.50–3.50
Dress: Zydeco Festival T-shirts, shorts, bandanas, bowling shoes
Food available: New Orleans bar food: cheese fries, shrimp po'boys, buffalo wings
Disabled access: No

Hours: For bowling, seven days a week. For music, Wednesday–Saturday, noon–2 A.M.

What goes on: Bizarre story. Johnny Blancher, a down-on-his-luck crawfish broker, makes a pilgrimage in the late '80s to Medjogore, the Jugoslavian village where the Virgin Mary is said to appear to the Catholic faithful. He asks for a sign, something to dig his family out of debt. Back home, he is approached about the sale of an old bowling alley. The sellers—the Knights of Columbus! He figures that's the sign he was waiting for. He buys this charming but crooked alley above a strip shopping center, starts booking bands, and in short time, is running the happiest and most interesting bar in the city. It's a hotbed of zydeco music Wednesday and Thursday nights. On weekends, the playlist is pumped-up R&B, soul, and more zydeco. It's loud, lively, fun, frenetic, and, quite frankly, the best bar in America. Do not miss it. If you go nowhere else in New Orleans, go here.
Setting & atmosphere: It's a place lost in time, a bowling alley where you still keep score in pencil. There's plenty of dancing room, and plenty of places to get off your feet. Tom Cruise's rental shoes hang alongside portraits of Elvis and the Virgin Mary. Let's just say there's nothing like this where you come from. Saturday nights and peak seasons, Blancher opens up a dance hall underneath the alley, called Bowl Me Under (get it?) and books more zydeco. On big nights, he'll book four bands from around southwest Louisiana.
If you go: Look for Blancher—he's the guy in the pink bowling shirt doing the funky chicken. He'll get you a lane or teach you how to two-step, whatever you want. Don't be intimidated by the local dancers; they're real good and they know it. Fake it, stumble over your feet, give it a whirl—no

one will laugh at you. We recommend going early and locking in a lane for the night. The ten bucks an hour is worth it. Once you have zydeco-stomped to Nathan and the Zydeco Cha-Chas in bowling shoes, you will never be the same.

MOLLY'S ON THE MARKET

French Quarter watering hole, media hangout

Who Goes There: The press, their sources, pols, tattoos, locals, former profesional athletes, video poker junkies, gutter punks

1107 Decatur Street
525-5169   Zone 1 French Quarter

Cover: None	Dress: Suits to grunge
Minimum: None	Specials: Frozen Irish coffee, $3
Mixed drinks: $2.75–5	Food available: A full Thai menu
Wine: $2.50	Disabled access: Yes
Beer: $1.25–3.75	

Hours: Daily, 10 A.M.–6 A.M.

What goes on: Local and visiting media have established Molly's as a news bureau of sorts, where rookies and old pros trade stories and shooters. On Thursday nights there's usually a celebrity bartender from the worlds of journalism, sports, or politics, and a complimentary cocktail for members of the working press. The rest of the week offers a general mix of French Quarter regulars: tourists, a few local drunks, a skinhead or two, and often a pretty good political argument at one of the raised tables.

Setting & atmosphere: Nothing fancy. A pub atmosphere with a long bar down one side and a few tables with bar stools up the other. The walls are crammed with press clippings about the place, from *Esquire* to *Le Monde* to the local *Times-Picayune*. The jukebox plays mostly rock, oldies, and New Orleans music. The open-air window on the sidewalk makes for quality people-watching on this busy nightlife stretch of the Quarter.

If you go: Don't fear the skinhead bartenders; they won't bite. Remember, they're somebody's kids also.

MULATE'S

Who Goes There: Bus tours, Kansans, local two-steppers, folks too short on time to drive to Lafayette

201 Julia Street
522–1492   Zone 2 Central Business District

Cover: None
Minimum: One drink
Mixed drinks: $2.75–5
Wine: $3.75 and up
Beer: $2.75 and up
Dress: Last year's Festivals Acadiens
 T-shirt, bermudas, cotton

Food available: Full-service Cajun
 restaurant—blackened catfish,
 gumbo, couscous, crawfish
 salad
Disabled access: Yes

Hours: Daily, 11 A.M.–11 P.M. Music: Monday–Thursday, 7–10:30 P.M.; Friday–Sunday, 7–11 P.M.

What goes on: The first Mulate's opened nearly 20 years ago in the little town of Breaux Bridge, La., and, along with New Orleans chef Paul Prudhomme and the famed bayou band Beausoleil, it helped put Cajun culture in the forefront of the American pop culture landscape. The recipe was simple: good, hot Cajun food and nightly dancing. The Breaux Bridge location's remarkable success in sales and patronage has been duplicated in Baton Rouge and at this New Orleans location. Mulate's takes great care to book the best available Cajun musicians, importing them nightly from southwest Louisiana.

Setting & atmosphere: There's no way anyone can reproduce the old-time Cajun dance halls of Acadiana here in the city, but Mulate's nearly pulls it off. It's huge, and they've tried their best to give it a country feel, with attention to faux-rustic detail and artworks by some of Cajun country's notable painters like George Rodrigue—he of Blue Dog fame—and Francis Pavy, "the zydeco painter."

If you go: Lose your fear and dance. There are enough locals on-hand to show you how to Cajun two-step. It is more fun than it looks, and it looks very fun. Caveat: Cajun dancing is a contact sport—be tolerant of the occasional butt-bounce from the couple next to you. And never, ever be afraid to ask a stranger to dance in a place like this. That's why strangers come here.

NAPOLEON HOUSE

French Quarter institution

Who Goes There: Writers, intellectuals, tourists, yuppies, bar flies, and storytellers

500 Chartres Street
524-9752   Zone I French Quarter

Cover: None	Dress: Whatever you're wearing
Minimum: None	Food available: Salads, jambalaya, po'-boys, and the best muffuletta in town
Mixed drinks: $3.50 and up	
Wine: $3 and up	
Beer: $2.50 and up	Disabled access: Yes

Hours: Monday–Thursday, 11 A.M.–midnight; Friday and Saturday, 11 A.M.–1 A.M.; Sunday, 11 A.M.–7 P.M.

What goes on: Nothing, and that's the joy. It's a place to sit and think, or sometimes just sit. The building was secured in the nineteenth century to be the great Emperor Bonaparte's residence in exile after his defeat at Waterloo, but he died before ever making it to the States. Now it's just a French Quarter corner bar, albeit a classic, where locals and visitors alike gather to cool their heels.

Setting & atmosphere: Sublime. The building is hundreds of years old, dark, with fading paint and chipped plaster. And plenty of artworks of Napoleon. The stereo—a turntable!—spins classical and opera recordings from morning until closing. It is sultry, romantic, and intimate. The staff is indifferent at best, surly at worst.

If you go: There is no better way to beat the city heat than to duck into any of the dark tavern or patio corners and sip a Pimm's Cup, a New Orleans standard made of ginger-spiced gin, lemonade, and 7-Up with a slice of cucumber. Totally refreshing. If you're on a fast track, stay away—conversation is the currency of the club and few here are in a hurry, including the waiters.

O'FLAHERTY'S

Live Irish music club and entertainment complex

Who Goes There: 30–75, beer drinkers, dart players, tourists, neo-folkies, trivia buffs, and sing-along lovers

514 Toulouse Street
529–1317   Zone 1 French Quarter

Cover: Thursday–Sunday only, $3–5
Minimum: One drink per set in music club
Mixed drinks: $1.75 and up
Wine: $2–4

Beer: $1.50–$3.75
Dress: Casual
Food available: Shepherd's pie, Irish stew, and such
Disabled access: Yes

Hours: Daily, noon–3 A.M.; music starts at 7:30.

What goes on: Plenty. One room holds the lively music club, which features local, national, and international Celtic performers seven nights a week. Another room is a traditional Irish pub with darts on the wall, slow-rolling Guinness on tap, and traditional dancing on Saturday nights. There's also a sultry courtyard in the back for lounging about, and a gift shop selling not only souvenirs but Irish groceries as well.

Setting & atmosphere: A grand old eighteenth-century building and courtyard, O'Flaherty's presents traditional exposed-brick French Quarter comfort with a hint of Old World decadence. An added attraction is the four ghosts said to inhabit the premises, from spurned lovers to old generals. They live upstairs. For more on that, ask proprietor Danny O'Flaherty to fill you in.

If you go: The folks are friendly here, but won't hesitate to remind you to be respectful of the music. If you want to sing the chorus, fine. If you want to chatter, head for the pub. For the trivia-minded, the pub hosts congenial three-person trivia team contests on Sundays nights from March to October, with loads of gifts and giveaways. While prizes are Irish—mugs and glasses, beer, travel prints, and such—the questions cover all bases, from world history to quantum physics to college sports.

PALM COURT JAZZ CAFE

Jazz bar and restaurant

Who Goes There: 35–75, jazz pilgrims, hipsters, Europeans

1204 Decatur Street
525-0200   Zone 1 French Quarter

Cover: $5 for table seat; free to lean on the bar
Minimum: None
Mixed drinks: $4–6
Wine: $3.50–6

Beer: $2.50–3.50
Dress: Casual to casually elegant
Food: Traditional Creole and international cuisine
Disabled access: Yes

Hours: Wednesday–Sunday, 7–11 P.M.

What goes on: George Buck gave his wife Nina a birthday present back in the '80s, something she always wanted—a jazz club. Now Nina Buck runs the classiest traditional jazz joint in town, while upstairs, George presides over the industry's largest independent jazz record distributorship. Together, they have developed *the* headquarters for traditional New Orleans Jazz. This is where Danny Barker, Pud Brown, and Louis Nelson finished their careers, and where their legacy plays on five nights a week from the likes of rising jazz masters Lucien Barbarin, Gregg Stafford, and Lionel Ferbos.

Setting & atmosphere: With its expansive tiled layout, mahogany bar, Steinway piano, and overhead lamps, the Palm Court reaches into Roaring '20s decor. It's a wide-open place with plenty of seats and a comfortable bar to lean on. Nina Buck sets the tone for the night; if she breaks out her umbrella and handkerchief for a second-line, fall in behind. Between sets, there's plenty of history to soak up from the paintings, photographs, and record albums on display throughout the hall. The records—that's right, vinyl!—are for sale.

If you go: Make a night of it. The food is good, and the shows are top-class performances by the old generals and young lions of New Orleans tradjazz. Every night is a celebration of the city's vibrant musical history.

PRESERVATION HALL

Old-time jazz hall

Who Goes There: Tourists—all of them

---

726 St. Peter Street
  522-2841   Zone 1 French Quarter

Cover: $4	Beer: None
Minimum: None	Dress: Casual
Mixed drinks: Drinks are prohibited	Food available: None
Wine: None	Disabled access: Yes

Hours: Daily, 8 P.M.–midnight

What goes on: Although the building—and the musicians—appears to have been standing here since the dawn of jazz, the place actually opened in 1961. Since that time, it has become synonymous with the great tradition of New Orleans Dixieland jazz, and deservedly so, for the musicians are top-notch. The club rotates bands and musicians nightly, and also puts together national and world tours of musicians under the name Preservation Hall Jazz Band. Everyone who was anyone during the past 30 years has been associated with this place, including Danny and Blue Lu Barker, Kid Thomas, Tuba Fats, and the Olympia Brass Band.

Setting & atmosphere: Comfort is not a premium here. It's a small room with very limited seating—just a few benches. Overflow sits on the floor and stands around the walls on the side and in back. The band's enthroned on chairs in the front, looking every bit like a 50-year-old postcard.

If you go: Be prepared to invest time in this one; lines can be long. The hall does not serve refreshments of any kind, and there is no smoking. We suggest a cocktail sipped from one of the city's famed "go-cups" while you wait in line. This is one of those "must-see" deals in guidebooks and travel stories, and apparently readers take the recommendation seriously. The show is only about 40 minutes long before they quickly usher you out and the next crowd in, but we've never heard people complain about the brevity, perhaps because they were getting thirsty toward the end.

THE SHOWCASE

Silky smooth blues, jazz, and soul club

Who Goes There: 30–60, music lovers, buppies, working folks from the neighborhood

1915 N. Broad Avenue
945-5612   Zone 6 Mid-City/Gentilly

Cover: $5–15
Minimum: None
Mixed drinks: $3.50–6
Wine: $3
Beer: $2.25
Dress: Collars, suits, fedoras, rhinestones

Specials: Weekday happy hour, drinks half-price
Food available: Kitchen under construction
Disabled access: Adequate

Hours: Opens 4 P.M. daily. Music starts at 7:30 Tuesday, Wednesday, Thursday, and Sunday at 9, Saturday at 10. Friday nights is Deejay Night, with golden oldies and classics beginning in early evening. No music Mondays.

What goes on: This is a formerly unknown neighborhood juke joint that has transformed into a vital player on the live jazz and blues scene over the past few years, offering a steady and reliable fare of contemporary jazz and blues to mature folks who've grown weary of the monotonous bass solos, meandering trumpet licks, and loud volume of some modern ensembles. Local favorites Marva Wright, Walter Payton—trumpet phenom Nicholas' father—and chanteuse Sharon Martin and pianist Davell Crawford enchant listeners here regularly, laying down cool, mellow riffs for a mostly local and loyal crowd.

Setting & atmosphere: Neighborhood soul with a piano-shaped bar, red vinyl seat covers, and red runner lights flashing in syncopation to the music. Little tables are huddled about, and the setting and feeling cast back to a time when there were dozens of clubs like this around town, only to be run off by crime and evolving tastes in urban music. This is a survivor.

If you go: You'll know you're there when you come upon dozens of cars parked in corners, on sidewalks, and on the neutral ground (median). It's away from downtown and not near any other landmarks you're likely to visit during your stay, so we recommend taking a cab.

SNUG HARBOR

Jazz club

Who Goes There: Hipsters, buppies, mellow fellows, and anyone named Marsalis

626 Frenchmen Street
949-0696   Zone 5 Downtown/St. Bernard

Cover: Varies, usually $8–20
Minimum: One drink per set
Mixed drinks: $4 and up
Wine: $4
Beer: $3 and up
Dress: Classy but comfortable

Food available: A separate dining room full of meat and seafood entrees, salads and soups, and such. Killer burgers.
Disabled access: Yes

Hours: Daily, 5 P.M.–about 2 A.M. Shows at 9 and 11 P.M.

What goes on: Marsalis, Connick, Batiste, Neville, Payton—this is where the great names of modern New Orleans jazz gather and grow. Snug is the link between the city's past and present musical forms, the serious contemporary jazz club in town, low-down and cool. It's a sit-down joint, not much for hootin' and hollerin', but more prone to an evening of Scotch-sipping, finger-snapping solos, and such. It's where the next toast of New York is playing tonight in New Orleans. You can say you saw them when.

Setting & atmosphere: Very cozy, befitting the name. The outer bar is dark, cool, and romantic—an ideal spot for a starter drink. Inside the small, two-tiered music hall, it is warmly lit and mirrored. Tables are small and tightly packed, and upstairs has some view-obstructed seats and tables, hence the big mirror on the stage-left wall.

If you go: Parking's tight. It's only two blocks out of the safe side of the Quarter, so walking is fine. There's usually two shows a night, so call and check it out. Arrive early if a big name is on the bill; prime seating can make all the difference. Ellis Marsalis—that's Wynton and Branford's daddy—is one of the city's sublime performers, a Snug regular, and one heck of a lot more fun to watch than his uptight kids.

TIPITINA'S

New Orleans' quintessential music club

Who Goes There: Frat boys and debs, mods and rockers, aging hippies, and people who actually saw Professor Longhair play

501 Napoleon Avenue
895-8477   Zone 4 Uptown on Napoleon

Cover: Varies from occasional free weeknight shows to about $15 for big names
Minimum: None
Mixed drinks: $3 and up
Wine: $3 and up

Beer: $2 and up
Dress: Khakis, old Jazz Fest T-shirts, tie-dyes, and suits
Food available: Burgers, red beans and rice, cheese fries
Disabled access: Yes

Hours: Sunday, 5–10 P.M.; Monday–Thursday, 5 P.M.–2 A.M.; Friday and Saturday, 5 P.M.–3 A.M.

What goes on: Tip's is the heart and soul and somewhat faded glory of the city's musical renaissance of the '70s, when Fess, James Booker, Dr. John, and the Neville Brothers got everybody hip to the city's non–Dixieland jazz musical heritage. Although the House of Blues has definitely altered Tip's ability to book big-name talent, it's still the place to go for New Orleans R&B, rock, and the occasional big name from the college circuit. The Sunday afternoon fais-do-do (Cajun dance) with Bruce Daigrepont is a New Orleans institution—good, sweaty family fun.

Tipitina's has a new venture called Tipitina's Warehouse (310 Howard Avenue, 568-1702), which is destined to pull in big-name bands to compete with the House of Blues. It is still a young venue but could prove to be a hip scene. You'd better call for current information before you go.

Setting & atmosphere: Wide-open spaces and the checkerboard floor give it an old dance-hall feel. There are stools down the two side bars, and that's about it for seating. Pressure from the House of Blues finally forced Tip's to put up a new coat of paint, fix up the rest rooms, get new refrigeration, and increase the cool air circulation, so the place is darn near comfortable these days. For big shows, the balcony upstairs offers a respite from the crowd.

If you go: Prepare for the occasional lapses in service. Move slowly and take in the amazing history of the club's performance posters plastered all over the walls. Check out the Professor Longhair memorial across the street. And, if you go to the Sunday fais-do-do, you may want to bring a second, dry shirt to wear home. It can be a barn burner.

WHISKEY BAR

Airport lounge masquerading as a speakeasy

Who Goes There: 25–40, Armani fashion victims, Mira Sorvino look-alikes, singles who wish they'd never moved back from L.A.

730 Common Street
525-6660   Zone 2 Central Business District

Cover: None	Specials: Wednesday features a
Minimum: None	Louisiana Philharmonic quartet
Mixed drinks: $5–8	from 5 to 7 P.M.
Wine: $6	Food available: None
Beer: $3–4	Disabled access: Yes, through the back
Dress: Oscar night	door of the First NBC building.

Hours: Monday–Thursday, 5 P.M.–3 A.M.; Friday, 5 P.M.–6 A.M.; Saturday, 9 P.M.–6 A.M.

What goes on: Singles and couples clutch expensive drinks and talk about bulls and bears. It's the newest chic retro/martini/cigar lounge in town, in an out-of-the way downtown fortress, mobbed, if nothing else, for its newness and power-mingling.

Setting & atmosphere: It sort of feels like a waiting room in here, but what everyone's waiting for we're not sure. Mirrors on one wall help alleviate the closed-in feeling of the room, and the semi-erotic photos along the wall suggest a decadence not quite befitting the posturing clientele. The doorman posing as a hitman with his sunglasses at night and audio headset seems completely out of place in a lounge this mellow. The vases of fresh-cut roses are a nice touch.

If you go: How do we suggest this? Go to the bathroom. They are the most exotic in town, black-tiled and dimly lit with a solitary rose for accent. And get this: Another headset-toting doorman keeps order here, directing patrons from a line into a hallway of unisex water closets. It is one of the most surrealistic toilet experiences you can have outside of New York's train stations.

PART NINE

Exercise and Recreation

A few years ago, it would have seemed silly to put a chapter on exercise in a vacation guide—particularly a guide to a city as famed for self-indulgence as New Orleans. But most of us at the *Unofficial Guides* are into some form of aerobic exercise, if only as a matter of self-preservation: It reduces stress, helps offset those expense account and diet-holiday meals (no, it's not true that food eaten on vacation has no calories), and even ameliorates some of the effects of jet lag. Even more remarkably, we have discovered that jogging, biking, and just plain walking are among the nicest ways to experience a city on its own turf, so to speak, and we're happy to see that more and more travelers feel as we do.

However, remember what we said in the beginning about the climate of New Orleans—hot and humid, cool and damp. In the summer months, it's really a good idea to schedule exercise early in the day or in the first cool of the evening; those late-afternoon showers can make a nice difference. (On the other hand, insects prefer the cooler hours, too, so pack some bug spray—better yet, double up and get sunscreen with repellent built in.) It's rarely too cold for a run even in January, but again it may be damp, so pack a weather-resistant layer. And a first-aid kit: We go nowhere without sports-style adhesive strips, ibuprofen or some other analgesic, petroleum jelly, and a small tube of antiseptic. Blisters can ruin the most perfect vacation. We know.

■ Walking ■

Considering how strongly we've urged you to walk at least the French Quarter, you may have already guessed that we find not agony but ecstasy in the feet. And in addition to the neighborhood walks, New Orleans has several picturesque options, starting with the roughly two miles of **Riverwalk** from Esplanade Avenue to the Spanish Plaza, which takes you past Jackson Square, the various cruise ships, and a wonderful assortment of vendors and relaxing natives. (Keep an ear out; this is also popular among rollerbladers.) If you take the St. Charles Avenue Streetcar to where St. Charles ends, you'll discover the tracks take a sharp right turn onto Carrollton

Avenue; that's because the Mississippi River takes a hard right as well, and you can get off and walk the levee there, too, before exploring the shops and cafes of the **Riverbend** neighborhood.

City Park covers 1,500 acres, twice the size of New York's sweeping Central Park, and you can wander pretty much as long as you like. If you like those walking trails with built-in exercise stations such as chin-up bars and stretching posts, go to **Audubon Park;** part of the macadam bike trail over by the duck pond has 18 mild challenges.

■ Running and Jogging ■

Again, the riverfront area is a common draw for runners who deal in limited distance, and the long, lovely stretch of **St. Charles Avenue** down through the Garden District is a great possibility. You could run as far as you like and then ride back—the annual Crescent City 10K starts in Jackson Square and ends at the zoo—or even go half-marathon distance by running to Audubon Park, circling the two-mile path around the golf course, and returning.

In addition to its pleasure paths, City Park has two 400-meter polyurethane tracks built for the 1992 Olympic trials and 1993 NCAA championships, one inside **Tad Gormley Stadium** (482-4888) and one outside.

At the **Chalmette Battlefield** there is a dirt track that is ideal for runners of the contemplative sort; although the car gate is locked at dusk, there is a smaller pedestrian gate next to the national cemetery that will give you access.

And if you're used to running with a club, contact the **New Orleans Track Club** (482-6682) or **Southern Runner Productions** (899-3333) for event schedules.

■ Biking ■

We already mentioned (in "Getting Around New Orleans") that it's easy to rent a bike or even a two-seater in the French Quarter. **Bicycle Michael's** on Frenchman Street has a 25-mile map for serious bikers that goes out Esplanade Avenue to City Park, around the lake, through mid-city to Audubon Park and the university area, and back along St. Charles. And that two-mile track in Audubon Park is very popular with rollerbladers and bikers, particularly on weekends.

■ Tennis ■

There are public courts in both **City Park** (483-9383), which has 39 lighted synthetic-surface courts (making it the largest public facility in the South), USPTA instructors, and even racquet rentals; and in **Audubon Park** at the Magazine Street end (895-1042), which has 10 clay courts and is nice but not lighted. Both charge fees and accept reservations, but they are not required.

There are 11 courts, 3 outdoors, at the **Rivercenter Racquet and Health Club,** which is in the Hilton Riverside at 2 Poydras Street (556-3742), but even hotel guests have to pay the $8 club fee and court time is hard to get. On the other hand, it has a stringing service and a match-a-partner service as well, so if you can make arrangements in advance, it's a good place to go. The club also has squash and racquetball courts. The **YMCA** on St. Charles at Lee Circle also has racquetball courts (568-9622).

■ Golf ■

Like much of the South, this is strong golf territory, and as usual, you can start at City Park, where **Bayou Oaks** club (483-9396) is the (again) largest municipal facility in the South. It offers four 18-hole courses, PGA teaching pros, and a huge, 100-tee double-decker driving range open until 10 P.M. **Audubon Park** (865-8260) has only one 18-holer but the advantage of being near the zoo, so you can grab a round while the kids go on safari. There is a course a little farther away in Pontchartrain Park, **Joe Bartholemew Course,** in the northeast part of the city, which charges around a $10 greens fee and $18 per cart (288-0928). There are also three public courses just across the river on the West Bank: **Plantation Golf Course** (392-3363), which charges $5.50 to $7.50 for greens and $14 for carts; the **Brechtel Park** course (362-4761), which charges $7.75 to $10 for greens and $14 for carts; and **Bayou Barriere** (394-0662), which charges a combined $29.

The PGA-sanctioned New Orleans Open is played in early April at **English Turn** (391-8030), which is on a curve of the Mississippi, a pretty drive down St. Bernard Highway.

■ Gyms and Health Clubs ■

The YMCA at Lee Circle (568-9622) has a relatively expansive half-mile track, large pool, machines, sauna-steam-whirlpool, and aerobics: $5 for outsiders and free to Y hotel guests with a valid hotel key.

The **New Orleans Athletic Club** on North Rampart (525-2375) opens its doors to out-of-towners for one-day $20 visas, in effect. It's 125 years old, but the club has, thankfully, been brought into the 1990s. It even has a restaurant, in the old fashion (definitely clean up first). The **Downtown Fitness Center** in the Canal Place complex has aerobics, treadmills, bikes, stair machines, free weights and leveraged machines, saunas, and even personal trainers, and you can get weekly or three-day rates averaging out to $8 a day, as well as daily passes for $10 (525-2956).

In addition to the courts listed above, the **Rivercenter Club** at the Hilton has massage therapists, a whole list of name-brand machines, salon treatments, and even a tanning bed. The somewhat smaller but equally shiny club at **Le Meridien Hotel** on Canal Street (525-6500) is also open to outsiders ($9), although here the guests play free.

■ **Other Recreational Activities** ■

If you want to swim and are not staying in a hotel with a pool (which only a few in the French Quarter or Garden District have), check with the Y or the health and fitness clubs. There is a public swimming pool at **Audubon Park** as well.

If you like a little outdoor entertainment, but don't go for regimented exercise, you have a couple of other choices. You can ride at a few stables including, of course, **City Park** (483-9398), which has only a ring, and Audubon Park's **Cascade Stables** (891-2246), which goes out into the park a bit.

You may be wondering what else City Park offers. Well, **canoes** and **paddleboats**; a little light **catfish and bass fishing** (you have to get a license at the boat dock behind the park casino, which is the only so-called casino in town without a deck of cards to its name; 483-9371); **soccer** fields; **baseball** diamonds; and a **batting cage** at the four-field softball center.

If you want to take up rollerblading or just rent a pair, head to **Park Skate** (6108 Magazine Street near Audubon Park, 891-7055).

And if you're interested in serious fishing and hunting a little farther outside the city, perhaps for your second New Orleans visit, there are dozens of guides and charters. The two most famous names, or at least faces, in the fishing biz are former TV weatherman Nash Roberts of **Fishhunter Guide Service,** which will not only supply you with everything you need but come and get you at the hotel (call (800) 887-1385 or (504) 837-0703); and TV sportsfishing series character Phil Robichaux of **Captain Phil's Saltwater Guide Services** (348-3264), whose charters run from the Lafitte Marina near the Barataria unit of the Jean Lafitte National Historic Park and Preserve, about an hour's drive from the French Quarter. You can probably get several other names and numbers out of promotional brochures or by calling marinas and fishing stores, but we suggest you contact the New Orleans Visitors Bureau for a list of guides whom they believe are reliable. Remember, you *do* need a permit from the Department of Wildlife and Fisheries, available from most sporting goods stores, marinas, and guide companies.

■ Spectator Sports ■

New Orleans is not a great football town—which may mean that it's a *great* football town for tourists. Although in most cities with NFL franchises, tickets are sold-out well in advance and have to be scalped at the scene, the **New Orleans Saints** do not sell out and there are regularly seats available. Not only that, but they are at home in the legendary (and newly spiffed-up) Superdome, of course, so you can also call TicketMaster at 522-5555 for information. **Tulane University** also plays its Saturday home games at the Superdome, and every other year, there's a rousing, old-fashioned, rah-rah LSU-Tulane grudge match there; call the Dome offices at 587-3810 for schedules and ticket information. You can also inquire about tickets for the **Sugar Bowl** collegiate duel if you have plenty of advance notice.

However, there are times when New Orleans is a super football town, that is, during the years when the **Super Bowl** is played there (8 times in 31 years). It's a long shot, but you can try to get in on the ticket lottery not by besieging the Superdome itself but by sending a certified letter to the National Football League offices at 410 Park Avenue, New York, NY 10022.

New Orleans does better in baseball with the **New Orleans Zephyrs** (the Houston Astros AAA affiliate). Zephyr Stadium in East Jefferson, which opened for the 1997 season, cost $23 million and seats 12,000 in the height of retro-stadium style. For game schedules and ticket information, call the Zephyrs office at 734-5155.

It also does well by the blue-blooded sport of horse racing (as you might expect from such a royalist colony). The **Fairgrounds** (944-5515) near City Park hosts thoroughbred racing from Thanksgiving to mid-April, when it gives way to the Jazz and Heritage Festival.

There are more good sports in the offing: The **New Orleans Sports Arena,** an $84 million multipurpose facility right behind the Superdome, is scheduled to open before the end of the decade, with seating for 20,000 for concerts, 18,500 for basketball (Tulane University games at first and possibly collegiate or professional tournaments), and 17,500 for ice hockey. Like many mid-sized cities, New Orleans is angling to lure a professional sports team.

PART TEN

Shopping in New Orleans

What's Your Bag?

Probably the only reason visitors to New Orleans spend any less time shopping than they do eating and drinking is that the stores close earlier—and even at that, you'll find a surprising number of merchants open until 8 or even 10 P.M. After all, trade and conspicuous consumption are at the heart of New Orleans history: In the mid-eighteenth century, it was the third-busiest port in the United States and had the highest per capita income of any city in the country, according to some figures.

So you can easily shop until you drop. Stores and galleries go wall to wall with bars and restaurants all over the Vieux Carré, making for spectacular window-shopping, and that can be the danger as well. Just as there is a tendency to keep eating because you can smell all that food around you, there's a tendency to keep falling in love with jewelry and posters and rings and masks. (And remember, alcohol loosens your inhibitions, including the financial ones.) If you have a budget, or if you are looking for something particular, it's best to know in advance where you want to go, or you might get sidetracked.

Also, if you think of shopping by "type"—high-end antiques or specialty stores, upscale supermalls or souvenir troves—you can head to the neighborhood with the most options. If you have a couple of days to spare, then you can range a little farther, but even then, if you don't have a background in antiques, a knowledgeable companion, or a friend who lives in town, you're probably not going to stumble onto a hidden treasure.

Among the neighborhoods with good browsing are the most famous shopping strip in New Orleans, Royal Street; the entire riverfront strip from the Farmers Market to the Convention Center; and Magazine Street uptown from Canal over to Audubon Park, all areas described below. You might also enjoy the somewhat more relaxed Riverbend District in Carrollton, which you can stroll as part of the St. Charles streetcar tour (see "Sight-Seeing and Tours").

There is also one of those consumer-era super outlet malls in Slidell, on the north shore of Lake Pontchartrain about 30 minutes from New Orleans off I-10 East, but these are becoming so common it's a shame to leave the city for that. For more information, call 646-0756.

Incidentally, sales tax in New Orleans is 9%, so if what you're buying is large, you might consider having it shipped to you; the handling charge may well be less than the tax. If you are visiting from another country, you can take advantage of Louisiana's Tax-Free Shopping, although this will mean carrying your passport with you instead of putting it in the hotel vault. Here's how it works: If the store posts an LTFS sticker (or ask at the counter), show the passport and ask for the special refund voucher. You'll still pay the tax, but when you get to the airport, stop by the LTFS counter and show them your receipts and refund slips. Up to $100 will be refunded in cash (minus a service charge), up to $500 by check; over $500, the check will be mailed to your home.

■ The French Quarter ■

As Bourbon Street is to nightlife, so **Royal Street** is to antiques — and if it's not there, it's probably on Chartres. That's an exaggeration, of course, but the Royal antiques row goes back three and four generations, on both the selling and buying sides. Royal Street makes for the most riveting window-shopping in the city: cases of earrings, necklaces, cufflinks, and enamels; chandeliers and gold leaf, crystal, and silver; china dolls, silver-headed walking sticks, and sterling cigarette cases, all glittering with the mystique of Creole culture. Some of these stores advertise all over the country (which is a consideration that cuts both ways—*somebody* has to pay for all that publicity); still others capitalize on Royal Street's reputation to embellish both the value and the actual cost of their goods.

Many hotels and visitors' centers have a brochure put out by the Royal Street Guild listing members (or call the guild at 524-1260), but the choices are almost overwhelming, so visitors should start with these reputable dealers:

One of the oldest names in the antiques game here is **Keil's** (325 Royal Street; 522-4552), founded before the turn of the century and still among the best choices for French and English art and furnishings, chandeliers, and decorative arts. It remains a family concern, and other stores in the clan's hands are **Royal Antiques** (307–309 Royal Street; 524-7033), its annex around the corner (715 Bienville Street), and **Moss Antiques** (411 Royal Street; 522-3981). Another good spot is the **French Antique Shop** (225 Royal Street; 524-9861), whose collection of bronzes, chandeliers, and Baccarat crystal loom out of the dark to draw you in.

For Asian art and antiquities, contact **Diane Genre,** a member of the International Association of Appraisers and a specialist in Japanese woodblock prints, temple carvings, lacquer work, and extraordinary Japanese and Chinese textiles, including such gold- and silver-embroidered dragons as would bring your fantasies to life. She has closed her retail store but is working out of an apartment showroom on Royal (595-8945).

If you're interested in fine estate jewelry, Deco, Nouveau, or just retro, check into **Gerald D. Katz Antiques, Inc.** (505 Royal Street; 524-5050) or consult Nancy Kittay, who runs her jewelry business, specializing in Victorian and Early American pieces, from inside the **Waldhorn Company** (343 Royal Street; 581-6379).

(This used to be the financial heart of the Vieux Carré, and several of the old financial institutions are into their second lives as antiques stores. The three-floor Waldhorn building, for example, was originally designed as the Bank of the United States in 1800, and the Manheim Galleries building at Royal and Conti Streets was designed in 1820 by Benjamin Latrobe as the Louisiana State Bank.)

For the hostess with the mostess, nothing could be more fun than a lesson in preparing an absinthe cocktail—and the sharp-tipped, perforated absinthe spoons are only $45—from Patrick Dunne, proprietor of **Lucullus** (610 Chartres; 528-9620). Lucius Licinius Lucullus was a famous Roman epicure, and Dunne's shop stocks cookware, silver, and culinary objets d'art dating to the seventeenth century.

The old **M. S. Rau** store has taken to offering one-day "specials," a la the Manhattan merchants, on such items as walking sticks, music boxes, and decanters; pick the right day, and you might pick a prize (630 Royal Street; 523-4662).

Kurt E. Schon, Ltd. (523 Royal Street; 524-5462) has what he advertises as the largest inventory of nineteenth-century European paintings in this country, particularly featuring works by Impressionist, Postimpressionist, French Salon, and Royal Academy artists, and the price tags are as breathtaking as the collection. (If your budget only goes up to $100,000 or so, you don't even want to know about the six floors of private showrooms, open by appointment only, on St. Louis.) If you love the styles, but can't quite afford the Schon prices, try the **Vincent Mann Gallery** (713 Bienville

Street; 523-2342), which specializes in the second rank, but high second rank, of predominantly French Postimpressionists.

Books, Records, and Prints

Not surprisingly, a literary town like New Orleans is rich in bookstores, particularly those specializing in out-of-print titles, first editions, and rare publications. **Faulkner House Books** is in the building overlooking St. Anthony's garden, where William Faulkner lived while writing *Soldier's Pay* and various short stories set in New Orleans. It naturally features first editions of his works and other important Southern literature (624 Pirate's Alley; 524-2940). The house where Tennessee Williams wrote *A Streetcar Named Desire,* coincidentally, is right through Exchange Alley in the next block at 632 St. Peter Street.

Other good book shops, especially for those who love to linger among the shelves, include **Beckham's** (228 Decatur Street; 522-9875) and its sibling **Librarie** (823 Chartres Street; 525-4837); **Arcadian Books and Art Prints** (714 Orleans Street; 523-4138); and **Dauphine Street Books** (410 Dauphine; 529-2333).

Of special interest is **Old Children's Books** (724 Royal Street; 525-3655), where you can find that out-of-print story you used to love, as well as children's editions ranging back more than 100 years. Incidentally, these stores belong to an association of antiquarian and second-hand booksellers, and any one of them can give you a list and a simple map of the others.

In the same way, a musical town like this is a great place to dig up old recordings. For jazz (mostly rerecorded and available on cassette or CD), stop by the shop at the Old U.S. Mint on Esplanade. The outlet of the **GHB Jazz Foundation** in the French Market (525-1776) carries Dixieland, traditional jazz, and classic jazz recordings, both old and remastered.

For classic rock and R&B, jazz, blues, zydeco, country, music hall, and novelty records—nearly every record you've ever heard and some you never would—plus old posters and T-shirts, the name is **Record Ron's** (1129 Decatur Street; 522-2230). This is a particular haven for "real" records, that is, the old 45's and LPs, which is why this is the place "Where Vinyl Lives!" New converts to the regional sounds of zydeco, Cajun, blues, swamp pop, and gospel sounds may also want to flip through the goods at **Louisiana Music Factory** (225 North Peters; 523-1094).

If you're interested in photographs, either vintage or contemporary, **A Gallery of Fine Photography** (322 Royal Street; 568-1313) carries works by such artists as Berenice Abbott, Eadweard Muybridge, Edward Weston, Yousuf Karsh, Edward Steichen, Henri Cartier-Bresson, Diane Arbus, Ansel

Adams, and Helmut Newton. For fine mezzotints and other vintage prints, try the **Stone and Press Galleries** (238 Chartres; 561-8555).

Stamp collector extraordinaire **Raymond H. Weill** sold his entire collection to a London firm ten years ago for a staggering $14 million, and has been restocking ever since (407 Royal Street; 581-7373).

For maps, fine art prints, architectural drawings, star charts, medical diagrams, and official documents—layers and layers of them—try the **Centuries Antique Prints and Maps,** which lives up to 500 years of its name (517 St. Louis Street; 525-5564).

Other French Quarter Collectibles

Once you get into New Orleans music, you'll want to join the parade. So for a really unusual souvenir, consider a "second-line" umbrella—the ones you see waving behind the band in those parades—or a fine plantation-worthy parasol. The two names, unfortunately confusing, are Lane's and Laines': Anne B. Lane, the **Umbrella Lady** (1107 Decatur Street; 523-7791), whose fashionable wares can often be seen on the balcony overlooking the street, if she herself is not waving them in an impromptu kickline; and the funkier **Laine's** (810 Royal Street; 423-2911).

Weapons and ammunitions—flintlocks, pistols, muzzle loaders, swords, bayonets, sabers, shot, and even cannonballs—are the signature stock at the fourth-generation **James H. Cohen & Sons** (437 Royal Street; 522-3305). Perhaps a little cruelly, the entrance is guarded by a wooden Indian.

For those who prefer their warfare a little less realistic, **Le Petit Soldier Shop** (528 Royal Street—or as they continue to put it, 528 Rue Royale; 523-7741) carries not only vintage lead and more modern toy soldiers of the familiar Civil War and Napoleonic eras, but figures of Sherlock Holmes and Watson, "Kagemusha"-style samurai, Roman emperors, Winston Churchill, and even Hitler, along with service decorations and pilots' wings. For dolls, check out **Boyers Antiques & Doll** shops (241 Chartres Street; 522-4513) or the **Little Toy Shoppe** (900 Decatur Street; 522-6588), which has a dazzling supply of blocks, tops, puzzles, and so on. For dollhouse furniture and miniatures, stop by **Boyers Miniature Shop** (330 Chartres Street; 566-7046), the **Black Butterfly** (727 Royal Street; 524-6464), or the **Ginja Jar Too** (607 Royal Street; 523-7614).

What would a trip to the voodoo capital of the country be without a little mysticism? For charms, potions, mojo dolls, and the most atmospheric palm or tarot readings, head to the **New Orleans Historic Voodoo Museum** (724 Dumaine Street; 523-7865), which despite the name is more theater than museum; the **Witches Closet** (521 St. Phillip Street; 593-9222); or **Marie Laveau's House of Voodoo** (739 Bourbon Street; 581-

3751). If you prefer to walk on the sunnier side, the **Bottom of the Cup Tearooms** stock crystals, wrought-iron stands and heavy crystal balls, and scores of tarot decks reproduced from various countries and centuries (732 Royal Street; 523-1204 and 616 Conti Street; 524-1997). There are readers at both, but New Orleans insiders swear by the gentle Alta, a Native American who works out of the Conti Street shop. You can even follow up with a phone call, in a sort of higher-class psychic's hotline.

Another New Orleans "must" is pralines, those brown sugar–pecan sweets. While there are several fine and old confectionaries, the **Old Town Praline Shop** (627 Royal Street; 525-1413) has even more than its candy to recommend it—hometown ladies behind the counter and a lovely courtyard in the back, one of the few still open to visitors and a welcome respite from the shopping grind. French Opera diva Adelina Patti, who set Creole hearts aflame during the 1860 season, used the house as her residence, and photos of her triumphal tour dot the walls.

This is the coffee generation, as they say, and Café du Monde and French Market coffee is everywhere. But for the real bean freaks, there is no better shop than **Kaldi's Coffee House** (941 Decatur Street; 586-8989), which not only sells (and ships) green coffee beans for home roasting but offers advice on the process. Try the web site at www.coffeebiz.com. This is also one of the nicest, quietest hangouts in the French Quarter, the sort of place residents still read the morning paper over espresso.

Among New Orleans veterans, there is no more revered name than Zula Fricks, even though the eponymous lady herself long ago departed this world. But that probably makes her the patron saint of lost buttons, because **Zula Fricks' Button Shop** (328 Chartres Street; 523-6557) has every sort of insignia, enamel, hand-painted, horn, ivory, oversized, understated, and unique fastenings imaginable.

Although it's now in the Pontalba complex next to the 1850 House, **Bourbon French Perfume** (525 St. Anne Street; 522-4480) used to be on the street it's named for—back in 1843, when it opened. You can either get French scents like those preferred by Creole society (see the super economy-sized bottles in the Hermann-Grima House, for fun) or have one blended for you.

There are masks and Mardi Gras paraphernalia all over, but unless you just want a mass-produced version, head for the **Little Shop of Fantasy** (523 Dumaine Street; 529-4243), which stocks all handmade masks and costumes by about two dozen local artists. This is also where you can get those Victorian stovepipes and ubiquitous *Cat in the Hat* toppers, if you must.

If your boss is the sort of guy who has everything, here are a few leather items that might save you the annual Christmas list blues: hanging suit bags for $335; golf bags, tooled or smooth, for $345; tennis racquet bags for $80, and even cellular phone carriers for $115. The smartest idea yet is a leather duffel weekender that folds flat into itself so you can pack it inside another suitcase for souvenirs. All, as well as belts, shoes, totes, and purses, are at **Leather Creations** (837 Decatur; 527-0033).

Finally, for those interested in restoring old homes, it's worth heading over to **Architectural Antiques** (4531 North Rampart Street; 942-7000) to look over the mantelpieces, corbels, and columns. **Sigle's Antiques and Metalcraft** is stocked with balcony iron and ornamental hangings and brackets (935 Royal Street; 522-7647). **Bevolo Gas and Electric Lights** has been turning out lamps, including the gas-look fixtures around Jackson Square, for half a century (521 Conti Street; 522-9485). And **Architectural Angel** near the French Market can supply your patio with all the fountain statues, wall sconces, and spirits you can dream of; they even have a banner reading "Angels and Gargoyles Made Fresh Daily" (1132 Decatur Street; 524-0302).

■ **Magazine Street** ■

In recent years, with rising rents and stiffer competition, many antiques dealers have either moved off the main drag or out of the French Quarter altogether. A number of stores and galleries have opened on **Magazine Street** in the Uptown/University area, and the Magazine Street merchants have been promoting their association with brochures and maps.

Which brings up a sticky point: There are a great number of interesting stores along Magazine Street, to be sure, but whether it actually makes sense for visitors to the city, especially those staying only a few days, to venture over there is another issue.

For one thing, despite the promotional brochures raving about "six miles of antique shops, art galleries, restaurants, and specialty shops in Historic Uptown New Orleans," the road is still primarily residential; there is a block or two with a lot of stores, and then it may be several blocks before another cluster. If you don't have a car, it's difficult to see more than a few stores at a time. The confusion is increased by the fact that Magazine Street begins in the new Warehouse/Arts District near the Convention Center, so that some visitors believe they can walk to the antiques strip, whereas it's quite a hike to the real clusters.

Second, alongside many of the nicer stores are still lower-scale salvage shops, more like flea market or "granny's attic" affairs. So if you don't already know something about antiques, and if you aren't willing to spend a couple of hours sorting through showrooms and comparing prices, you may be disappointed.

(One other possibility is to hire a professional antiquing companion, such as **Macon Riddle** of Let's Go Antiquing, who's made a career of designing half- or full-day shopping tours geared to your interests. For $50 an hour, minimum three hours, you get her expert advice, too; call 899-3027.)

If you do want to go, here are a few clusters of specialty shops of particular interest, so you can make at least some sort of park-and-walk visit or walk over from the streetcar without exhausting yourself. Or consult with the Regional Transit Authority about bus routes and VisiTour passes, as described in "Getting Around New Orleans."

Start off at the corner of St. Andrew Street with **Jim Smiley's Fine Vintage Clothing** store (2001 Magazine; 528-9449), the sort of place which knows the difference between "vintage" and merely used. Smiley's runs the gamut from haute couture dresses to '40s suits, serious antique wedding gowns and bodices, silk step-ins, and even bloomers—and has some riotous hats to boot.

Next stop is **Bush Antiques,** which has an amazing assortment of ecclesiastical remnants, so to speak: gilded high altars, heavy bishops' chairs, old chapel statuary, including the Virgin Mary and various saints, iron crucifixes from cemeteries, stained glass, and even vestments (2109–2111 Magazine; 581-3518). If you're attracted to the vividly painted bayou folk art of the sort that adorns the House of Blues, for instance, be sure to step through to the courtyard for a look at the "studio" there.

Across the street are **Hands** (2042 Magazine; 522-2590), whose owner Rachel Dalessandro specializes in pre-Columbian art and artifacts as old as 3,000 years (some astonishingly affordable) and **Gerry White Glass** (2036 Magazine; 522-3544), the showroom/studio of a man whose custom architectural glass, etched and carved, ranges from tables to standing screens. (The panels in the window, etched to look like venetian blinds, won him his wife.)

A few blocks farther is **George Herget Books,** which is one of the most important rare and secondhand bookstores outside the French Quarter, housing an estimated 20,000 volumes (3109 Magazine Street; 891-5595). Right next door is **Magazine Arcade Antiques** (3017 Magazine; 895-5451), stocking thousands of music boxes, home furnishings, high-end bric-a-brac, porcelain, and cloisonné, and a mix of American, European, and Asian antiques. And if you've got the money, honey, they've got the time: **Kohlmaier and Kohlmaier** (1018 Harmony Street, just off the 3200 block of Magazine Street; 895-6394) specializes in standing and cabinet clocks, mantel clocks, and personal timepieces.

Another few blocks out is a cluster for decorators with an eye for ethnic and folk arts. Pottery fans will be torn between the studio showrooms of **Charles Bohn** at Shadyside Pottery (3823 Magazine Street; 897-1710), who served his apprenticeship in Japan but who also loves classical Greco-Roman styles; and **Casey Willems Pottery** (3919 Magazine; 899-1174), who throws his more rustic, but elegantly utilitarian, pottery on a wheel and fills custom orders from the Guggenheim Museum gift shop. In between, if you dare, see the beautifully finished pieces by furniture designer **Mario Villa** (3908 Magazine; 895-8731); it was Villa who made the sconces for the Contemporary Arts Center, which gives you an idea how highly his peers regard his work.

For collectors of African art, the **Davis Gallery** (3964 Magazine Street; 897-0780) is a must-see: Household items, baskets, personal items, cookware, and masks from Central and West Africa—all actually used, not mass-manufactured—are displayed in a museum-quality setting. The nearby **Private Connection** does a similar good turn for Indonesian artifacts—shadow puppets, "flying" temple figurines, batik fabrics, and jewelry—along with colonial-era antiques (3927 Magazine Street; 899-4944).

And if you've become one of the retro–tea party crowd, visit **Jon Antiques** (4605 Magazine Street; 899-4482), which specializes in smaller, more portable but elegant items such as eighteenth- and nineteenth-century porcelains, tea caddies, and fireplace screens.

■ The Warehouse District ■

Another neighborhood emerging as a shopping center is the old Warehouse/Arts District, a loosely defined area roughly squared off by the convention center, Lafayette Street to Lafayette Square, St. Charles Avenue between Lafayette and Lee Circle, and Howard Avenue from Lee Circle back to the convention center. A number of former mills, machinery suppliers, and storehouses have been gutted and refurbished as art spaces and condominiums, although there are still pockets of industry all over. Taking most of its impetus from the 1984 World's Fair (which was a *succès d'estime* if not an economic one), this neighborhood is an intriguing combination of retail and residential, the home of Emeril's Restaurant (and chef Emeril Lagasse, himself), the area where you'll find the Contemporary Arts Center and the new Louisiana Children's Museum, as well as the Civil War Museum and such historic landmarks as St. Patrick's Cathedral. (See the profiles in "New Orleans Attractions.")

The main strip, nicknamed **Gallery Row,** is along Julia Street between

St. Charles and the Convention Center. Since art is definitely a matter of taste, you'll just have to wander around the galleries and check them out. You can get to the Warehouse District from the French Quarter by riding the Riverfront Streetcar to the Julia Street stop; and if you're not tired afterwards, you can wind up at St. Charles and take that streetcar for a spin out to the Garden District.

Some of the best-known galleries here belong to **Marguerite Oestreicher** (626 Julia Street; 581-9253), who has the sculpture from the estate of Milton Avery, among others; **Simonne Stern** (518 Julia; 529-1118), who was one of the first, and remains one of the premier, dealers in contemporary regional art; and the **New Orleans Auction Galleries** (801 Magazine Street at Julia; 566-1849), which innovatively employs only women auctioneers.

Aside from the art galleries and studios, there are a couple of particularly noteworthy addresses. The **New Orleans School of GlassWorks & Gallery** (727 Magazine Street just off Julia; 529-7277) is the largest contemporary glass arts studio in the South, and it offers glassblowing classes to the public—not only six-week courses, but two-day intensive introductions to the art and even private tutoring. Exhibitions go on constantly, and the studio shares space with fine bookmakers and print- and paper-makers, who also offer exhibitions and workshops. This is a first-class family attraction as well as an art gallery.

And although it may be a little fine for beginners, good amateur and even professional musicians should make a special trip to **International Vintage Guitars** (1011 Magazine Street; 524-4557), which has used and vintage Martin, Rickenbacher, Fender, and Gibson instruments, along with accessories, amplifiers, etc.

■ Malls of the Americas ■

New Orleans has developed an almost continuous line of those prepackaged, upscale-label shopping malls stretching along the waterfront from Jackson Square to the Convention Center, or commercially speaking, from the French Market to the Riverwalk Marketplace. This baby-boomer boomtown also includes those most notorious of souvenir franchises, the Hard Rock Cafe and Planet Hollywood, which look across Decatur Street at two other quintessential '90s trend-shops, a brewpub (Crescent City) and New York's Fashion Cafe, founded by fashion supermodels Cindy Crawford, Linda Evangelista, and Naomi Campbell. The whole area is sort of bookended by two other theme-sales centers: the Jimmy Buffett shop, filled with Parrothead paraphernalia at the corner of Decatur and Ursuline, and the

House of Blues souvenir store on Decatur past Bienville; so if your idea of souvenir heaven is a Hard Rock–New Orleans T-shirt, you scarcely need lose sight of Jackson Square.

This Great Wall o' Malls winds in and out among the various riverside promenades, cruise ship landings, and the Aquarium of the Americas, and in good weather the kite flyers and rollerbladers wind in and out of tourists hefting huge shopping bags and wielding baby strollers like human machetes. This can be somewhat wearing, whether or not you're actually purchasing anything, so it's best to stop periodically and admire the river, or get a 15-minute neck massage or a hair-wrap.

Starting at the east end of the French Quarter and stretching along North Peters Street to the Café du Monde at Jackson Square is the **French Market,** which legend says was a trading post for Native Americans long before the Europeans arrived. Nowadays the complex comprises a half-dozen nicely restored pink stucco buildings housing everything from high-priced souvenirs to jazz bars to orange juice stands. The building closest to Barracks Street is the **Old Farmers Market** — or, rather, what is now called the Old Farmer's Market. The crates of live poultry, rabbits, turtle, and squid that locals used to buy right off the dock have pretty much been replaced by stands of pepper sauce and braided ropes of garlic being sold at inflated prices to credulous tourists as "Cajun hot garlic."

The next stretch of the market, which spills out into the street on week-ends, is the **Community Flea Market,** a grab bag of tie-dyed dresses, carved masks, old chairs, and mass-produced "stained glass" that for most people provides all the cheap souvenirs their officemates can stand. Inside these buildings are scores of vendors offering voodoo dolls, T-shirts, earrings, cheap ties (including Jimi Hendrix patterns and copies of Nicole Miller designs for $5), rock posters, sunglasses, blackface pecan-shell magnets, reproduction grocery labels, fabric pins, mobcaps, novelty ballpoint pens (including some that resemble syringes), rubber-band guns, and sports caps. Hot sauce and Cajun spice fans can find stalls like the **N'awlins Cajun & Creole Spices** (1101 North Peters Street; 566-2325 or (800) 237-2325) selling hundreds of gumbo mixes and seasonings bearing both old names (Zatarain's, McIlhenny) and new celebrity imprints (Paul Prudhomme's and Emeril's). You can even have your name inscribed on a grain of rice for only $8.

As you work your way toward Jackson Square, you'll find some clothing boutiques, indoor-outdoor bars (there are usually at least two jazz trios playing at any given time), and gift shops with pralines and pepper sauce and cutesy statuettes of Louis Armstrong. (Note that the similarly styled building a little behind the French Market at about St. Philip Street is the Jean

Lafitte National Park Visitors Center; see "Sight-Seeing and Tours.") Beyond the legendary **Café du Monde,** where you can buy chicory coffee and beignet mix right from the source, the commercial strip briefly gives way to Washington Artillery Park and the wooden Moonwalk promenade along the river. Of course, down along the Square, the sidewalks will be full of mule carriages, caricaturists, and clowns, and Artillery Park will probably have some street theater or music going on, but that's just for fun.

Then the shopping picks up again at the old **Jackson Brewery,** onetime house of Jax beer (as it's familiarly known) and now the home of **Planet Hollywood,** and its twin the **Millhouse;** one parking lot over is the **Marketplace,** similarly the outpost of the **Hard Rock Cafe.** The installation of Planet Hollywood pushed out most of the smaller vendors who were in the complex, but there are a couple of entertainments remaining, notably one of the city's teaching kitchens, the **New Orleans School of Cooking** (731-6100 or (800) 237-4841) in the Jax building, where you can make your lunch and eat it too, if you make your reservations in advance. The school has its own **Louisiana General Store,** too, so you can take the ingredients home for an encore. The Marketplace is big-time retail media: **Tower Records & Video** and **Bookstar.**

There is another pretty stretch—Waldenburg Park—which meanders over to the Aquarium of the Americas; just west of the Aquarium, the Spanish Plaza segues into the huge **Riverwalk Marketplace** complex, an upscale Rouse development of 200 boutiques and eateries that connects to the Hilton Hotel and the **Flamingo** floating casino. Most of these stores seem to come as a package deal now, and even in duplicate: the **Disney Store** and **Warner Bros., the Gap** and **Banana Republic, Sharper Image** and **Brookstone, Eddie Bauer** and **Abercrombie & Fitch, Victoria's Secret** and . . . well, you get the idea. For something a little less predictable, look into the shop of **Yvonne LaFleur,** who not only carries upscale fashions but custom-designed hats, cocktail dresses, evening gowns, and even wedding dresses. From the river, you can see where the facade of Riverwalk was torn away by the runaway barge—it looks a little like an intentional architectural model, actually—but you'd never know from strolling through the glossy mall inside that anything had ever happened.

At the foot of Canal Street, across the streetcar tracks from the Aquarium, is **Canal Place,** a new, lushly appointed and label-conscious mall that blazons the logos of its **Gucci, Saks,** and **Lord & Taylor** tenants large and loud. Be sure to browse through **RHINO,** which is an acronym for "Right Here in New Orleans," describing where the store's crafts were made. It's a nonprofit shop, but the clothing and art are extemely attractive. Canal Place is also the home of hometown jewelry designer **Mignon Faget,** whose creations in silver, 14-karat gold, and bronze d'or for both men and women are highly prized.

There is another upscale mall called the **New Orleans Centre** at 1400 Poydras by the Superdome, but there isn't much reason to make a trip unless you want to tour the stadium and eat in the food court there.

PART ELEVEN

Sight-Seeing and Tours

The nice thing about sight-seeing is that you can choose your own pace, looking closely at what intrigues you, gazing appreciatively at what only pleases you, and pushing right on past what stirs not a flicker of interest. New Orleans is particularly well suited to walking tours, and that's what we recommend, especially for the French Quarter. So the latter portion of this chapter is given over to introductory walks around the most important (at least, to visitors) neighborhoods, with a little background flavor and a few landmarks for orientation. We've also suggested ways to customize your visit according to your own interests, by zeroing in on just the military sites, the other-worldly media, etc. The "inside stuff"—museums, historic houses, and so on—are described in more detail in the next part on "New Orleans Attractions," which also includes some general walking-tour tips.

But as we said in the introduction, we know that not everybody prefers do-it-yourself tours. Some people find it distracting to try to read directions and anecdotes while walking, and others use packaged tours as a way of getting a mental map of the area. So first we'll run through some of the guided tours available. (These are surely not all of them: Tourism is a boom industry in New Orleans, and you'll see flyers for new tours every month. If you want to take a guided tour, check through the material at the information desks and visitors' centers or even your hotel lobby; you may find a discount coupon.)

In New Orleans, you can tour by land or sea, mule carriage or coach. You can see historic spots or "haunts," literary sites or cemeteries, battlefields or bayous. And you can pay nothing or, well, something.

The last thing to consider is that New Orleans is not one-size-fits-all. Walking is wonderful if you're young and fit, but if your party includes children or seniors, make sure to pace yourself. Build in a timely stop in a park; split the touring day into "shifts," so that if necessary, those with less stamina can head back to the hotel for a rest while the others continue. Or lay out the schedule on the democratic scheme —that is, put the attractions everyone wants to see first, the could-be-missed intermediate ones later, and the only-for-fanatics excursions last. That way, whoever wants to drop out can.

If each member of the party has his own must-see's, then set a particular hour to split up and a clearly understood place to regroup—General Jackson's statue, for example. If you're worried about a teenager getting completely wound up in whatever museum or exhibit he's into and losing track of the time, schedule this separate tour session just before lunch; there are few things that can override a kid's stomach alarm.

Finally, because the food and beverage lures are everywhere, avoid stomach overload or whining children by carrying a supply of snacks in plastic bags.

Guided Sight-Seeing

■ **Walking Tours** ■

To be honest, when it comes to overviews, the best tours in life are free. Rangers from the **National Park Service** lead two walks every day (except Christmas and Mardi Gras), one covering the French Quarter and one the Garden District, and frequently a third "tour du jour" with a changing theme rather than a geographic structure.

The French Quarter Walks, which emphasize the history and succession of cultures in the Vieux Carré, begin at 10:30 A.M. and last about 90 minutes; the distance covered is about a mile. These are first-come, first-served tours, and rangers allow a maximum of 30 in each party. You must have a pass (and all members of your party must get a pass in person—you can't just send a representative). Passes are available beginning at 9 A.M. at the ranger station at 916 North Peters Street behind the French Market (near where Decatur runs into North Peters).

The Garden District Walk begins at 2:30 and also lasts about 90 minutes and covers one mile. Again, you must make reservations (589-2636), and since these are popular tours, we suggest you call a couple of days in advance if possible. The walk begins in the Garden District, so you must make your way to the corner of Washington and Prytania Streets. The nicest way to do it is to take the St. Charles Streetcar (board at Carondelet and Canal or on St. Charles at Common Street, a block west of Canal) to the Washington Street stop, turn left (south), and walk one block to Prytania.

The tour du jour, which is offered only when sufficient rangers are available, begins at 11:30 A.M. and takes about 90 minutes, but the distance varies. Ask at the station for the day's topic; they may also know a few days in advance what other subjects—legends of New Orleans, origins of streets names, balconies and ornamentation—will be covered that week. The rangers are informative guides, and when you remember that the entire French Quarter is part of the National Park System, you'll see why.

Incidentally, only the most extreme weather halts these tours, and they are conducted entirely outdoors, so dress accordingly.

Members of the nonprofit **Friends of the Cabildo** lead two-hour walks that focus on the more important historic exteriors and also some of the state museum system's exhibits (see more detail on the Louisiana State Museums below and in "New Orleans Attractions"). Admission is called a "donation," and the quality of the work that has been done on the museums in recent years gives resonance to the word; besides, it costs only $10 for adults and $5 for those over 65 or between 13 and 20 (children free). You can either buy tickets in advance at the Museum Store on St. Ann Street in Jackson Square (523-3939) or just arrive with the funds on-hand. Tours begin daily at 10 A.M. and 1:30 P.M., except Mondays (1:30 P.M. only) and holidays.

Anne Rice's New Orleans Tours group has added a French Quarter walking tour to its Garden District tour, but since both of them have a whiff of brimstone, we've described them with the "Dark Side" packages below.

■ Bus Tours and Trolleys ■

Gray Line Tours (call (800) 535-7786 or (504) 587-0861) offer a variety of packages, including walking tours of the French Quarter and Garden District, plantation tours, and a combination tour with lunch aboard the steamboat *Natchez*. The bus tour covers the whole city, but you don't get out and really see anything; the main advantages are that a large group can arrange a tour in advance, and the buses make pick-ups from the major hotels. Their trolley tour is nicer and covers the French Quarter, City Park, and Longue Vue House and Gardens; here you can jump off and back on the tour whenever the desire for a closer look overtakes you ($15 for a one-day pass, $25 for two days).

Tours by Isabelle (391-3544) uses minivans, so space is obviously more limited; call as far in advance as possible. The three-hour tours, 9 A.M. and 1:30 P.M. daily, are among the most comprehensive, covering the French Quarter, the cemeteries, City Park, the Lakefront, Bayou St. John, the Garden District and university neighborhood, and even the Superdome; tours cost $30 per person or $35 for a "combo tour" that also includes Longue Vue.

New Orleans Tours (592-0560) is almost a subcontractor—they can arrange walking tours, cruises, nightlife jaunts, swamp tours, and combos.

■ Carriage Tours ■

These are becoming common in many cities around the country (and elsewhere—imagine Florence by buggy), but they're still the sort of thing that grabs at your nostalgic heartstrings every once in a while. The French

Quarter, especially at night, lends itself to such time-traveling. A relatively quick two-mile route does help orient you a little, and if you have children, they will definitely enjoy this.

Most of the carriages just line up along Decatur Street around Jackson Square; the cost is $8 for adults and $5 under 12. There are a few things to note about such tours, however: "Local color" definitely doesn't stop at the bridle ribbons. The quality—the factual accuracy, not necessarily the entertainment quotient—varies tremendously, which is one reason there is a movement afoot to license carriage drivers as entertainers rather than as tour guides. And most of the horses are really mules, which doesn't really affect the ride but might affect your view if you're a horseflesh fan. (And some seem more aromatic than horses, but that may be imagination.) On the other hand, there are usually drivers around until midnight, so you can fit this into your schedule at almost any time.

If you want a more elaborate (more expensive) personal tour, contact **Good Old Days Buggies** (523-0804); they will pick you up at your hotel or even at some of the major restaurants.

■ Special Interest Tours ■

Heritage City Tours offers a "Roots of Heritage City" tour twice daily, Thursday-Saturday, that stops by Marie Laveau's tomb, Congo Square, and so on; $28 adults, $23 children. Also offered is a "Roots in the Night" tour which includes a blues and jazz show, Thursday–Saturday. Prices for that tour vary depending on the package you choose. A third tour, "Roots in the Church," is available twice every Sunday; $55 adults, $45 children. Call (888) 33ROOTS or (504) 596-6889 for more information or to schedule a tour Monday–Wednesday (groups of six or more). Also contact **Le'Ob's Tours** (288-3478) for tours with special connections to African-American culture and its contribution to the city.

Hidden Treasures Tours (529-4507), which range through both the Upper and Lower Garden District, emphasize women's history, including monuments and authors' homes. Advance reservations are required, and tickets are $12 apiece.

UNO professor Kenneth Holditch of **Heritage Tours** will lead you through a tour of literary-interest sites and homes (by appointment; 949-9805). **Gay Heritage** tours are irregular (in both senses of the word), but great if you can get one. They are generally offered on weekends, leaving from Alternatives at 907 Bourbon Street, and promise to dish the gossip on Tennessee Williams, Truman Capote, Claw Shaw, and even Lillian

Hellman. Call 945-6789 for information. And in fact, if you read the French Quarter self-guided walking tour we've laid out below, you'll find quite a few of the literary spots listed.

Finally, music lovers should call **Cradle of Jazz** tours to get the score on New Orleans' earliest masters (by appointment; 282-3583).

Walking on the Dark Side

Haunted tours, voodoo tours, and cemetery tours are all the rage in New Orleans, and you can go at practically any hour (and with guides in full capes and pointy-toothed glory, if you want).

On the straight side is **Save Our Cemeteries** (525-3357), a nonprofit group whose proceeds go toward the restoration of these "cities of the dead." SOC offers a serious and informative tour of St. Louis No. 1 every Sunday at 10 A.M., leaving from Royal Blend Coffee and Tea Room at 623 Royal Street, and leads tours of Lafayette Cemetery in the Garden District every Monday, Wednesday, and Friday at 10:30 A.M.

The longest-running haunted tours are probably those offered by the **New Orleans Historic Voodoo Museum** at 724 Rue Dumaine (523-7685 or www.voodoomuseum.com or e-mail, voodoo@voodoomuseum.com). The cemetery tour not surprisingly focuses on Marie Laveau's still-revered tomb and allows you to participate in a wishing ritual, but also explains why the "cities of the dead" are all above ground and shows off various personalities' resting places. The 90-minute tours begin at 10:30 A.M. and 1 P.M. daily (Sundays 10:30 P.M. only) and cost $12 apiece. (Subtract 20% from all Voodoo Museum tour prices for groups of 10 or more and 30% for teenagers or AARP members.) Arrive 20 minutes early for any of these tours, and you can tour the museum for free as well.

The "voodoo walking tour" also visits the great voodoo priestess's tomb, but also covers haunted houses, Congo Square—emphasizing its history as a voodoo ritual meeting ground rather than its musical roots—and a Catholic church with a voodoo saint among its statues, given Monday through Saturday at 1 P.M. and Sunday at 10:30 A.M. This is a two-and-a-half-hour tour for $18 per person.

And its "original" voodoo tour, the "Tour of the Undead" route, includes a visit to a voodoo temple, a live witch, and witchcraft and voodoo shops, and each participant gets a gris-gris bag to wear for protection throughout the two-and-a-half-hour tour ($25).

Magic Walking Tours (593-9693) offer a similar barrage of mystery-history—a voodoo tour, a haunted house roundup, a cemetery tour, a vampire tour, and a ghost hunt, in addition to relatively straight neighborhood walks—but they are generally accurate as such things go (they do not mistake one old mansion with a calm history for its sanguine neighbor, as do some self-anointed tour guides). You don't have to make reservations, but the meeting place for each tour differs, so call ahead. Adult tickets range from $9 to $13; kids come along for free.

The lightest-hearted tour group is probably **Millennium Tours** (569-9002), which pokes cheerful fun at itself and other tours with a two-hour "party on legs" through the French Quarter that tosses together historical facts, ghost stories, stops at Marie Laveau's tomb and TV and movie locations, and "the latest Anne Rice gossip," a genre that has itself become a New Orleans addiction. "We carefully analyzed each walking tour, eliminated the boring parts and cleverly combined all the really good stuff!" boasts the flyer. Millennium promises licensed tour guides with personality, and you should be glad for both. Tours leave daily at 9:30 A.M. and 2:30 and 9 P.M. from the Hauntings Today Ghost Expedition courtyard at 635 Toulouse Street just off Royal; no reservations are required, but be there about 15 minutes early. (For more on Hauntings Today, see "The Great Hereafter" in the next chapter). Tickets are $15, $10 for ages 13–16, and free for 12 and under. Note that the nighttime tours do not cover St. Louis Cemetery—a safety precaution.

Anne Rice has become a New Orleans industry in her own write, so to speak. Currently **Anne Rice's New Orleans Tours** (899-6450) offers four packages, all punctuated by Rice-flavored stops. "The French Quarter Haunts" is a two-hour walking tour that begins in the courtyard of the New Orleans Pharmacy Museum on Chartres, winds around the Vieux Carré, with special attention to the exotic sites, and ends at the Gallier House Museum, which is the fictional home of the Vampire Lestat. Tours begin at 10 A.M. Tuesday through Saturday, and at 2 P.M. on Sunday; tickets are $20, $12 ages 6–12, and with the tickets comes discounted admission to Gallier House, though with a more staid tour guide.

The Garden District tour is subtitled "A Stroll with the Mayfair Witches," referring to the clan that populates the *Witching Hour/Lasher* series. Among the stops are the gardens of Rice's own home at Chestnut and First Street, which was described at length in *The Witching Hour,* and her more recent acquisition of the Claiborne Cottage on St. Charles, which is the setting for *Violin.* It winds up at Lafayette Cemetery, where Lasher's cast-iron tomb is, if you follow such things. Garden District walking tours are two-and-a-half hours, beginning at 10 A.M. and 1:30 P.M. daily; $20 adults, $12 children 6–12.

"Anne's Lost New Orleans" tour ranges farther, all the way to Destrehan Plantation, the oldest plantation in Louisiana, and the house used in filming *Interview with the Vampire.* Other stops include Bayou St. John, where an earlier settlement was attempted; the Pitot House, a stucco-covered brick house built in 1799 in the West Indies plantation style (there is a similar house in *The Witching Hour*); and the Esplanade Ridge. This is a nice alternative tour, even for Rice novices, as it includes several lovely houses not usually included in packaged tours. The three-hour tour is offered only Thursdays and Saturdays at 1 P.M.; $45 per adult, or $25 ages 6–12.

If you religiously tour beautiful churches or seek out stained glass, sign up for the "Inside the World of Anne Rice" tour. The partially restored St. Alphonsus Church in the Irish Channel—"the Mayfair family church," and Rice's family's church as well—has some of the most astonishing stained glass panels you will ever see, a contemporary but slightly smaller replica of the Black Madonna, and at least one of the graves of Pere Antoine. (Tourmaster Billy Murphy, Rice's cousin, has forgotten more about the church than most people have ever known, and is rumored to have been the model for Uncle Julian Mayfair.) The tour also stops by the Rice properties in the Garden District and includes lunch at Commander's Palace. It begins on Wednesdays and Fridays at 10 A.M.; adult admission costs $80 and $42 for children 6–12.

■ Swamp Tours ■

The bayous of Louisiana are among the nation's great natural treasures, filled with herons and ospreys, bald eagles, wild hogs, turtles, nutria and mink, deer, bear, and of course alligators, and several companies offer guided boat tours. Among the most popular is **Lil' Cajun Swamp Tours** (call (800) 725-3213 or (504) 689-3213), whose guide, Captain Cyrus Blanchard, is as authentic as his Cajun accent and intimately familiar with the twists and turns of his home. If you can take the tour from the boat launch in Crown Point, it's $16 for adults, $14 for seniors, and $12 for children, but it's probably better to arrange with Blanchard for transportation, even though it kicks in another $14 per adult.

Honey Island Swamp Tours of Slidell (641-1769) offers professional naturalists as guides through this rich area; $20 adults, $10 under age 12, but like Lil' Cajun, you'll pay extra for transportation from the city. **Gator Swamp Tours** also operate out of Slidell (call (800) 875-4287 or (504) 484-6100), and go through and even a bit beyond Honey Island Swamp with a short nature walk thrown in; $20 for adults, $10 for kids, and the usual extra charge for pick-up.

A little farther afield, **Half Pint's Swamp Adventures** are somewhat theatrical in delivery, but gorgeous in their presentation of the Atchafalaya Basin (and come to think of it, the swamp is pretty theatrical, too). They leave from Breaux Bridge; call (318) 228-2384 for information.

Other swamp tours are offered by Jean Lafitte Swamp Tours (592-0560) and Gray Line (569-1401). For fishing tours of the bayou, see page 176 in Part Nine.

If you prefer the walking tour approach to wildlife, the **Barataria Unit of the Jean Lafitte National Park** (689-2002) has trails and boardwalks through three different "ecosystem" routes: bottomland hardwoods, a cypress swamp, and a freshwater marsh. There are fine exhibits in the visitors center as well; take US 90 south and west of the city to state Highway 45/Barataria Boulevard and continue about seven miles.

Almost directly across Lake Pontchartrain from New Orleans, about 45 miles away on Highway 51, is the **Joyce Wildlife Management Area;** there a 1,000-foot boardwalk strikes deep into Manchac Swamp and offers great vistas for bird watching, nature photography, and sketching. It's open sunrise to sunset. Stop by the Tangipahoa Parish visitors center (542-7520) at the Exit 28 ramp from I-55 for a free map and birding and animal guide.

A little farther is the **Global Wildlife Center** (796-3585) on Highway 40, about 15 miles east of I-55, one of only three preserves for endangered and threatened species of birds and animals in the country. It covers 900 acres and is devoted to safe breeding and free-ranging of zebras, giraffes, llamas, gazelles, impalas, and even kangaroos. Staffers will drive you right up to the animals for a photo op, and since many of the animals have learned to beg for treats, you may get quite a close-up. (Admission to the park is free, though guided tours are not.) If you really want to feel "out there," arrange to spend the night at the Safari Lodge, which provides dinner and breakfast, wagon tours, photo safaris, and moose or giraffe "roundups." Just try *that* in the French Quarter.

■ River Cruises ■

Several boats cruise the nearby Mississippi River, some with meals, some with music, but to put it bluntly, a port is not the most scenic of sites. Huge tankers, rusting wharves, and old smokestacks are not exactly what Mark Twain saw when he fell in love with "Life on the Mississippi."

The steamboat *Cajun Queen* (call (800) 445-4109 or (504) 524-0814), for example, offers a 90-minute cruise leaving from in front of the IMAX/Aquarium complex to Chalmette Battlefield, site of the Battle of New Orleans. The boat churns past the old Jackson Barracks (where Robert E. Lee, U.S. Grant, and all did Army time); the Doullut Houses, twin glazed white brick "Victorian Steamboat Gothic" mansions; the Greek Revival–cum–French Colonial home of Rene Beauregard, planter son of the general; and Pitot House. But the Doullut and Pitot houses are surrounded by smokestacks in a way that is much more obvious from a distance. The Beauregard House is now the battlefield visitors' center, so you can see it up-close (and walk the battlefield itself) and visit the homes, too, if you like. (See "Zone 5" in "New Orleans Attractions" on page 252.) And once you're there, the boat turns around, the haphazard narration ends, and you go back past the old naval cruiser *Cabot,* onetime berth of President Bush, and the wharves to Poydras Street. At $14 (kids, $7), we really can't recommend it.

The sister-ship paddle wheeler *Creole Queen,* which offers a jazz dinner cruise at 7 P.M., covers the same territory but at least with a little more spunk, for $39 and $18). Call for daily times and availability, or go to the ticket booth by the berth in front of the IMAX.

The *Natchez* (call (800) 233-BOAT or (504) 586-8777), a three-deck stern-wheeler that docks behind the Jax Brewery, also offers daytime and jazz dinner cruises with optional buffet (adults about $18.75, not including dinner). Call for schedules.

The compromise cruises, especially for those with children (since a couple of hours can be a long time to have to sit still), are probably the *John James Audubon* Aquarium-Zoo cruise or the free Canal Street Ferry across to Algiers (and perhaps Blaine Kern's Mardi Gras World). The *John James Audubon* cruises the seven miles between the Aquarium of the Americas and the Audubon Zoo (that's upriver from the French Quarter, while Chalmette is downriver). It leaves the Aquarium at 10 A.M., noon, and 2 and 4 P.M., and comes back from the zoo at 11 A.M. and 1, 3, and 5 P.M. One-way tickets are $10.50 for adults and $5.25 for children 2–12; round-trip fares are $13.50 and $6.75, but there are various combination fares that save you more money. Boat/aquarium/zoo passes are $26.50 and $13.25, saving adults $5.50, and so on. In fact, if you buy tickets to all four related attractions, the zoo, the aquarium, IMAX, and a round-trip cruise ticket, you may save $8 or so. For more information call (800) 233-BOAT or (504) 586-8777.

The **Canal Street Ferry** just putters back and forth every day except Christmas to Algiers, touching the foot of Canal Street every half-hour from 6 A.M. to 11:30 P.M., with the last trip returning at midnight. (The ferry spends the night in Algiers, which you don't want to do.) If you want to visit Mardi Gras World, you can pick up a free shuttle bus at the Algiers dock.

There are also various overnight trips on the paddle wheelers *Delta Queen, Mississippi Queen,* and their younger sibling, the *American Queen.* The *Delta Queen* is a true wooden ship, while the two larger ones are steel-ribbed, but all have etched glass, bright trim, antebellum-costumed staff, and so on. These are three-day to fortnight-long trips, and obviously take you out of New Orleans, although if you want to see Natchez and Memphis, you might be interested (call (800) 543-1949 or (504) 586-0631).

Self-Guided Tours

■ Exploring New Orleans' Diversity ■

New Orleans has a pleasant case of multiple personality syndrome. Even in between the big festivals, you can indulge in self-designed tours spotlighting Mardi Gras, music or literature, Creole society, or history; or you can fill your days (and nights) dabbling in that suddenly pervasive supernatural stuff, hauntings and voodoo and vampire lore. If you're sticking to the family-rated attractions, such as those mentioned in "Planning Your Visit to New Orleans," you'll be pleased to see how many of them are indoors, so you won't have to worry about the rainy-day blahs, which always hit kids the hardest.

Of course, not all attractions are encased in cemetery stone or museum glass. One easy thing to do is to check through the local papers for announcements of the week's cultural offerings (this is true for music, garden, church, and home tours and special receptions and taste-of-the-town events, many of which may be held in historic sites or houses of special interest).

The *Times-Picayune* newspaper, like many in the country, puts together a special section on Fridays called "Lagniappe," which lists the best events—concerts, exhibits, tastings, art openings, even flea markets—of the weekend; this is also where you'll find cultural calendars. And remember that bookstores and coffeeshops are traditionally neighborhood "bulletin boards" for such events.

But for a few informal do-it-yourself tour ideas, read on.

Mardi Gras and Music

Hangover-wary veterans of Carnival celebrations, or those who prefer the more sophisticated Mardi Gras parades of earlier decades, can get their fill of the frills by visiting the **Old U.S. Mint,** the free **Germaine Cazenave Wells Mardi Gras Museum** at Arnaud's Restaurant, both in the French Quarter; **Blaine Kern's Mardi Gras World** across the river, where the floats are made; and perhaps the smaller **Mardi Gras Museum** in Rivertown. There are also a few Mardi Gras outfits at the **House of Broel** on St. Charles in the Garden District.

You could also browse through mask and costume shops all over town, notably **MGM Costume Rentals** (1617 Chartres Street; 581-3999), which has thousands of outfits from the studio's old storerooms; the **Mardi Gras Center** (831 Chartres; 524-4384); or the **Little Shop of Fantasy** (523 Dumaine Street; 529-4243).

If you're interested in the history of jazz, surprisingly, there isn't as much as you might expect. Start by calling **Cradle of Jazz** tours to make an appointment with one of their guys on the beat (282-3583). The first museum stop for you is also the **U.S. Mint,** which has a rare collection of early instruments; then browse the bins at area record stores (see "Shopping in New Orleans"). There is no trace of the famed Storyville red-light district, where jazz is generally said to have been born, although there is a re-creation and figures of some famous musicians in the **Musée Conti Wax Museum. Congo Square** in Armstrong Park still hosts some concerts, but it is not a neighborhood to visit without knowledgeable company. At night, however, be sure to check out **Preservation Hall,** a sort of living history music museum.

Cruise Bourbon Street and you can still find a little Dixieland struggling to be heard through the rock and roll din: Try the **Famous Door** at Bourbon and Conti Streets, **Maxwell's Cabaret** on Toulouse between Chartres and Royal, the **Mystick Den** in the Royal Sonesta Hotel, or **Lafitte's Blacksmith Shop. Donna's Bar & Grill** on North Rampart presents only brass bands, but good ones. Sunday jazz brunches are popular all over town (the **Court of Two Sisters** offers a jazz buffet for lunch every day). If you're more into zydeco or Cajun or gumbo music, make sure to check the schedules at the legendary **Tipitina's** on Tchoupitoulas Street and the **House of Blues** on Decatur or go take a free Cajun dance lesson at happy hour at **Patout's** bar on Bourbon Street. For more on jazz and music clubs, see the profiles in the nightlife section.

Despite the city's history, literary tours are a little harder self-directed, primarily because only a few of the former writers' haunts are identifiable from the street (but we've pointed some out in the walking tours). Your best bet is to sign up for a literary and gleefully gossipy outing from **Heritage Tours,** designed by University of New Orleans professor Kenneth Holditch (by appointment; 949-9805), or check into special-topic walks by local organizations. The **Gay Heritage** folks (945-6789) have been known to dish a pretty funny one.

Anyone interested in black Southern culture should take the subway out to **Tulane University's Amisted Research Center,** the world's largest collection of arts and letters on race history, both in this country and elsewhere. More contemporary black art is the specialty of **La Belle Galerie,** the black art collection at 309 Chartres (529-3080).

History and Culture

American history buffs have an easy time setting their agenda: The **Cabildo** and **Presbytere** complex on Jackson Square; the **Historic New Orleans Collection;** the **Confederate Museum, Jackson Barracks military museum,** and **Chalmette Battlefield.**

As for historic houses, there are a number to choose from that are maintained as museums and decorated with original or period furnishings. For a quick-time dance through New Orleans history, compare the 1792 **Merieult House** of the New Orleans Historic Collection (a must-see); the West Indies plantation-style **Pitot House,** circa 1800; the **Hermann-Grima House,** which shows the influence of early nineteenth-century American society on traditionally Creole architecture; the **Beauregard-Keyes House,** an 1826 "raised cottage" that in its time sheltered both Gen. P.T.G. Beauregard and novelist Frances Parkinson Keyes; and the 1857 **Gallier House Museum,** home of one of the city's premier architects, another best bet. There is also the **1850 House,** a restored middle-class residence in the Pontalba Apartments on Jackson Square, and **Longue Vue Gardens,** though the house itself is more modern. All these sites are profiled in other chapters, along with a few that are open for viewing only by appointment. And throughout the book, certain buildings of interest are cited as you may come upon them.

As famous as the Garden District is, few buildings there are actually open to the public—but then, the exteriors are what really distinguish them. We have put together a limited walking tour later in the chapter, and a bit of streetcar touring.

If you have time, you should take an excursion to the great plantations west of town, but that requires some extra planning, especially if you want to spend the night in the country, or need professional guidance. See the section on plantation tours below. Similarly, if you're captivated by Cajun culture, you'll want to head a few hours west to Lafayette and its environs, but that almost certainly requires two days. See "Cajun Country Festivals."

Don't overlook the **New Orleans Museum of Art** in City Park. On the off chance that you happen to be a particular fan of the Impressionist painter Degas, note that the **Edgar Degas House** at 2306 Esplanade Avenue, where he may have finished as many as 17 works, has recently been restored as a bed-and-breakfast, but visitors are welcome to look around (821-5009 or e-mail, www.degashouse.com). In fact, there are several houses in town with Degas connections: The building that now houses Brennan's Restaurant was originally built for his maternal grandfather, José Faurie; the Musson House at 1331 Third Street in the Garden District was built for his aunt's husband; the Pitot House once belonged to his great-grandmother; and some sources claim the Waldhorn Galleries building on Royal Street was built for his great-grandfather. There's a tour in itself.

The Great Hereafter

If you love old churches, make sure to see **St. Louis Cathedral** in Jackson Square, **St. Patrick's** in the Warehouse/Arts District, and the remarkable but only partly restored **St. Adolphus** in the Irish Channel; for quirkier saints, visit **Our Lady of Guadalupe** in the Central Business District and the **Chapel of St. Roch's** east of the French Quarter. If you're particularly interested in stained glass, which is the real treasure at St. Adolphus, be sure to contact the Preservation Resource Center (604 Julia Street; 581-7032) to see when their next "Stained Glass in Sacred Places" tour is scheduled. Otherwise, sign up for one of the Anne Rice tours (see page 196 under "Walking on the Dark Side"). Also, see the Garden District walking tour for directions to the Tiffany Glass at Tulane University.

If, on the other hand, it's cemeteries you love, you can either experience them straight or gussied up with vampire and voodoo lore. You can visit several of the "cities of the dead," the most famous being **St. Louis Cemetery No. 1** (where the tomb of the city's famous voodoo madam Marie Laveau still gets nightly petitions) and **Lafayette Cemetery** in the Garden District (where Anne Rice's creation Lasher is "buried" in a cast-iron tomb) by yourself, but as mentioned above, you should never go after dark, and preferably go in a group even during the day. Your best bet is to drive out to **Lake Lawn Metairie Cemetery,** which has all the extravagant tombs you could want to see. You can tour **Gallier House,** but the guides there probably won't mention the sometimes residence there of the Vampire Lestat.

If voodoo queens and vampire lovers are your thing, you can, uh, drink your fill. There are now probably as many "haunted," "voodoo," or "magic" tours of New Orleans as general history ones, though not all are particularly serious; see "Walking on the Dark Side" for more information. You can even participate in an expedition to "record" (generally, via your own imagination, flashlights, thermometers, and a compass) paranormal activity in houses and hotels where hauntings or violent events are said to have occurred. For that, contact the **Society for Paranormal Research** and ask about the Hauntings Today investigations and ghost expeditions (635 Toulouse Street; 522-0045). It was good enough for ABC, and it might be just the "channeling" you're looking for, too.

■ **Neighborhood Walking Tours** ■

Okay, this is the fun part, at least as far as we're concerned—putting the "tour" back in the "tourist," so to speak. We've designed three routes for you, one laying the French Quarter open, one giving the flavor of the Garden District, and a third to help orient you to the newer pleasures of the Warehouse Arts/District and a bit of the Central Business District (CBD) at the same time.

How long they will take you depends on your pace and whether you stick to the sidewalk; you can, of course, stop at any museum or site that interests you. But none is either exhausting or exhaustive (to be frank, we think most walking tours tell you more than you need or want to know). These are just pleasant, informative, and intriguing strolls—a little history, a bit of legend, some literary notes, architectural details, and anecdotes. The French Quarter walk is the longest, of course, but then there are the greatest number of opportunities to sit, get something to eat or drink (remember, alcohol dehydrates), or duck into a store. The Garden District tour is the shortest, but it gives onto several other options, including Audubon Park, the zoo, the Riverbend neighborhood, etc.

The Vieux Carré/French Quarter (Zone 1)

It's nicer to think of the Quarter as the "old block" because there are so many influences at play on the tour: Spanish, German, American, and African-Caribbean as well as French. Our route is divided into two double-loop halves, somewhat as though a huge E-3 monogram had been printed over the map with the two middle strokes meeting in front of St. Louis Cathedral. The longer part comes first, so that you can stop midway if you like and have an easier return. (This is also designed to help you get the layout of the Quarter in your head and not worry about going too far astray, because the loops go out and come back within eyeshot of the cathedral spire.)

The tour begins in the heart of **Jackson Square,** with a mental salute to the statue of Gen. Andrew Jackson. As pointed out in the "Too-Brief History," this was originally called Place d'Armes by the French, re-accented to Plaza de Armas by the Spanish, and altered permanently after the glorious victory of 1815. It was also the "inspiration," or in-spite-ation, for Lafayette Square in the American sector.

Straight before you is **St. Louis Cathedral,** the oldest cathedral in the United States (and even at that, the third church to occupy that space). The flagstone piazza just outside the church doors is officially called Place Jean Paul Deux, to commemorate the 1987 visit of Pope John Paul II.

To the left of the cathedral is the **Cabildo,** so named because during the Spanish administration, the governing council, or Cabildo, met here. To the left of that is the **Arsenal,** built in 1803 on the site of what had been a Spanish prison, and now, like the Cabildo, it is part of the Louisiana State Museum complex.

Walk around the corner of the Arsenal onto St. Peter, and then turn right into the short **Cabildo Alley** and left again into **Pirates Alley.** This is one of several places in which Jackson and Jean Lafitte are frequently said to have plotted strategy for the Battle of New Orleans, but unfortunately, the alley wasn't cut through until 1831. Its real name is Ruelle d'Orleans, Sud—Little Orleans Way, South. However, there are two spots of interest here: **Faulkner House Books,** at 624 Pirates Alley, is not only a fine Southern literature bookstore but also the house where Faulkner lived while working on his first novel. And it borders **St. Anthony's Garden,** officially named the Cathedral Garden but long considered a memorial to the Capuchin Father Antonio de Sedella, the beloved Pere Antoine, who arrived in 1779 and served the colony for nearly a half-century. (The good father's garden was also, oddly, the most popular dueling ground for young aristocrats.) The monument in the middle of the garden was erected by the government of Napoleon III to honor 30 French marines who died serving as volunteer nurses during one of the great yellow fever epidemics.

Pirates Alley ends at Royal Street; turn left onto Royal and begin enjoying the old buildings around you. Walk a block and cross St. Peter Street. In the next block, on your right at 627 Royal Street, is the **Old Town Praline Shop,** on the site of an apartment that once was home to nineteenth-century French opera prodigy Adelina Patti and that still sweetly opens its lovely old courtyard to the public. Just beyond that at 613 Royal is the **Court of Two Sisters,** which a century ago was the shop of Emma and Bertha Camors and is now a restaurant and jazz bar with its own fine courtyard and informal aviary.

At the next intersection, turn right onto Toulouse Street. On the left at 710 Toulouse, in what is now the Coghlan Gallery, is the house known as the **Court of Two Lions,** named for the two royal beasts that mount the gate pillars. It was bought in 1819 by Vincent Nolte, whose autobiography inspired the huge, and at one point hugely popular, novel-turned-movie *Anthony Adverse.* Across the street, in a literary small-world coincidence, is the **Hotel Maison de Ville,** which incorporates restored slave quarters including the room, No. 9, in which Tennessee Williams lived and wrote.

At the next corner, turn left onto Bourbon Street (you can't miss it!), and after one block turn right again onto St. Louis Street. Halfway up on the left at 820 St. Louis is the **Hermann-Grima Historic House,** one of the finest examples of early American architectural shifts and well worth coming back to tour.

At the corner of Dauphine Street, look catty-corner across to 509 Dauphine and the **Audubon Cottages,** also run by the Hotel Maison de Ville; John James Audubon lived in No. 1 while writing and painting his 1821 masterpiece, *Birds of North America*. In the next block of Dauphine Street (turn left) are some buildings with less illuminated histories: At 415 Dauphine is the Dauphine Orleans, whose lounge, **May Bailey's Place,** used to be a bordello (and they can prove it). And at the corner of Conti Street is the **Déjà Vu** bar, said to be haunted and more reliably said to have housed an 1880s opium den.

At the corner of Conti look right; halfway up the block is the Musée Conti Wax Museum, but it's not worth staring at unless you're ready to visit it. If not, keep strolling along Dauphine to Bienville Street and turn left, back toward Bourbon Street. Halfway down on the left is the **Arnaud's** complex, which includes not only the restored old mansion of a restaurant (potted palms and ceiling fans, leaded glass, and mosaic tile) and a fine old-fashioned bar, but the **Germaine Wells Mardi Gras Museum,** a free and fine collection of Carnival costumes.

When you get to Bourbon Street, look diagonally across the intersection to the **Old Absinthe House** on the corner. This 1805 house (it looks every day of it, and proud of it, too) is another of the places that Jackson and Lafitte are supposed to have met. Stroll another block back to Royal Street and turn left.

Now, remember that Royal Street was once the financial center of town. On the right at 334 Royal Street is the **French Quarter Police Station,** housed in the 1826 Bank of Louisiana (it has also served as the state capitol, among other things). On the left at 343 Royal Street is the **Waldhorn Company** antique store, a huge, balconied, and wrought iron–decorated three-story Spanish Colonial edifice built around 1800 as the Bank of the United States. And in the next block, just past Conti Street, is **Manheim Galleries,** designed in 1820 by U.S. Capitol architect Benjamin Latrobe as the Louisiana State Bank (look for the "LB" entwined in the forged ironwork on the balcony).

Across the street at 417 Royal is the celebrated **Brennan's Restaurant,** known in historical circles as Casa Faurie because it was supposedly built around the turn of the nineteenth century for Edgar Degas' Spanish grandfather José Faurie. A few years later it was sold and turned into yet another bank office, the Banque de la Louisiane, and gained its own wrought-iron monogram in the balcony, a "BL." A few years after that it was sold back as the private residence of the socially prominent Martin Gordon—Andrew

Jackson danced here several times when he returned to the city in 1828—but when Gordon went bankrupt, it was sold again, at auction, to Judge Alonzo Morphy (perhaps not coincidentally, he was the son-in-law of the auctioneer). Morphy is interesting for two reasons: In the 1850s, his son Paul became the world chess champion at 21, and before buying the house at 417, he lived in what is now the Beauregard-Keyes House (see below).

At **437 Royal,** in what is now the Cohen rare coins gallery, was the Masonic Lodge where pharmacist Antoine Peychard served his fellow Masons his special after-dinner drink, poured out into little egg cups. The word for the cups was "coquetier," which some people believe became "cocktail," and Peychard himself became immortalized as a brand of bitters. (His tonic included absinthe and Sazerac-de-Forge cognac, the original Sazerac cocktail.)

The huge white building that takes up the whole **400 block of Royal** on your right is a hotly debated millstone that was built just after the turn of the century as the civil courts building. Later it housed the Louisiana Department of Wildlife and Fisheries and its wildlife museum; the U.S. Circuit Court of Appeals for the Fifth Judicial District; and was most recently (having been wrested back from the feds by the state) expensively renovated for the Louisiana Supreme Court. However, the state has had second, or third, thoughts, and at press time, nobody was sure what would happen to the building.

Cross St. Louis Street to the TV station building at **520 Royal** and walk through to the fine four-sided courtyard; take note of the "S" worked into the fan-shaped ironwork at the left corner of the third-floor balcony. In the early nineteenth century, this was built for wine merchant and furniture maker Francois Seignouret, who always used to carve that same initial into his furniture. The straightforward Spanish building at **536 Royal** was constructed just after the second great fire, in 1794, and the three-story Maison LeMonnier at **640 Royal,** built in 1811, was considered the city's first "skyscraper." (The fourth story was added in 1876.) Note the initials "YLM," for Dr. Yves LeMonnier, in the wrought iron of the balcony.

Across the street at 533 Royal is the **Historic New Orleans Collection** and the **Merieult House.** The Collection, which faces onto Royal, often has fine historical exhibits (a small but first-class assortment of Mardi Gras costumes and early propaganda posters promising streets of gold to would-be settlers) and is open and free. It also houses the finest research archives in the city, open to scholars only. Behind it is the late-eighteenth-century Merieult House, one of only two important structures to survive the great fire of 1794, and a nineteenth-century cottage, which are now open for tours with paid admission. Madame Merieult, née Catherine McNamara, had a head of Irish copper that made her the toast of New Orleans. And when she and her husband visited Paris, Napoleon offered her her own castle in return for parting with her hair, which he wanted to make into a wig to woo the Sultan of Turkey (who himself wanted to woo a reluctant harem lady with the bright beauty) into an alliance. The high-spirited Merieult refused, however.

Walk back along Royal Street and stop at the corner of St. Peter Street. The **Royal Cafe** building, one of the most popular postcard and photograph subjects in town, is sometimes called the LaBranche House, and its oak-and-acorn-pattern wrought-iron balconies are in very fine condition. Actually, there are 11 LaBranche row houses altogether, built in the 1830s by a sugar planter, that run from the corner of Royal around the block of St. Peter toward Pirates Alley.

Turn right down St. Peter Street. On the right, at the corner of Chartres Street, is **Le Petit Théâtre du Vieux Carré,** home to the country's oldest continuously operating community theater (dating from a 1916 production in the Pontalba Apartments). The whole building is a sort of theatrical set: Built in 1922, it's a faithful reproduction of the eighteenth-century residence of Joseph Xavier de Pontalba, last Spanish governor of New Orleans. The chandeliers and the courtyard fountain are of more recent origin; the wrought-iron balcony rail inside the theater is real, though, made in 1796. Le Petit Théâtre is believed to be haunted by a *Phantom*-like, well, phantom, in the balcony, who has been "photographed"; the Society for Paranormal Research has recorded him several times.

Glance across the corner at the back of the Arsenal, and you will see that we have looped back toward Jackson Square for the first time. Now turn your back again and head out along Chartres Street, which is full of strange and wonderful shops and old facades. After you cross Toulouse, look left; at 514 Toulouse is the **New Orleans Pharmacy Museum,** housed in the 1816 shop (believed to have been designed by architect J.N.B. DePouilly) of apothecary Louis Defilho, Jr. A little beyond, at the corner of Chartres and St. Louis Streets is the **Napoleon House,** which may look as though the entire plaster interior were about to collapse but which has probably seen more hard living than even its French Quarter peers and remains a favorite of locals despite the tourists. It owes its name to the loyal sentiments of pirate Jean Lafitte (yes, again), New Orleans mayor Nicholas Girod, and various other Creole leaders who fixed up the 1797 house and offered it to the deposed emperor, who was then languishing on the island of St. Helena. A plot was under way to rescue him when he died in 1821. (The third-floor "Appartement de l'Empereur" has been restored in real style, but can only be rented for private functions.)

If you're a fan of Paul Prudhomme, you can walk one more block and sniff the spicy air outside **K-Paul's Louisiana Kitchen** at 416 Chartres; then turn left at Conti Street and head toward Decatur Street. Turn left again onto Decatur and the "new New Orleans," the big-name franchise promenade, stretches out before you. As you head back toward Jackson Square, you pass the Hard Rock Cafe opposite St. Louis Street, the Crescent City Brewhouse, the Millhouse/Jax Brewery complex with its Planet Hollywood, Hooters, the only Fashion Cafe outside New York City, and so on. By the time you make it to the square, and see those silly mules in their hats and ribbons, you'll be delighted to look right and mount the steps up to **Washington Artillery Park** and the **Moonwalk** overlooking the river.

Now settle yourself in for a cup of reviving coffee at the **Café du Monde,** tour the caricaturists or just relax in Jackson Park. This is the end of Loop 2, and intermission time for the tour.

Here beginneth Loop 3, as they used to say; the cross-hatch of the figure 8, or however you want to think of it. Walk up St. Ann Street from Decatur toward Chartres, looking up at the **Pontalba Apartments.** Halfway up the block at 525 St. Ann is the **1850 House,** a restored three-story apartment showing how a middle-class Creole family lived at the time the Baroness Micaela Almonester Pontalba built her still-sought-after apartments. This is another part of the Louisiana State Museum, and tickets can be bought here for all LSM buildings. Right next to it at 529 St. Ann is a **Louisiana visitors center,** with scores of brochures, maps, and coupons. Intriguingly, the state of Louisiana owns the block of apartments along St. Ann; the city of New Orleans owns the opposite block along St. Peter, including No. 540, where in the mid-1920s, Sherwood Anderson wrote *Dark Laughter.*

At the corner of St. Ann and Chartres is the **Presbytere,** the fourth Louisiana State Museum property right on Jackson Square, and the most conventional of the buildings in that it hosts both permanent and rotating exhibits about New Orleans and Louisiana history, maritime culture, society, portraiture, and decorative arts. The first building there was a small Capuchin monastery, but the building was destroyed by the fire of 1788 and, partly rebuilt, by the fire of '94. It was actually never completed until 1913 and never actually served as the parish residence it was named for. Its most famous possession is Napoleon's death mask.

Walk past the door of the Presbytere and turn right up the 1830s flagstone walkway called **Pere Antoine's Alley,** which borders St. Anthony's garden on the other side. (Like Pirates Alley, its official name is more pedestrian: Ruelle d'Orleans, Nord.) Jog left onto Royal and then right onto Orleans Street to the Bourbon Orleans Hotel on your right. The **Orleans Ballroom,** which has now been restored within the hotel complex, was built by entrepreneur John Davis in 1817 to house theatrical productions and opera—and, although some of the official walking tours don't mention it, it was also the site of the famous Quadroon Balls, where Creole aristocrats formally courted mixed-race beauties for their concubines (see "A Too-Short History of a Fascinating Place"). It apparently served, as did many public buildings, as a hospital during the Civil War, and in 1881 was acquired by an order of black nuns to serve as an orphanage and school. The order sold the building about 30 years ago to the hotel, and there have been rumored ghost sightings, including one of a Confederate soldier and another of a young woman, about the building.

Turn right at Bourbon Street and there on the corner is **Marie Laveau's House of Voodoo,** one of the more popular spots for tarot readings, charms, and souvenirs. Keep strolling past St. Ann and Dumaine Streets to St. Philip; on the left at 941 Bourbon is **Lafitte's Blacksmith Shop,** yet another probably apocryphal site but much loved. The story is that the Lafitte brothers, Jean and Pierre, used the blacksmith shop as a front for their smuggling network, but although there are deeds of ownership on the property dating to the early 1770s, none indicates a smithy. Still, it's architecturally interesting—one of the last bits of post and brick construction, which means that the bricks were set inside a wooden frame because the local clay was so soft—and is still a great candlelight jazz bar that draws locals even more than tourists. (It's such an old reliable that a few years ago, three sheriff's deputies were moonlighting behind the bar when a fugitive came in for a drink; they arrested him on the spot.) It was also the favorite watering hole of Tennessee Williams.

Continue down Bourbon two more blocks to Gov. Nicholls Street and turn right. Glance across to 721 Gov. Nicholls Street and the **Thierry House,** built around 1814 to a design proffered by Benjamin Latrobe when he was only 19 years old. Its neoclassical Greek style inspired the whole Greek Revival that so characterized Creole architecture.

At the end of the block turn the corner right again onto Royal. On the left corner at 1140 Royal is what is still known as the **LaLaurie House,** and to tour guides as *the* Haunted House. In 1834, it was the home of Delphine LaLaurie, a sort of Creole Elizabeth Bathory, who hosted many brilliant and elaborate soirées there, which despite their popularity fueled gossip about the pitiable appearance of many of her servants. Several of these slaves committed suicide, or so LaLaurie said. One neighbor reported that LaLaurie had savagely beaten a young black girl, who shortly thereafter "fell" from the roof to her death, but a court merely fined her. But on April 10, 1834, when the house caught fire, neighbors hearing the screams of slaves broke in to find them chained in a secret garret, starving and bearing the marks of torture. Rumors spread that Madame LaLaurie herself might have set the fire. The house was stormed, and she and her family barely escaped, making their way to Europe. She never returned in life, although the house was rebuilt, but her body was smuggled back to New Orleans and secretly buried. Some people swear they have heard the shrieking of slaves and the snapping of whips at night, and it is a very popular late-night tourist stop. Madame LaLaurie is so famous, in fact, that she is memorialized at the Musée Conti Wax Museum.

The neighboring buildings have a much finer reputation, fortunately. Just alongside at 1132 Royal Street is the **Gallier House Museum,** built in 1857 by James Gallier, Jr., son of the architect of the city hall and a prominent architect himself. He designed the building itself, with many ingenious and then-rare fixtures. The house is administered as a museum by Tulane University.

Continue on Royal past St. Philip to 915 Royal, where the wrought-iron fence that gives the **Cornstalk Hotel** its name. It was cast in the 1830s in Philadelphia for Dr. Joseph Biamenti as a present for his homesick Midwesterner wife, and its twin can be seen in the Garden District in front of the house at 1448 Fourth Street.

Across the street at **900, 906,** and **910 Royal** are the three Miltenberger houses, built in 1838 and now housing art galleries. The granddaughter of one Miltenberger was Alice Heine, the Barbara Hutton or Pamela Harriman of her day; she married first the Duc de Richelieu and then moved on to Prince Louis of Monaco.

Turn right onto Dumaine and duck up to the **New Orleans Historic Voodoo Museum** at 724 Dumaine, which is part museum (some pretty grisly), part souvenir shop/fortune telling temple, and part tour central. Then double back down a block to 632 Dumaine and **Madame John's Legacy,** which is put forth by many historians as the oldest existing building in the lower Mississippi River valley. It was originally built between 1724 and 1726, but was either repaired or entirely rebuilt to the same design (hence the debate) after the Good Friday fire of 1788. In either case, it is a fine example of French Colonial architecture of the style called a "raised cottage," with a steeply pitched room and dormers, living quarters high above flood level, and storage below (also brick and post). The name comes from "Tite Poulette," a short story by the nineteenth-century writer George Washington Cable, about a beautiful quadroon whose white lover wills her the house on his deathbed. It is now part of the state museum complex.

At the corner of Chartres glance right—there it is, Jackson Square— and then turn left onto Chartres for the final loop. At Ursuline Street, turn the corner just long enough to peek at the Hotel Villa Convent, 616 Ursuline Street. It's a respectable guest house now, but legend points to it as the famous **House of the Rising Sun** bordello. Now go back down Ursuline to Chartres and turn left. Just around the corner at 1113 Chartres is the **Beauregard-Keyes House,** built by wealthy auctioneer Joseph Le Carpentier and his son-in-law Judge Alonzo Morphy (see Brennan's, above). In its time it was home to Confederate hero Gen. P.G.T. Beauregard and novelist Frances Parkinson Keyes. Keyes wrote two novels about previous occupants while living here (perhaps she was haunted); the better-known is about Beauregard, *Madame Castel's Lodger,* and the one about Paul Morphy is titled simply, *The Chess Player.*

Across the street on the corner of Ursuline and Chartres is the **Old Ursuline Convent,** the strongest candidate for oldest building in Louisiana. Designed in 1745 and completed in 1752, it is the only structure that we know for sure survived the great fires at the end of the eighteenth century. (The Sisters of St. Ursula themselves arrived in 1727, and lived in the meantime in a building at Bienville and Chartres.) It was not only the first nunnery in the state, it was the first orphanage, the premier school for Creole children, and the first school for black and Indian children as well. And, between 1831 and 1834, it housed the state legislature—the ultimate proof of charity.

Continue down Ursuline to Decatur and turn right, back toward Jackson Square. The **French Market** runs along your left, with the tracks of the Riverfront Streetcar beyond it; shops and restaurants line Decatur on both sides. At St. Philip Street look left and locate the **National Park Service** office peeking through from North Peters; then keep on back to the Café du Monde or stop at any of the little cafes along the way. And you're back at ground zero.

The Garden District (Zone 3)

Although some guidebooks list scores of homes in the Garden District as historically or architecturally important, they are mainly so to real devotees, especially as virtually all are private residences and can only be glimpsed from the outside. You may well see all you want to see by just staying on the St. Charles Avenue Streetcar on the way to Audubon Park. So we have designed only a fairly limited walk-through, one that will give you the flavor of the district and several of the celebrity highlights. If you go in the later morning, you may find a lunch stop at the famous Commander's Palace convenient. If you are enjoying the stroll, you can just keep wandering and admiring the facades. (If the present owners are working in the yard, you might stop and ask if they know much about the history of their homes;

most of them are quite knowledgeable.) If you are seriously interested, contact the New Orleans Visitors Bureau about the Spring Fiesta, which stars the Friday after Easter and includes many garden and house tours.

The Garden District is usually said to be bounded by St. Charles Avenue and Magazine Street (on the north and south sides, more or less) and Jackson and Louisiana Avenues on the east and west. But neighboring streets continue to claim relationship, and there is now what is sometimes called a "Lower Garden District"—lower as in Downtown—to the east back toward Lee Circle. Its look is so different from the French Quarter that it almost seems like another country, and in fact it almost was. This was the "American Quarter," the area where the rich, the *nouveau riche,* and the well-connected from all over the United States built extravagant mansions to show up their new fellow citizens of the Creole aristocracy.

We suggest you start by taking the St. Charles Streetcar to Jackson Street. Start off down Jackson in the same direction to 2220 St. Charles and the **House of Broel,** which is both a dollhouse museum and a full-sized one, as well as a bridal and haute couture salon. It was originally built as a two-story pied-à-terre for a planter and his family, but in the 1890s, tobacco tycoon Simon Hernsheim had the whole building lifted and added a new Victorian first floor. It is open for tours, if you want to stop or circle back (522-2220).

Across the street at the end of the block, on the corner of Philip Street at **2265 St. Charles,** is a house that was designed by James Gallier, Jr., for Lavinia Dabney in the late 1850s, about the time his own home in the Vieux Carré (see above) was completed. Gallier designed it as Greek Revival; the Ionic columns and side galleries were added later. Across Philip at **2336 St. Charles** is, for comparison, a Greek Revival raised cottage designed by his father, James Gallier, Sr., at just about the same time.

At the corner of First Street turn left, walk a block to Prytania, and turn the corner. At 2343 Prytania is the Second Empire–style **Louise S. McGehee School,** also known as the Bradish Johnson House after the wealthy sugar trader for whom it was built, for a then-astonishing $100,000, in 1872, probably by New Orleans–born, Paris-trained architect James Freret. It has been a prestigious girls' school since 1929; the carriage house is the gymnasium, and the stables have been turned into a cafeteria. According to legend, none of the girls, or anyone else, has been born, died, or married within its walls.

Across the street from the school at **2340 Prytania** is what sometimes is called Toby's Corner, built sometime before 1838 for Philadelphian Thomas Toby, and believed to be the oldest house in the Garden District. It is put in the shade in both senses, however, by the huge Spanish moss–draped live oak on the grounds, which is several hundred years old.

Continue down First Street, noting the ornate cast iron in front of the circa 1869 Italianate home at **1331 First Street** and the matching galleries at the remarkably similar house at **1315 First Street;** both were designed by Irish immigrant Samuel Jamison in 1869.

Just past Chestnut Street, on the corner at **1239 First Street,** is the 1857 mansion once known as the Rose-Brevard House—it was built for merchant Albert Brevard, and its elaborate ironwork has a rose pattern—but now far more famous as the residence of novelist Anne Rice and the setting of the best-selling book *The Witching Hour.* The original structure cost only $13,000 (the hexagonal wing was added a few years later); restoring the gates would cost that now.

Across the street at **1236 First Street** is a gorgeous Greek Revival mansion built as a wedding gift in 1847. Walk another block to Camp Street and look across the corner to the house at **1134 First Street,** built about 1850 for Judge Jacob Payne. It is also the home where onetime U.S. senator and former president of the Confederate States of America Jefferson Davis died in 1889.

Turn right onto Camp Street and walk to Third Street, turning right again at the corner. The arched and eaved mansion at **1213 Third Street** was built during the Reconstruction for Irish carpetbagger Archibald Montgomery, president of the Crescent City Railroad. Continue on to the Italianate home at **1331 Third Street,** designed in 1853 by James Gallier, Sr., for New Orleans postmaster Michel Musson, who married Edgar Degas' aunt. (The elaborate cast-iron galleries were added later.)

Across Coliseum at **1415 Third Street** is the Robinson House, one of the Garden District's largest and most attractive homes: Its curving front seems especially spacious because both stories are the same height, with identical iron balconies and columns. It was built just before the Civil War by architect Henry Howard for Virginia tobacco trader Walter Robinson, and is thought to have been one of the first homes in New Orleans to have indoor plumbing.

Turn left onto Coliseum Street and walk two blocks to Washington Street. On the corner is **Commander's Palace,** where you can stop for lunch or just cast an admiring glance at the courtyard (or finish the tour and circle back around). This stately old-liner of the Brennan's restaurant fleet has been a restaurant for well over a century, and owes its name not to a naval officer but to owner Emile Commander. It's terribly respectable now —it claims to be the birthplace of oysters Rockefeller, and nobody much has contested it—but back during Prohibition, the second story was a high-stakes, high-society bordello.

Behind the high brick walls of Washington and Coliseum is, obviously,

Lafayette Cemetery, named for the American sector it served, then the City of Lafayette. Laid out in 1833, it was designed for the well-to-do, and its wide aisles were intended to carry extravagant funeral processions to elaborate tombs. But it was nearly filled within 20 years by victims of repeated epidemics. It has many fine examples of the above-ground tombs that are New Orleans trademarks, including the cast-iron tomb Anne Rice uses for the elemental spirit Lasher (the cemetery itself served as a setting for scenes from the movie version of *Interview with the Vampire*), the Jefferson Fire Company No. 22 tomb with its bas-relief firetruck, and other monuments that might look familiar to fans of the seminal film, *Easy Rider*. (Eternal rest or eternal bliss? In 1980, a Neiman Marcus executive and his bride were married here, on Friday the 13th of June, wearing full black.) Unfortunately, even this cemetery is no longer safe to wander without company, and in any case the gate may be locked. However, if you are waiting at the Washington Street gate at 10:30 A.M. Monday, Wednesday, or Friday, you can probably hook onto the Save Our Cemeteries tour or contact one of the commercial tour groups mentioned above in "Walking on the Dark Side."

Walk along the cemetery wall to Prytania and turn back to the right. (Actually, if you're a literary type, turn left and go to **2900 Prytania,** at Sixth Street; that boardinghouse was where Jazz Age icon F. Scott Fitzgerald lived in 1919–1920.) Glance down Fourth Street to **No. 1448** if you want to see the wrought-iron twin to the fence at the Cornstalk Hotel in the French Quarter. Continue on to **2605 Prytania** at the corner of Third Street: The guest house of this pointy-arched Gothic Revival house, designed by the senior Gallier in 1849, is a perfect miniature of the main house.

Just across Third Street at **2521 Prytania** is the former Redemptorist Fathers chapel, Our Lady of Perpetual Help—"former" because the Italianate home, built in 1857 for a coffee merchant, had fallen into disrepair and has now been purchased, like several other dilapidated historic buildings in the District, by Anne Rice. Across from that at **2520 Prytania** is the Gilmour-Parker home, a Palladium-fronted house built in 1853 for an English cotton trader named Gilmour and later sold to John Parker, father of a future governor. (The building around the corner at **1417 Third Street** used to be its carriage house, but has been considerably expanded.)

The Queen Anne–Greek Revival–style hybrid **Women's Opera Guild House,** at the far end of the block at 2504 Prytania Street, was designed by William Freret (father of James) in 1858, except for the octagonal turret, which was added toward the end of the century and holds a music room and bedrooms. It was bequeathed to the Opera Guild by its last inhabitant, Nettie Seebold, and its collection of eighteenth- and nineteenth-century antiques, along with some Guild mementos, can only be viewed Mondays from 1 to 4 P.M. (a small donation is requested).

Turn left onto Second Street, walk back to St. Charles, and turn left again. At 2524 St. Charles, on the corner of Third Street, is what is known both as the Dameron House and more romantically—and thanks to the publication of Anne Rice's *Violin,* far more widely—known as the **Claiborne Cottage.** That story has it that the Greek Revival raised cottage was the home of Bernard Xavier Phillipe de Marigny de Mandeville, son of one of the wealthiest and more influential Creoles of old New Orleans society, and his wife Louise Claiborne, daughter of the diplomat who would become the first American governor of Louisiana. Their match marked the first great union of the two societies of New Orleans, but Marigny, who had inherited so much land and money, gambled so obsessively that he is said to have lost a million dollars—not in modern money, but a million dollars *then*—by the time he was 20. In fact, it may have been Marigny who brought back dicing from England: It became known to the Americans as "Johnny Crapaud's game," something like "the Frog's game," and eventually "craps." (He tried to name Burgundy Street Craps Street, but it didn't take.) Unfortunately, the more people he taught it to, the more people he lost to. He still managed to live well, but by the time he died at 83, he was a pauper; the neighborhood of Faubourg Marigny is almost the last reminder of his huge holdings. Meanwhile, the house became a convent, a guest house, a rectory, and a school, and was nearly razed several times under various development schemes. However, in the '50s, when Anne Rice was a teenager, her parents rented the house for several years, and *Violin* is about her haunted time there. She has, needless to say, now purchased the property.

And here you are back at the streetcar.

The Warehouse/Arts and Central Business District (Zone 2)

This is a somewhat mixed tour, primarily pointing out historical buildings, but with a few arts sites thrown in. It has a rather dramatic finale, especially if you schedule it for the afternoon and wind up around dusk. If you are a more serious student of contemporary art, you should also plan to take a walk up and down Julia Street from Commerce to St. Charles, where there are many fine galleries and studios.

For the general tour, begin by paying tribute to the Maid of Orleans— **Joan of Arc,** whose gold-plated image, astride her fearless steed, stands in the median in front of the World Trade Center as a gift from the French government. With the Trade Center on your left, walk along Convention Center Boulevard to Lafayette Street. Look left down Poydras Street as you pass to flash a victory "V" back to the statue of **Winston Churchill** (the green is called English Place). Turn right at Lafayette and walk two blocks to South Peters Street and the **Piazza d'Italia.** (Remember the Spanish Plaza by the river? They don't call it the World Trade Center for nothing.) The Piazza d'Italia was designed by Charles Moore, and its fountain (shaped like the map of Italy) and partial arches were supposed to suggest a classical ruin, but the heavy and in many cases unresolved construction in the neighborhood has added rather unkindly to the effect.

Continue on Lafayette another two blocks until it runs into **Lafayette Square,** laid out in 1788 and named for the noble marquis who had joined the American Revolution. On the right is a 1974 sculpture by Clement Meadmore entitled "Out of There," and straight ahead just inside the park is the Benjamin Franklin monument created in 1871 by Hiram Powers. The statue in the center of the park of statesman Henry Clay, dedicated in 1860, originally stood at the intersection of St. Charles and Canal (and the place of honor in this park, oddly, once belonged to a statue of the king of Spain); Clay was moved here in 1901. And at the far side of the square, facing St. Charles Avenue, is the John McDonogh monument, portraying the philanthropist, who in the mid-nineteenth century endowed several public schools, as surrounded by grateful children (although until his will was known, he was considered a cranky old miser with radical ideas about educating slaves).

Turning left onto Camp Street (from Lafayette Street) notice the building on the left between Lafayette and Capedeville. The more or less Italian Renaissance building is now the **U. S. Court of Appeals for the Fifth Circuit,** but was built in 1914 as the post office.

Continue on Camp past Girod Street to **St. Patrick's Church** and its rectory. The high and narrow Gothic Revival building, built in the 1830s and for many years the undisputed high point of the area, was modeled after England's York Minster Cathedral by Irish architects Charles and James Dakin, and meant as a rival and rebuke to the close-minded French communicants of St. Louis Cathedral. (The shorthand for this class in ethnic division is, "God speaks only in French," though how He felt about canonical Latin is unclear.) Their revenge was complete in 1851, when because St. Louis Cathedral was being rebuilt, Bishop Antoine Blanc was ordained as archbishop in St. Patrick's. The design was completed by James Gallier, Sr. (born James Gallagher in Dublin), who was responsible for the high, vaulted interior and ribbed sanctuary ceiling with floral bosses. The stained glass over the altar and the three large murals, painted in 1840 by Leon Pomarede, are very fine. The Italianate rectory to the church's left was built by Garden District and plantation architect Henry Howard in 1874.

At the end of the block, catty-corner across Julia Street, you can see what's called **Julia Row** or **the Thirteen Sisters,** a block of 13 red brick rowhouses of a type that was extremely popular among upper-class residents of the American sector from about 1825 (these were built in the early 1830s) to about 1885. Notice the fan-light transom windows, attic cornices, and iron balconies. These are among the most important buildings being restored in the Warehouse District, and in fact the offices of the Preservation Resource Center of New Orleans are at 604 Julia. (You might stick your head in and ask about their walking tour maps, too, if you'd like to see more.)

Continue along Camp past St. Joseph Street to 900 Camp Street and the **Contemporary Arts Center.** This renovated 40,000-square-foot, turn-of-the-century warehouse is both a "living museum," with studios for practicing artists and rotating exhibits, and a theater, with two stages and sometimes concerts. Even the furniture is art—the glass-wave front desk, the lobby information board, the elevator panels, and the lighting sconces are all creations of fine local artists.

At the other end of the block at 929 Camp Street is the **Confederate Museum,** which has the second-largest collection of Confederate memorabilia (after Richmond's Museum of the Confederacy) in the nation. It is also the oldest museum in the state, designed in 1891 with a cypress hallway, 24-foot ceiling, and fireproof cases for its collection of restored battle flags. The body of Jefferson Davis, who died here in 1889 (see the Garden District tour above), lay in state at the museum before being taken to Richmond, and many of his family effects are here, along with uniforms, weapons, insignia, and photographs.

Turn the corner right onto Howard Avenue and you will see the greatest Confederate of them all, Robert E. Lee, on eternal vigilant guard against invasion from the north in the center of **Lee Circle.** (Talk about revered— he's not just on a pedestal, he's on a 60-foot pedestal.) The memorial was dedicated in 1884, and Jefferson Davis and New Orleans hometown hero P.T.G. Beauregard were still around for the ceremony.

(This is becoming an even more important arts district: As you approach Lee Circle you will pass the Howard Memorial Library, an 1888 sandstone extravaganza by Romanesque Revival champion Henry Hobson Richardson that is being renovated as the **Roger Ogden Museum of Southern Art,** scheduled to open in 1998. And facing the circle to the left of Howard Avenue is the **Lee Circle Center for the Arts,** scheduled to open in 1998.)

On the circle to Lee's back is the **K&B Plaza,** an indoor-outdoor sculpture garden including Isamu Noguchi's granite "Mississippi," commissioned for the plaza, and other pieces by an international group of artists including George Rickey, Frank McGuire, Michael Sandle, and Pedro Friedeberg. (The indoor gallery is open weekdays 8:30 A.M. to 4:30 P.M.)

Swing around Lee Circle, watching out for streetcars, and head back downtown along St. Charles. Many of these buildings have great but sad histories—the three-story brick Greek Revival townhouse at **827 St. Charles** is the only survivor of three—but within a few years, many of them will be prime commercial territory again.

At 545 St. Charles, looking out toward Lafayette Square, is **Gallier Hall,** designed in the late 1840s by the senior James Gallier as City Hall for the Second Municipality (i.e., the American Sector) and one of the most beautiful examples of the Greek Revival style in the city—and many believe in the entire country. The figures on the pediment represent Justice, Liberty, and Commerce (the one toting barges and lifting bales). It is now a private office building with a theater in the basement.

Stay on St. Charles Avenue for several blocks to Common Street; turn left for two blocks and then go right onto Baronne Street. At 132 Baronne is the outlandish Alhambra-Moscovy romantic **Church of the Immaculate Conception,** informally known as the Jesuit Church. The original church, erected in the mid-nineteenth century, had so much wrought and cast iron, some 200 tons of it, that it had nearly collapsed after five years. It was replaced in 1930 by an almost identical structure which still has the old church's cast-iron pews and the bronze-gilt altar, designed by James Freret, which won first prize at the Paris Exposition of 1867. And except for rude intervention of the French Revolution of 1848, the statue of the Virgin Mary would have been installed at the Tuileries.

Go to the corner, turn right onto Canal Street, and head back toward the river. This was for many years "the" shopping area for upper- and middle-class New Orleanians ("I wore white gloves to come here," says one native), and after a dispiriting decline, Canal Street is coming back to life with a raft of brand-name shops and luxury hotels.

Past Decatur at 423 Canal Street is the **U.S. Customs House,** begun in the 1840s (when the Mississippi was within eyeshot) but not usable until 1889, and not fully completed until 1913. The statuary niches along the Decatur Street side are still unfilled. In the meantime, it housed Confederate prisoners of war during the Union occupation. The huge third-floor Marble Hall, with its 55-foot skylight and 14 marble columns, is breathtaking.

Finally, walk one last block of Canal and turn back onto Convention Center Boulevard. Top off your tour at **Top of the Mart,** a slowly rotating 500-seat bar on the 33rd floor of the World Trade Center building. It takes 90 minutes to make a complete circuit, and the view of New Orleans—

from the riverfront around the business districts to the genteel old French Quarter—is especially attractive at night, when the bridges seem hung with Christmas lights (all those poor commuters) and the cathedral spire salutes the sky. It's open until midnight most days and 2 A.M. on Saturdays; however, no one under 21 is admitted, so families will have to go instead to the 31st floor and use those giant telescopes made famous by the Empire State Building.

Plantation Tours and Excursions

It is unlikely that you will have enough time to visit the plantations as part of a business trip, and unless you have figured such an excursion into your family vacation schedule (and unless you have or are planning to rent a car), you may have to settle for a half-day group tour.

There are some good tour packagers who can bus you to a few of the houses, among them **Tours by Isabelle** (391-3544), which offers a couple of different expeditions including an eight-hour, three-home tour; and **New Orleans Tours, Inc.** (call (800) 543-6332 or (504) 592-0560). **Gray Line Tours** (call (800) 535-7786 or (504) 587-0709) offers a seven-hour tour of Nottoway and Oak Alley, but the price of lunch is not included in the $50 fee, so bring extra. **Anne Rice's New Orleans Tours** (899-6450), which currently includes Destrehan Plantation in its three-hour Lost New Orleans tour, is also planning to start offering a more in-depth tour with overnight accommodations. (There are also steamboat tours, but they generally offer no more than a glimpse of the houses from the water, and so are not very satisfying for the time they require.)

However, if you would like to strike out by yourself, we have laid out a few options, including a half-day's drive, a full day's tour, and an overnight route that would be a romantic highlight.

Altogether, there are a half-dozen houses along what is usually called River Road, and a seventh a bit to the south; what makes this statement a little misleading, however, is that some are on one side of the Mississippi, and the rest on the other. In fact, there is no great single "River Road." There is instead a pair of two-lane roads, one on each side of the river—generally Route 44 on the north bank and Route 18 on the south—called various names as you continue west. Just try to keep a sense of where the river is, and watch for the house signs. It's not as difficult as it may sound—these are, after all, major tourist attractions and are well marked.

Because the tour companies are on tight schedules, they usually take Interstate 10 at least part of the way into plantation territory. However, we suggest you try a slightly more scenic route: Head west out of New Orleans on River Road (also marked as Route 48 or Jefferson Highway) and stay on the north side of the Mississippi River past Destrehan, San Francisco Plantation, Tezcuco Plantation, and Houmas House. Then cross the Sunshine

Bridge (Route 70) to the southern bank of the river, taking Route 1 a bit farther west to Nottoway and then heading back east, mostly on Route 18 past Oak Alley and back to the city.

The ideal trip would be overnight, stopping for lunch at Texcuco (or holding out for dinner at Lafitte's Landing) and taking a room at Nottoway Plantation, where you can either have dinner or do the big breakfast thing. You can see Destrehan without really leaving town; you could drive an hour or so and spend the night at Oak Alley. Or you could probably see Destrehan, San Francisco, Tezcuco, and Houmas and be back in New Orleans for dinner.

All the plantation homes described here have been immaculately restored and are open for tours. However, if you keep your eyes open, you will see many other fine old homes that are still private residences.

The first and closest is **Destrehan Manor** at 13034 River Road/La. 48, just eight miles west of the airport in Kenner (764-9315). Built in 1787 in the French Colonial style by a free man of color, it was given its wings just after the turn of the nineteenth century and renovated by the next generation into a Greek Revival style. Its Doric columns, double porch, and hipped roof will look very familiar to fans of the film, *Interview with the Vampire,* and many of the haunted–New Orleans tours mention sightings and even alleged photos of phantasmic shapes here. Destrehan is the oldest intact plantation in the Lower Mississippi Valley. Admission is $6; open daily 9:30 A.M.–4 P.M.

San Francisco Plantation (535-2341) on Highway 44 a little beyond Reserve is an old and elaborately Gothic Creole-style home begun in the mid-1850s by a planter named Edmond Marmillion and finished in the most fantastical manner—double galleries, widow's walk, highly decorative mouldings and painting, carved woodwork—by his sons, one of whom remarked at the end of the construction that he was now "sans fruscin," or "without a penny." So the house was first called St. Frusquin, eventually corrupted to San Francisco. Its elaborate, almost paddle-wheeling look inspired the setting of Frances Parkinson Keyes' *Steamboat Gothic.* Admission: $7 adults, $4 ages 12–17, $2.75 ages 6–11, age 5 and under free; open daily 10 A.M.–4 P.M.

About 25 miles farther at 3138 Highway 44 is **Tezcuco Plantation** (562-3929), one of the bed-and-breakfast facilities (for $60–$160, you can stay in one of the cottages or in a room in the main house, take a tour, drink some welcoming wine, etc.). It also has a restaurant where you can have breakfast or lunch if you're going on. This was built just before the Civil War, using bricks made on the grounds, local timber, and, of course, slave labor. The outbuildings include a Civil War museum, a life-sized dollhouse, a chapel, and more. Admission: $6 adults, $5.50 seniors and ages 13–17, $3.25 ages 4–12, age 3 and under free; open 9 A.M.–5 P.M. The name, incidentally, comes from the Aztecs and means "place of quiet rest."

A couple of miles farther along 44/River Road at Highway 942 is **Houmas House** (522-2262), which was named for the Indians who originally owned the land and was for decades the largest sugar plantation in Louisiana. The original house was only four rooms; what looks like the main house now, the two-and-a-half-story Greek Revival mansion with columns around three sides, was added on the front in 1840. Built to the fancy of a South Carolinian, it, too, was a film set, in this case for the Southern Gothic *Hush, Hush Sweet Charlotte* with Bette Davis. The hexagonal houses on either side are called "garconnieres," which were used either by the bachelor sons of the family (the "boys") or house guests. Admission: $7 adults, $5 children ages 13–17, $3.50 ages 6–12, age 5 and under free; open 10 A.M.–5 P.M. (closes at 4 P.M. November through January).

Retrace Highway 44 to Highway 70, cross the Sunshine Bridge over the Mississippi River, and look right at Frontage Street. The restaurant there, **Lafitte's Landing** (473-3007), is a first-rate neocontinental dining spot, but it also has historical romantic interest, as you may have guessed from the name. It used to be in Donaldsonville, where it was known as the Old Viala Plantation, and was supposed to have been one of the pirates' bases. In any case, his son and entrepreneurial successor, Jean Pierre Lafitte, married the Viala heiress. The Sunshine Bridge is so named because it was a former governor of Louisiana, Jimmy Davis, who wrote, "You Are My Sunshine.")

From Lafitte's Landing, turn onto Highway 1/Mississippi River Road and head west again for about 15 miles. Near White Castle is **Nottoway Plantation Inn & Restaurant,** a spectacular and almost unique building which was called "the white castle" and so gave its name to the town. Nottoway, built in 1859 by John Hampden Randolph, is the largest plantation home in the South, a hybrid neoclassical beauty with 64 rooms, 22 enormous columns, and a series of staggered porches and bays. Inside is a spectacular ballroom with hand-carved Corinthian columns, plaster friezes, and crystal chandeliers, and a surprising list of then-rare conveniences such as hot and cold running water and gas lights. As the name suggests, you can have lunch or dinner (and swim in the walled garden that once held roses), or stay overnight with breakfast and a tour tossed into the $125–$250 room rate. Otherwise, the admission is $8, $3 ages 12 and under; open 9 A.M.–5 P.M. with the last tour at 4:30 P.M.

(Incidentally, when you get as far as Nottoway Plantation, you are only about another 30 miles from Baton Rouge, around which are other plantations and attractions. If you want to go on, contact the Baton Rouge Convention and Visitors Bureau, P.O. Box 4149, Baton Rouge, LA 70821, or 383-1825, and ask for their tour brochures.)

To return to New Orleans, take Highway 1 back east toward Oak Alley.

Here's yet another option: If you have the time, or haven't worn out yet, you could instead go south from the Sunshine Bridge on Highway 70, to Spur 70 and Highway 308, to **Madewood Plantation** on Bayou Lafourche (call (800) 749-7131 or (504) 568-1988), a widely admired 1848 Greek Revival manor whose modern travel-mag style restoration has earned it high ratings from *Travel & Leisure,* etc. Again, you can stay in the main house or the cottages and have dinner in the original dining room and a continental breakfast before moving on. Otherwise, admission is $6 for adults, $4 for children; open 10 A.M.–5 P.M.

Back on the Route 1/River Road, drive about 15 miles and look for Highway 18 and the signs to **Oak Alley** (call (800) 44-ALLEY or (504) 265-2151), another Greek Revival beauty whose long drive between rows of 300-year-old live oaks, which gave it its nickname, has become famous through photographs as an example of antebellum architecture. (The real name was Bon Séjour.) It was built in 1839, and has as many Doric columns, 28, as the oaks themselves. It also has several outbuildings that have been turned into overnight rooms ($85–115) and a restaurant open for breakfast and lunch if you just want to drive over from New Orleans. Admission is $7 adults, $4 students, $2 ages 6–12, age 5 and under free; open 9 A.M.–5:30 P.M. (closes at 5 P.M. November through February).

You can take Highway 18/River Road back to town, and at the intersection of Route 90, take the Huey Long Bridge across the Mississippi back into New Orleans.

PART TWELVE

New Orleans Attractions

As you can tell from the walking tours and our suggestions in "Planning Your Visit" about designing your own special-interest tour, New Orleans is a lot more, and a lot more interesting, than Bourbon Street. Some of the finest attractions, such as City Park and the New Orleans Museum of Art, the Historic New Orleans Collection, the Jackson Barracks Museum, and Longue Vue House and Gardens, are often overlooked as tourists rush to the more obvious sites. So we've tried to evaluate most of the attractions in a way that may help you choose what you want to see depending on who's in the party, what your interests are, and how in-depth you would like to get.

For convenience in cross-referencing, these profiles are grouped by zone and alphabetically. However, keep in mind that some cross-zone transportations—the St. Charles Avenue streetcar, the *John James Audubon,* and the Canal Street ferry—are attractions in themselves.

Incidentally, remember that most museums are closed on state as well as federal holidays, and in New Orleans, that also means Mardi Gras and frequently All Saint's Day (November 1) as well as the more familiar dates such as Christmas. Many places have group ticket rates, so if you are traveling with more than just your immediate family, call ahead and ask about discounts. Also remember that ticket prices have a way of inching up without warning, so carry a little extra with you or call in advance.

■ **Zone 1: The French Quarter** ■

Aquarium of the Americas/IMAX Theater

Type of Attraction: A state-of-the-art and interactive marine museum with a good mix of science and fun

Location: Along the Mississippi Riverfront at the foot of Canal Street

Admission: Aquarium alone: $10.50 adults, $8 seniors, $5 kids 12 and under. IMAX alone: $7.50 adults, $6.50 seniors, $5 kids 12 and under. Combination tickets: $15 adults, $12 seniors, $9 children. Additional discount tickets available for boat/aquarium/zoo packages or boat/zoo/aquarium/IMAX.

Hours: Aquarium: Sunday–Thursday, 9:30 A.M.–6 P.M.; Friday and Saturday, 9:30 A.M.–7 P.M. IMAX (shows every two hours): Sunday–Thursday, 10 A.M.–6 P.M.; Friday and Saturday, 10 A.M.– 8 P.M.

Phone: 861-2537

When to Go: Early, if not to see it before it gets crowded, at least to get timed tickets for later in the day, when the air conditioning may be welcome

Special Comments: One of the '90s generation of marine installations, very pleasant and user-friendly and a best bet for mixed-age groups

Overall Appeal by Age Group:

Pre-School	Grade School	Teens	Young Adults	Over 30	Senior Citizens
★★½	★★★★	★★★★	★★★★	★★★★	★★★

Author's Rating: Visually and intellectually stimulating, with unusual care taken to make legends both legible and intelligible. ★★★★

How Much Time to Allow: At least an hour for the aquarium, even if you have restless children; two hours for IMAX, counting standing in line

Description and Comments It's hard to go wrong here unless you are so blasé that you can't get a thrill out of stroking the tough-suede skin of a small sand shark (one of the most popular queues) or of marveling at the beautiful, transparent, and snowflake-complex bodies of lacy jellyfish, one of the more astounding exhibits. The museum houses several large permanent exhibits, including a multilevel, multispecies Amazon rain forest, a penguin house, Caribbean reef and Mississippi River environments (look for the rare white alligator), and a 400,000-gallon saltwater mini–Gulf of Mexico with 14-foot glass walls and all the sharks and stingrays any kid could desire. There is a cafe on the second floor and the usual concessions at the IMAX. The IMAX rotates at least two movies a day, mostly on environmental themes; a few viewers may find the super-realistic wide-angle photography dizzying.

Touring Tips Wear comfortable shoes with no-slip soles; although the ramps in and out of various environments are not slick, you may be distracted by all that's going on around you. This is a nice spot to meet in the afternoon if the party wants to split up during the day because you can buy timed IMAX tickets in advance. Everything is wheelchair accessible, another fact worth noting in a city as old and often inconvenient as New Orleans.

The Beauregard-Keyes House

Type of Attraction: Restored nineteenth-century "raised cottage" and former residence of Gen. P.T.G. Beauregard and novelist Frances Parkinson Keyes, with personal effects and open gardens

Location: 1113 Chartres Street, between Ursulines and Gov. Nicholls Streets

Admission: $4 adults, $3 seniors and students, $1.50 kids 12 and under

Hours: Monday–Saturday, 10 A.M.–3 P.M.

Phone: 523-7257

When to Go: Anytime

Overall Appeal by Age Group:

Pre-school	Grade School	Teens	Young Adults	Over 30	Senior Citizens
none	★★	★★★	★★★	★★★	★★★★

Author's Rating: Low-key but lovely and a little sad if you know your history. ★★★

How Much Time to Allow: No more than an hour, including guided tour and stroll around the gardens

Description and Comments   This is a lovely old home, even without its many historical connections (see the self-guided walking tour of the French Quarter for more details), built in 1826 in raised-cottage style with a lovely twin staircase, Doric columns, and elegant side gallery. The formal gardens probably date back to the 1830s, when it belonged to the Swiss consul. It was a boardinghouse during the Civil War, and when Confederate general and native son Pierre Gustav Toutant Beauregard returned to the area, his own plantation in ruins, he and several members of his family lodged there for about 18 months. It was almost demolished in the 1920s, but a group of ladies lobbied for its restoration, and in 1944 the novelist Frances Parkinson Keyes moved in and began meticulous reconstruction, eventually turning the big house over to a charitable foundation and living in the rear cottage, also part of the tour. Many of the furnishings and personal effects belonged to

Beauregard. The gift shop has copies of most of Keyes' books, many of them historical novels dealing with Creole society and the house itself.

Touring Tips   Like many New Orleans homes, this is strictly a guided tour, with costumed docents. But now that PBS has made *The Civil War* so lively again, even students may find Beauregard's old study intriguing. The gardens make for a nice respite, as well.

The Cabildo and Arsenal

Type of Attraction: Flagship building of the Louisiana State Museum complex in the city. Entrance to the Arsenal, which only occasionally has exhibits, is through the Cabildo.

Location: On Chartres Street facing Jackson Square

Admission: $4 adults; $3 seniors, students, and active military; free for kids 12 and under. Tickets to all four state museum facilities currently open (several more will be added in the future) are $10 adults and $7.50 seniors, students, and military.

Hours: Tuesday–Sunday, 9 A.M.–5 P.M.

Phone: 568-6968

When to Go: Anytime

Special Comments: Be sure to check at the front desk for information on changing exhibits or exhibits in the Arsenal.

Overall Appeal by Age Group:

Pre-school	Grade School	Teens	Young Adults	Over 30	Senior Citizens
none	★★	★★	★★★	★★★	★★★

Author's Rating: Not terribly engaging, and sometimes stiffly explained, but if you skim through, picking up the more intriguing exhibits, particularly some of the more subtle folk-art pieces, mildly entertaining. ★★½

How Much Time to Allow: 30–60 minutes

Description and Comments   This is not a very hands-on museum, and compared to the new-generation facilities it can be rather dry; you will probably find yourself skimming through unless you stop to watch videos. But there are a few particular exhibits that may hold even a child's attention, such as the Indian pirogue; weapons and uniforms from the Civil War and the Battle of New Orleans; that apocryphal symbol of slavery, the cotton gin; a lock of Andy Jackson's hair; antique medical tools, including a leech jar; a young child's casket; and Napoleon's death mask, with a dark and surprisingly philosophical visage unfamiliar from the typical portraits. African-Americans and Native Americans may find the exhibits devoted to their contributions a little stiff but well-intentioned. The building itself has historical significance: The official transfer of the Louisiana Territory from France to the United States was signed here, and since it also housed the State Supreme Court from 1868 to 1910, it saw the arguing of several famous legal cases, including *Plessy v. Ferguson*.

Touring Tips   The Cabildo is wheelchair accessible, and even offers wheelchairs for use; visitors with other disabilities should check in at the front counter for assistance.

The 1850 House

Type of Attraction: Mid-nineteenth-century middle-class apartment with period furnishings

Location: In the Pontalba Apartments at 523 St. Ann Street facing Jackson Square

Admission: $4 adults; $3 seniors, students, and active military; free for kids 12 and under. Tickets to all four state museum facilities currently open (several more will be added in the future) are $10 adults and $7.50 seniors, students, and military.

Hours: Tuesday–Sunday, 9 A.M.–5 P.M.

Phone: 568-6968

When to Go: Anytime, though this might qualify as rainy-day stuff

Special Comments: One of the most intriguing things about these apartments is that they are still occupied, and there's still a waiting list. Also note the Spring Fiesta Association house at 826 St. Ann; open by appointment only (945-2744, or Fridays 581-1367).

Overall Appeal by Age Group:

Pre-school	Grade School	Teens	Young Adults	Over 30	Senior Citizens
none	★	★	★★	★★	★★

Author's Rating: Just a snapshot of social history, but oddly chilly—less palpably lived-in than the Hermann-Grima or Gallier houses. ★½

How Much Time to Allow: 15–20 minutes

Description and Comments   This is a sort of single museum exhibit expanded over several stories, a real-sized dollhouse, in a way. If you are not curious about the evolution of American social customs, you may not get much out of it. However, some of its antiques, particularly the rococo revival bedroom furniture and the rare complete 75-piece set of Vieux Paris tableware will be very significant to some and merely pretty to others. What is intriguing is the apartment's history: Baroness Micaela Almonester de Pontalba, daughter of the Spanish grandee who rebuilt the Presbytere, Cabildo, and Cathedral after the great fires of the late eighteenth century, wanted both to transform the square from a military parade ground into a European-style public plaza and to improve the value of her land in the declining old city. She went through several of New Orleans' best architects, including James Gallier, Sr., and Henry Howard, and micromanaged the contractors who survived (if you see the portraits of the baroness in the Presbytere, you won't be surprised); but the row houses were ultimately a great success, 16 on each side and all with storefronts on the sidewalk level, just as they are today. Note the entwined "A" and "P" cartouche—for Almonester de Pontalba—in the balcony railing.

The apartments did eventually become fairly run-down, but were restored by massive WPA projects. The Louisiana State Museum owns the Lower Pontalbas (the side including the 1850 House), and the city owns the Upper Pontalbas.

Touring Tips   This museum is not wheelchair accessible, and the rather steep and narrow stairs may be difficult for older or physically limited visitors. The booklet given to visitors for the self-guided tour offers a great deal of information about the original facilities and decoration.

Gallier House Museum

Type of Attraction: Period-correct restoration of the house designed by prominent architect James Gallier, Jr., for his own family

Location: 1118–1132 Royal Street, between Ursulines and Gov. Nicolls Streets

Admission: Adults $4, $3 seniors and students, $2.25 ages 5–11, free under 5

Hours: Monday–Saturday, 10 A.M.– 4 P.M. (last tour begins at 3:30 P.M.)

Phone: 525-5661

When to Go: Anytime, although unlike most historic houses, it's difficult in the rain because you have to go along the upstairs gallery.

Special Comments: Particularly interesting because Gallier designed so many more elaborate homes in the Garden District for American patrons.

Overall Appeal by Age Group:

Pre-school	Grade School	Teens	Young Adults	Over 30	Senior Citizens
none	★	★	★★	★★★	★★★

Author's Rating: House tours are a particular sort of attraction, requiring a fair amount of imagination (or desire for imitation), but Gallier's design is both gracious and clever, crammed full of fine architectural and decorative detailing. ★★★½

How Much Time to Allow: 30–45 minutes

Description and Comments   Administered by Tulane University, this is one of the most meticulously correct restorations in town, partly because Gallier's own designs and notes have been preserved. Though not perhaps as wealthy as many of his patrons, Gallier would certainly qualify as comfortably well-off. His house was very up-to-date in many ways—the chandeliers were gas-burning, the bathroom had hot running water, and the whole house had a sort of primitive air-conditioning system with vents and ice-cooled air—but it is also revealing about customs of the times, with its servants' quarters, dish pantry, summer matting vs. winter carpets, children's sickroom, high brick garden walls, etc. The faux painting of the cypress to resemble pine is also very characteristic. The decorative molding and plaster work, gilded capitals, 12-foot ceilings, marble, and paneling are very fine, and the docents here are extremely knowledgeable about the entire inventory. The work on outbuildings continues, but be sure to admire the carriage in the alley between the two buildings.

Touring Tips   Not wheelchair accessible, but not uncomfortable.

Hermann-Grima House

Type of Attraction: Beautifully restored home from the early Federal period, with unusually extensive outbuildings

Location: 818–820 S. Louis Street between Bourbon and Dauphine Streets

Admission: Adults $4, seniors and students $3, free for kids 8 and under

Hours: Monday–Saturday, 10 A.M.–4 P.M. (last tour leaves at 3:30 P.M.)

Phone: 525-5661

When to Go: Anytime

Special Comments: Occasionally there are special cooking demonstrations in the rear kitchen; ask at the ticket counter in the carriage house.

Overall Appeal by Age Group:

Pre-school	Grade School	Teens	Young Adults	Over 30	Senior Citizens
none	★	★★	★★★	★★★	★★★

Author's Rating: An unusual house and one that says quite a bit about its owners; more fun when the live demonstrations are scheduled. ★★★

How Much Time to Allow: 45 minutes–1 hour

Description and Comments   This is an unusual home in that it represents the style of the so-called Golden Age of New Orleans, meaning the first great commercial boom under U.S. administrations. Though it's usually hard to get younger people interested in old homes, the peculiarities of this one—the shared bathroom, the outdoor kitchens, the young woman's furnishings—make it more accessible than most. The house was built in 1831 for a wealthy merchant named Samuel Hermann. It was constructed in the Federal style, with a central doorway and divided rooms rather than the earlier side-hall style; the exterior plaster is scored to look like brick, which was very expensive and showy. (Much of the decorative work was produced by the free men of color then flourishing in New Orleans.) The house was sold in 1844 to Judge Felix Grima, whose family remained there for five generations. The period furniture is very fine. The master bedroom actually faces the street and has a pocket-door opening to the middle hall and second bedroom for ventilation. The long garden, outbuildings for cooking and household work, and even the original carriage house (the one used for tickets and souvenirs comes from the house next door) are finely restored.

Touring Tips   Since you can buy timed tickets in advance, you may want to ask the guides if there are any large groups already scheduled for a particular tour. You can also stop by in the morning and get tickets for the time of your choice, pass them out, and meet at the appointed hour. Since you don't get to go upstairs, this is a good choice for those with physical limitations, although there are a few steps; those unable to mount the front steps might ask at the counter if they can be brought through from the courtyard.

Historic New Orleans Collection

Type of Attraction: A complex of free exhibits, a late-eighteenth-century residence and a nineteenth-century residence remodeled for 1940s society.

Location: 533 Royal Street between Toulouse and St. Louis Streets

Admission: Williams galleries free; Williams residence and Louisiana History Galleries in the Merieult House $4

Hours: Tuesday–Saturday, 10 A.M.–4:30 P.M.; tours at 10 and 11 A.M. and 2 and 3 P.M.

Phone: 523-4662

When to Go: Anytime

Special Comments: One of the most satisfying tours in town, histori-cally and culturally

Overall Appeal by Age Group:

Pre-school	Grade School	Teens	Young Adults	Over 30	Senior Citizens
none	★	★★	★★★★	★★★★	★★★

Author's Rating: If you have limited time and want to get a flavor of the social, cultural, and historical evolution of New Orleans, this is the tour to take. Even if you have lots of time, it's the one. ★★★★½

How Much Time to Allow: Up to 2 hours including tours

Description and Comments This is partly a research center, partly a group of restored architectural gems, and a bit of an art gallery as well. The entrance-level Williams galleries have first-class rotating exhibits on Mardi Gras, renovation, arts and crafts, etc., that are free for the browsing. Behind that is the glorious 1792 Merieult House of roman-tic legend (see the walking tour of the French Quarter), whose airy rooms now house rare materials from the landmark collection of the late Kemper and Leila Williams, including maps, documents concern-ing the Louisiana Purchase, wildly inflated propaganda posters, rare photographs, and so on. (The extraordinary bulk of their collection is now housed in its own lovely library, the Williams Research Center, at

410 Chartres.) The nineteenth-century brick cottage at the end of the courtyard was the Williams' residence, which they had renovated to suit their own high standards of comfort and hospitality, and to showcase their collections of fine porcelain, antique furniture, and textiles.

Touring Tips This is a one-stop whirlwind tour of New Orleans history, and a particularly evocative one, since you literally step off Royal Street into a gracious residence of two centuries' standing. Even the gifts in the shop have some historical appeal. Wheelchair access available; ask at the counter.

Musée Conti Wax Museum

Type of Attraction: Pretty much what it sounds like, a Madame Toussaud's of New Orleans history with a little requisite scary stuff mixed in and some surprising Mardi Gras outfits as a lagniappe

Location: 917 Conti Street, between Dauphine and Burgundy Streets

Admission: $5.75 adults, $4 seniors and students, $3.50 ages 4–17, free for kids 3 and under

Hours: 10 A.M.–5:30 P.M.

Phone: 525-2605

When to Go: Anytime, though this makes a very diverting rainy-day stop and a cool one on the hottest afternoons.

Special Comments: The special "haunted dungeon" of more or less horrific stuff is off to one side, so young or susceptible children don't have to see it.

Overall Appeal by Age Group:

Pre-school	Grade School	Teens	Young Adults	Over 30	Senior Citizens
★★	★★★	★★★	★★★	★★	★★

Author's Rating: This is not the sort of attraction to visit twice (unless you're a kid), but the first time around, it has its fun moments. ★★½

How Much Time to Allow: 45 minutes

Description and Comments Wax museums may be corny, but they have a certain appeal to even the youngest of kids, who are fascinated by their immovability, and seniors, for whom they represent the attractions of an earlier, more innocent age. These are pretty good as such things go, with German glass eyes, human hair imported from Italy, and figures straight from Paris. Many of the exhibits are purely historical —Andy Jackson and Jean Lafitte (and the Battle of New Orleans in panorama), and the hilarious vision of the Emperor Napoleon, ensconced in his bathtub, impulsively offering to sell the entire Louisiana Territory— while others are more theatrically gory (Marie Laveau leading a voodoo ritual and lovely Delphine LaLaurie gloating over her chained slaves). A few are downright cheerful: There are wax models of Louis Armstrong, Pete Fountain, Huey Long, and Mardi Gras Indian Chief Montana. Even the long-lost Storyville has its moment in the artificial sun. Dracula, the Wolf Man, Frankenstein, and two dozen or so of their friends are kept off to one side.

Touring Tips　Consider before taking small children; a few will find the peculiar, almost-real quality of these mannequins spooky even before they get to the chamber of horrors. International travelers may be surprised at the variety of translated tours available for rent.

New Orleans Historic Voodoo Museum

Type of Attraction: Part museum, part weird-camp souvenir shop— or to put it simply, part shock, part schlock

Location: 724 Dumaine Street, between Royal and Bourbon Streets

Admission: $5 adults, $4 seniors and students (if you sign up for a guided tour, the museum tour is free)

Hours: 10 A.M.–5 P.M.

Phone: 523-7685

When to Go: Anytime

Special Comments: One of the hot spots for psychic readings and gris-gris charms as well as "voodoo tours"

Overall Appeal by Age Group:

Pre-school	Grade School	Teens	Young Adults	Over 30	Senior Citizens
★	★★	★★★	★★★	★★	★★

Author's Rating: This absolutely requires that you get into the spirit of things; think of it as an adventure, rather than as a museum per se. ★★★

How Much Time to Allow: 30 minutes

Description and Comments　If something like the Historic New Orleans Collection is the quintessential above-board museum, this is the height of neo–New Orleans exotica—rather grim and sometimes grisly artifacts, strange bones and potions, a voodoo altar, plenty of Marie Laveau lore, stuffed cats and live snakes, low light, and sometimes local low life as well. If you like atmosphere, you'll love this; in fact, if it weren't so dim and dilapidated, they'd have to curse it.

Touring Tips Children are generally fascinated by the grotesque, but take your own kids' sensitivities into account. Teens and novice occultists will probably think it very cool, but seniors may find it all a little too grim. The museum staff not only arranges readings and tours but occasional "rituals."

New Orleans Pharmacy Museum

Type of Attraction: Restored apothecary with period exhibits, old potions, and pharmaceutical supplies
Location: 514 Chartres Street, between Toulouse and St. Louis Streets
Admission: $2
Hours: Tuesday–Sunday, 10 A.M.–5 P.M.
Phone: 565-8027
When to Go: Anytime; good rain alternative
Special Comments: Exhibit rooms on the upper floor are still under renovation.

Overall Appeal by Age Group:

Pre-school	Grade School	Teens	Young Adults	Over 30	Senior Citizens
★	★★	★★	★★	★★	★★★

Author's Rating: This is another of those "atmospheric" venues that has to draw you. The subject may seem somewhat limited, but it's quite intriguing if you're not squeamish. ★★★
How Much Time to Allow: 30 minutes

Description and Comments This was the pharmacy of the very first apothecary to be licensed in the United States, Louis Dufilho, who was certified in 1816 and opened this store in 1823. It's an impressive piece of restoration, with German mahogany cases, antique handblown canisters and apothecary jars, a leech pot, and such famous patent medicines of the past as Pinkham's pills, the vitamin concoctions of Miss Lydia Pinkham that were supposed to resolve both ladies' vapors and, though not said openly, sexual indifference; and Spanish fly, the male equivalent still hotly sought after today. The black and rose marble soda fountain, made in Italy in 1855, is a nostalgic highlight.

Touring Tips Bring your sense of humor. This will be of some interest to most ages, since the idea of applying leeches and trepanning skulls to relieve pressure (or possession) has a perverse appeal. The courtyard is a nice place to sit for a few minutes, and with the revival of interest in botanicals and alternative medicine, almost trendy. In a funny way, however, this has more appeal to older visitors who recognize more of the names and may even remember tales of defunct medical techniques.

Old Ursuline Convent/Archbishop Antoine Blanc Memorial

Type of Attraction: A 250-year-old complex incorporating several religious sites, formal gardens and archives

Location: 110 Chartres Street, at the corner of Ursulines Street

Admission: $4 adults, $2 seniors and students, free 8 and under

Hours: Tuesday–Friday, 10 A.M.–3 P.M. (tours on the hour); Saturday and Sunday, tours at 11:15 A.M. and 1 and 2 P.M. only

Phone: 529-3040

When to Go: Anytime

Special Comments: Not a lively, elaborate, or particularly varied site, but oddly atmospheric; obviously appeals more to Catholic visitors

Overall Appeal by Age Group:

Pre-school	Grade School	Teens	Young Adults	Over 30	Senior Citizens
none	none	★	★	★★	★★

Author's Rating: Of more historical and religious than visual appeal; an unusually serene tour. ★★

How Much Time to Allow: 1 hour

Description and Comments This is the only surviving example of pure French Creole construction, begun in 1745, and most people believe it's the oldest surviving building in New Orleans of any sort; it was saved from the fire of 1788 by Pere Antoine and his bucket brigade. The Sisters were the guiding social hand of the city's young people for centuries, educating not only the children of aristocrats (Micaela Almonester, for example) but blacks, Indians, and orphans as well. They served as religious guides, chaperones (it was they who brought over the "casket girls" as brides to the early settlers), nurses, housekeeping instructors, and welfare workers, braving epidemics and massacres alike. Andrew Jackson sent word to the Sisters to ask them to pray for his forces on the eve of the Battle of New Orleans; they responded by spending the entire night in prayer at the chapel here before a statue of the Virgin Mary, and were still there when the messenger brought word of victory. Jackson came in person to thank them, and to this day a celebratory Mass is said on January 8 at the Ursulines' other chapel, the **National Shrine of Our Lady of Prompt Succor** at State Street and South Claiborne. The lovely old cypress spiral staircase, antique furniture and relics, medicinal garden, and restored chapel, known variously as Our Lady of Victory Church, St. Mary's Italian Church, and the Archbishop's Chapel, are very pretty—but again, of somewhat limited appeal. Incidentally, in the early years of U.S. government, the convent seemed threatened by anti-Catholic educational reforms; the Mother Superior wrote first to President Jefferson and again to President Madison, asking that the school be allowed to continue, and both wrote back assuringly. The Shrine of Our Lady has not only her petitions, but both presidential responses.

Touring Tips　This is pleasant, but rather a lot of walking for the effect.

The Old U.S. Mint

Type of Attraction:　Another part of the Louisiana State Museum complex, an imaginatively reconditioned installation housing two of the city's best-kept secret exhibits

Location:　400 Esplanade Avenue, at Decatur Street

Admission:　$4 adults; $3 seniors, students, and active military; free for kids 12 and under. Tickets to all four state museum facilities currently open (several more will be added in the future) are $10 adults and $7.50 seniors, students, and military.

Hours:　Tuesday–Sunday, 9 A.M.–5 P.M.

Phone:　568-6968

When to Go:　Anytime

Special Comments:　Because of its music exhibits, the museum sometimes hosts concerts of jazz, big band, spirituals, and early ballroom music; inquire at the desk. Also browse through the music collection in the gift shop.

Overall Appeal by Age Group:

Pre-school	Grade School	Teens	Young Adults	Over 30	Senior Citizens
★★★	★★★★	★★★★	★★★★★	★★★★★	★★★★★

Author's Rating: This is virtually the only exhibit on New Orleans music, and requires perhaps a little personal knowledge for the fullest effect, but even the tone-deaf will be floored by the Mardi Gras rooms. ★★★★★

How Much Time to Allow: 1–2 hours

Description and Comments   The building itself, a huge but not clumsy Greek Revival facade with Ionic details, was designed during Andrew Jackson's administration by William Strickland, the most prominent public architect of the day. Its polished flagstone floors, double staircase, and rear galleries are still pretty impressive (although it has to be admitted that engineer P.T.G. Beauregard had to be called in to perform a little facelift in the 1850s). One side of the second floor holds the jazz collection, which arranges old photographs of Jelly Roll Morton, King Oliver, Sidney Bechet, and Fate Marable's Orchestra alongside early instruments (including Louis Armstrong's first cornet), sheet music, and other memorabilia. Snatches of vintage recordings play overhead, and the often overlooked women of early music are also saluted. (Be sure to notice the copy of the notorious "Blue Book," the social register of Storyville ladies, and the delicate stained-glass panels rescued from a demolished bordello.) The other side of the building houses the Mardi Gras exhibit, an astonishing cornucopia of mocked-up floats and authentic costumes, scepters, crowns, krewe decorations and "honors," hat pins, watches, and Carnival favors. The lavish outfits are made of gold lamé, fake fur, appliquéd satin, beads, feathers, velvets, and silk tassels. Even if your kids can resist the music rooms, they'll be stunned by the chief of the Wild Tchoupitoulas in all his glory, and the picture of Louis Armstrong as King of the Zulu Krewe in 1949. Look also at the paintings depicting the duel between rival club owners (that spelled the beginning of the end of Storyville) and the third-floor hallway mural with many famous faces from the musical past. Down in the basement, where the remnants of the mint equipment can be seen, are a few intriguing exhibits as well, including the carved hearse, built at the turn of the nineteenth century.

Touring Tips   This is good wheelchair access territory, with wide aisles and new bathrooms. And if you like old homes, take the time to wander up and down Esplanade Avenue. Although the neighborhood is in mid-revival, it is likely to be the next Garden District. Take particular note of the house at **704 Esplanade**, at Royal Street: The Gauche House (so called for owner John Gauche, not as an editorial comment) was built in 1856 supposedly from a drawing by Albrecht Dürer, including cast-iron balconies, cupids, and all. Also note that you are very near the end of the Riverfront Streetcar line, if you're getting tired or want to get across the Quarter easily.

The Presbytere

Type of Attraction: Of the Louisiana State Museum properties in the French Quarter, the most traditional, with both permanent and rotating exhibits

Location: 751 Chartres Street, facing Jackson Square

Admission: $4 adults; $3 seniors, students, and active military; free for kids 12 and under. Tickets to all four state museum facilities currently open (several more will be added in the future) are $10 adults and $7.50 seniors, students, and military.

Hours: Tuesday–Sunday, 9 A.M.–5 P.M.

Phone: 568-6968

When to Go: Anytime

Overall Appeal by Age Group:

Pre-school	Grade School	Teens	Young Adults	Over 30	Senior Citizens
none	★	★	★★★	★★★	★★

Author's Rating: Like the Cabildo, you have to follow your nose to what interests you, but the rotating exhibits can be very intriguing. ★★★

How Much Time to Allow: 45 minutes–1½ hours

Description and Comments   This is a somewhat mongrel building, architecturally speaking, though not unattractive—it has been renovated and expanded several times—and most recently its really fine plank floors have been reconditioned to fine advantage. Intended to be used as an ecclesiastical residence, it wound up as a courthouse; the mansard room and (hurricane-demolished) cupola were supposed to mirror the Cabildo. Its exhibits are a somewhat haphazard but cheerful mishmash: portraits of influential Creoles, such as Don Almonester and his formidable daughter, Baroness de Pontalba; fine decorative arts, from an eighteenth-century gold- and silver-embroidered velvet altar cloth and local art glass, to wrought iron from the staircase of the great domed (and doomed) St. Charles Hotel; crosses, cameos, and earrings; hand-tinted Audubon plates; silver table settings; etc. Among the busts are two faces of Beauregard, one young and confident, the other older and wiser.

Touring Tips   Although the age rating shows low for children, it does depend somewhat on the subject of the rotating exhibits. Among fairly recent examples, the collection of very elaborate to-scale builders' ship models, haute couture (a la the Metropolitan Museum in New York), or antique maps might interest certain youngsters, and the rather weird *Tales from the Crypt* effect of the bust-lined second-floor arcade gallery might tickle others' fancy.

Germaine Wells Mardi Gras Museum

Type of Attraction: Costume and jewelry collection

Location: Upstairs at Arnaud's Restaurant at 813 Bienville Street, between Bourbon and Dauphine Streets

Admission: Free

Hours: Monday–Friday, 11:30 A.M.–2:30 P.M. and 6–10 P.M.; Saturday, 6–10 P.M.

Phone: 523-0611

When to Go: Anytime

Overall Appeal by Age Group:

Pre-school	Grade School	Teens	Young Adults	Over 30	Senior Citizens
★	★★	★★	★★★	★★★	★★

Author's Rating: This covers less territory than the Mardi Gras exhibit in the Old U.S. Mint, since it's primarily his-and-her gowns, but they speak volumes about the lost sophistication of old New Orleans. As a fast, free diversion, hard to beat. ★★★

How Much Time to Allow: 20 minutes

Description and Comments   The family of restaurateur Arnaud Cazenave, and particularly his daughter, Germaine Cazenave Wells, were mainstays of the old-society Carnival for decades; Germaine alone reigned as queen of nearly two dozen balls, more than anyone else in history. Her collection of royal outfits and jewelry, many of them astonishingly luxurious and accompanied by pictures of the corresponding ball, has been rescued and placed in glass cases in a pretty but simple wing. When you find the spangled gown she wore as the 1954 Queen of Naiades, tip your hat: She loved the gown so much she was buried in a replica of it. A small case outside displays some of her almost equally exuberant Easter bonnets.

Touring Tips   The costumes are fragile, so the air conditioning is often up pretty high.

■ **Zone 2: The Central Business District** ■

We've said several times that you should not venture into St. Louis Cemetery without a tour group or at least several friends. One way to get a glimpse of its setting and historic role is to visit **Our Lady of Guadalupe**, which was once used as a virtual assembly line for yellow fever victims. Unfortunately, the other important site in this area, **Louis Armstrong Park**, can't be recommended as a tourist attraction either, although plans to renovate and secure it in the future may change that. The park is a sort of ghost of Storyville (now vanished under an eyesore of a housing project). It is bordered on one side by Basin Street and includes Congo Square, the legendary tribal gathering spot turned jammin' ground; a bandstand (where off and on, free Sunday concerts are scheduled), a community center, and several historic buildings; a jazz and blues radio station (WWOZ 90.7); and even a performing arts center, not to mention the 12-foot statue of Satchmo himself. The neighborhood is gradually reviving, partly thanks to the sentimental "homecoming" of many musicians, but it is not a good idea to walk here. If you do want to hear and see this historic area, contact **Cradle of Jazz Tours** (282-3583).

Confederate Museum

Type of Attraction: Traditional but unusually large and somber Civil War museum

Location: 929 Camp Street, at Howard Avenue

Admission: $4, $2 for kids 12 and under

Hours: Monday–Saturday, 10 A.M.– 4 P.M.

Phone: 523-4522

When to Go: Anytime

Overall Appeal by Age Group:

Pre-school	Grade School	Teens	Young Adults	Over 30	Senior Citizens
none	★	★★	★★★★	★★★★	★★★★

Author's Rating: Moving and interesting. ★★★

How Much Time to Allow: 1½ hours

Description and Comments   "Everybody thinks it's a church, but it's not," says the staffer about this medievally somber shrine to the Glorious Cause, the oldest Civil War museum in the country. Homegrown architect Thomas Sully designed it as a complement to the Romanesque Howard Memorial Library next door (itself becoming a museum, as noted in the walking tour of the Warehouse/Arts District), and it looks every bit the sepulcher—as it surely must have in 1893 when 50,000 mourners came to pay respects to the body of Jefferson Davis. There's no substitute for artifacts in a museum: That ineffable dignity that lingers in objects handled by long-dead humans suffuses the most sophisticated installation, and in such items the museum, also known as Confederate Memorial Hall, is rich indeed. Its collection, the second largest in the country, turns arms and armaments into an eloquent commentary on the social impact of the war on men and women alike. Among the most moving items are the frock coats worn by generals Beauregard and Braxton Bragg, their physical slightness a poignant counterpoint to the magnitude of the conflict; the modest headgear of one Landon Creek, who survived 7 battles and 3 wounds to make it to his 15th birthday; a pair of boots, long interred with its owner and now on eerie, empty display; a child's Zouave-style jacket from Marshall Field's, a high-fashion flirtation with rebellion; and part of Lee's battlefield silver. Among the women honored here are those who resisted the occupation of "Beast" Butler's troops by spitting or recoiling in their presence.

Touring Tips   Street parking available.

Louisiana Children's Museum

Type of Attraction: State-of-the-art children's activity center
Location: 420 Julia Street, at Constance Avenue
Admission: $5
Hours: Tuesday–Saturday, 9:30 A.M.–4:30 P.M.; Sunday, noon–
  4:30 P.M.; Monday (June–August only), 9:30 A.M.–4:30 P.M.
Phone: 523-1357
When to Go: After lunchtime, when the daytrippers and school
  groups have left

Overall Appeal by Age Group:

Pre-school	Grade School	Teens	Young Adults	Over 30	Senior Citizens
★★★★★	★★★★★	½	½	½	½

Author's Rating: The way early learning is supposed to be—fun and exciting. ★★★★

How Much Time to Allow: 1½–2 hours

Description and Comments In a colorful, noisy converted warehouse, this science- and math-oriented facility teaches kids the inner workings of things by letting them simply have a good time. Pulleys, gears, wind machines, bubble rings, and sound-wave amplifiers are offered, along with an innovative and kindly minded exhibit introducing kids to the difficulties of handicapped—but not limited—life: They shoot baskets from a wheelchair, stack blocks wearing thick, clumsy gloves, etc. There are *Sesame Street*–style areas, such as the cafe where they can pretend to cook, a grocery store, a Cajun cottage, and an art gallery. There's a special room for toddlers, so siblings don't feel tied down.

Touring Tips Being subjected to constant battering means some of the hands-on exhibits need maintenance; just move on to the next thing. Food is limited to vending machines. Street parking available.

Louisiana Superdome

Type of Attraction: Enclosed sports arena also used as a concert and convention venue

Location: 1500 Poydras Street, at LaSalle Street

Admission: $6 adults, $5 seniors, $4 ages 5–10, free for kids 4 and under

Hours: 10 A.M.–4 P.M. (tours on the hour)

Phone: 587-3810

When to Go: When something's scheduled.

Special Comments: The New Orleans Centre, a three-story pseudo-neo-Disney Victorian crystal exposition hall inside an office building, connects to the Superdome like the super souvenir/concession wing. A new Sports Arena complex is being constructed behind the Superdome to bring in even more games.

Overall Appeal by Age Group:

Pre-school	Grade School	Teens	Young Adults	Over 30	Senior Citizens
none	★½	★½	★	★	none

Author's Rating: Strictly for sports-stats freaks. It may be big, and the numbers the tour guides spout are impressive, but hey—if you've seen one stadium, you've seen 'em all.

How Much Time to Allow: 30–45 minutes

Description and Comments   The Superdome is, as you will hear repeatedly, one of the largest buildings in the world, 27 stories high, with no obstructing support posts (admittedly impressive, if rather unnerving) and 13 acres' worth of AstroTurf, here called Mardi Grass. It can seat more than 76,000 people, but if there are only 20 or so of you walking around behind a tour guide, it seems a little . . . dumb. And it seems even worse when there are about 20 busloads of tourists looking around, staring.

Touring Tips   Plenty of parking.

New Orleans Contemporary Arts Center

Type of Attraction: Multidisciplinary arts and performing arts complex

Location: 900 Camp Street, at St. Joseph Street

Admission: $5 adults, $2 seniors and students; free on Thursdays. Performance ticket prices vary.

Hours: Monday–Saturday, 10 A.M.–5 P.M.; Sunday, 11 A.M.–5 P.M.

Phone: 523-1216

When to Go: After lunchtime on weekdays to avoid school class groups

Overall Appeal by Age Group:

Pre-school	Grade School	Teens	Young Adults	Over 30	Senior Citizens
½	★★	★★★	★★★★	★★★★	★★★★

Author's Rating: Worth a visit for the high caliber of exhibitions.
★★★★

How Much Time to Allow: 1–1½ hours

Description and Comments   The CAC's gallery spaces total 10,000 square feet and rotate about every six to eight weeks among international as well as national and local artists' exhibits. It also includes spaces for theatrical, musical, and dance performances, as well as some cutting-edge performance art. Call for a schedule of events. That's the up-side. The slight down-side is that this somewhat raw, accessible renovated warehouse can be very loud when groups of school kids come in.

Touring Tips   Street parking available.

Our Lady of Guadalupe/Shrine of St. Jude

Type of Attraction: Simple but quirky little chapel built to serve St. Louis Cemetery, but with a couple of not-so-strict saints in charge
Location: 411 North Rampart Street, at Conti Street
Admission: Free (donations welcome)
Hours: 7 A.M.–6 P.M.
Phone: 525-1551
When to Go: Anytime
Special Comments: This is the official chapel of the city's fire and police departments, so don't be surprised by any uniforms.

Overall Appeal by Age Group:

Pre-school	Grade School	Teens	Young Adults	Over 30	Senior Citizens
none	½	½	★½	★½	★★

Author's Rating: An eccentric but lively side trip. ★★½
How Much Time to Allow: 15 minutes; also tours by appointment

Description and Comments This little chapel, built in 1826 as the Chapel of the Dead and originally opening directly onto the cemetery (there's a street between now), is intriguing for several reasons. First, because in the days of continual epidemic, it operated at tragic speed: Bodies were brought in, a swift service was said, and they were shipped right into the waiting graves. (The victims were brought here instead of St. Louis Cathedral in a vain effort to limit contagion.) The second intriguing aspect, for those who take saintly intercession with a grain of salt, is that the shrine is now dedicated to St. Jude—he of the lost causes—who despite his connections (he may have been the brother of either Jesus or James) has lost a little status, although the petitions and published notices of thanks continue to flow in. Third, this is also the shrine of the one and only (as far as anyone knows) St. Expedite, whose statue arrived at the chapel without its papers or even an address. He had no identifying attributes, and no other church in New Orleans claimed to be expecting a new saint, so the only thing written on the packing crate—Expedite!—was carved into the base by the confused workers, who didn't speak much English. Gradually petitioners began taking him at his word. The legend goes that if you have a request, you go out toward St. Louis Cemetery and say five rosaries; if your prayer is answered (it will be within 36 hours, or probably not at all), you return to the chapel and leave a teaspoon of salt and a slice of pound cake.

■ **Zone 3: Uptown below Napoleon (Garden District)** ■

Unless you have several days, are making a return trip, or have a real shopping "jones," it is unlikely you will spend much time around here. The run of Magazine Street from the Central Business District through Zone 3 to Audubon Park in Zone 4 is often touted as the new antiques center, though it is extremely drawn out; you could get off the St. Charles streetcar and walk about three blocks south (that is, turning left as you face "uptown" from the French Quarter). If you love stained glass, however, jump off at St. Andrew Street and walk four blocks to Constance for St. Alphonsus.

St. Alphonsus Church

Type of Attraction: Stunning partially restored chapel with extraordinary stained glass

Location: 2029 Constance Street, at St. Andrew

Admission: None

Hours: Thursday–Saturday, 10 A.M.–2 P.M.

Phone: 522-6748

When to Go: Anytime

Overall Appeal by Age Group:

Pre-school	Grade School	Teens	Young Adults	Over 30	Senior Citizens
none	★★	★★	★★★	★★★	★★★

Author's Rating: Absolutely beautiful. ★★★★★

How Much Time to Allow: 30–45 minutes alone

Description and Comments   It's astonishing to consider by what scrimping and sweating the Irish immigrants of the mid-nineteenth century managed to erect this lovely church. Note the unusual "repertory cast" of faces used in the stained-glass windows, shamrocks in the floor tiles, and tomb of the popular Redemptorist priest, Father Francis X. Seeles, who is credited with several miracles (for more info see the section on Anne Rice tours, page 197).

Touring Tips   To get the most information about St. Alphonsus, hook up with tour guide Billy Murphy of Anne Rice's "Inside the World of Anne Rice" tour. Or contact the Preservation Resource Center (604 Julia Street; 581-7032) to obtain info on their next "Stained Glass in Sacred Places" tour.

■ Zone 4: Uptown above Napoleon/University ■

Although they do not qualify as "attractions" in the usual sense, the campuses of both **Loyola University** and **Tulane University** make for nice strolling if you happen to be in the neighborhood. They sit virtually side by side at streetcar stops 36 and 37 on St. Charles Avenue across from Audubon Park. (The statue that greets you at the entrance to Loyola, which seems to be running with its arms flung high, has been known on campus for decades as "the touchdown Jesus.") On the Tulane campus is the Amistad Research Center, which has the world's largest collection of documents, letters, diaries, photographs, and even art concerning civil rights and black history; the collection is open to the public, and is housed in the three-story Tilton Hall right at the St. Charles entrance (865-5535). And there are a few Tiffany studio stained-glass windows at Tulane's Rogers Chapel, which is about four blocks off St. Charles on Audubon Place.

If you take the streetcar out to Audubon Park, you may want to notice a few buildings (although there are so many fine fronts that the ride itself qualifies as an attraction). At 3811 St. Charles, between Penniston and General Taylor Streets, is the sweeping double-porch-fronted **Columns** hotel, designed by architect Thomas Sully in 1883 for a wealthy tobacco merchant and used as the setting for, among other movies, *Pretty Baby.* (If you want to jump off and admire the interior, *Esquire* magazine once rated its Victorian Lounge the best bar in the city.) At **4010 St. Charles**, between General Taylor and Constantinople Streets, is the Queen Anne home Sully designed for himself. He also designed some three dozen houses along St. Charles, but unfortunately only a few remain. What is now the **New Orleans Public Library** at 5120 St. Charles, between Soniant and Dufossat, is a fine turn-of-the-century house that was home to, among others, aviator Harry Williams and his film star wife Marguerite Clark; the reading rooms still have their ceiling murals and chandeliers. And just past the edge of the park at Walnut Street is the **Park View** hotel, an ornate Victorian that was originally built to accommodate visitors to the 1884 World Cotton Exposition in Audubon Park.

Finally, you may want to spend a few hours wandering the **Riverbend** neighborhood for a window-shopping variety as nice as the Quarter's but much less touristy. Take the St. Charles streetcar just past the big right turn onto South Carrollton Avenue (or ask for stop 44), and start strolling up and down Maple Street and then a little farther along Carrollton. There are fine artisan shops here, including boutiques from both Mignon Faget and Yvonne LaFleur; cafes and coffee shops; bookstores; and bars. Among local favorites: Brigtsen's for a Cajun and Creole dinner (chef Frank Brigtsen is a protégé of Paul Prudhomme) and the Camellia Grill for a locally popular version of steak tartare called the "Cannibal Special."

Audubon Park

Type of Attraction: Public green and pedestrian retreat with riding stables, conservatory, swimming pool, miniature train, playgrounds, golf course, bandstands, soccer fields, jogging path, etc.

Location: Entrances at 6800–7000 St. Charles Avenue and 6500 Magazine Street

Admission: Free

Hours: 6 A.M.–10 P.M.

Phone: 861-2537

When to Go: Anytime except after dark, no matter what the signs say

Special Comments: One of the reasons to choose to stay in the Garden District instead of the French Quarter; not quite as fine a facility as City Park but very close

Overall Appeal by Age Group:

Pre-school	Grade School	Teens	Young Adults	Over 30	Senior Citizens
★★★	★★★	★★★	★★★★★	★★★★	★★★

Author's Rating: If you're staying in town long enough to seek out exercise and recreation, this is prime; even a jog or hour's reading in one of the shady gazebos can be an essential break for a visiting executive. And, of course, it has something for everyone in a family. ★★★★½

How Much Time to Allow: Varies by activity

Description and Comments   This is the classic ideal of a public green, built on what was originally a sugar plantation (in the very beginning, it belonged to the Sieur de Bienville himself) and which still boasts live oaks from before the city's founding, along with magnolias, lagoons, formal plantings, hothouse flowers (the Heymann Memorial Conservatory, 891-2419), benches, and trails. The 365-acre park was laid out in the 1890s by John Olmstead, son of the architect of New York's Central Park, after the Cotton Exposition of 1884 was held there. Cars are prohibited around the St. Charles end, so you can wander without fear. Across the railroad tracks toward the Mississippi is the less-publicized area called River View, popular for picnics or jogging. For more on the sport and exercise facilities, see "Exercise and Recreation" on page 173.

Touring Tips Most of the more organized activities and the zoo are at the Magazine Street end of the park. It's a fairly long walk from St. Charles Avenue if you're only trying to get from here to there, but the zoo operates a shuttle van from St. Charles around to the parking lot.

Audubon Zoo

Type of Attraction: Popular and professionally acclaimed zoological park with naturalistic environments, hands-on exhibits, a tropical bird house, live-animal feedings, etc.

Location: 6500 Magazine Street in Audubon Park

Admission: $8 adults, $4 seniors and ages 2–12

Hours: 9:30 A.M.

Phone: 861-2537

When to Go: Anytime

Overall Appeal by Age Group:

Pre-school	Grade School	Teens	Young Adults	Over 30	Senior Citizens
★★★	★★★★	★★★	★★★½	★★★	★★★

Author's Rating: Extremely well designed and stocked, with huge family appeal. ★★★★

How Much Time to Allow: 2–3 hours

Description and Comments There are nearly 2,000 animals here, many of them rare or endangered species, in carefully re-created environments such as the 6 ½-acre Louisiana Swamp, crisscrossed with boardwalks so you can spy on the white alligators. It's only a short stroll to other continents, however: the Asian Domaine, with its Indian temple, rhinos, elephants, and a white tiger; the African Savannah; the South American pampas, the primate house . . . well, you get the idea. For kids of the *Jurassic Park* generation, there's good info on dinosaurs, a group of "living dinosaurs," Komodo dragons, and so on. And all around, the keepers offer chances to stroke or feed the tamer animals.

Touring Tips The Cypress Knee Cafe has better food than the concessions at many facilities, and even some of the restaurants around. Remember to consider the package tickets available combining zoo admission with a cruise from the aquarium, etc.

■ Zone 5: Downtown/St. Bernard ■

We remind you again that cemeteries, as distinct a New Orleans feature as they are, can be dangerous places for solitary visitors or even small groups. However, if you are seriously intrigued by the offbeat, stop by **St. Roch Cemetery** (945-5961) at Derbigny Street and St. Roch Avenue, modeled on Campo Santo dei Tedeschi near the Vatican in Rome. The story begins with the French-born St. Roch (or Rocco) who, at the beginning of the fourteenth century, gave away all his possessions and turned to nursing victims of the plague, often curing them by making the sign of the cross. When he himself fell ill, he was kept alive by a dog who brought him food (he's the patron saint of dog-lovers); nevertheless, he was so altered that when he went home he was thrown into prison (he's also the patron of prisoners). Visited in his cell by an angel for five years, he finally died there. In Europe, VSR ("Viva Saint Roch") was often carved over doorways to ward off disease.

So when yellow fever broke out in 1868, Father Thevis of nearby Holy Trinity Church prayed to St. Roch, promising to build a monument with his own hands if the saint would intercede. The epidemic ended, and Father Thevis built this little chapel, which is now absolutely crammed with prostheses, crutches, glass eyes, and bandages from those who have come here praying for recovery from their injuries. And that's just what's arrived recently; there are hundreds of such offerings in storage.

Also, if you are with a group and call in advance, you may be able to get inside the **Doullut Steamboat House** on Egania Street near the river (949-1422). It and its neighbor, built just after the turn of the century by Milton Doullut, are two of the most extravagant examples of what is called Victorian Steamboat Gothic architecture, with cypress furbelows, glazed brick, marching columns, great steamboat-style galleries, and glass pilot houses perched on the tops.

Chalmette National Battlefield

Type of Attraction: Scene of the Battle of New Orleans, Jackson's famous victory over the British in 1815

Location: 8608 St. Bernard Highway (Rampart/St. Claude extended)

Admission: Free

Hours: 8:30 A.M.–5 P.M.

Phone: 589-4430

When to Go: January 7–8 to see the battle reenactment; otherwise anytime

Special Comments: Although the car gate closes at 5 P.M., there is a pedestrian entry near the cemetery.

Overall Appeal by Age Group:

Pre-school	Grade School	Teens	Young Adults	Over 30	Senior Citizens
none	★★	★★	★★½	★★★	★★★

Author's Rating: Admittedly, battlefields (and military cemeteries) don't appeal to everyone, but if you do find wandering such grounds moving, this is an unusually reassuring and well-marked route—an unalloyed, Hollywood-cheery victory, not a haunting experience like revisiting Antietam, for example. And you can't beat the scenery. ★★★

How Much Time to Allow: 1–2 hours

Description and Comments The bare bones of this battle, so to speak, are familiar to most Americans, by film and pop-music history, if nothing else. Here, on January 8, 1815, British forces under Lt. Gen. Edward Pakenham, brother-in-law of the great Duke of Wellington, were crushed (and Pakenham killed) by the ragtag coalition of Tennessee volunteers, other Southern regiments hustled down for support, free men of color, and Barataria pirates under the able and often ruthless Andrew Jackson. More than 2,000 British were killed on that last day (there had been skirmishes since before Christmas), but only 13 Americans were lost, all but 2 of them black. The other ironies are almost as well-known: The Treaty of Ghent, ending the war, had been signed on Christmas Eve, making the battle moot; Jackson made several errors in judgment that might easily have thrown the victory the other way; and Jackson, who had unsuccessfully tried to persuade President Jefferson to name him governor of Louisiana, wound up far more famous as a result of the battle—the city threw him a triumphal parade modeled on those of the conquering Caesars—which was in effect the first great stroke of his own presidential campaign. It also marked a great turning point in the city's history, uniting Creoles and Americans (and pirates) against a common threat. The annual reenactment is highly theatrical, beginning the night before with staged "spying" on Pakenham and Jackson. Oddly, the adjoining Chalmette National Cemetery dates from the Civil War, and holds only 2 veterans of the Battle of New Orleans; most of the other bodies, some 14,000 of them, are Union soldiers.

Touring Tips   You can just drive past the landmarks, but the visitors' center, once the plantation home of Rene Beauregard, son of the general, holds good exhibits that help you understand the battle's waves, a half-hour film, and well-informed rangers. Be sure to walk over to the levee and look onto the Mississippi River.

Jackson Barracks Museum

Type of Attraction: Military museum with antique and modern armaments and aircraft from the Revolutionary War through the 1990s.

Location: 6400 St. Claude Avenue (Rampart Street extended)

Admission: Free

Hours: Monday–Friday, 7:30 A.M.–3:30 P.M.

Phone: 271-6242

When to Go: Anytime

Overall Appeal by Age Group:

Pre-school	Grade School	Teens	Young Adults	Over 30	Senior Citizens
★	★★★★	★★★	★★★★	★★★★	★★★★

Author's Rating: Fantastic variety of exhibits in this small space, and one almost guaranteed to make kids happy. And since even Operation Desert Storm is represented here (by a Phantom jet and a Russian-made tank abandoned in the Gulf War), veterans or students of any war in U.S. history will find something to marvel at. ★★★★

How Much Time to Allow: 1½ hours

Description and Comments   Tanks, artillery, jets, battle flags, decorations, uniforms, maps. . . . This military museum seems to have acquired relics from every skirmish and siege in the nation's history, but without the sometimes morbid touch of the Confederate Museum. The museum's main building is a powder magazine dating to 1837, but not surprisingly, it had to expand into an annex. The presence of Guardsmen may make this even more realistic for youngsters.

Touring Tips   This is now headquarters for the National Guard, and subject to "internal business," so it wouldn't hurt to call ahead. As you pass the Jackson Barracks next door, you may feel the ghosts even more strongly: The base was built by order of (President) Andy Jackson, and Civil War generals Robert E. Lee, P.T.G. Beauregard, Ulysses S. Grant, and George McLellan were all stationed here as young West Point graduates.

Zone 6: Mid-City/Gentilly

Pitot House

Type of Attraction: Historic, early-nineteenth-century home
Location: 1440 Moss Street
Admission: $3 adults, $2 seniors, $1 children under 12
Hours: Wednesday–Saturday, 10 A.M.–3 P.M.
Phone: 482-0312
When to Go: Anytime

Overall Appeal by Age Group:

Pre-school	Grade School	Teens	Young Adults	Over 30	Senior Citizens
none	½	★	★★½	★★★	★★★

Author's Rating: Evocative and in fine condition. ★★★
How Much Time to Allow: 1–2 hours, depending on your interest

Description and Comments   When it was built in 1799 for Degas' great grandmother (it's named for James Pitot, first mayor of the city, who bought it soon after), this West Indies–style home — encircled by porches, protected by full shutters — was a block away where the Catholic school now stands. It was used in this century as a convent by Mother Francis Xavier Cabrini, the first canonized saint of the United States. It has been beautifully restored to its original condition and furnished with period antiques.

Touring Tips   Under the aegis of the State Landmarks Society, who moved it in the 1960s, this house has been made wheelchair accessible.

■ Zone 7: Lakeview/West End/Bucktown ■

If you're headed toward City Park, and you should be, you can visit **Lake Lawn Metairie Cemetery** on Pontchartrain Boulevard at Metairie Road (486-6331), probably the only safe cemetery for tourists to explore (but don't just wander off by yourself, even here). It's younger than the others, built after the Civil War, and not so crowded, but it houses some of the most elaborate sepulchers around: Moorish, Japanese, Greek, Egyptian, Gothic, you name it. (At the foot of the 85-foot obelisk are four statues, because although grieving widower Daniel Moriarty was told there were only three Graces, he insisted there be one at each side, so they've been nicknamed Faith, Hope, Charity and Mrs. Moriarty.) You can borrow a general recorded tour at the funeral home, as well as one that locates Civil War veterans and statesmen.

City Park

Type of Attraction: Municipal park with a variety of recreational and cultural attractions

Location: 1 Palm Drive off I-10 (City Park/Metairie exit)

Admission: Park free; museum, botanical gardens, and some recreational centers have fees.

Hours: Sunrise to sunset

Phone: 482-4888

When to Go: Anytime

Overall Appeal by Age Group:

Pre-school	Grade School	Teens	Young Adults	Over 30	Senior Citizens
★★★	★★★★★	★★★	★★★★★	★★★★★	★★★

Author's Rating: An unrivaled family venue, with attractions for kids, jocks, picnickers, nature-lovers, and general romantics.
★★★★★

How Much Time to Allow: 1–4 hours

Description and Comments   This is an extraordinary municipal gift, 1,500 acres from the old Allard Plantation (presented to the city by John McDonough, whose statue stands in Lafayette Square) and home to the largest stand of mature live oaks in the world. As mentioned elsewhere, City Park has an almost unequaled variety of recreational facilities, golf courses, tennis courts, batting cages, riding stables, lagoons, etc., plus a bandstand (the Beatles played here in 1964!), the **New Orleans Museum of Art**, the **Botanical Gardens,** and the famous **Dueling Oaks** beneath which hundreds of formal duels were fought during the nineteenth century. However, the park has many simpler attractions, including the **Storyland Amusement Park**, an old-fashioned but swell children's fairyland where they can climb over, around, and into the larger-than-life storybook exhibits and hear the out-loud stories straight from the "books'" mouths. (*Child* magazine calls this one of the top ten playgrounds in the United States) Next door is the **Carousel Gardens,** known to locals as "The Flying Horses," one of the few surviving carved wooden merry-go-rounds in the country. And beyond that is a kid-scaled Ferris wheel, miniature trains, bumper cars, roller coaster, and so on.

Touring Tips From Thanksgiving through New Year's, nearly a million tiny lights are strung among the trees, and the Carousel stays lighted and alive into the evening. Long lines of locals make this an annual holiday event. That's Beauregard at the front gate, of course. Also be sure to notice the WPA symbols, chisels, hammers, and so on, worked into the iron of the bridges around the grounds.

Longue Vue House and Gardens

Type of Attraction: Historic home, decorative arts museum, and formal gardens
Location: 7 Bamboo Road off I-10 (Metairie Road exit)
Admission: $7 adults, $6 seniors, and $3 students and children
Hours: Monday–Saturday, 10 A.M.– 4:30 P.M. (last tour at 4); Sunday, 1–5 P.M. (last tour at 4:15)
Phone: 488-5488
When to Go: Anytime, but flowering gardens peak in spring.
Special Comments: Check out the web page at www.longuevue.com.

Overall Appeal by Age Group:

Pre-school	Grade School	Teens	Young Adults	Over 30	Senior Citizens
½	★	★★	★★★	★★★★★	★★★★★

Author's Rating: Elegant, interesting, and satisfying. ★★★★★
How Much Time to Allow: 2 hours (1 each for house and gardens)

Description and Comments The sumptuous Greek Revival home of philanthropist Edgar Bloom Stern and Edith Rosenwald Stern, daughter of Sears tycoon Julius Rosenwald, was constructed with the express idea that it would be left as a museum. It was designed by William and Geoffrey Platt, and the gardens were laid out by Ellen Biddle Shipman, who also oversaw much of the interior decoration, which features important antiques, rice-paper wall coverings, needlework, Oriental carpets, and Wedgwood creamware. (The house also offers rotating exhibits in its galleries.) Among the gardens are the Spanish Court (modeled after the gardens of the Alhambra), the Portuguese Canal, the Wild Garden, and the Walled Garden.

Touring Tips   The home is wheelchair accessible and a good choice for older visitors. Tour guide brochures are available in French, German, Italian, Spanish, and Japanese, as well as large print. Educational programs are offered for both children and adults; inquire at the desk.

New Orleans Botanical Gardens

Type of Attraction: Formal gardens and conservatory
Location: Victory Avenue in City Park, across from the tennis center
Admission: $3 adults, $1 ages 5–12, free for age 4 and under
Hours: Tuesday–Sunday, 10 A.M.–5 P.M.
Phone: 483-9386
When to Go: Anytime; seasonal exhibits
Special Comments: A quiet respite, not as elaborate as Longue Vue
    Gardens, but only a few minutes' stroll from, and emotionally well
    paired with, the New Orleans Museum of Art

Overall Appeal by Age Group:

Pre-school	Grade School	Teens	Young Adults	Over 30	Senior Citizens
★	★★	★★	★★★★	★★★★	★★★★★

Author's Rating: A fine refuge. ★★★★
How Much Time to Allow: 15 minutes–1 hour

Description and Comments   This was the city's first public classical gardens, an Art Deco–style WPA creation marrying art and nature. Today its 10 acres house about 2,000 varieties of plants grouped into theme gardens and settings, among them a tropical conservatory, aquatic gardens, an azalea and camellia garden, a rose garden, cold frames, and horticultural trails.

Touring Tips   The Garden Study Center offers 90-minute educational programs and how-to's for about $10; call 483-9427 for a schedule.

New Orleans Museum of Art

Type of Attraction: Wide-ranging fine arts and decorative arts
    collection
Location: Lelong Avenue and Dueling Oak Drive in City Park
Admission: $6 adults, $5 seniors, $3 children; free admission
    Thursdays
Hours: Tuesday–Sunday, 10 A.M.–5 P.M.

Phone: 488-2631

When to Go: Anytime

Special Comments: An all-ages introduction-to-art exhibit called "The Starting Point" is as good as it gets.

Overall Appeal by Age Group:

Pre-school	Grade School	Teens	Young Adults	Over 30	Senior Citizens
★	★★★	★★★	★★★★★	★★★★★	★★★★★

Author's Rating: Art lovers should not miss this. ★★★★★

How Much Time to Allow: 1–3 hours

Description and Comments   This neoclassical building, commissioned in 1910 by Jamaican-born New Orleans philanthropist Isaac Delgado to benefit "rich and poor alike," lives up to its mission, housing more than 35,000 works by not only the premier American and European artists—Picasso, Miro, and Degas, whose studio was nearby—but African, Japanese, Chinese, and Native American art as well. Its "Art of the Americas" collection, ranging from pre-Columbian through Spanish Colonial times, is one of the largest, as is its decorative glass works. There are miniatures, furnishings, and regional arts and crafts from the nineteenth century to today—you can even find the trendy Faberge represented. Sketching of these masterworks is welcome, but in dry media only (pencil, charcoal, etc.) and on a single tablet no larger than legal size. One wing is devoted to rotating exhibits. General tours and special exhibition lectures are offered daily; the courtyard cafe serves lunch and afternoon beverages.

Touring Tips   Free parking.

■ Zone 8: New Orleans East ■

Louisiana Nature & Science Center

Type of Attraction: Nature preserve and planetarium

Location: Joe W. Brown Memorial Park, 11000 Lake Forest Boulevard (off I-10)

Admission: $4 adults, $3 seniors, $2 children

Hours: Tuesday–Friday, 9 A.M.–5 P.M.; Saturday, 10 A.M.–5 P.M.; Sunday, noon–5 P.M.; planetarium laser "concerts" Friday and Saturday at 9 and 10:30 P.M. and midnight

Phone: 244-4663; planetarium schedule, 246-STAR

When to Go: Anytime

Special Comments: Parts of the trails have wheelchair-accessible boardwalks.

Overall Appeal by Age Group:

Pre-school	Grade School	Teens	Young Adults	Over 30	Senior Citizens
★★	★★★	★★	★★½	★★	★★★

Author's Rating: A rare urban reserve. ★★½

How Much Time to Allow: 1–2 hours

Description and Comments   This may be one of those places you don't get to until the second trip, but it would be worth visiting: an 86-acre forest and wetlands reserve with trails, greenhouses, changing science exhibits in the center, and a hands-on "Discovery Loft" with fossils, skeletons, etc., plus some live specimens. Local wildlife can be observed either from the trails or from window overlooks at the Wildlife Garden.

Touring Tips   Weekend visitors should inquire about special activities such as canoeing, bird-watching, etc.

■ Zone 10: Metairie above Causeway/Kenner/ ■ Jefferson Highway

If you are staying out near the airport, **Destrehan Manor** is very near, about eight miles farther west. However, since most people consider the River Road plantations as "out-of-town" attractions, we have included it with the other plantation homes in "Sight-Seeing and Tours," which can be found on pages 222–25.

Rivertown

Type of Attraction: Family amusement/education complex, with a dozen small museums and activity centers along three blocks in suburban Kenner

Location: Welcome center at 405 Williams Boulevard off I-10

Admission: All-complex pass $10 adults, $5 seniors and children 12 and under; single venues $3 adults, $2 seniors and children 12 and under

Hours: Tuesday–Saturday, 9 A.M.–5 P.M.; Sunday, 1–5 P.M.; observatory, Thursday–Saturday, 7:30–10:30 P.M.

Phone: 468-7231 or (800) 473-6789

When to Go: Anytime

Special Comments: Business travelers bringing the family along may find this a good reason to stay in an airport-area hotel instead of looking in town.

Overall Appeal by Age Group:

Pre-school	Grade School	Teens	Young Adults	Over 30	Senior Citizens
★★	★★★★★	★★★	★★★★	★★★★	★★★

Author's Rating: A mixed bag, but at least something for everyone. ★★★★

How Much Time to Allow: 2–4 hours

Description and Comments Families with children can duck the Bourbon Street barrage for at least a half-day by heading toward this Victorian village–style complex a half-mile from the airport. The **Louisiana Toy Train Museum** is one of the all-ages attractions, with a half-dozen large dioramas crisscrossed with tracks for the vintage Lionel, American Flyer, and other small-gauge collections (most dating to the '50s). The **Mardi Gras Museum** conveys the trashy, flashy fever of Carnival at safe and PG-rated distance, with costumes, beads, a simulated costume shop, and lots of live-action video. Probably only the most hard-core football fans, or small children, will find more than a few minutes' entertainment at the **New Orleans Saints Hall of Fame**, which is primarily a giant locker room of helmets, uniforms, game balls, etc. The **Daily Living Science Center**, a hands-on if lightweight introduction to car engines, weather, dental hygiene, commercial laundries, and other strange and sundry aspects of everyday life and a full-sized NASA space station, complete with weightlessness chamber, is scheduled to open in April of 1998. It also has a planetarium and an observatory, which is open Thursday through Saturday, 7:30–10:30 P.M. (582-4000). On the other hand, the **Louisiana Wildlife Museum and Aquarium** is well organized and attractive, with over 700 preserved specimens of indigenous mammals and reptiles and a 15,000-gallon tank holding marine life. Literally in the backyard of the Wildlife Museum is the **Cannes Brulee Native American Center of the Gulf South,** a living history installation that re-creates a Native American village, complete with live hogs, poultry, rabbits, and crayfish, and staffed by serious and well-spoken native craftsmen and "residents." There is also a 300-seat **Repertory Theatre,** and the **Children's Castle** offers puppet shows, magic displays, and storytelling.

Touring Tips   Like many children's museums, this tends to be busier before lunch than after. Walk across to LaSalle's Landing for a good view of the mighty Mississippi.

■ Zone 11: West Bank ■

Blaine Kern's Mardi Gras World

Type of Attraction: Year-round "factory" of flamboyant Mardi Gras floats and costumes

Location: 223 Newton Street, Algiers (across the river from the World Trade Center)

Admission: $5.50 adults, $4.50 seniors, $3.25 children ages 3–12

Hours: Daily, 9:30 A.M.–4:30 P.M.

Phone: 361-7821

When to Go: Anytime

Special Comments: One of the four major year-round ways to experience Mardi Gras, and a sure-fire kids' favorite, especially combined with the free ferry ride

Overall Appeal by Age Group:

Pre-school	Grade School	Teens	Young Adults	Over 30	Senior Citizens
★★★	★★★	★★★	★★★	★★★	★★★

Author's Rating: Impressive and fantastical, if a little static. ★★★

How Much Time to Allow: 1½–2 hours

Description and Comments   Blaine Kern & Co. goes back to the late '40s, and since then has become among the busiest float-makers in the world, responsible for not only the floats and multistory-sized figures for Mardi Gras, but also for Macy's Thanksgiving Day parade, the Bastille Day celebrations in Cannes, France, and more than 40 other parades. The sculpture company was founded right before the 1984 World's Fair in New Orleans to build the giant characters for that event, and now works for amusement parks all over the world. These huge warehouses, more than 500,000 square feet of them, called "dens," are filled with props, celebrity statues, royal regalia, and the artists creating them; you can even dress in costume and have your picture taken alongside one of the characters.

Touring Tips   Take the Canal Street Ferry across and look for the shuttle bus. For older visitors, the architecture of the Algiers neighborhood may hold some interest, but it is not a great area to walk around, especially late in the day.

PART THIRTEEN

Dining in New Orleans

I used to work for a New Orleans newspaper whose masthead motto quoted a French philosopher: "Localism alone leads to culture." That could serve as a slogan for Orleanians, who live lives quite different from those of other Americans. Not just on Mardi Gras, and not only among certain classes, either. The style that gave New Orleans its nickname "The Big Easy" imbues every aspect of local society.

Here's a classic New Orleans story. A guy leaves town for a better job in a more stable place. After a year or so, though, he returns to a lower salary and less promise for the future because he can't stand not being able to get gumbo or an oyster poorboy when he wants.

Food is of incalculable importance to Orleanians. The degree to which that is true can be observed in any restaurant. Conversations that seem from a distance to be about sports, politics, or business are actually, more often than not, about eating: what was eaten yesterday, where eating will occur tomorrow, and whether this place is as good as it was last time. Although a seemingly equivalent kind of gustatory consciousness has swept across the country in recent years, the interest in food in New Orleans wells up from a much deeper place, through six or seven generations of genes.

But, to return to that motto . . . The main appeal of New Orleans' food is in its localism. You'd have to travel to Europe to find its like. In just the way that French or Italian towns offer their local culinary styles to the near-exclusion of anything else, so too is New Orleans obsessed with Creole and Cajun food. And that's nothing new. Creole was America's first regional gourmet cuisine. Over a century ago, books were being written that identified Creole cooking as both fairly comprehensive and a thing apart.

The question that everybody who gets interested in New Orleans eating wants answered is: "What's the difference between Creole food and Cajun food?" A colossal amount of discussion on this matter has transpired—usually in restaurants—and nobody, regardless of his claims to authority, has ever been allowed to nail anything down.

But I'll try. Creole is the cooking style of New Orleans proper, which has been a cosmopolis for almost 200 years. Creole cuisine is based on

French cuisine, but with powerful influences from Spain and Africa (the latter by way of the Caribbean). Other nationalities have added their touches, most significantly the Germans and Italians.

The Cajuns are also French, but they're different French: Acadians expelled from Nova Scotia two centuries ago. Living in almost complete isolation and poverty on the bayous of South Louisiana for two-thirds of the time since then, they have developed a culture of survival. They had a lot of seafood and farm products, but they had to sell the best of them to stay alive, and were forced to invent a unique style of cooking to make the inferior stuff taste good. Even today, real Cajun food—as delicious as it is— looks pretty bad. Which is why it has only rarely translated in authentic form to restaurant menus.

So Creole is city food and Cajun is country. A big fillet of fish with a complicated sauce draped over it is more likely to be found in a Creole milieu; the Cajun restaurant will tend more toward its étouffées and other slow-cooked pot dishes. Okay, okay. Now let's abandon the issue. Creole and Cajun have influenced each other so much in recent years that you find the same menus and flavors throughout Southeast Louisiana, save for a few unreconstructed pockets of hyper-localism here and there. And any argument over which is better is bound to end in trouble.

Creole and Cajun cooking have one notable distinction in common: the raw materials. The cooking of Southeast Louisiana is in large part defined by its native seafoods. Principal among them are oysters, shrimp, crabs, and crawfish. And there's a large cast of finfish from local waters. While restaurants in most other cities thrive on the tide of fish delivered by fast airplanes, there's nothing quite like the freshness of seafood that came to the general vicinity of your plate by way of a beat-up old truck that only had to drive a few miles. There are restaurants in New Orleans where you can eat a fish while watching his relatives swim and jump in the waters right outside the window.

I suppose you're expecting me to define the Creole taste now. Well, I give up. I'm blinkered by having eaten Creole food all my life, which makes me think of it as totally normal. What I can tell you is what I miss in the food I eat when I travel. I find non-Creole American food lacking in salt, pepper, richness, and general intensity of flavor.

One of the explanations for this is the amount of salt, pepper, cream, butter, and other fats in classic Creole cooking. Indeed, an often-cited characteristic of New Orleans recipes is that they have a way of beginning: "First you make a roux." (Roux, a blend of flour and oil, butter, or other fat, cooked to various shades of brown, is the main active ingredient in dishes from gumbo to oysters Rockefeller.) As a result, much of Creole and

Cajun cooking in the old style is high in all the things the food police tell us to stay away from.

But during the past decade there's been a revolution in Creole cooking, spurred by intense competition from the hundreds (this is no exaggeration) of new restaurants that have opened. Diners have come to expect new dishes, ingredients, and flavors, and the younger, higher-profile chefs have been happy to invent them. Most of the new Creole cuisine is incomparably lighter than the old standards. Even roux is becoming rare. Occasionally it's left out of gumbos, a state of affairs my mother—like every other old-time Creole cook—would consider heresy.

The current crop of chefs takes two different routes to their innovations. Most of them are one-worlders, importing ingredients, flavors, and techniques from exotic places. Many of them incorporate those outside influences into dishes that are still quite recognizably Creole. But more than a few are serving food that has no local connection at all—sometimes not even local ingredients. That is a completely new development in a city where diners historically haven't accepted even French or Italian food until it hybridized with Creole. At the same time, purveyors of unusual ethnic cuisines in New Orleans are finding success for the first time.

If this causes you to cock an eyebrow and wonder whether our island of culture will lose its distinctiveness, rest easy. No matter how enthusiastic even the most sophisticated New Orleans diner waxes about some new Vietnamese-Mexican fusion bistro, you can be sure that in his most relaxed moments he's still munching down poorboy sandwiches, boiled crawfish, jambalaya, and bread pudding—as will all other aficionados of Creole food from near or far because we all know that, like all the world's other great ethnic cuisines, great Creole and Cajun cooking is only found in the land of its birth.

■ A Few Things You Should Know ■

Because the cuisine of New Orleans is so intimately tied to the indigenous ingredients, it's important to pay attention to the seasons. Although many restaurants serve, say, crawfish year-round, there's no question that crawfish are incomparably better in the peak of their natural cycle. Here's the schedule:

Crawfish   Christmas through the Fourth of July, with the peak of quality in April and May.

Crabs, soft-shell and otherwise   April through October. The peak is unpredictable, but usually the warmer it is, the better the crabmeat.

Oysters   Good year-round, but a little off during the spawn in July and August. (In other words, forget that months-with-an-R myth.)

Shrimp   There are several species, so seasons click on and off. The best times are May through August and October through December. The only poor month for shrimp is March.

Tuna   May through September.

Pompano   July through October.

Creole tomatoes   These meaty, sweet, gigantic, sensual tomatoes have a short season, in April and May, but are worth waiting for.

The calendar is also reliable in predicting when restaurants will be at their best. Absolutely the worst time to eat in New Orleans is during the Mardi Gras season, which extends three weeks before the movable Ash Wednesday (in February or early March). The city's restaurants are stretched thin at that time of year by tourists, conventions, and Mardi Gras balls. What's more, waiters and other restaurant personnel tend to be heavy participants in Carnival hijinks and are, shall we say, not at their peaks.

The best times for a serious eater to come to town are the months of October and April. The weather is beautiful for patio dining, the food supplies are at their best, and the conventions aren't overwhelming. Also good are the summer months, especially July and September. The heat and humidity convince tourists and conventions to stay away (despite the fact that there may be no better air-conditioned city on earth), and the restaurants are eager to please.

Also of note are two superb food festivals. The New Orleans Jazz and Heritage Festival takes place on the last week of April and the first week of May, with an outdoor surfeit of music and indigenous food. Then, in late June, the New Orleans Wine and Food Experience brings you indoors for an extended weekend of special feasting with the city's best chefs and drinking with the world's best winemakers.

■ Tourist Places ■

In the restaurant profiles that make up most of this section, you may notice that a few well-known or highly visible restaurants are missing. This is not an oversight. The following restaurants may come to your attention, but in my opinion they're not as worthwhile as other comparable options.

Caribbean Room   2031 St. Charles Avenue 524-0581
Once a great favorite of local diners, the dining room of the Pontchartrain Hotel has been truncated and its menu jerked around so much that it's lost its appeal.

Central Grocery   923 Decatur 523-1620
As this old emporium of imported food has allowed its floor space to become taken over by the vending of muffulettas to tourists, both the store and the muffulettas have declined.

Deanie's Seafood   1713 Lake Avenue, Bucktown 831-4141
Deanie's is immensely popular, but what brings that about is the eye-popping size of its indifferent seafood platters.

Hard Rock Cafe   440 North Peters 529-5617
Although the burgers, roasted chicken, and ribs are not bad, the New Orleans edition of the international chain is much more of a place than a restaurant.

Jackson Square Cafe   801 Decatur 523-5061
This place has a great location in the Lower Pontalba Building on Jackson Square, and its menu promises all the clichéd New Orleans food you'd ever want, but it's not very good.

Jimmy Buffett's Margaritaville Cafe   1104 Decatur 592-2565
A must for Parrotheads—but only after eating somewhere else.

Kabby's   Riverside New Orleans Hilton, 2 Poydras 584-3880
Assuming a ship hasn't pulled alongside, this big restaurant offers a great view of the river, but they change the concept of the menu so often that eating here is chancy at best.

Kristal Seafood   600 Decatur 522-0336
At the top of the Jackson Brewery, with a fine view of the river and the Quarter, this place serves forgettable seafood.

Landry's Seafood House   400 North Peters 558-0038
A regional chain, Landry's has the look of a great old middle-of-nowhere Louisiana roadhouse, but the food is strictly formula and not very good.

Mulate's   201 Julia 522-1492
A mammoth place copied from the original Cajun dance restaurant in Breaux Bridge, Mulate's does indeed have good Cajun music, but the food is only occasionally interesting.

Patout's Cajun Cabin   501 Bourbon 524-4054

They occupy the space where Al Hirt plays when he's in town with gilded versions of Cajun food. Although it can be quite good, the inconsistency is so extreme as to make the place unrecommendable.

Planet Hollywood   Jackson Brewery 522-7826

This chain of rock and roll glitz palaces has a New Orleans chef running its food operations, and he installed a very heavy emphasis on local food. This is admirable, but the seasoning levels are so high they're less convincing than offensive.

Ralph & Kacoo's   519 Toulouse 522-5226

It started as a fine seafood house upriver and expanded into a chain of very large, somewhat overpriced, and mediocre food factories.

■ **New Places** ■

Here are some restaurants that haven't established enough of a track record for full review. I think, however, they will prove worthy of your attention, especially if you like hot, new places.

Breakwater Bistro

This is the second, more casual, more seafood-oriented restaurant by the guys who brought you the Steak Knife. It's near the marina and has a lively bar, as well as good, basic, New Orleans food. In Zone 7—Lakeview.

Dominique's

The chefs from the Bistro at the Maison de Ville have a way of leaving to open new places of their own. This is the latest such venture, the creation of Chef Dominique Macquet. A wide range of styles are presented preciously but with great originality. In Zone 1—French Quarter.

House of Saigon

Vietnamese restaurants are suddenly popular, and this is the first of them to appeal to mainstream New Orleans. A lovely dining room serves a menu that's short by Vietnamese standards but sufficiently ethnic to keep you interested. Not far from the airport in Zone 10—Kenner.

Metro Bistro

The owners of the Cajun restaurant, Charley G's (profiled), stretched a good deal with this reasonably authentic French bistro. It offers cassoulet, bouillabaisse, bourride, and all the rest of that stuff, all of which is rare in New Orleans. In Zone 2—Central Business District.

Mystic Cafe

A good-looking Turkish restaurant with a slick, intriguing, and very good menu. Order light: The portions are very large. It can be noisy when full. In Zone 3—Uptown below Napoleon.

Red Fish Grill

Ralph Brennan, one of the creators of Mr. B's, opened a seafood-intensive cafe in what looks like the shell of an old department store. (It's really the work of a designer.) Simple and very New Orleans. In Zone 1—French Quarter.

The Restaurants

■ Our Favorite New Orleans Restaurants: ■
Explaining the Ratings

We have developed detailed profiles for the best restaurants (in our opinion) in town. Each profile features an easily scanned heading which allows you to check out the restaurant's name, cuisine, star rating, cost, quality rating, and value rating very quickly.

Star Rating The star rating is an overall rating which encompasses the entire dining experience, including style, service, and ambiance in addition to the taste, presentation, and quality of the food. Five stars is the highest rating possible and connotes the best of everything. Four-star restaurants are exceptional, and three-star restaurants are well above average. Two-star restaurants are good. One star is used to connote an average restaurant that demonstrates an unusual capability in some area of specialization, for example, an otherwise unmemorable place that has great barbecued chicken.

Cost To the right of the star rating is an expense description that provides a comparative sense of how much a complete meal will cost. A complete meal for our purposes consists of an entree with vegetable or side dish, and choice of soup or salad. Appetizers, desserts, drinks, and tips are excluded.

Inexpensive	$14 and less per person
Moderate	$15–25 per person
Expensive	$26–40 per person
Very Expensive	Over $40 per person

Quality Rating To the right of the cost rating appears a number and a letter. The number is a quality rating based on a scale of 0–100, with 100 being the highest (best) rating attainable. The quality rating is based expressly on the taste, freshness of ingredients, preparation, presentation, and creativity of food served. There is no consideration of price. If you are a person who wants the best food available, and cost is not an issue, you need look no further than the quality ratings.

Value Rating If, on the other hand, you are looking for both quality and value, then you should check the value rating, expressed in letters. The value ratings are defined as follows:

A   Exceptional value, a real bargain
B   Good value
C   Fair value, you get exactly what you pay for
D   Somewhat overpriced
F   Significantly overpriced

Location   Just below the restaurant name is a designation for geographic zone. This zone description will give you a general idea of where the restaurant described is located. For ease of use, we divide New Orleans into 12 geographic zones.

Zone 1.   French Quarter
Zone 2.   Central Business District
Zone 3.   Uptown below Napoleon
Zone 4.   Uptown above Napoleon
Zone 5.   Downtown/St. Bernard
Zone 6.   Mid-City/Gentilly
Zone 7.   Lakeview/West End/Bucktown
Zone 8.   New Orleans East
Zone 9.   Metairie below Causeway
Zone 10.   Metairie above Causeway/Kenner/Jefferson Highway
Zone 11.   West Bank
Zone 12.   North Shore

If you are in the French Quarter and intend to walk or take a cab to dinner, you may want to choose a restaurant from among those located in Zone 1. If you have a car, you might include restaurants from contiguous zones in your consideration. (See pages 10–23 for detailed zone maps.)

■ Our Pick of the Best New ■ Orleans Restaurants

Because restaurants are opening and closing all the time in New Orleans, we have tried to confine our list to establishments—or chefs—with a proven track record over a fairly long period of time. Those newer or changed establishments that demonstrate staying power and consistency will be profiled in subsequent editions.

The list is highly selective. Non-inclusion of a particular place does not necessarily indicate that the restaurant is not good, but only that it was not ranked among the best or most consistent in its genre. Detailed profiles of each restaurant follow in alphabetical order at the end of this chapter. Also, we've listed the types of payment accepted at each restaurant using the following codes:

AMEX	American Express	DC	Diners Club
CB	Carte Blanche	MC	MasterCard
D	Discover	VISA	VISA

	The Best New Orleans Restaurants				
Restaurant/Type	Star Rating	Price	Quality Rating	Value Rating	Zone
Breakfast					
Brennan's	★★★	Very Exp	82	F	1
Coffee Pot	★★	Mod	71	C	1
Cajun					
Bon Ton Cafe	★★★	Mod	79	B	2
Chinese					
China Blossom	★★★★	Mod	87	B	11
Trey Yuen	★★★★	Exp	85	D	12
Mr. Tai's	★★★	Mod	83	C	9
Kung's Dynasty	★★★	Mod	82	C	3
Creole					
Le Parvenu	★★★★	Exp	89	C	10
Vizard's	★★★★	Exp	88	B	4
Tujague's	★★★★	Exp	87	C	1
La Cuisine	★★★	Mod	87	B	7
Gallagher's	★★★	Exp	86	C	12
Begue's	★★★	Exp	83	C	1
Gumbo Shop	★★★	Mod	80	B	1
Coffee Pot	★★	Mod	71	C	1
Creole French					
Christian's	★★★★	Exp	90	B	6
Galatoire's	★★★★	Exp	90	C	1
Arnaud's	★★★★	Exp	86	D	1
Antoine's	★★★★	Exp	83	D	1
Brennan's	★★★	Very Exp	82	F	1
Creole Italian					
Vincent's Italian Cuisine	★★★★	Mod	90	A	10
Mosca's	★★★★	Exp	88	C	11

The Best New Orleans Restaurants (continued)

Restaurant/Type	Star Rating	Price	Quality Rating	Value Rating	Zone
Creole Italian (*continued*)					
Sal & Judy's	★★★★	Exp	86	B	12
Pascal's Manale	★★★★	Exp	85	B	4
Bacco	★★★★	Mod	84	C	1
Eclectic					
Pelican Club	★★★★★	Exp	96	C	1
Windsor Court Grill Room	★★★★★	Very Exp	94	F	2
Bella Luna	★★★★	Very Exp	92	C	1
Bayona	★★★★	Exp	96	B	1
Nola	★★★★	Exp	90	C	1
Gautreau's	★★★★	Exp	89	C	4
Mike's on the Avenue	★★★★	Very Exp	89	D	2
Bistro at Maison de Ville	★★★	Exp	84	C	1
French					
La Provence	★★★★★	Exp	98	C	12
Crozier's	★★★★★	Exp	93	C	10
La Crêpe Nanou	★★★★	Mod	87	A	4
Louis XVI	★★★★	Very Exp	87	D	1
Martinique	★★★	Mod	85	B	4
Greek					
Odyssey Grill	★★★	Mod	87	B	7
Indian					
India Palace	★★★	Mod	83	C	10
Shalimar	★★★	Mod	82	C	1
Italian					
Irene's Cuisine	★★★★	Mod	89	B	1
Andrea's	★★★★	Exp	87	C	9
La Riviera	★★★★	Exp	83	C	10
Ristorante Carmelo	★★★	Mod	79	C	1
Japanese/Sushi Bar					
Shogun	★★★★	Mod	86	C	9
Little Tokyo	★★★	Mod	82	C	3

The Best New Orleans Restaurants (continued)

Restaurant/Type	Star Rating	Price	Quality Rating	Value Rating	Zone
Lebanese					
Byblos	★★★★	Mod	83	A	9
Mexican/Southwestern					
Vaqueros	★★★	Mod	90	C	4
Neighborhood Cafe					
Liuzza's	★★★	Inexp	79	B	6
Mandina's	★★★	Mod	75	A	6
Nouvelle Cajun					
K-Paul's Louisiana Kitchen	★★★★	Very Exp	91	D	1
Charley G's	★★★	Exp	83	D	9
Nouvelle Creole					
Emeril's	★★★★★	Very Exp	98	C	2
Commander's Palace	★★★★★	Exp	97	B	3
Dakota	★★★★	Exp	94	C	12
Gabrielle	★★★★	Exp	93	B	6
Brigtsen's	★★★★	Exp	92	B	4
Rib Room	★★★★	Very Exp	91	D	1
Clancy's	★★★★	Exp	90	B	4
Mr. B's	★★★★	Exp	90	C	1
Nola	★★★★	Exp	90	C	1
Upperline	★★★★	Exp	88	C	4
Broussard's	★★★★	Very Exp	84	D	1
Sclafani's	★★★★	Mod	91	A	1
Palace Cafe	★★★	Exp	84	C	2
Kelsey's	★★★	Mod	82	B	3
Nouvelle French					
Peristyle	★★★★★	Exp	98	B	1
Nouvelle Italian					
G&E Courtyard Grill	★★★★	Exp	93	B	1
Cafe Giovanni	★★★★	Exp	87	B	1
Sandwiches					
Uglesich's	★★★★	Mod	86	D	3

The Best New Orleans Restaurants (continued)

Restaurant/Type	Star Rating	Price	Quality Rating	Value Rating	Zone
Sandwiches (continued)					
Mother's	★★★	Mod	83	D	2
Napoleon House	★★	Inexp	74	B	1
Seafood					
Bozo's	★★★★	Inexp	86	B	9
Uglesich's	★★★★	Mod	86	D	3
Drago's	★★★★	Mod	85	C	10
Barrow's Shady Inn	★★★	Inexp	84	B	4
Sid-Mar's	★★★	Mod	83	A	9
Mike Anderson's	★★★	Mod	80	C	1
Bruning's	★★★	Inexp	79	A	7
Spanish					
Lola's	★★★	Mod	80	A	6
Steak					
Ruth's Chris Steak House	★★★★	Very Exp	90	D	6, 10
Tavern on the Park	★★★	Exp	80	C	6
Thai					
Siamese	★★★	Mod	84	C	10
Vegetarian					
Chicory Farm Cafe	★★★★	Mod	83	C	4
Vietnamese					
Kim Son	★★★★	Mod	87	A	11

■ More Recommendations ■

Best Restaurants for Sunday Brunch

Arnaud's   813 Bienville 523-5433

Bacco   310 Chartres 522-2426

Begue's   Royal Sonesta Hotel, 300 Bourbon 586-0300

Brennan's   417 Royal 525-9711

Cafe Sbisa   1011 Decatur 522-5565

Cafe Volage   720 Dublin 861-4227

Charley G's   111 Veterans Boulevard, Metairie 837-6408

Commander's Palace   1403 Washington Avenue 899-8221

Court of Two Sisters   613 Royal 522-7273

Dakota   629 North US 190, Covington (504) 892-3712

Feelings   2600 Chartres 945-2222

House of Blues   225 Decatur 529-2583

La Gauloise   Le Meridien Hotel, 614 Canal 527-6712

Mr. B's   201 Royal 523-2078

Palace Cafe   605 Canal 523-1661

Praline Connection   901 South Peters 523-3973

Rib Room   Omni Royal Orleans Hotel, 621 St. Louis 529-7045

Sazerac   Fairmont Hotel, University Place 529-7111

Vaqueros   4938 Prytania 891-6441

Veranda   Hotel Inter-Continental, 444 St. Charles Avenue 522-5566

Windsor Court Grill Room   300 Gravier 523-6000

Best Breakfasts

Bacco   310 Chartres 522-2426

Bailey's   123 Baronne 529-7111

Begue's   300 Bourbon 586-0300

Bluebird Cafe   3625 Prytania 895-7166; 7801 Panola 866-7577

Brennan's   417 Royal 525-9711

Cafe Pontchartrain   2031 St. Charles Avenue 524-0581

Camellia Grill   626 South Carrollton Avenue 866-9573

Coffee Pot   714 St. Peter 524-3500

La Gauloise   614 Canal 527-6712

La Madeleine   547 St. Ann 568-9950; 601 South Carrollton Avenue 861-8661

Louis XVI   730 Bienville 581-7000

Mother's   401 Poydras 523-9656

Peppermill (Riccobono's)   3524 Severn Avenue, Metairie 455-2266

Petunia's   817 St. Louis 522-6440

Tally-Ho   400 Chartres 566-7071

Tiffin Inn   6601 Veterans Boulevard, Metairie 888-6602

Veranda   Hotel Inter-Continental, 444 St. Charles Avenue 522-5566

Windsor Court Grill Room   300 Gravier 523-6000

Best Hamburgers

Bud's Broiler   500 City Park Avenue 486-2559; 6325 Elysian Fields Avenue 282-6696; 2800 Veterans Boulevard, Kenner 466-0026; 3151 Calhoun 861-0906; 4101 Jefferson Highway, Jefferson 837-9419; 112 Sauve Road, River Ridge 738-2452; 9820 Lake Forest Boulevard 244-6866; 5100 Lapalco Boulevard 348-0492

Camellia Grill   626 South Carrollton Avenue 866-9573

Doug's Place   748 Camp 527-5433

Hard Rock Cafe   440 North Peters 529-5617

Hummingbird Grill   804 St. Charles Avenue 561-9229

Katie's   3701 Iberville 488-6582

Lee's Hamburgers   904 Veterans Boulevard 836-6804

Michael's Mid-City Grill   4139 Canal 488-2878

New Orleans Hamburger & Seafood Co.   1005 South Clearview Parkway, Jefferson 734-1122; 6920 Veterans Boulevard, Metairie 455-1272; 817 Veterans Boulevard, Metairie 837-8580

Port of Call   838 Esplanade 523-0120

Snug Harbor   626 Frenchmen 949-0696

Straya   4517 Veterans Boulevard, Metairie 887-8873; 2001 St. Charles Avenue 593-9955

Ye Olde College Inn   3016 South Carrollton Avenue 866-3683

Restaurants with Most Unusual Architecture

Allegro   1100 Poydras 582-2350

Antoine's   713 St. Louis 581-4422

Arnaud's   813 Bienville 523-5433

Bacco   310 Chartres 522-2426

Bella Luna   914 North Peters 529-1583

Brennan's   417 Royal 525-9711

Broussard's   819 Conti 581-3866

Cafe Sbisa   1011 Decatur Street 522-5565

Christian's   3835 Iberville 482-4924

Commander's Palace   1403 Washington Avenue 899-8221

Emeril's   800 Tchoupitoulas 528-9393

Nola   534 St. Louis 522-6652

Restaurant des Familles   LA 45 at LA 3134, Crown Point 689-7834

Tavern on the Park   900 City Park Avenue 486-3333

Upperline   1413 Upperline 891-9822

Vaqueros   4938 Prytania 891-6441

Veranda   Hotel Inter-Continental, 444 St. Charles Avenue 522-5566

Best Cafes for Dessert and Coffee

Angelo Brocato   214 North Carrollton Avenue 486-1465; 537 St. Ann 525-9676

Cafe du Monde   800 Decatur 525-4544

Churros Cafe   3100 Kingman, Metairie 885-6516

Coffee Cottage   2559 Metairie Road, Metairie 833-3513

Coffee Rani   2324 Veterans Boulevard, Metairie 833-6343

Croissant d'Or   617 Ursulines 524-4663

La Madeleine   547 St. Ann 568-9950; 601 South Carrollton Avenue 861-8661

La Marquise   625 Chartres 524-0420

Maurice's French Pastries   3501 Hessmer Avenue, Metairie 885-1526

Morning Call Coffee Stand   3325 Severn Avenue, Metairie 885-4068

Plantation Coffeehouse   5555 Canal Boulevard 482-3164

Best Restaurants for Dining with Children

Assunta's   2631 Covington Highway (US 190), Slidell (504) 649-9768

Bozo's   3117 21st Street, Metairie 831-8666

Brick Oven Cafe   2805 Williams Boulevard, Kenner 466-2097

Bruning's   West End Park 282-9395

Cafe Atchafalaya   901 Louisiana 891-5271

Cavallino's   1500 South Carrollton Avenue 866-9866

Copeland's   1001 South Clearview Parkway, Jefferson 733-7843; 701 Veterans Boulevard, Metairie 831-3437; 4338 St. Charles Avenue 897-2325; 1700 Lapalco, Harvey 364-1575; 1337 Gause Boulevard, Slidell (504) 643-0001

Corky's   4243 Veterans Boulevard, Metairie 887-5000

Delmonico   1300 St. Charles Avenue 525-4937

Doug's Place   748 Camp 527-5433

Fausto's   530 Veterans Boulevard, Metairie 833-7121

Figaro Pizzerie   7900 Maple 866-0100

Golden Lake Chinese Restaurant   1712 Lake Avenue, Bucktown 838-8646

La Gauloise   614 Canal 527-6712

Louisiana Pizza Kitchen   615 South Carrollton Avenue 866-5900

Mark Twain Pizza Landing   2035 Metairie Road, Metairie 832-8032

Peppermill (Riccobono's)   3524 Severn Avenue, Metairie 455-2266

Semolina   3242 Magazine 895-4260; 5080 Pontchartrain Boulevard 486-5581; Oakwood Mall (197 West Bank Expy.), Gretna 361-8293; 3501 Chateau Boulevard, Kenner 468-1047

Sid-Mar's   1824 Orpheum, Bucktown 831-9541

Straya   4517 Veterans Boulevard, Metairie 887-8873; 2001 St. Charles Avenue 593-9955

West End Cafe   8536 Pontchartrain Boulevard 288-0711

Ye Olde College Inn   3016 South Carrollton Avenue 866-3683

Best Restaurants for Local Color

Antoine's   713 St. Louis 581-4422

Arnaud's   813 Bienville 523-5433

Bon Ton Cafe   401 Magazine 524-3386

Bozo's   3117 21st Street, Metairie 831-8666

Brigtsen's   723 Dante 861-7610

Broussard's   819 Conti 581-3866

Bruning's   West End Park 282-9395

Cafe du Monde   800 Decatur 525-4544

Cafe Sbisa   1011 Decatur Street 522-5565

Casamento's   4330 Magazine 895-9761

Clancy's   6100 Annunciation 895-1111

Coffee Pot   714 St. Peter 524-3500

Commander's Palace   1403 Washington Avenue 899-8221

Court of Two Sisters   613 Royal 522-7273

Dooky Chase   2301 Orleans Avenue 821-0600

Doug's Place   748 Camp 527-5433

Galatoire's   209 Bourbon 525-2021

Joey K's   3001 Magazine 891-0997

Liuzza's   3636 Bienville 482-9120

Mandina's   3800 Canal 482-9179

Mosca's   4137 US 90, Waggaman 436-9942

Napoleon House   500 Chartres 524-9752

Pascal's Manale   1838 Napoleon Avenue 895-4877

Praline Connection   542 Frenchman 943-3934; 901 South
Peters 523-3973

Rocky & Carlo's   613 West St. Bernard Highway, Chalmette 279-8323

Sid-Mar's   1824 Orpheum, Bucktown 831-9541

Tujague's   823 Decatur 525-8676

Uglesich's   1238 Baronne 523-8571

Best Muffulettas
Cafe Buon Giorno   830 Third Street, Gretna 363-9111

Compagno's   7839 St. Charles Avenue 866-9313

Giovanni's Sausage Co.   1325 Veterans Boulevard, Metairie 835-4558

Italian Pie   417 South Rampart 522-7552

Joey K's   3001 Magazine 891-0997

Johnny's Po-Boys   511 St. Louis 524-8129

Katie's   3701 Iberville 488-6582

Landry's   789 Harrison Avenue 488-6476

Messina's   200 Chartres 523-9225

Napoleon House   500 Chartres 524-9752

Best Restaurants with Oyster Bars
Acme Oyster House   724 Iberville 522-5973

Bozo's   3117 21st Street, Metairie 831-8666

Bruning's   West End Park 282-9395

Casamento's   4330 Magazine 895-9761

Drago's   3232 North Arnoult Road, Metairie 888-9254

Felix's   739 Iberville 522-4440

Messina's   200 Chartres 523-9225

Mike Anderson's   215 Bourbon 524-3884

Pascal's Manale   1838 Napoleon Avenue 895-4877

Remoulade   309 Bourbon 523-0377

Uglesich's   1238 Baronne 523-8571

Best Restaurants for Outdoor Dining

Bayona   430 Dauphine 525-4455

Broussard's   819 Conti 581-3866

Cafe Degas   3127 Esplanade 945-5635

Cafe Volage   720 Dublin 861-4227

Court of Two Sisters   613 Royal 522-7273

G&E Courtyard Grill   1113 Decatur 528-9376

Louis XVI   730 Bienville Street 581-7000

Martinique   5908 Magazine 891-8495

Vaqueros   4938 Prytania 891-6441

Best Pizza

Brick Oven Cafe   2805 Williams Boulevard, Kenner 466-2097

Cafe Buon Giorno   830 Third Street, Gretna 363-9111

Cafe Italiano   3244 Magazine 891-4040

Cavallino's   1500 South Carrollton Avenue 866-9866

Figaro Pizzerie   7900 Maple 866-0100

Italian Pie   417 South Rampart 522-7552

Louisiana Pizza Kitchen   615 South Carrollton Avenue 866-5900

Mama Rosa's   616 North Rampart 523-5546

Mark Twain Pizza Landing   2035 Metairie Road, Metairie 832-8032

Mona Lisa   1212 Royal 522-6746; 874 Harrison Avenue 488-0133

Mr. Roma   4421 Clearview Parkway, Metairie 455-8010

New York Pizza   5201 Magazine 891-2376

Roman Pizza   7329 Cohn 866-1166

Tailgators Cafe   933 Metairie Road, Metairie 832-0122

Tower of Pizza   2104 Veterans Boulevard, Metairie 833-9373

ANDREA'S

Northern Italian	★★★★	Expensive	QUALITY
			87

3100 19th Street 834-8583   Zone 9, Metairie below Causeway

		VALUE
		C

Customers: Businessmen at lunch; daters
Reservations: Recommended
When to go: Anytime
Entree range: $10–24
Payment: All major credit cards
Service rating: ★★★★
Friendliness rating: ★★★

Parking: Free lot adjacent
Bar: Full bar
Wine selection: Substantial list, mostly Italian and French; a bit overpriced
Dress: Jacket recommended but not required
Disabled access: Full

Brunch: Sunday, 11 A.M.–3 P.M.
Lunch & Dinner: Monday–Thursday, 11:30 A.M.–10 P.M.; Friday, 11:30 A.M.–11 P.M.; Saturday, 4–11 P.M.; Sunday, 11 A.M.–9 P.M.

Setting & atmosphere: The collection of dining rooms has a suburban look, but the environment is sophisticated and comfortable.

Recommended dishes: Antipasto (especially marinated vegetables); oysters Andrea; vitello tonnato; pasta with smoked salmon; mussels or clams marinara; pasta fagioli soup; fresh cheese salad; fish (especially red snapper, trout, or pompano) with basilico, fresh herb, or cream pesto sauces; veal chop Valdostana; roast duck with green peppercorns; steak with three-pepper sauce; panéed veal Tanet. Tiramisu; strawberry cake; fruit flan; chocolate mousse.

Entertainment & amenities: Strolling accordionist at Sunday brunch.

Summary & comments: Andrea's revolutionized the Italian restaurant scene when it opened in the mid-eighties by giving Italian food the same shrift that the best French places always had. Few restaurants can match the quality and freshness of its raw materials, particularly seafood and vegetables. The menu is enormous—too big, really—and the chef offers to fix you anything that might not be on it. When it's at its best, Andrea's serves food at the five-star level, but it's a bit inconsistent. The monthly regional Italian menus are fascinating. Sunday brunch is more likely to be an off-meal than any other here.

ANTOINE'S

			QUALITY
Creole French	★★★★	Expensive	**83**

		VALUE
713 St. Louis Street 581-4422	Zone 1, French Quarter	**D**

Customers: Tourists, some locals
Reservations: Recommended
When to go: Lunch and early evenings; avoid days before holidays
Entree range: $13–26
Payment: All major credit cards
Service rating: ★★★
Friendliness rating: ★

Parking: Pay garages nearby
Bar: Full bar
Wine selection: Distinguished cellar with tremendous inventory, French-dominated; many older vintages; the wine cellar presents a great visual.
Dress: Jacket required at dinner
Disabled access: Limited

Lunch: Monday–Saturday, 11:30 A.M.–2:30 P.M.
Dinner: Monday–Saturday, 5–9:30 P.M.

Setting & atmosphere: The front room is fine at lunchtime, when the place is rarely busy; in the evenings, the larger annex is where the action is. But there are so many other interesting rooms that they make for a fascinating tour.

Recommended dishes: Oysters Rockefeller; oysters Foch; escargots bordelaise; shrimp rémoulade; crawfish cardinale; grilled pompano; soft-shell crabs Colbert; chicken Rochambeau; chicken bonne femme; tournedos marchands de vin; lamb chops béarnaise. Baked Alaska.

Summary & comments: The oldest restaurant in America, Antoine's was founded in 1840 by the great-great grandfather of the present proprietor. Extraordinarily old-fashioned, usually in a good way, Antoine's requires a certain taste for and patience with antiquity for fullest enjoyment. The best dishes, once common elsewhere, can only be found here now. Meat and poultry dishes tend to be better than seafood. Antoine's is at its best if you're either a regular or in the company of one.

ARNAUD'S

Creole French	★★★★	Expensive	QUALITY
			86

813 Bienville Street 523-5433   Zone 1, French Quarter

	VALUE
	D

Customers: Tourists, some locals
Reservations: Recommended
When to go: Anytime
Entree range: $13–40 (median: $20)
Payment: All major credit cards
Service rating: ★★★★
Friendliness rating: ★★★
Parking: Validated (free) at garage

(corner of Dauphine and Iberville)
Bar: Full bar
Wine selection: Distinguished cellar, good international balance; a bit pricey
Dress: Jacket recommended but not required
Disabled access: Full

Brunch: Sunday, 11 A.M.–3 P.M.
Lunch: Every day, 11:30 A.M.–2:30 P.M.
Dinner: Every day, 6–10 P.M.

Setting & atmosphere: The distinctive decor of tiled floors, beveled glass, and ceiling fans are classic Old New Orleans.

Recommended dishes: Shrimp Arnaud (rémoulade); oysters Arnaud (an assortment of five); turtle rillettes; shrimp Bellaire; oyster stew in cream; trout meunière; pompano David; pompano en croûte; Cornish hen Twelfth Night; rack of lamb. Crème brûlée; bananas Foster; bread pudding.

Entertainment & amenities: Strolling jazz trio at Sunday brunch.

Summary & comments: One of the great restaurants of the first half of this century, Arnaud's had steeply declined by the sixties, and was rescued in the nick of time in the late seventies. It was beautifully restored in both premises and cuisine and has been remarkable ever since. The menu is encyclopedic and requires much explanation from the waiters. In the past couple of years, Arnaud's has become a bit touristy and its prices have risen steeply, but it's still a great taste of the old style.

BACCO

Creole Italian	★★★★	Moderate	QUALITY
			84

310 Chartres Street 522-2426	Zone 1, French Quarter	VALUE
		C

Customers: Mostly locals, a few tourists
Reservations: Recommended
When to go: Anytime
Entree range: $10–20
Payment: All major credit cards
Service rating: ★★★★
Friendliness rating: ★★★★
Parking: Free valet parking in hotel garage

Bar: Full bar
Wine selection: Substantial list, mostly Italian and California; many interesting, offbeat bottles
Dress: Jacket recommended but not required
Disabled access: Full

Breakfast: Every day, 7–10 A.M.
Brunch: Sunday, 11 A.M.–3 P.M.
Lunch: Every day, 11:30 A.M.–2:30 P.M.
Dinner: Every day, 6–10 P.M.

Setting & atmosphere: The premises are striking, with unusual spaces shaped largely from concrete. In the rest rooms, you can learn Italian.

Recommended dishes: White-cheese pizza; grilled eggplant; baked oysters; pasta "rags" with spinach and chicken; crawfish ravioli; grilled fish; grilled veal T-bone; roasted pork tenderloin; hickory-grilled duck breast. Tiramisu; homemade ice creams.

Summary & comments: An atypical restaurant for the Brennan family, Bacco started out a very authentic Italian trattoria and has become more and more Creole. The menu is dominated by dishes prepared in a wood-burning oven; these include not only pizza, but also roasts of meat, poultry, and fish. Lots of good grilled dishes, also accomplished over burning wood. The wine list is exceptionally good, particularly for Italian wines. Breakfast is one of the best in town.

BARROW'S SHADY INN

Seafood	★★★	Inexpensive	QUALITY
			84
			VALUE
			B

2714 Mistletoe Street 482-9427
   Zone 4, Uptown above Napoleon

Customers: Neighborhood people
Reservations: Not accepted
When to go: Anytime
Entree range: $10
Payment: No credit cards
Service rating: ★★

Friendliness rating: ★★★
Parking: Free lot adjacent
Bar: Full bar
Wine selection: A few house wines
Dress: Anything goes
Disabled access: Limited

Lunch & Dinner: Tuesday and Wednesday, 5–10 P.M.; Thursday–
   Saturday, 11 A.M.–10 P.M.

Setting & atmosphere: It looks like a neighborhood bar with a lot of
tables. Only place in town with lava lamps (originals!) as serious interior
decor.

Recommended dishes: Fried catfish with potato salad (only dish available).

Summary & comments: A family-run catfish specialist since 1943, Bar-
row's serves the lightest, most addictive fish in town, with an interesting
glow of red pepper. Also on the plate is a fine, mildly flavored homemade
potato salad. That's the only menu option; its current price is posted on the
walls.

BAYONA

Eclectic	★★★★	Expensive	QUALITY
			96
			VALUE
			B

430 Dauphine Street 525-4455   Zone 1, French Quarter

Customers: Mostly locals, a few
   tourists
Reservations: Required
When to go: Anytime
Entree range: $14–25
Payment: All major credit cards
Service rating: ★★★★★
Friendliness rating: ★★★
Parking: Validated ($3) at adjacent
   garage

Bar: Full bar
Wine selection: Distinguished,
   with many interesting, offbeat
   bottles; many by-the-glass
   selections
Dress: Jacket recommended but not
   required
Disabled access: Limited

Bayona (continued)

Lunch: Monday–Friday, 11:30 A.M.–2:30 P.M.
Dinner: Monday–Saturday, 6–10 P.M.

Setting & atmosphere: The several small dining rooms are beautifully designed. In decent weather you may also dine al fresco.

Recommended dishes: Grilled shrimp with coriander; sweetbreads (as appetizer or entree); toad-in-the-hole (foie gras and quail egg in brioche); roasted garlic soup; salads; shrimp curry; salmon with choucroute and Gewürztraminer sauce; pork, lamb, or veal chops; quail with dried cherries and foie gras sauce. Lemon tart; apple-almond gratin with spice ice cream; orange-scented crêpes with vanilla gelato.

Summary & comments: This is the personal cuisine of Susan Spicer, who likes the food of the Mediterranean, India, and France, and combines these flavors in highly creative and unerringly tasteful ways. The menu will probably underwhelm you—the concoctions are understated and subtle—but almost anything you order will come across with surprising satisfaction. The wine list is full of rare and unusual bottles, all at affordable prices.

BEGUE'S

Creole	★★★	Expensive	QUALITY 83
300 Bourbon Street 586-0300	Zone 1, French Quarter		VALUE C

Customers: Tourists, some locals; mostly local for Sunday brunch
Reservations: Recommended
When to go: Anytime; Friday's lunch buffet is particularly inviting
Entree range: $12–22
Payment: All major credit cards
Service rating: ★★★★

Friendliness rating: ★★★★
Parking: Validated free in Royal Sonesta garage, downstairs
Bar: Full bar
Wine selection: Decent list, good international balance
Dress: Jacket recommended but not required
Disabled access: Full

Breakfast: Every day, 7–10 A.M.
Brunch: Sunday, 11 A.M.–3 P.M.
Lunch: Monday–Saturday, 11:30 A.M.–2:30 P.M.
Dinner: Every day, 6–10 P.M.

Setting & atmosphere: The principal restaurant of the picturesque and luxurious Royal Sonesta Hotel occupies the south face of its lush courtyard. Beyond that, its design is airy and fresh.

Begue's (continued)

Recommended dishes: Smoked salmon; crab cakes; shrimp and crabmeat rémoulade in an avocado; spinach salad; tomato and tasso bisque; seafood gumbo; baby salmon with potato cakes; sautéed shrimp with refried grits and spinach; grilled double pork chop; roasted lamb chops with spaetzle; steamed lobster on fettuccine with vanilla beurre blanc. Sorbets; ice creams; chocolate pecan pie.

Entertainment & amenities: Pianist plays throughout dinner and at Sunday brunch.

Summary & comments: They serve all three meals here, and although the menu seems at first to be standard hotel fare, the food here is actually quite original and good, using first-class local ingredients. Of particular note are the seafood buffet at lunch on Fridays and the Sunday brunch buffets, both of which are far better than buffets tend to be. Service is a little lackluster, but the restaurant is always a pleasure.

BELLA LUNA

Eclectic/Southwestern	★★★★	Very Expensive	QUALITY
			92

914 N. Peters Street 529-1583	Zone 1, French Quarter	VALUE
		C

Customers: Mostly locals, a few tourists; couples
Reservations: Recommended
When to go: Anytime
Entree range: $14–25
Payment: All major credit cards
Service rating: ★★★★
Friendliness rating: ★★★
Parking: Validated free for French Market lot, immediately adjacent
Bar: Full bar
Wine selection: Distinguished cellar, many interesting, offbeat bottles; many by-the-glass selections
Dress: Jacket recommended but not required
Disabled access: Limited

Brunch: Sunday, 11 A.M.–3 P.M.
Dinner: Monday–Saturday, 6–10 P.M.

Setting & atmosphere: One of the town's two or three most striking restaurants, Bella Luna is on the second floor of a building in the French Market and, from that vantage point, offers a superb view of the Mississippi River and its activity.

Recommended dishes: Entire menu is always changing, but at last look: crab cakes with chipotle rémoulade; fettuccine with aged Reggiano. Barq's-marinated baby back ribs; eggless Caesar salad; shrimp quesadillas; black bean soup; grilled or blackened tuna; veal T-bone; osso buco; grilled pork

Bella Luna (continued)

tenderloin with ancho-chile polenta; veal T-bone with herb-infused olive oil; any game special. Dessert assortment; fudge brownie cappuccino pie; warm apple tart with cinnamon ice cream.

Summary & comments: The food is every bit the equal of the environment. Chef Horst Pfeifer unites Italian, Southwestern, and Creole flavors into singular creations. Much grilling, roasting, and smoking of foods goes on, and plates are finished off with delightfully unexpected flavoring ingredients. The wine list is first-rate and the service usually pleasing, although the front-desk greeting could be better.

BISTRO AT MAISON DE VILLE

Eclectic	★★★	Expensive	QUALITY 84
733 Toulouse Street 528-9206	Zone 1, French Quarter		VALUE C

Customers: Mostly locals, a few tourists

Reservations: Recommended

When to go: Anytime

Entree range: $14–21

Payment: All major credit cards

Service rating: ★★★★

Friendliness rating: ★★★

Parking: Several pay lots within two blocks

Bar: Full bar; many single-malt Scotches, cognacs, Armagnacs

Wine selection: Decent list, many interesting, offbeat bottles; many by-the-glass selections

Dress: Jacket recommended but not required

Disabled access: Limited

Brunch: Sunday, 11:30 A.M.–3 P.M.

Lunch: Monday–Saturday, 11:30 A.M.–2:30 P.M.

Dinner: Every day, 6–10 P.M.

Setting & atmosphere: A tiny, somewhat claustrophobic, but nicely designed cafe, dominated by banquettes along one wall. There are a few tables on the small courtyard.

Recommended dishes: Entire menu changes every two or three months; all of the following will be gone by the time you go there, but this is a typical menu: gravlax with dill yogurt and wasabi caviar; crawfish with spicy aïoli; tuna tartare; chicken stuffed with Boursin and leek confit; seared pompano with saffron couscous; filet mignon with green-peppercorn mustard sauce; grilled sea scallops with wild mushroom galette. Crème brûlée; flourless chocolate cake.

Bistro at Maison de Ville (continued)

Summary & comments: The Bistro made its name by hiring hot young chefs who established the place as a source of fascinating and good food. Trouble is, these chefs have had a way of opening their own restaurants after a year or two here, so there have been some ups and downs. At the moment the place is pretty good but, as always, the menu is utterly unpredictable. The service, wine list, and admirable list of single-malt Scotches, cognacs, and other spirits, are all orchestrated by a maître d' who survived each change in the kitchen.

BON TON CAFE

			QUALITY
Cajun	★★★	Moderate	**79**
			VALUE
401 Magazine Street 524-3386	Zone 2, Central Business District		**B**

Customers: Mostly locals at lunch, mostly tourists at dinner
Reservations: Recommended
When to go: Anytime
Entree range: $12–18
Payment: All major credit cards
Service rating: ★★★
Friendliness rating: ★★★★

Parking: Pay lot and curbside (metered)
Bar: Full bar
Wine selection: A few house wines
Dress: Jacket recommended but not required
Disabled access: Limited

Lunch: Monday–Friday, 11:30 A.M.–2:30 P.M.
Dinner: Monday–Friday, 5–9 P.M.

Setting & atmosphere: A brick-walled dining room full of tables with red-checked tablecloths and an easygoing style.

Recommended dishes: Turtle soup; fried catfish fingers; shrimp rémoulade; Cajun Caesar salad; crawfish dinner (crawfish four ways: étouffée, bisque, fried, and omelette); crabmeat au gratin; redfish Bon Ton; oysters or soft-shell crab Alvin; pan-broiled oysters; shrimp étouffée. Bread pudding.

Summary & comments: It seems strange now, but for years the Bon Ton was just about the only nice restaurant in New Orleans that would serve you crawfish. The style is Cajun, but it's the rather mild Cajun cooking of the Bayou Lafourche area. It's also very old-fashioned, and you'll see touches you haven't been treated to since the early sixties. (The service staff is definitely from that era.) It's a charming, unaffected place delivering good food and value.

BOZO'S

Seafood/Oyster Bar	★★★★	Inexpensive	QUALITY 86
3117 21st Street 831-8666 Zone 9, Metairie below Causeway			VALUE B

Customers: Mostly locals, a few tourists
Reservations: Not accepted
When to go: Anytime except the very busy Fridays
Entree range: $6–12
Payment: MC, VISA

Service rating: ★★★
Friendliness rating: ★★★★
Parking: Free lot adjacent
Bar: Full bar
Wine selection: A few house wines
Dress: Casual
Disabled access: Full

Lunch: Tuesday–Saturday, 11:30 A.M.–3 P.M.
Dinner: Tuesday–Saturday, 5–10 P.M.

Setting & atmosphere: A little too squeaky-clean a restaurant to house a classic old-style seafood house. Lots of action at the oyster bar.

Recommended dishes: Oysters on the half shell; boiled crawfish or shrimp in season; chicken andouille gumbo; fried oysters; fried catfish; broiled shrimp; stuffed shrimp; stuffed crab; hot sausage po'boy. Bread pudding.

Summary & comments: Bozo's sets the standard for fried seafood in New Orleans. Not only is everything fresh, but everything is extraordinarily well selected. The catfish, for example, are exclusively small, wild fish from Des Allemands, which have a much more interesting flavor than bigger, farm-raised cat. They also have a great source of oysters, served raw at the bar or fried at the table. All the fried stuff is prepared to order and comes out crackly and hot. Each variety of seafood is fried in a separate pot of constantly cleaned oil. The meticulousness of the kitchen can be observed through its large windows. In season, they also have great boiled crawfish here. The portions are not as gargantuan as elsewhere, but the quality is beyond reproach.

BRENNAN'S

Creole French/Breakfast	★★★	Very Expensive	QUALITY 82
417 Royal Street 525-9711 Zone 1, French Quarter			VALUE F

Customers: Mostly tourists; a few local regulars and wine buffs
Reservations: Required

When to go: Late mornings or lunchtime
Entree range: $20–40

Brennan's (continued)

Payment: All major credit cards
Service rating: ★★★★
Friendliness rating: ★★★★
Parking: Validated free for Omni
Royal Orleans garage (Chartres at
St. Louis)
Bar: Full bar
Wine selection: Easily the finest

restaurant wine cellar in New
Orleans; tremendous inventory,
variety, and depth; lots of
unusual, rare, and older wines,
very well stored; prices are alarmingly low.
Dress: Dressy casual
Disabled access: Full

Brunch: Every day, 8 A.M.–2:30 P.M.
Breakfast & Lunch: Every day, 7 A.M.–2:30 P.M.
Dinner: Every day, 6–10 P.M.

Setting & atmosphere: The founding establishment of the Brennan dynasty is a magnificent, historic French Quarter building surrounding an ideal courtyard. The best rooms are downstairs, just past the bar and alongside the courtyard. Avoid the upstairs rooms.

Recommended dishes: Breakfast: Oyster soup; eggs Sardou; eggs Hussarde; eggs St. Charles; grillades and grits; crêpes Fitzgerald. Dinner: Oysters Rockefeller; oysters casino. Buster crabs with pecans; seafood crêpes Barbara; turtle soup; Jackson salad; filet mignon Stanley; filet mignon Diane; veal Kottwitz; fish Jaime. Bananas Foster; chocolate suicide cake.

Summary & comments: Brennan's is famous the world over for its breakfast, a lengthy meal whose menu includes more specialty egg dishes than you'd ever imagine existing. Brennan's is renowned among oenophiles for its wine cellar, certainly the best in New Orleans and among the best in the country. But to most locals Brennan's is notorious as a place they'd love to go more often if the prices weren't so high (they're at the top of the scale) and if the waiters didn't treat them like the tourists who make up most of the clientele. The food at dinner can be terrific but, even for regulars, is very inconsistent. Breakfast is always perfect.

BRIGTSEN'S			
Nouvelle Creole	★★★★	Expensive	QUALITY 92
723 Dante Street 861-7610 Zone 4, Uptown above Napoleon			VALUE B

Customers: Mostly locals, a few
tourists
Reservations: Required
When to go: Early evenings

Entree range: $10–22
Payment: All major credit cards
Service rating: ★★★★
Friendliness rating: ★★★★★

Brigsten's (continued)

Parking: Curbside
Bar: Full bar
Wine selection: Modest list, but
  wines well-chosen for the food

Dress: Jacket recommended but not
  required
Disabled access: Limited

Dinner: Tuesday–Saturday, 5:30–10 P.M.

Setting & atmosphere: The restaurant was built in a 150-year-old residence that was originally constructed from the lumber from disassembled Mississippi River flatboats. All the rooms are small, but claustrophobia is kept in check.

Recommended dishes: (Menu changes daily, so not all of this may be available.) Grilled rabbit tenderloin with spinach; shrimp rémoulade; sesame-encrusted foie gras; any soup, especially gumbos or seafood bisques; panéed rabbit; any veal special; any grilled, broiled, or pan-sautéed fish; tournedos of beef with Port and blue cheese; chicken with hot and sweet peppers. Banana bread pudding; ice creams; double chocolate cake.

Summary & comments: Frank and Marna Brigtsen are the most illustrious graduates of the hot era at K-Paul's. They opened their restaurant about a decade ago, and from that day forward kept all the little rooms filled with happy eaters. The style is Creole, but with a freshness and imagination that grabs you not only in your mouth but in your mind. It's always an agony to decide what to order here, because so many dishes sound irresistible. Because the menu changes daily and the chef loves to experiment, you'll find dishes here you've never heard of, along with a predominance of more common eats. The service staff treats you like a live-in guest. The wine list is short but good and attractively priced.

BROUSSARD'S				
Nouvelle Creole	★★★★	Very Expensive	QUALITY	84
819 Conti Street 581-3866	Zone 1, French Quarter		VALUE	D

Customers: Tourists, some
  locals
Reservations: Recommended
When to go: Anytime
Entree range: $17–26
Payment: All major credit cards
Service rating: ★★★

Friendliness rating: ★★★
Parking: Validated (free) at adjacent
  garage
Bar: Full bar
Wine selection: Decent list,
  good international balance;
  a bit overpriced

Dress: Jacket recommended but not required

Disabled access: Full

Dinner: Every day, 6–10 P.M.

Setting & atmosphere: Three handsome dining rooms, each designed differently, surround a lovely French Quarter courtyard.

Recommended dishes: Delice ravigote (a combination plate with crawfish ravigote, shrimp rémoulade, and gravlax); shrimp and crab cheesecake with roasted red pepper and dill cream; daube glacé (Creole-spiced cold beef); baked oyster trio; sweet potato, corn, and shrimp bisque; duckling Normandy; poussin Rochambeau (with ham and marchands de vin and béarnaise sauces); pecan-stuffed salmon; pompano Napoleon; veal filet on braised leeks; wild game grill. Chocolate pava; crêpes Broussard; bananas Foster.

Summary & comments: Broussard's is a bona fide product of the grand era of New Orleans restaurants, having opened in 1920. But among locals it's something of a mystery, having catered mainly to visitors for so long. In the past few years its owners have tried to change that by breathing some life into the menu, and they've succeeded admirably: The dishes are the ones you'd expect of a place of this vintage, but updated to current tastes and ingredients.

BRUNING'S

Seafood	★★★	Inexpensive	QUALITY
			79

West End Park 282-9395	Zone 7, Lakeview/West End/Bucktown	VALUE
		A

Customers: Locals; families
Reservations: Not accepted
When to go: Anytime, but Fridays are very crowded.
Entree range: $8–16
Payment: All major credit cards
Service rating: ★★

Friendliness rating: ★★★★
Parking: Free lot adjacent
Bar: Full bar
Wine selection: A few house wines
Dress: Anything goes
Disabled access: Limited

Lunch & Dinner: Every day, 11 A.M.–10 P.M.

Setting & atmosphere: Quite possibly the oldest fried-seafood house in the world, Bruning's opened in 1859 at West End Park, at that time a resort reachable from New Orleans only by rail or boat. Now owned by the fifth generation of the founder's family, it's still in the same old building on stilts over Lake Pontchartrain's waters. Check out the mammoth antique bar on the way in.

Recommended dishes: Oysters on the half shell; seafood gumbo; boiled crabs, crawfish, or shrimp in season; whole broiled flounder; whole fried trout; fried seafood platter; fried chicken. Bread pudding.

Summary & comments: Things change little here over the decades. The menu consists of the archetypal platters of fried seafood, mounds of boiled seafood, and one distinctive specialty: a very large whole flounder, fried or broiled. A very casual place for eating, drinking, and reveling in the New Orleans life.

BYBLOS			
Lebanese	★★★★	Moderate	QUALITY 83
1501 Metairie Road 834-9773	Zone 9, Metairie below Causeway		VALUE A

Reservations: Accepted	Parking: Free lot adjacent
When to go: Anytime	Bar: Full bar
Entree range: $8–14	Wine selection: A few house wines
Payment: AMEX, MC, VISA	Dress: Casual
Service rating: ★★	Disabled access: Full
Friendliness rating: ★★★	Customers: Locals

Lunch & Dinner: Monday–Saturday, 11 A.M.–10 P.M.

Setting & atmosphere: The dining room has a lofty ceiling and a comfortable, uncluttered look.

Recommended dishes: Hummus; baba ghanoush; stuffed kibbeh; falafel; stuffed cabbage rolls; cheese pie; tabbouleh salad; beef shawarma; beef kabob; chicken kabob; kafta kabob; fried kibbeh; kibbeh nayyi. Ashta (flaky dessert pastry).

Summary & comments: This is the best Middle Eastern restaurant we've ever found in New Orleans. The ingredients are first-class (i.e., filet mignon is used for the beef kabob), and the cooking is careful and light. The appetizer "meza" brings forth an assortment of some 15 appetizers for 4 to 6 people—a great way to eat.

CAFE GIOVANNI

Nouvelle Italian	★★★★	Expensive	QUALITY 87

117 Decatur Street 529-2154   Zone 1, French Quarter

VALUE **B**

Customers: Mostly locals, a few tourists
Reservations: Recommended
When to go: Anytime
Entree range: $14−22
Payment: All major credit cards
Service rating: ★★★
Friendliness rating: ★★★★

Parking: Valet (free)
Bar: Full bar
Wine selection: Substantial list, mostly Italian; many by-the-glass selections
Dress: Jacket recommended but not required
Disabled access: Full

Dinner: Every day, 6–10 P.M.

Setting & atmosphere: The dining room is an atrium built between two old French Quarter buildings. This clever, romantic space has an appeal that comes from the hidden, tucked-away feeling it gives.

Recommended dishes: Oysters Giovanni; baked seafood casino with apple-smoked bacon; Sicilian wedding soup; crabmeat Siciliana salad; pasta Gambino with rock shrimp and three cheeses; pasta absolutely (with shrimp and scallops in a vodka-basil sauce); cioppino; grilled marinated seafood assortment; filet mignon Abruzzo; roast chicken with rosemary and garlic. Dessert pastries (change daily).

Summary & comments: A very good trattoria operated by Duke LoCicero, a young but well-traveled chef with a strong sense of creativity and polish. What's interesting about his style is that he eschews the currently popular Northern Italian flavor in favor of the much-maligned Sicilian culinary traditions. What results is a fascinating, unique menu full of flavors familiar to New Orleans eaters (especially those of Italian descent) but with lots of fresh, original touches. An especially attractive option here is to let the chef feed you an assortment of small portions of the day's specials.

CHARLEY G'S

Nouvelle Cajun	★★★	Expensive	QUALITY
			83

			VALUE
111 Veterans Boulevard 837-6408	Zone 9, Metairie		**D**
below Causeway			

Customers: Businessmen at lunch; couples and foursomes at dinner
Reservations: Recommended
When to go: Anytime
Entree range: $10–17
Payment: All major credit cards
Service rating: ★★★★
Friendliness rating: ★★★★
Parking: Free lot adjacent
Bar: Full bar

Wine selection: Substantial list, assembled with great pains to match the food; the list shows extensive cross-referencing with the menu; many by-the-glass selections
Dress: Jacket recommended but not required
Disabled access: Full

Brunch: Sunday, 11 A.M.–3 P.M. (menu, with blues music)
Lunch: Monday–Friday, 11:30 A.M.–2:30 P.M.
Dinner: Every day, 6–10 P.M.

Setting & atmosphere: The split-level dining room offers more booth seating than most places, as well as a view of the open kitchen.

Recommended dishes: Sausage mixed grill; duck-andouille gumbo; crab cakes; shrimp rémoulade salad; crabmeat or crawfish fettuccine; veal with grilled portobello mushrooms; wood-grilled fish. Bullwinkle (chocolate mousse) pie; almond tuile; white chocolate bread pudding.

Entertainment & amenities: Pianist at dinner Tuesday–Saturday. Blues combo at Sunday brunch.

Summary & comments: The second location of a very successful Lafayette restaurant, Charley G's has all the elements of a fine restaurant: an interesting, comfortable dining room, an outgoing service staff, a menu of good local specialties prepared in original (but not too original) ways, an extensive wine list (ingeniously cross-referenced to the menu!), and even live music. The prices seem a touch high, but the best specialties are entirely satisfying, and I've never had a bad meal here.

CHICORY FARM CAFE

			QUALITY
Vegetarian	★★★★	Moderate	**83**

		VALUE
723 Hillary Street 866-2325	Zone 4, Uptown above Napoleon	**C**

Customers: Locals and college students
Reservations: Accepted
When to go: Anytime
Entree range: $7–15
Payment: MC, VISA
Service rating: ★★★

Friendliness rating: ★★★
Parking: Curbside
Bar: Beer and wine
Wine selection: Limited list of ordinary wines
Dress: Casual
Disabled access: Limited

Brunch: Sunday, 10 A.M.–2 P.M.
Lunch: Tuesday–Saturday, 11:30 A.M.–2:30 P.M.
Dinner: Tuesday–Saturday, 5:30–10 P.M.

Setting & atmosphere: An old Creole cottage, renovated far better inside than outside. Seating is at funny little tables with mismatched chairs.
Recommended dishes: Shiitake Rockefeller; cheese plate; house salad; yam and potato salad; celery root and leek rémoulade; gumbo z'herbes; smoked mushroom grillades and grits; vegetable shepherd's pie. Dessert specials.
Summary & comments: There really is a Chicory Farm. It's located a hundred miles north of town, and raises various milk-giving animals from which a host of fresh and aged cheeses—long favored by local chefs—are made. They also grow mushrooms and vegetables. All of that and more finds its way into this ambitious cafe, which cooks vegetarian dishes in the style and with the talent of the gourmet Creole bistros.

CHINA BLOSSOM

			QUALITY
Chinese	★★★★	Moderate	**87**

		VALUE
1801 Stumpf Boulevard, Gretna 361-4598	Zone 11, West Bank	**B**

Reservations: Accepted
When to go: Anytime
Entree range: $7–15
Payment: AMEX, MC, VISA
Service rating: ★★★
Friendliness rating: ★★★
Parking: Free lot adjacent

Bar: Full bar
Wine selection: Limited list of ordinary wines
Dress: Casual
Disabled access: Full
Customers: Locals

China Blossom (continued)

Lunch: Tuesday–Sunday, 11:30 A.M.–2:30 P.M.
Dinner: Tuesday–Sunday, 6–10 P.M.

Setting & atmosphere: Despite the location in a modest strip mall, the dining rooms are understated and comfortable.

Recommended dishes: Spring roll; five-spiced cold beef; hot and sour soup. Tong-cho shrimp, trout, oysters, or soft-shell crab; spicy flaming chicken; sesame chicken. Wor shu op (crisp half duck); Ming steak; beef with oyster sauce. Lotus banana.

Summary & comments: When Trey Yuen closed its Jax Brewery restaurant, much of the staff got together to open this restaurant, one of the best Chinese places in the area. The menu covers many styles of Chinese cooking, but the best dishes involve fresh local seafood: oysters, shrimp, crawfish, trout, and even alligator. Many of the dishes involve interesting tableside preparations.

CHRISTIAN'S

Creole French	★★★★	Expensive	QUALITY
			90

3835 Iberville Street 482-4924	Zone 6, Mid-City/Gentilly	VALUE
		B

Customers: Mostly locals, a few tourists; couples; gourmets
Reservations: Recommended
When to go: Early evenings
Entree range: $12–23
Payment: All major credit cards except Discover
Service rating: ★★★★
Friendliness rating: ★★★

Parking: Free lot adjacent
Bar: Full bar
Wine selection: Substantial list, about equally French and California; very attractive prices
Dress: Jacket recommended but not required
Disabled access: Limited

Lunch: Tuesday–Friday, 11:30 A.M.–2:30 P.M.
Dinner: Tuesday–Saturday, 6–10 P.M.

Setting & atmosphere: With a name like Christian's, the fact that this restaurant occupies a small old church may seem like a joke. Indeed, pews are used as banquettes, the cry room as the bar, and the pulpit as a waiter's stand. But the place was called Christian's before it moved in here (it's the name of the owner), and they stop well short of using the decor as a gimmick.

Christian's (continued)

Recommended dishes: Oysters Roland; oysters en brochette; shrimp rémoulade; smoked salmon; smoked soft-shell crab; shrimp-and-crabmeat-stuffed fish; stuffed eggplant; braised sweetbreads with Port sauce; roast duck with blackberry vinegar sauce; veal Christian; trout meunière amandine; quenelles of fish Nantua. Crème caramel; homemade ice creams.

Summary & comments: But this is not only a serious restaurant, it's a very consistent and original one that offers terrific value. Proprietor Chris Ansel combines the style of his family's restaurant Galatoire's with that of classic French cooking and some new ideas from the current young chef. The result is a collection of dishes as distinctive as the premises. The service staff has an easy style, the wines are sold at bargain prices, and the early-evening special menu is almost too good to be real. Complaints: The dessert selection is uninteresting, and some diners may find the deuces along the perimeter a little too cramped.

CLANCY'S

Nouvelle Creole	★★★★	Expensive	QUALITY
			90

	VALUE
	B

6100 Annunciation Street 895-1111
   Zone 4, Uptown above Napoleon

Customers: Locals; gourmets
Reservations: Recommended
When to go: Anytime
Entree range: $13–22
Payment: All major credit cards
Service rating: ★★★★
Friendliness rating: ★★★★
Parking: Curbside

Bar: Full bar
Wine selection: Substantial list, full of oddities; the owner is an oenophile, and buys many short-lot wines; many by-the-glass selections
Dress: Dressy casual
Disabled access: Limited

Lunch: Tuesday–Friday, 11:30 A.M.–3 P.M.
Dinner: Monday–Saturday, 6–10 P.M.

Setting & atmosphere: An old neighborhood bar was buffed up in the early eighties to create an only modestly gentrified cafe, populated by a highly social group of regulars.

Recommended dishes: Oysters with Brie and spinach; crabmeat ravigote; shrimp rémoulade; house salad; smoked soft-shell crab with crabmeat; smoked shrimp with ginger; seafood pasta specials; veal liver Lyonnaise; veal and lamb chops; smoked duck; filet mignon with Port sauce and Stilton. Crème caramel.

Clancy's (continued)

Summary & comments: One of the first nouvelle Creole bistros, Clancy's remains one of the best such restaurants around. It boasts a few unique specialties, an easy, engaging style, a wine list full of offbeat bottles, and enough innovation to keep curiosity piqued. Clancy's was the first local eatery to use a smoker as a major kitchen appliance, and they still smoke foods well. Only locals eat here because only they know where it is.

COFFEE POT			
Creole/Breakfast	★★	Moderate	**QUALITY** 71
714 St. Peter Street 524-3500	Zone 1, French Quarter		**VALUE** C

Customers: Tourists, a few Quarterites
Reservations: Not accepted
When to go: Anytime
Entree range: $7–15
Payment: AMEX, MC, VISA
Service rating: ★★

Friendliness rating: ★★★
Parking: Pay garages nearby
Bar: Full bar
Wine selection: A few house wines
Dress: Casual
Disabled access: None

Open: Sunday–Thursday, 8 A.M.–midnight; Friday and Saturday, 8 A.M.–1 A.M.

Setting & atmosphere: The parlor and carriageway of a modest Creole townhouse serve as the dining areas.

Recommended dishes: Salad Jayne; seafood gumbo; red beans and rice. Fried chicken; fried seafood platter; daily blackboard specials; omelettes. Bread pudding; fruit cobblers.

Summary & comments: This Creole cafe dates back to the forties, and although it has long catered heavily to the tourist business, it remains a good place to sample local home cooking. The place is still a neighborhood hangout for Quarterites, who mainly come for the very good breakfasts. One thing never changes: The coffee, by New Orleans standards, is awful.

COMMANDER'S PALACE

			QUALITY
Nouvelle Creole	★★★★★	Expensive	**97**

	VALUE
1403 Washington Avenue 899-8221	**B**

Zone 3, Uptown below Napoleon

Customers: Half tourists, half socializing locals; couples
Reservations: Required
When to go: Lunch and weekday dinners
Entree range: $15–26
Payment: All major credit cards
Service rating: ★★★★
Friendliness rating: ★★★

Parking: Valet (free)
Bar: Full bar
Wine selection: Distinguished cellar, good international balance; many rare wines (but not many older ones) from France and California
Dress: Jacket required at dinner
Disabled access: Limited

Brunch: Saturday–Sunday, 11 A.M.–3 P.M.
Lunch: Monday–Friday, 11:30 A.M.–2 P.M.
Dinner: Every day, 6–10 P.M.

Setting & atmosphere: Dining rooms of quite different styles fill a nineteenth-century mansion. The upstairs Garden Room gives a view through the boughs of the mammoth live oak tree to the courtyard below. The kitchen serves as a passageway to the bar and holds a single table for serious foodies.

Recommended dishes: A very substantial number of the best dishes here are daily specials, to which I draw your attention. Regularly offered greats: shrimp rémoulade; shrimp with tasso; smoked fish cake; fish Lyonnaise; sauté of crawfish; turtle soup; grilled fish; sautéed fish with pecans; veal chop Tchoupitoulas; veal Marcelle; filet mignon Adelaide; roasted strip sirloin steak; rack of lamb. Bananas Foster; bread pudding soufflé; chocolate fudge Sheba.

Entertainment & amenities: Strolling jazz trio at Sunday brunch.

Summary & comments: If there were no Commander's Palace, the dining scene in New Orleans would be much different. For the past two decades it's been the consistent favorite of both local diners and frequent visitors. Culinary substance here runs deep, and Commander's innovations have influenced almost every other Creole restaurant. The menu combines both old and new styles of Creole cooking; either route is rewarding. The wine list is strong in both French and American bottles. And Commander's is an extraordinary value: A four-course dinner can be had for $30, lunch for $14. The service is a little too methodical, but the staff is entirely responsive to special requests.

CROZIER'S

			QUALITY
French Bistro	★★★★★	Expensive	**93**

	VALUE
3216 W. Esplanade Avenue 833-8108	**C**
Zone 10, Metairie above Causeway/Kenner/Jefferson Hwy.	

Customers: Locals; couples
Reservations: Recommended
When to go: Weeknights
Entree range: $13–20
Payment: AMEX, DC, MC, VISA
Service rating: ★★★★
Friendliness rating: ★★★★

Parking: Free lot adjacent
Bar: Full bar
Wine selection: Decent list, French-dominated
Dress: Dressy casual
Disabled access: Full

Dinner: Tuesday–Saturday, 6–10 P.M.

Setting & atmosphere: The present dining room belies its strip-mall exterior by being charming and very French. The two dining rooms are quiet, unexpectedly elegant, and intimate.

Recommended dishes: Pâté maison; cassoulet of shrimp or crawfish; magret of duck with pink peppercorn sauce; escargots bourguignonne; onion soup gratinée; salade maison; poached pompano or salmon hollandaise; coq au vin; sweetbreads Grenobloise; veal Crozier; beef tournedos Gerard; steak au poivre; filet mignon á la périgourdine. Lemon tartelette; crème caramel; gâteau de pain au whiskey (bread pudding).

Summary & comments: Gerard Crozier opened New Orleans' first pure French restaurant—no Creole flavors at all. The specific style is classic bistro food from his hometown of Lyons. No nouvelle cuisine. Despite this conventionality (or perhaps because of it), Crozier's food is some of the best around. It is certainly the most consistent: The dish the chef cooked for you a decade ago is cooked the same today, even though the restaurant itself has moved twice. Service and presentations are understated. Not entirely casual, although it's easy to mistake such unrelieved Frenchness for formality.

DAKOTA

Nouvelle Creole	★★★★	Expensive	QUALITY 94

629 N. US 190, Covington (504) 892-3712
   Zone 12, North Shore

VALUE
C

Customers: Locals; couples; gourmets
Reservations: Recommended
When to go: Weeknights
Entree range: $13–24
Payment: AMEX, MC, VISA
Service rating: ★★★★★
Friendliness rating: ★★★★
Parking: Free lot adjacent
Bar: Full bar

Wine selection: Distinguished cellar, emphasis on California; many excellent boutique wines; the owner, a wine buff, travels to look for the good stuff
Dress: Jacket recommended but not required
Disabled access: Full

Brunch: Sunday, 11 A.M.–3 P.M.
Lunch: Monday–Friday, 11:30 A.M.–2:30 P.M.
Dinner: Monday–Saturday, 6–10 P.M.

Setting & atmosphere: Dakota's two major dining rooms are furnished and decorated with uncommon attention to detail; even the way the silverware is laid is distinctive. It appears from the outside to be affiliated with the motel next door; it's not.

Recommended dishes: Sweet potato nachos with lamb and Roquefort; smoked shrimp and Brie polenta cake; sea scallops with cayenne caviar; grilled rabbit tenderloin; smoked chicken gumbo; fish with smoked artichoke and roasted bell pepper butter with rock shrimp; stuffed soft-shell crab; honey and rosemary–roasted chicken; cane-syrup-glazed smoked pork tenderloin with bourbon barbecue butter; mixed grill; rack of lamb. Bread pudding; dessert pastries.

Summary & comments: Dakota's is rivaled only by La Provence for the honor of Best Place to Eat on the North Shore. The chef, despite his origins on the Great Plains (hence the name), cooks Creole food in its most intensely flavorful forms, and shows no shyness about using salt, pepper, cream, butter, smoke, or anything else that might make your palate say howdy. You may also taste some flavors from exotic lands in some of the dishes here. Good daily specials and a great Sunday brunch menu. Service is attentive to an almost absurd degree. The wine list is riddled with offbeat bottles, all priced reasonably. Loaded with originality and polish.

DRAGO'S

			QUALITY
Seafood/Oyster Bar	★★★★	Moderate	**85**

	VALUE
3232 N. Arnoult Road 888-9254	**C**
Zone 10, Metairie above Causeway/Kenner/Jefferson Hwy.	

Customers: Locals; families
Reservations: Accepted
When to go: Anytime
Entree range: $7–16
Payment: All major credit cards
Service rating: ★★
Friendliness rating: ★★★

Parking: Free lot, sometimes full at lunch
Bar: Full bar
Wine selection: A few house wines, including a few from Croatia
Dress: Casual
Disabled access: Full

Lunch: Monday–Friday, 11:30 A.M.–2:30 P.M.
Dinner: Monday–Saturday, 5–10 P.M.

Setting & atmosphere: Except for the flea-market art on the walls, this is a much handsomer dining room than is found in typical seafood houses.
Recommended dishes: Raw oysters; char-grilled oysters; seafood gumbo; shrimp Ruth (sautéed with herbs over fresh tomatoes); shrimp fondue; salad with feta vinaigrette; garlic-pepper shrimp; drumfish Tommy (grilled and stuffed); fried or broiled seafood platter (great tartar sauce); boiled lobster. Lunch specials.
Summary & comments: A step up from the average casual seafood restaurant, Drago's has unusually excellent oysters, which shows in its raw bar and its original char-broiled oysters (grilled in the shell, basted with garlic-herb butter). Almost everything else in the way of local seafood is available here, usually in some interesting, garlic-laced preparation. For about $30 per person, there's an unending seafood feast of the best specialties. The service can bog down at times.

EMERIL'S

			QUALITY
Nouvelle Creole/Eclectic	★★★★★	Very Expensive	**98**

	VALUE
800 Tchoupitoulas Street 528-9393	**C**
Zone 2, Central Business District	

Customers: Mix of tourists and locals; hip, gourmet crowd
Reservations: Required

When to go: Lunch and early evenings
Entree range: $16–26

Emeril's (continued)

Payment: All major credit cards
Service rating: ★★★★
Friendliness rating: ★★
Parking: Valet (free)
Bar: Full bar
Wine selection: Distinguished cellar,
with many well-known but rarely
seen bottles; many by-the-glass
selections
Dress: Dressy casual
Disabled access: Full

Lunch: Monday–Friday, 11:30 A.M.–2:30 P.M.
Dinner: Monday–Saturday, 6–10 P.M.

Setting & atmosphere: The main room is in an old, interestingly renovated factory; it is noisy to incredibly noisy. At one end, on the other side
of the stoves where they cook the a la minute items, is the food bar; this is
a great place for the single gourmet.

Recommended dishes: Specials here are often the most interesting possibilities. Current regular items: barbecue shrimp; parfait (a salad, really) of
shrimp rémoulade; smoked trout dumplings; gumbo of the day; andouille-
crusted redfish; panéed quail. "A study of duck" (breast, foie gras, leg confit, mushroom bread pudding); filet of beef with blue cheese; double-cut
pork chop with green chile mole. Banana cream pie; chocolate pecan pie;
chocolate Grand Marnier soufflée; cheeses.

Summary & comments: After establishing himself at Commander's Palace
for almost a decade, Emeril Lagasse opened his own dining room and
kitchen five years ago. Ever since, he's presided over the dining scene as its
leading innovator. Emeril's menu is grounded in Louisiana flavors, gaining
distinction by concentrating hard on ingredients: Many of the meats, vegetables, and seafoods are raised especially for the restaurant; sauces and
condiments that most restaurants would buy already prepared are made on
the premises. The result is a palette of very big flavors in unimpeachably
fine foodstuffs. The wine list is fantastic. Prices and smugness levels climb
in step with the chef's fame.

G&E COURTYARD GRILL			
Nouvelle Italian/Eclectic	★★★★	Expensive	QUALITY 93
1113 Decatur Street 528-9376	Zone 1, French Quarter		VALUE B

Customers: Mostly locals, a few
  tourists; couples; gourmets
Reservations: Required
When to go: Early evenings, Friday
  lunch
Entree range: $10–21

Payment: All major credit cards
Service rating: ★★★★
Friendliness rating: ★★★★
Parking: French Market pay lot, one block
Bar: Full bar

Wine selection: Modest list, mostly Italian and California; wines well-chosen for the food; many by-the-glass selections
Dress: Dressy casual
Disabled access: Full

Lunch: Friday, 11 A.M.–3 P.M.

Dinner: Sunday–Thursday, 6–10 P.M.; Friday and Saturday, 6–11 P.M.

Setting & atmosphere: In an old row house built by the Ursuline nuns almost two centuries ago, the G&E maintains two dining areas: a lovely parlor with an antique bar and travertine floors, and a fine little covered courtyard. The latter is in greater demand; not only is it lush with flowers, fresh herbs, and other greenery, but the aromas from its grill and rotisserie whet the appetite.

Recommended dishes: Antipasti; soft-shell crab roll with caviar and wasabi; fried oyster Caesar salad; oyster Rockefeller soup; turtle soup. Rotisserie chicken (finished a different way every day); pasta puttanesca; pasta with Italian-style lamb sausage; any lamb dish: rack, chops, leg o', etc; any treatment of grilled fish; daily specials. All desserts are daily specials, but usually good.

Summary & comments: The anticipation built by the aromas in the courtyard is fulfilled in spades by the most innovative and interesting Creole-Italian cooking around. Although the chef likes to fiddle with Asian flavors here and there, the main line is the robust but fresh flavors of herbs, olive oil, and crushed red pepper. Nobody does lamb better, and anything off the rotisserie or grill (particularly thick fish steaks) will be memorable. A subtle joy.

GABRIELLE

Nouvelle Creole	★★★★	Expensive	QUALITY
			93
			VALUE
3201 Esplanade Avenue 948-6233	Zone 6, Mid-City/Gentilly		**B**

Customers: Locals; couples; gourmets
Reservations: Required
When to go: Early evenings, weeknights

Entree range: $14–22
Payment: All major credit cards
Service rating: ★★★★
Friendliness rating: ★★★★
Parking: Curbside

Gabrielle (continued)

Bar: Full bar
Wine selection: Modest list, mostly California; wines well-chosen for the food; many by-the-glass selections; attractive prices
Dress: Dressy casual
Disabled access: Limited

Lunch: Friday, 11:30 A.M.–2:30 P.M.
Dinner: Tuesday–Saturday, 6–10 P.M.

Setting & atmosphere: This miniscule restaurant is a little frantic—the triangular dining room makes movement complicated—but once you're seated things are comfortable, if a bit loud.

Recommended dishes: Menu changes weekly. Oysters Gabie (baked with artichokes & bread crumbs); sausage mixed grill; grilled rabbit tenderloin; blackened steak; blackened tuna; jerked pork chop; roasted poussin stuffed with duck sausage. Bread pudding; lemon chess pie.

Summary & comments: One of the most interesting new-style Creole bistros, Gabrielle's food is fresh and imaginative, and usually downright exciting—more so when it arrives than when you're reading about it on the menu (certainly better than the other way around). Owners chef Greg Sonnier and wife Mary run things in a highly personal but down-to-earth way. Tough to get a reservation at times; the place has lots of enthusiastic regulars, and with good reason.

GALATOIRE'S

Creole French	★★★★	Expensive	QUALITY 90
209 Bourbon Street 525-2021	Zone 1, French Quarter		VALUE C

Customers: Tourists, locals, regulars who know each other
Reservations: For parties of 8 or larger, and then only Tuesday–Thursday
When to go: To avoid the line, go late lunch through early dinner
Entree range: $12–24 (median: $18)
Payment: AMEX, MC, VISA, DC
Service rating: ★★★
Friendliness rating: ★★
Parking: Pay garage nearby
Bar: Full bar; drinks are generously poured and modestly priced
Wine selection: Peculiar list of French and California wines with the absolute minimum of identification of maker and vintage; very attractive prices
Dress: Jacket and tie required at dinner and all day Sunday
Disabled access: None

Lunch & Dinner: Tuesday–Sunday, 11:30 A.M.–9 P.M.

Setting & atmosphere: The single long dining room, flanked on both sides by large mirrors surmounted by naked light bulbs and motionless ceiling fans, is bright, noisy, happy, and well dressed.

Recommended dishes: Shrimp rémoulade; crabmeat maison; canapé Lorenzo; oysters Rockefeller; oysters en brochette; green salad with garlic; trout meunière or amandine; grilled pompano; poached salmon or drum hollandaise; shrimp Marguery; crabmeat Yvonne; chicken Clemenceau; filet or strip steak béarnaise; lamb, veal, or pork chop. Crème caramel; crêpes maison.

Summary & comments: A truly indispensable restaurant, Galatoire's has changed more in the last 5 years than in the previous 50. Although they still don't take reservations, they do now accept credit cards. And, in a shocking concession to modern modes, a fish grill was installed a few years ago. Still, the standards of simple but excellent French-Creole cooking that the founders established at the turn of the century remain in force. Although seafood has always been the main draw, they cook everything deftly, to the point that every regular Galatoire's diner can recommend one or two sleeper specialties in the catalog-like menu. The old-fashioned service style includes a bit of food-slinging; try to ignore it.

GALLAGHER'S

Creole	★★★	Expensive	QUALITY
			86
			VALUE
			C

1630 N. US 190, Covington (504) 892-1444
  Zone 12, North Shore

Customers: Locals; gourmets; couples
Reservations: Accepted
When to go: Anytime
Entree range: $12–20
Payment: All major credit cards
Service rating: ★★★

Friendliness rating: ★★★
Parking: Free lot adjacent
Bar: Full bar
Wine selection: Decent list, emphasis on California
Dress: Dressy casual
Disabled access: Limited

Lunch: Monday–Friday, 11:30 A.M.–2:30 P.M.
Dinner: Monday–Saturday, 6–10 P.M.

Setting & atmosphere: The several small dining rooms are intimate, comfortable, and surprisingly urbane for what is still essentially a rural area.

Recommended dishes: Crab cakes; fried baby soft-shell crabs; baby back ribs; smoked duck and andouille gumbo; charcoal-grilled tuna with smoked tomato salsa; trout Winner's Circle (topped with artichokes and lemon cream sauce); grilled quail; smoked duckling; veal St. Tammany (mushrooms and garlic); chicken Lafayette (rich sauce with tasso). Different desserts daily.

Summary & comments: A revival of the style proprietor Pat Gallagher made rather famous at two now-deceased editions of the Winner's Circle, among a few other places. The emphasis is on grilled foods, which are s easoned very nicely and cooked with excitement. The Creole basics like gumbo, seafood platters, and steaks with sauces are also prepared with verve. Now let's hope the place stays open a little longer than Pat's last few places.

GAUTREAU'S

Eclectic	★★★★	Expensive	QUALITY **89**
1728 Soniat Street 899-7397	Zone 4, Uptown above Napoleon		VALUE **C**

Customers: Locals; couples; gourmets
Reservations: Recommended
When to go: Anytime
Entree range: $18–24
Payment: All major credit cards
Service rating: ★★★★
Friendliness rating: ★★★★

Parking: Valet (free)
Bar: Full bar
Wine selection: Modest list, but well-chosen for the food
Dress: Jacket recommended but not required
Disabled access: Limited

Lunch: Monday–Friday, 11:30 A.M.–2 P.M.
Dinner: Monday–Saturday, 6–10 P.M.

Setting & atmosphere: The building is a former antique pharmacy, and some of the fixtures from that era remain: the pressed-tin ceiling, the wood display cabinets (now filled with wine). Smallish, but not as earsplitting as it once was.

Recommended dishes: Menu changes seasonally. Here's what was best at this writing: crisp duck confit with mustard and sage; seared sea scallops; Gorgonzola and artichoke tart; tuna carpaccio; chilled curried tomato soup; roasted grouper with braised fennel, tarragon, and crabmeat in fish broth; roasted chicken with wild mushrooms; seared beef tournedos with artichoke ragout; roasted lamb chops with truffle risotto. Crêpes with cherry fig sauce; crème brûlée.

Gautreau's (continued)

Summary & comments: Gautreau's supplies a loyal clientele with an exacting and highly individualistic cuisine. The menu, while not especially long, seems to have one of just about everything, whipped up in a generally nouvelle style with a light Creole influence. The best dishes tend to be the least exotic, oddly; for example, I've never had less than a wonderful filet mignon or roast chicken. Since so many of the customers are regulars, the service has a rather chummy style. It's often difficult to get a table here on short notice, and there's no comfortable place to wait. It's curious that although there have been two major changes of ownership and chefs, the record of consistency is spotless.

GUMBO SHOP

Creole	★★★	Moderate	QUALITY
			80

630 St. Peter Street 525-1486	Zone 1, French Quarter	VALUE
		B

Customers: Tourists, some locals
Reservations: Not accepted
When to go: Middle of the afternoon or evening
Entree range: $7–14
Payment: All major credit cards
Service rating: ★★★

Friendliness rating: ★★★
Parking: French Market pay lot, one block
Bar: Full bar
Wine selection: A few house wines
Dress: Casual
Disabled access: Limited

Lunch & Dinner: Every day, 11 A.M.–11 P.M.

Setting & atmosphere: This best-named of all New Orleans restaurants isn't as old as it looks, with its yellowed murals surrounding the antique dining room. But if you eat here you'll feel as if you've dined in Old New Orleans.

Recommended dishes: Shrimp rémoulade; seafood gumbo; jambalaya; red beans and rice; crawfish pie; crawfish étouffée; redfish Florentine; blackened redfish. Pecan pie; bread pudding.

Summary & comments: If it's traditional everyday New Orleans eats you want, this is the place to get them; gumbo and the other homestyle Creole specials are very credibly done every single day. Prices are lower than they could be, given the popularity and great location of the restaurant.

INDIA PALACE

			QUALITY
Indian	★★★	Moderate	83

	VALUE
3322 N. Turnbull Street 889-2436 Zone 10, Metairie above	C

Causeway/Kenner/Jefferson Hwy.

Customers: Locals
Reservations: Accepted
When to go: Anytime
Entree range: $8–20
Payment: All major credit cards
Service rating: ★★★

Friendliness rating: ★★★
Parking: Free lot adjacent
Bar: Full bar
Wine selection: A few house wines
Dress: Casual
Disabled access: Full

Brunch: Sunday, 11:30 A.M.–3 p.m; buffet with music
Lunch: Every day, 11:30 A.M.–3 P.M.
Dinner: Every day, 5–10 P.M.

Setting & atmosphere: The city's newest Indian restaurant is its most handsome—slick, informal, and comfortable, with little in the way of ethnic decor.

Recommended dishes: Vegetable or chicken pakoras (fried cutlets); samosas (small pastries stuffed with meat or vegetables); tandoori chicken or prawns, roasted in charcoal-fired claypot ovens; the entire range of curries, including the very hot vindaloo curries; saag paneer (homemade cheese in a creamed spinach sauce); lamb or chicken saagwala (sauce similar to saag paneer); yogurt-marinated lamb rack; naan (tandoor-baked bread). Cream cheese and pistachio pudding; mango sundae.

Summary & comments: If you come for lunch, you may be tempted to do the buffet, but resist this: The food is good, but is never quite as hot (either from the stove or pepper) as it should be. The entire range of Indian standards is here, from the almost absurdly healthy tandoori roasts, to the relatively oil-free fried foods, to the curries and other stews. All are served with appropriate and first-class condiments and sauces. The staff is very helpful, if not always polished.

IRENE'S CUISINE

			QUALITY
Italian	★★★★	Moderate	89

	VALUE
539 St. Philip Street 529-8811 Zone 1, French Quarter	B

Customers: Mostly locals, a few
   tourists; many Quarterites

Reservations: Not accepted
When to go: Early evenings

Irene's Cuisine (continued)

Entree range: $11–19
Payment: All major credit cards except Discover
Service rating: ★★★
Friendliness rating: ★★★
Parking: Curbside

Bar: Full bar
Wine selection: Decent list, mostly Italian
Dress: Casual
Disabled access: Full

Dinner: Every day, 6–10 P.M.

Setting & atmosphere: A small, largely unadorned dining room was once the office of a paper warehouse. Borderline mysterious.

Recommended dishes: Mussels marinara; oysters Irene (baked with bacon, herbs, Parmesan cheese); grilled shrimp and panéed oysters with spinach; roasted chicken with rosemary, garlic, and brandy; cannelloni; veal Sorrentina (eggplant, mushrooms, prosciutto, mozzarella); roast duck with spinach and mustard; sautéed soft-shell crab and pasta; steak pizzaiola. Tiramisu; Italian ice creams.

Summary & comments: Irene DiPietro ran a few local kitchens (most notably the Brick Oven Cafes) before opening this trattoria in the French Quarter. Although the food is quite different, the spirit of the cooking here is reminiscent of that of Mosca's: lots of roasting of simple main ingredients with generous sufficiencies of olive oil, garlic, rosemary, basil, and oregano. Although the red-sauced dishes are good here, they're in the minority and not specialties. Even though the dining room is orchestrated by former Sazerac maitre d' Tommy Andrade (a co-owner), the restaurant is so small and popular that there's a certain frantic edge which, frankly, adds to the excitement of the meal.

K-PAUL'S LOUISIANA KITCHEN

Nouvelle Cajun/Eclectic	★★★★ Very Expensive	QUALITY
		91
416 Chartres Street 524-7394 Zone 1, French Quarter		VALUE
		D

Customers: Mostly tourists, a few locals; gourmets
Reservations: Not accepted downstairs; required upstairs
When to go: Lunch and during slack tourist and convention periods

Entree range: $22–30
Payment: AMEX
Service rating: ★★★★
Friendliness rating: ★★
Parking: Jackson Brewery pay lot, one block
Bar: Very limited

K-Paul's Louisiana Kitchen (continued)

Wine selection: Just one wine (it
varies) downstairs; a little more
variety upstairs

Dress: Casual
Disabled access: Full

Lunch: Monday–Saturday, 11:30 A.M.–2:30 P.M.
Dinner: Monday–Saturday, 6–10 P.M.

Setting & atmosphere: In the hypercasual downstairs dining room, small parties share tables with other small parties, and amenities are minimal. The new upstairs dining room offers everything local diners had been complaining that they wanted: tablecloths, private tables, and even reservations.

Recommended dishes: Stuffed, smoked soft-shell crawfish; chicken-andouille gumbo; Cajun popcorn with sherry sauce; shrimp or crawfish étouffée; stuffed soft-shell crab Choron; blackened tuna; fried mirliton and oysters with tasso hollandaise; roast duck with pecan gravy; pan-fried veal with roasted stuffed peppers; blackened beef tenders in debris sauce (during a three-day process, beef stock is reduced to a rich, brown gravy). Sweet potato pecan pie; bread pudding with lemon sauce; chocolate mocha cake.

Summary & comments: For years Chef Paul Prudhomme's fame as the archetypal Cajun chef has allowed his restaurant to make the point that you need him more than he needs you. But K-Paul's has become much friendlier: It's open for lunch and on Saturdays now, which shortened the lines. And in the new upstairs dining room, he plans an entire formal dinner for you. Either way, you get the unique cooking of Chef Paul, with his consistently impressive ability to make the first-class ingredients explode with flavor—not all of which is Cajun. Also still in place: some of the town's highest prices.

KELSEY'S			
Nouvelle Creole	★★★	Moderate	**QUALITY** 82
3923 Magazine Street 366-6722 Zone 3, Uptown below Napoleon			**VALUE** B

Customers: Youngish Uptowners;
couples
Reservations: Recommended
When to go: Anytime
Entree range: $9–18

Payment: All major credit cards
Service rating: ★★
Friendliness rating: ★★★
Parking: Free lot adjacent
Bar: Full bar

Kelsey's (continued)

Wine selection: Limited list of
    standards

Dress: Casual
Disabled access: None

Lunch: Tuesday–Friday, 11:30 A.M.–2 P.M.
Dinner: Tuesday–Saturday, 5–10 P.M.

Setting & atmosphere: A modest but pleasant dining room on the second floor of a nondescript office building.

Recommended dishes: Eggplant delight (fried, topped with spicy shrimp); shrimp Bombay pie; rabbit tenderloin; Creole gumbo; eggplant Kelsey (stuffed with seafood and herbs); grilled fish; barbecue drum; blackened ribeye; panéed rabbit with pasta; braised pork T-bone with apple butter. Chocolate hazelnut torte; orange poppyseed cheesecake; bread pudding.

Summary & comments: Chef Randy Barlow is a product of the new, upscale Creole-Cajun style of the early eighties. He established his version of it in a cafe on the West Bank, then polished it up after a move to Uptown. Flavors are very big, thanks to the profligate use of cream, intense seasoning blends, aromatic vegetables, and tasso—not to mention fresh seafood and vegetables. The flavors, epitomized by the eggplant with seafood in cream sauce, can get a little repetitive if you don't order carefully, but there's good variety here. Desserts are a little dull.

KIM SON

Vietnamese	★★★★	Moderate	QUALITY
			87
349 Whitney Avenue, Gretna 366-2489		Zone 11, West Bank	VALUE
			A

Customers: Locals; gourmets
Reservations: Accepted
When to go: Anytime
Entree range: $6–11
Payment: AMEX, MC, VISA
Service rating: ★★
Friendliness rating: ★★★★

Parking: Free lot adjacent
Bar: Full bar
Wine selection: Limited list of ordi-
    nary wines
Dress: Casual
Disabled access: Limited

Lunch: Monday–Saturday, 11:30 A.M.–2:30 P.M.
Dinner: Every day, 5–10 P.M.

Setting & atmosphere: A long, heavily windowed room with subtle but typical Asian decor, and a tank full of large, weird fish.

Recommended dishes: Imperial roll; spring roll; shrimp toast; Vietnamese hot and sour fish soup; charcoal-broiled beef over cold noodles; salt-baked crab; salt-baked scallops; fish cooked in clay pot; steamed whole fish with ginger and onion; shrimp (or chicken) with curry and coconut in clay pot; leaf-bound beef; beef fondued in boiled vinegar; beef on iron plate; gluten puffball (a sort of dumpling) in black bean sauce; eggplant and bean cake in clay pot.

Summary & comments: The oldest, best, and most accessible Vietnamese restaurant in the area, Kim Son's markedly underpriced menu is riddled with exciting food. The Vietnamese cuisine has a lot of the rapid wok cooking of China, but is distinctive in its heavy use of fresh herbs—to the point that some dishes are borderline salads. The best way to do this place is to come with six to eight people, both to make it an adventure and to get samples of all of Kim Son's specialties. These include charcoal-grilled, claypot, salt-baked, and noodle dishes along with the more familiar stir-fried jobs. The longest list of vegetarian dishes in town is also here. The staff is very friendly and unhesitating about either explaining or serving the restaurant's more unusual creations.

KUNG'S DYNASTY				
Chinese	★★★	Moderate	**QUALITY** 82	
			VALUE C	

1912 St. Charles Avenue 525-6669
   Zone 3, Uptown below Napoleon

Customers: Mostly locals, a few tourists
Reservations: Accepted
When to go: Anytime
Entree range: $6–17
Payment: AMEX, MC, VISA
Service rating: ★★★

Friendliness rating: ★★★
Parking: Curbside
Bar: Full bar
Wine selection: A few house wines
Dress: Casual
Disabled access: None

Lunch: Every day, 11:30 A.M.–2:30 P.M.
Dinner: Every day, 6–10 P.M.

Setting & atmosphere: The building is decidedly un-Chinese: a fine old Uptown mansion, with big windows looking out onto St. Charles Avenue.
Recommended dishes: Diced boneless squab packages (in lettuce); Peking duck appetizer; crabmeat fried won ton; ruby and crystal shrimp

Kung's Dynasty (continued)

(shrimp in two different sauces); soft-shell crab with ginger and garlic; oysters Szechuan style; Kung's chicken (plum sauce; crispy); imperial beef in spicy orange sauce; lemon chicken; pork Hunan style. Honey banana; almond bean curd.

Summary & comments: The food is on the ambitious side, employing very fine ingredients (especially in the seafood department) in well-made, refined sauces. The main style is Hunan, with its thick, translucent, subtly spicy-sweet sauces. Portions would be considered enormous even in places serving dishes of mush lesser quality. Service is ordinary.

LA CRÊPE NANOU				
French Bistro	★★★★	Moderate	**QUALITY** **87**	
1410 Robert Street 899-2670		Zone 4, Uptown above Napoleon	**VALUE** **A**	

Customers: Uptowners; Francophiles
Reservations: Not accepted
When to go: Early evenings
Entree range: $7–16
Payment: MC, VISA
Service rating: ★★★
Friendliness rating: ★★★

Parking: Curbside
Bar: Full bar
Wine selection: Substantial list, French-dominated; many by-the-glass selections; attractive prices
Dress: Casual
Disabled access: Limited

Dinner: Every day, 6–10 P.M.

Setting & atmosphere: It looks as if it was transported here from a Parisian backstreet, complete with mismatched everything in its collage of crowded, noisy dining spaces.

Recommended dishes: Pâté maison; mussels marinière; escargots de bourguignonne; onion soup au gratin; salad tropicale; crêpes, especially crab, crawfish, Florentine, and provençal; grilled salmon béarnaise; roast chicken; grilled quails with mushrooms; filet mignon with green peppercorn sauce; lamb chops with cognac sauce, sweetbreads with lemon, capers, and butter. Dessert crêpes, especially Antillaise, Belle Helene, and Calvados; baked Alaska for two.

Summary & comments: Evolved far beyond its origins as a crêpe shop, Nanou is a fix for Francophiles. Incredibly (and understandably) popular, meals here usually require at least a short wait for a table to open; the social scene during the delay is a latter-day version of the Uptown cocktail party that Manale's was in the seventies. The food is stereotypical bistro fare: fresh, very French, inexpensive, and more delicious than you anticipate. Crêpes —both entree and dessert varieties—remain a specialty that no other local restaurant can match.

LA CUISINE

Creole	★★★	Moderate	QUALITY
			87

	VALUE
	B

225 W. Harrison Avenue 486-7664
    Zone 7, Lakeview/West End/Bucktown

Customers: Locals, mostly on the older side
Reservations: Recommended
When to go: After 8 P.M.
Entree range: $9–20 (median: $14)
Payment: All major credit cards
Service rating: ★★★

Friendliness rating: ★★★★
Parking: Free lot adjacent
Bar: Full bar
Wine selection: Limited list of ordinary wines
Dress: Dressy casual
Disabled access: Limited

Lunch: Tuesday–Sunday, 11 A.M.–2:30 P.M.
Dinner: Tuesday–Saturday, 5–10 P.M.

Setting & atmosphere: The two main rooms are a bit too formal for today's tastes, but everything else about the place is easygoing.

Recommended dishes: Oysters Deanna (baked with garlic and bread crumbs); oysters trois faáon (baked with three different sauces); shrimp rémoulade; crab soup; crawfish bisque; crawfish étouffée; crabmeat Martin (a creamy, spicy casserole); trout meunière amandine; Joe's hot shrimp (stuffed with mozzarella and jalapeños); filet mignon; boiled beef brisket; osso buco; broiled chicken bordelaise. Bread pudding; lemon ice box pie.

Summary & comments: After 25 years spent assembling a loyal audience for its familiar, likeable Creole food, La Cuisine abruptly went out of business in 1994. The consternation of the faithful was salved when the place reopened with much of the same staff and the same old menu in 1995. The culinary style is quite out of vogue, but if you can get past the minor atrocities (iceberg lettuce salads, mushy vegetables, overuse of stuffing, and terrible wine service), you'll find a lot of honest flavor.

LA PROVENCE

French Creole	★★★★★	Expensive	QUALITY
			98

25020 US 190, Lacombe (504) 626-7662	Zone 12, North Shore	VALUE
		C

Customers: Gourmets from all over the area; couples
Reservations: Required
When to go: Sunday afternoon
Entree range: $14–24
Payment: AMEX, MC, VISA
Service rating: ★★★★
Friendliness rating: ★★★★

Parking: Free lot adjacent
Bar: Full bar
Wine selection: Distinguished cellar, French-dominated; the corkage policy is draconian
Dress: Jacket recommended but not required
Disabled access: Full

Dinner: Wednesday–Saturday, 6–10 P.M.; Sunday, 1–9 P.M.

Setting & atmosphere: If you have ever discovered an unexpectedly wonderful restaurant in a small European town, you'll recognize the scene at La Provence. Isolated in a pine forest on the old east-west highway on the North Shore, this is a lovely, comfortable, somewhat rustic, classy, and fully informal place to take a meal.

Recommended dishes: Merguez (lamb sausage); boudin noir with lentils; gravlax; baked oysters three ways; Madagascar-pepper shrimp cocktail; escargots bourguignonne; quail gumbo; Greek salad; quenelles of scallops; sautéed thyme-marinated quail. Duck à l'orange; rack of lamb; tournedos bordelaise; sweetbreads braised in Port wine. Diplomat pudding, dessert cart.

Entertainment & amenities: Pianist in lounge nightly.

Summary & comments: Chef-owner Chris Kerageorgiou, a beloved local character, blends his native French, ancestral Greek, and adopted Creole flavors in thrilling, original ways. You can participate not only by eating but by entering the showplace kitchen. There are occasional inconsistencies (the place gets a little too busy Saturday nights, for example), but dinner here is usually unforgettable. Our favorite time to go: late Sunday afternoon in winter, with the fireplace blazing.

LA RIVIERA

Italian   ★★★★   Expensive

QUALITY
83

VALUE
C

4506 Shores Drive 888-6238
   Zone 10, Metairie above Causeway/Kenner/Jefferson Hwy.

Customers: Locals; couples	Parking: Free lot adjacent
Reservations: Recommended	Bar: Full bar
When to go: Anytime	Wine selection: Substantial list,
Entree range: $9–22	mostly Italian
Payment: All major credit cards	Dress: Jacket recommended but not
Service rating: ★★★★	required
Friendliness rating: ★★★★	Disabled access: Full

Lunch: Monday–Friday, 11:30 A.M.–2:30 P.M.
Dinner: Monday–Saturday, 6–10 P.M.

Setting & atmosphere: The dining room is bright and formal in a dated, Metairie-anean kind of way, but the camaraderie among the customers prevents stuffiness from getting a toehold.

Recommended dishes: Crabmeat ravioli; fried calamari; fettuccine La Riviera (like Alfredo, but lighter); baked oysters Italian style; stuffed mushrooms; broiled trout; seafood-stuffed eggplant; soft-shell crab with crabmeat; spaghetti and meatballs; osso buco; veal pizzaiola; veal piccata; filet mignon with Madeira sauce. Spumoni; amaretto kiss.

Summary & comments: This was the first permanent home of true Italian (as opposed to Creole Italian) cooking in New Orleans. Chef Goffredo Fraccaro opened La Riviera 25 years ago and has since sold it, although he's still there cooking most of the time. The menu is pretty accessible—over the years, more than a few local Italian standards have crept in. (For example, it's the best plate of meatballs and spaghetti I've found.) More ambitious dishes abound, particularly among the specials. Rather popular with a devoted bunch of regulars.

LE PARVENU

			QUALITY
Creole	★★★★	Expensive	**89**
			VALUE
			C

509 Williams Boulevard, Kenner 471-0534
   Zone 10, Metairie above Causeway/Kenner/Jefferson Hwy.

Customers: People from Kenner, River Ridge, the Riverlands, the airport
Reservations: Recommended
When to go: Anytime
Entree range: $13–24
Payment: AMEX, DC, D, MC, VISA
Service rating: ★★★

Friendliness rating: ★★★
Parking: Curbside; small lot
Bar: Full bar
Wine selection: Short list of standard wines
Dress: Dressy casual
Disabled access: Full

Brunch: Sunday, 11:30 A.M.–3 P.M.
Lunch: Wednesday–Friday, 11:30 A.M.–2:30 P.M.
Dinner: Wednesday–Saturday, 6–10 P.M.

Setting & atmosphere: A comfortable (but perhaps a bit too snug) cottage in the oldest part of the old railroad town of Kenner. In nice weather, there's porch dining.

Recommended dishes: Crabmeat Patricia; mirliton, shrimp and crab bisque; artichoke-and-garlic cheese soup; broiled fish à la Rivertown; lobster Le Parvenu; veal with portobello mushrooms and spinach; lamb chops and sausage with cider mint sauce; filet mignon with shrimp and peppercorns. Lemon crêpes; crème brûlée.

Summary & comments: The chef-owner was formerly in charge of the kitchen at the now-closed five-star Versailles, and while he's toned down the snootiness of that place, his food retains all the polish. The style is inventive without going too far afield. Order one more course than you ordinarily would, because portions here are a touch small. This is the only really good restaurant anywhere near the airport, which is about a half-mile away.

LITTLE TOKYO

Japanese/Sushi Bar	★★★	Moderate	QUALITY
			82

		VALUE
1612 St. Charles Avenue 524-8535		**C**
Zone 3, Uptown below Napoleon		

Customers: Locals, tourists;
  businessmen at lunch
Reservations: Accepted
When to go: Anytime
Entree range: $8–13
Payment: All major credit cards
Service rating: ★★★

Friendliness rating: ★★★
Parking: Curbside (metered)
Bar: Full bar
Wine selection: A few house wines
Dress: Casual
Disabled access: Limited

Lunch: Every day, 11:30 A.M.–2:30 P.M.
Dinner: Every day, 6–10 P.M.

Setting & atmosphere: Somewhat utilitarian, with different scenes at the sushi bar, conventional tables, and tatami rooms.

Recommended dishes: Sunomono (seaweed with octopus and shrimp); tofu steak; shu mai (steamed shrimp dumplings); beef tataki; sushi; chirashi sushi (seafood on a bed of sushi rice); sashimi; una don (teriyaki eel on rice). Red bean ice cream.

Summary & comments: The most convenient-to-downtown sushi bar is only loosely associated with the Little Tokyo in Metairie, and a bit different in its food. This cafe offers a menu only slightly smaller than its bigger competitors, but with no sacrifice of goodness. The daily lunch box brings an interesting assortment of different specialties daily. The sushi bar is staffed by the owner, who has a deft hand and eye. At the tables they serve the entire range of Japanese specialties, including sukiyaki and its ilk. Pleasant, helpful servers.

LIUZZA'S

Neighborhood Cafe	★★★	Inexpensive	QUALITY
			79

		VALUE
3636 Bienville Street 482-9120 Zone 6, Mid-City/Gentilly		**B**

Customers: Neighborhood people;
  families
Reservations: Not accepted
When to go: Anytime
Entree range: $5–14

Payment: No credit cards
Service rating: ★★★
Friendliness rating: ★★★
Parking: Free lot adjacent and
  curbside

Liuzza's (continued)

Bar: Full bar
Wine selection: A few house wines

Dress: Anything goes
Disabled access: Limited

Lunch & Dinner: Monday–Saturday, 11 A.M.–9:30 P.M.

Setting & atmosphere: One of the oldest of the few remaining corner cafes, Liuzza's presents the classic neighborhood "bar & rest." aspect.

Recommended dishes: French fries; Italian breaded eggplant; oyster artichoke soup; Wop salad (sorry; that's really what they call it); fried seafood platters; roast beef poorboy; hot sausage poorboy; broiled ham and cheese poorboy; fried chicken; panéed veal and fettuccine; eggplant casserole with spaghetti and meatballs; daily specials. Bread pudding.

Summary & comments: Liuzza's most famous product is the large, heavy, frozen glass chalices in which they serve beer and root beer. But the food's pretty good, too, starting with a fine roast beef poorboy and moving up through interesting, very homely daily specials, seafood platters, and Italian dishes. The presence of fresh-cut French fries and the small window through which the finished orders are pushed both bear witness to the well-preserved old style for which this place is loved. Not always perfect in its food, but always authentic backstreet New Orleans.

LOLA'S				
Spanish	★★★	Moderate	**QUALITY**	80
3312 Esplanade Avenue 488-6946		Zone 6, Mid-City/Gentilly	**VALUE**	A

Customers: Locals, mostly young
Reservations: Not accepted
When to go: Early evenings
Entree range: $7–14
Payment: No credit cards
Service rating: ★★

Friendliness rating: ★★★
Parking: Curbside
Bar: No alcohol; bring your own
Wine selection: Bring your own
Dress: Casual
Disabled access: Limited

Dinner: Tuesday–Saturday, 6–10 P.M.

Setting & atmosphere: The scene here is defined by the miniscule size of the restaurant, which comes nowhere close to satisfying the demand for tables.

Recommended dishes: Pâté and cheese board; mussels vinaigrette; garlic soup; gazpacho; grilled fish with spicy sauce du jour; garlic chicken; paprika-marinated roast pork loin; paella (meat, seafood, and vegetarian versions are all fine); daily specials.

Summary & comments: This is the rebirth of the deceased Altamira, the city's only Spanish (as opposed to Latin American) restaurant. While much of the menu is still Spanish—gazpacho and paella are two specialties—more than a few dishes are from closer to home. (Creole and Spanish have a lot in common anyway.) Extremely popular, dining at Lola's almost always involves waiting for a table. Very cheap.

LOUIS XVI			
French	★★★★	Very Expensive	QUALITY 87
730 Bienville Street 581-7000		Zone 1, French Quarter	VALUE D

Customers: Mostly locals, a few tourists; couples; gourmets
Reservations: Recommended
When to go: Anytime
Entree range: $18–30
Payment: All major credit cards
Service rating: ★★★★★
Friendliness rating: ★★★

Parking: Validated ($3) in garage behind Mr. B's
Bar: Full bar
Wine selection: Wines here have never been quite as interesting or various as the food, and prices are too high
Dress: Jacket required
Disabled access: Full

Breakfast: Every day, 7–10 A.M.
Dinner: Every day, 6–10 P.M.

Setting & atmosphere: A pleasant dinosaur, Louis XVI is handsome and plush in a modern way. Mirrors in the small dining room reflect a geometry of indirect neon, and a wall of windows opens onto the hotel's courtyard. Tables on the covered, climate-controlled courtyard are available for dining.

Recommended dishes: Duck pâté with onion marmalade; marinated fish with peanut-ginger relish; feuilletage de crustaces (puff pastry layered with shellfish in sauce Nantua); escargots with hazelnuts and pecans; vegetable cream soup du jour; fillet de poisson Louisiane (with banana, red bell pepper, and meunière sauce); poached or grilled fish; sweetbreads with mushrooms; rack of lamb; Châteaubriand; filet mignon St. Hebert (pepper-and-currant sauce). Gâteau au noisettes; pastries.

Entertainment & amenities: Pianist in lounge nightly.

Summary & comments: First opened a quarter-century ago, this is the first local restaurant successfully to serve Escoffier-era, non-Creole French cuisine. The service, too, is French: Most dishes are presented and usually administered to at tableside. Big roasts of red meats for two are carved; sauces are brought to bubbling; and desserts are flamed before you. Corny by today's vogues, but still romantic and special. The menu is slowly updated, and there may be more than a few new dishes since your last visit, but it's still Louis XVI.

MANDINA'S				
Neighborhood Cafe/Italian	★★★	Moderate	**QUALITY** 75
3800 Canal Street 482-9179	Zone 6, Mid-City/Gentilly		**VALUE** A

Customers: Locals; families; businessmen at lunch
Reservations: Not accepted
When to go: Off-peak lunch and dinner hours to avoid waiting
Entree range: $9–17
Payment: No credit cards

Service rating: ★★
Friendliness rating: ★
Parking: Curbside
Bar: Full bar
Wine selection: A few house wines
Dress: Casual
Disabled access: Limited

Lunch & Dinner: Monday–Saturday, 11 A.M.–10 P.M.; Sunday, noon–9 P.M.

Setting & atmosphere: Mandina's comes closer than any other restaurant to the Orleanian's cherished ideal of the old-time neighborhood cafe. The front room is the busier, with tables vying for space with the customers waiting for their turn at the bar. In the back is a utilitarian dining room that's a bit quieter. The whole place is furnished with neon, old painted signs, beer clocks, and other relics.

Recommended dishes: Shrimp rémoulade; crab fingers in wine sauce; oyster and artichoke soup; fried soft-shell crab; trout amandine; spaghetti and Italian sausage. Daily specials, especially: red beans with Italian sausage (Monday); beef stew (Tuesday); braciolone (Thursday); stuffed crab (Friday); crabmeat au gratin (Sunday). Bread pudding.

Summary & comments: The best food on any given day will be the homestyle specials, with a further edge to non-seafoods. All portions are titanic, but somehow avoid grossness. The service staff has been here a long time; you cannot impress them.

MARTINIQUE

French Bistro/Caribbean	★★★	Moderate	QUALITY
			85

5908 Magazine Street 891-8495
   Zone 4, Uptown above Napoleon

	VALUE
	B

Customers: Locals; couples; gourmets
Reservations: Not accepted
When to go: Early evenings
Entree range: $12–17
Payment: MC, VISA
Service rating: ★★
Friendliness rating: ★★★

Parking: Curbside (metered)
Bar: Beer and wine
Wine selection: Modest list,
   but wines well-chosen for
   the food
Dress: Casual
Disabled access: Limited

Dinner: Tuesday–Sunday, 6–10 P.M.

Setting & atmosphere: Physically minimal in a charming way. The court-yard gives a bit more cheery an atmosphere than the darkish main room.
Recommended dishes: Grilled black bean cake with bell pepper coulis; oysters sautéed with lime and cayenne; mussels steamed in Chablis and herbs; salad of lamb sausage and lima beans; chicken stuffed with goat cheese and prosciutto; pork chop grilled with coconut and balsamic vinegar; sesame-seed-crusted salmon with pickled ginger; filet mignon with sautéed pecans and orange zest; scallops provençale. Desserts of the day.
Summary & comments: After creating an unlikely hit with L'Economie, Chef Hubert Sandot, a native of the French West Indies, moved Uptown. The menu is a bit different from that of L'Economie: There's an emphasis on Caribbean cuisine, although everything retains a distinct French accent. All of this is on the light side—neither cream nor butter are found in the recipes—but it's flavorful and fascinating. It's a coin-flip as to whether Martinique's tables or nearby parking places are harder to come by.

MIKE ANDERSON'S

Seafood	★★★	Moderate	QUALITY
			80

215 Bourbon Street 524-3884   Zone 1, French Quarter

	VALUE
	C

Customers: Tourists, some locals;
   businessmen at lunch
Reservations: Not accepted
When to go: Anytime
Entree range: $12–20

Payment: All major credit cards
Service rating: ★★
Friendliness rating: ★★★★
Parking: Pay garages nearby
Bar: Full bar

Wine selection: A few house wines   Disabled access: Limited
Dress: Casual

Lunch & Dinner: Every day, 11 A.M.–11 P.M.

Setting & atmosphere: The local branch of the Baton Rouge football hero's seafood restaurant is a big, long, narrow place on Bourbon Street, full of the trappings of hunting, fishing, and other Cajun stuff.

Recommended dishes: Oysters on the half shell; three-way alligator; baked oysters four ways; fried seafood platter; broiled seafood platter; crawfish, shrimp, or crab dinner; fish stuffed with crab and shrimp; jolie rouge (broiled fish topped with crabmeat).

Summary & comments: This is the best casual seafood joint in the Quarter. The best platters are assortments of several different dishes, in a total portion size so unreasonably large that, even though you might find a thing or two that's sub-par, there'll be more than enough good stuff to fill you up. The seven-way crawfish, crab, and shrimp platters are especially appealing.

MIKE'S ON THE AVENUE				
Eclectic	★★★★	Very Expensive	QUALITY	89
			VALUE	D

628 St. Charles Avenue 523-1709
    Zone 2, Central Business District

Customers: Hip, social crowd; gourmets; couples; businessmen at lunch
Reservations: Recommended
When to go: Anytime
Entree range: $14–23
Payment: All major credit cards
Service rating: ★★★★
Friendliness rating: ★★★

Parking: Lunch: curbside (metered); dinner: valet ($6)
Bar: Full bar
Wine selection: Substantial list, emphasis on California; many by-the-glass selections
Dress: Dressy casual
Disabled access: Full

Brunch: Sunday, 10:30 A.M.–3 P.M.
Lunch: Monday–Friday, 11:30 A.M.–2:30 P.M.
Dinner: Every day, 6–10 P.M.

Setting & atmosphere: The handsome, airy, white dining room features works of art by the chef on most walls, except for the one with big windows that look out onto Lafayette Square and Gallier Hall. A second dining room—located on the other side of the hotel lobby—is a bit plusher but less scenic.

Recommended dishes: Chinese shrimp dumplings with tahini; crawfish spring rolls; sushi; flash-fried oysters with green chile aïoli; barbecue oysters; blackened tuna Napoleon. Maytag blue cheese salad; crawfish and scallop cakes; U-12 barbecue shrimp; shellfish stew with Creole sausage and focaccia; panéed veal with portobello mushrooms and grilled eggplant; filet mignon with chile-lime butter and mashed potatoes. Dessert assortment; sorbets; crème brûlée.

Summary & comments: Mike Fennelly came from Santa Fe, where he made a name for himself by uniting Southwestern and Asian tastes into not just menus but individual dishes. He brought that act to New Orleans in 1991, adding enough other offbeat ideas of food and service to make it one of the most eclectic restaurants around. He has since moved to San Francisco, but he retains his interest and executive chef title here. Mike's serves the culinary equivalent of abstract art: You have to think about it a lot before you really can enjoy it. Indeed, most of the dishes have a sculptural aspect. Generally the eating here is very good to exciting; some of it is just weird. Not a good choice for the traditionalist. The crowd is lively and well connected.

MOSCA'S

Creole Italian	★★★★	Expensive	QUALITY 88
4137 US 90, Waggaman 436-9942		Zone 11, West Bank	VALUE C

Customers: Mostly locals (many regulars), a few tourists; families of adults

Reservations: Accepted but rarely honored on time

When to go: Weeknights; closed all of August

Entree range: $16–22

Payment: Cash only

Service rating: ★

Friendliness rating: ★

Parking: Free lot adjacent

Bar: Full bar

Wine selection: Decent list, almost entirely Italian; several Amarones

Dress: Casual

Disabled access: None

Dinner: Tuesday–Saturday, 5–10 P.M.

Setting & atmosphere: Mosca's seems to be a restaurant that a mystery novelist dreamed up. Set inconveniently past the last suburb on US 90, surrounded by marshes and their accompanying insect clouds and amphibian armies, the place has all the atmosphere of a roadhouse.

Recommended dishes: Marinated crabs; crab salad; chef's bean soup; oysters Italian style; shrimp Italian style. (The last two are totally different.) Chicken grandee (pan-roasted with garlic, potatoes, and artichokes); roast chicken; roast quail or squab; Italian sausage; filet mignon. Pineapple fluff.

Summary & comments: Don't expect sympathy from the staff for the length of your repose in the bar, or exceptions to the cash-only policy, even if the check rises well into three figures—which, for a party of six (the right size for maximum enjoyment here) is a certainty. But the food is great: all the olive oil, garlic, and rosemary you always wanted, scattered around roasted chicken, sausage, shrimp, and oysters. All this is served with a total lack of ceremony (indeed, service is a bit sullen), but nobody cares: It's a food orgy.

MOTHER'S

Sandwiches/Neighborhood cafe	★★★	Moderate	**QUALITY**	83
401 Poydras Street 523-9656 Zone 2, Central Business District			**VALUE**	D

Customers: Tourists, some locals; businessmen at lunch
Reservations: Not accepted
When to go: Anytime except around noon and during large conventions
Entree range: $6–14
Payment: No credit cards

Service rating: ★★
Friendliness rating: ★★★
Parking: Curbside; pay lot nearby
Bar: Beer
Wine selection: A few house wines
Dress: Anything goes
Disabled access: None

Open: Monday–Saturday, 5:30 A.M.–10 P.M.; Sunday, 9 A.M.–10 P.M.

Setting & atmosphere: The brick-walled, concrete-floored dining room is even smaller than it looks, a problem exacerbated by the usually long lines and the parade of cooks bringing hot food through breaks in the line to the cafeteria-style serving area up front. A long-noticed local miracle is how, when your food is ready, a space to sit will suddenly become available.

Recommended dishes: Breakfast special (eggs, grits, breakfast meat, biscuits); Mae's omelette (crusty ham, green onions, mushrooms); pancakes. Ham poorboy; ferdi poorboy (ham and roast beef debris); turkey poorboy; fried seafood poorboys; red beans and rice with Italian sausage; gumbo of the day; jambalaya; corned beef and cabbage. Bread pudding; brownies; muffins.

Summary & comments: Mother's is the most distinguished, busiest, and certainly most expensive sandwich and short-order place in town. It's a cut above most such places: Absolutely everything is cooked from scratch on the premises, with no regard to any considerations other than filling you up deliciously. There's a line most of the time. If there's not, the food will be off a bit—with one exception: Breakfast, which most tourists don't know about, is always wonderful. Don't come here on a diet or without at least $15 per person in cash.

MR. B'S			
Nouvelle Creole	★★★★	Expensive	QUALITY **90**
201 Royal Street 523-2078 Zone 1, French Quarter			VALUE **C**

Customers: Mostly locals, some tourists; gourmets; couples	Parking: Validated (free) at adjacent garage
Reservations: Accepted	Bar: Full bar
When to go: Early evenings	Wine selection: Substantial list, almost entirely West Coast
Entree range: $13–22	
Payment: All major credit cards	Dress: Dressy casual
Service rating: ★★★★★	Disabled access: Limited
Friendliness rating: ★★★★★	

Brunch: Sunday, 11 A.M.–3 P.M.
Lunch: Monday–Saturday, 11:30 A.M.–2:30 P.M.
Dinner: Every day, 6–10:30 P.M.

Setting & atmosphere: The single large, somewhat dim dining room has a certain amount of bustle, yet the place manages to preserve privacy and even a bit of romance.

Recommended dishes: Coconut and beer–battered shrimp; barbecue oysters; catfish fingers; gumbo ya-ya (chicken-andouille style); seasonal salads; pasta jambalaya; hickory-grilled fish; barbecue shrimp; hickory-roasted chicken with sweet garlic glaze; seafood-and-pasta specials. Bread pudding; Mr. B's chocolate cake; profiteroles and chocolate sauce.

Entertainment & amenities: Pianist at dinner nightly and at Sunday brunch.

Summary & comments: Mr. B's began a revolution when it opened in 1979: It served great Creole food in the tradition of Commander's Palace (same owners), but did so in a casual, chic environment and with an accelerated pace of innovation. (Grilling fish over burning wood was their most important new idea.) Now that casual gourmet restaurants dominate the dining scene, Mr. B's is unique no longer, but it still has consistently interesting food served in an engaging ambiance. So engaging, in fact, that at both lunch and dinner the place is usually filled right up to the bar, where one might well wait for a table. (The reservation system favors walk-ins.) The service staff and the wine list are both better than you might expect.

MR. TAI'S			
Chinese/Hunan	★★★	Moderate	**QUALITY** 83
701 Metairie Road 831-8610	Zone 9, Metairie below Causeway		**VALUE** C

Customers: Locals; businessmen at lunch
Reservations: Accepted
When to go: Anytime
Entree range: $8–15
Payment: All major credit cards
Service rating: ★★★

Friendliness rating: ★★★
Parking: Free lot adjacent
Bar: Full bar
Wine selection: A few house wines
Dress: Casual
Disabled access: Full

Lunch: Monday–Friday, 11:30 A.M.–2:30 P.M.
Dinner: Every day, 6–10 P.M.

Setting & atmosphere: Upstairs in a shopping mall is an uncommonly handsome, modern (no red velvet dragons) Chinese restaurant with waiters in tuxedos. There's even a bit of tableside service.

Recommended dishes: Fried dumplings; diced boneless quail; fried sesame fish; shredded chicken in assorted sauces; Hunan beef soup; stir-fried oysters in black bean sauce; Mr. Tai's whole fish; Hunan duck; chicken with spiced pecans; chicken chunks with sesame seeds; shrimp with pine nuts; bean curd with minced pork; Mr. Tai's lo mein. Honey crisp apple; sesame-fried banana.

Summary & comments: Many of the refined dishes served here are found in no other local restaurant. The main style is Hunan, with its elegant, translucent, spicy-sweet sauces. Entrees here tend to be the main two or three ingredients and little else—no filler of onions and anonymous vegetables. The place is not as consistent or as ambitious in its menu as it once was, but it's still one of the best Chinese restaurants in the area.

NAPOLEON HOUSE

Sandwiches	★★	Inexpensive	QUALITY 74
500 Chartres Street 524-9752		Zone 1, French Quarter	VALUE B

Customers: Mostly locals, a few tourists; late nighters; Quarterites
Reservations: Not accepted
When to go: Anytime
Entree range: $6–8
Payment: All major credit cards
Service rating: ★★★

Friendliness rating: ★★★★
Parking: Jackson Brewery pay lot, one block
Bar: Full bar
Wine selection: A few house wines
Dress: Casual
Disabled access: Full

Lunch & Dinner: Monday–Saturday, 11 A.M.–midnight; Friday and Saturday, 11 A.M.–1 A.M.

Setting & atmosphere: "Crumbling ruin" captures the essence of the two-century-old building, in which an apartment was once reserved for Napoleon in exile. (He never took the landlord up on the deal.) The Napoleon House today is mainly a bar where classical music plays, Quarterites complain about the failure of their last show, and everybody drinks Pimm's Cups without knowing why.

Recommended dishes: Seafood gumbo; muffuletta; pastrami sandwich; corned beef sandwich; jambalaya.

Summary & comments: The Napoleon House serves a small menu of sandwiches. Topping the list is what is to our taste the city's best muffuletta, well stuffed with good meats and cheeses and dressed with a fine olive salad.

NOLA

Eclectic/Nouvelle Creole	★★★★	Expensive	QUALITY 90
534 St. Louis Avenue 522-6652		Zone 1, French Quarter	VALUE C

Customers: A mix of hip, young tourists and locals
Reservations: Recommended
When to go: Anytime
Entree range: $12–24
Payment: All major credit cards
Service rating: ★★★★
Friendliness rating: ★★★★

Parking: Jackson Brewery pay lot, one block
Bar: Full bar
Wine selection: Substantial list, emphasis on California; many by-the-glass selections
Dress: Dressy casual
Disabled access: Full

Lunch: Monday–Saturday, 11:30 A.M.–2:30 P.M.
Dinner: Every day, 6–10 P.M.

Setting & atmosphere: Dining rooms are on three levels (with elevator service), and the whole place is filled with trendy fixtures, designs, sculptures, and paintings.

Recommended dishes: Menu changes frequently. At this writing: pizzas; crabcake with chile aïoli. Boudin stewed in beer; sautéed shrimp over pasta with warm rémoulade sauce; slow-roasted duck with andouille spoon bread and greens; Vietnamese-style seafood salad; cedar plank–roasted fish with citrus horseradish crust; double-cut pork chop; wood-roasted lamb shank; panéed veal with crabmeat ravioli. Coconut bread pudding; lemon chess pie; chicory coffee crème brûlée.

Summary & comments: This is the second restaurant of Chef Emeril Lagasse, one of the most celebrated of local culinary geniuses. The ingredient standards of Emeril's are applied with equal rigor here: Everything's fresh and made in-house. The scene at Nola is much looser and kickier, with a distinct pitch toward the younger gourmet. They use a wood-burning oven for baking pizzas and a few other things, a wood-burning grill for thick slabs of meat and poultry, and an open kitchen for everything else. Desserts are far more numerous than you're used to and good, as well.

ODYSSEY GRILL

Greek	★★★	Moderate	QUALITY
			87
6264 Argonne Boulevard 482-4092			VALUE
Zone 7, Lakeview/West End/Bucktown			**B**

Customers: Neighborhood people and members of the local Greek community
Reservations: Accepted
When to go: Anytime
Entree range: $8–16
Payment: All major credit cards
Service rating: ★★★

Friendliness rating: ★★★★
Parking: Free lot adjacent
Bar: Full bar
Wine selection: Decent list, several Greek wines among the Californias
Dress: Casual
Disabled access: Limited

Lunch: Tuesday–Sunday, 11:30 A.M.–3 P.M.
Dinner: Tuesday–Sunday, 5:30–10 P.M.

Odyssey Grill (continued)

Setting & atmosphere: The small room, its walls covered with subtle murals, is bright and chummy; the women of the Greek community have adopted the place as a lunchroom.

Recommended dishes: Saganaki (fried, flamed cheese); fried calamari with tzatziki (a yogurt, garlic, and cucumber sauce); hummus; spanakopita; Greek salad; Mediterranean lamb salad; pan bagnat (grilled vegetable sandwich, also good with grilled tuna); moussaka; grilled quail with Gorgonzola stuffing; whole grilled fish; grilled veal scaloppine; fish baked in phyllo; couscous with seven vegetables, chicken, lamb, and sausage. Galakto-boureko (Greek custard); yogurt cheese with honey and walnuts.

Summary & comments: As the name implies, most of the food here is brought to completion on the grill. The offbeat part of this is that the Odyssey is a Greek restaurant, with all the standards of that cuisine, cooked with elan. An unexpected specialty is the grilled fish, marinated or seasoned with a Greek spice complement and cooked to excitement, often in whole form. There's also a great French grilled vegetable sandwich here, available with grilled fish in it.

PALACE CAFE

Nouvelle Creole	★★★	Expensive	QUALITY 84
605 Canal Street 523-1661	Zone 2, Central Business District		VALUE C

Customers: A mix of locals and tourists; businessmen at lunch; families

Reservations: Recommended

When to go: Anytime

Entree range: $11–19

Payment: All major credit cards

Service rating: ★★★★

Friendliness rating: ★★★★

Parking: Validated (free) at Holiday Inn and Marriott garages

Bar: Full bar

Wine selection: Substantial list, almost entirely from the West Coast

Dress: Dressy casual

Disabled access: Full

Brunch: Sundays, 11 A.M.–3 P.M.
Lunch: Every day, 11:30 A.M.–2:30 P.M.
Dinner: Every day, 6–10:30 P.M.

Setting & atmosphere: Occupying two floors of the historic old Werlein's building on Canal Street, the dining area here is a spacious array of dark-wood booths on tiny-tiled floors. The acoustics are lively; when the place is full, it's loud. The upstairs tables offer a great view of New Orleans' main street; during the Carnival season, this is a great place to watch parades.

Palace Cafe (continued)

When the weather is tolerable, you can eat at sidewalk tables in a rough approximation of the Champs Elysees.

Recommended dishes: Shrimp rémoulade; blue cheese salad; catfish pecan; grilled tuna; roast duck. White chocolate bread pudding; warm chocolate pudding cake; fruit beignets with ice cream.

Entertainment & amenities: Unusually good player piano rolls all the time.

Summary & comments: This is the most casual restaurant run by the Commander's Palace side of the Brennan family. As such, there is difficulty with identity, as in: Should they serve red beans and rice or not? The efforts to raise homecooked Creole standards to Brennan standards of panache usually end in frustration. So stay with the unusual seafood concoctions, which have emerged as the specialty.

PASCAL'S MANALE

Creole Italian	★★★★	Expensive	QUALITY
			85

1838 Napoleon Avenue 895-4877	VALUE
Zone 4, Uptown above Napoleon	B

Customers: A mix of Uptown locals and tourists
Reservations: Recommended
When to go: Anytime
Entree range: $10–20
Payment: All major credit cards
Service rating: ★★★

Friendliness rating: ★★
Parking: Free lot adjacent
Bar: Full bar
Wine selection: Ordinary Italian wines
Dress: Casual
Disabled access: Limited

Lunch & Dinner: Monday–Friday, 11:30 A.M.–10 P.M.
Dinner: Saturday and Sunday, 4–10 P.M.; closed Sundays between Memorial Day and Labor Day.

Setting & atmosphere: This old restaurant shows its age the way an elder movie star with too many facelifts does: The attempts to hide the wear and tear are not entirely successful. But everybody feels comfortable here. Changing the concrete-floor bar, for example, might ruin the place.

Recommended dishes: Raw oysters on the half shell; stuffed mushrooms; crab and oyster pan roast; oysters Bienville; shrimp and crabmeat rémoulade; turtle soup; barbecue shrimp (baked in black pepper butter); broiled fish with crabmeat and hollandaise; veal Puccini (a very rich piccata); filet mignon; spaghetti Collins (with green onions and butter). Bread pudding; chocolate mousse.

Pascal's Manale (continued)

Summary & comments: Founded in 1913, Manale's is the archetype of the Creole-Italian restaurant. It became immensely popular in the fifties for a dish that's still its signature: barbecue shrimp. It's badly misnamed, since the shrimp are neither grilled nor smoked, and the sauce isn't anybody's BBQ sauce, but it's undeniably wonderful: gigantic heads-on jobs with a peppery butter sauce. After some problems in the eighties, Manale's bounced back strong and has become a terrific, casual place for eating some very convincing food. The prices have even become a good value—a big change from a decade ago. Service remains a bit inexact, and you may have to wait for a table on weekends. Good oyster bar. Avoid red-sauce dishes.

PELICAN CLUB

Eclectic	★★★★★	Expensive	QUALITY
			96

		VALUE
615 Bienville Street 523-1504	Zone 1, French Quarter	C

Customers: A mix of locals and tourists; couples; gourmets
Reservations: Recommended
When to go: Anytime
Entree range: $14–25
Payment: All major credit cards
Service rating: ★★★★
Friendliness rating: ★★

Parking: Validated (free) at Monteleone Hotel garage
Bar: Full bar
Wine selection: Substantial list, good international balance; many by-the-glass selections
Dress: Jacket recommended but not required
Disabled access: Limited

Dinner: Every day, 6–10 P.M.

Setting & atmosphere: A row of handsome dining rooms flanks semi-mysterious Exchange Alley, a French Quarter walkway that even Orleanians are unfamiliar with. Depending on what part of the restaurant you're in, the ambiance ranges from party-like (the first room) to romantic (the rear of the second room).

Recommended dishes: Scallop-stuffed artichoke with lemon garlic beurre blanc; beef and shrimp potstickers; escargots with crawfish, garlic, mushrooms, and puff pastry hats; Creole Caesar salad; Thai seafood salad; smoked duck and shrimp gumbo; clay pot of seafood with Thai rice; Louisiana bouillabaisse; grilled fish with ginger-lime glaze; filet mignon with Cabernet shiitake mushroom sauce; jambalaya. Dessert specials.

Summary & comments: This extraordinarily good restaurant keeps a low profile, although it can cook and serve with the best of them. Chefs Richard

Hughes and Chin Ling combine Creole, Italian, Chinese, Southwestern, and various other flavors into dishes using ingredients of unimpeachable goodness (pompano, lobster, prime beef, etc.). The result is immensely appealing, perhaps because a bit more familiarity of flavor is preserved than in similar restaurants. The dining room can get a bit noisy; many of the regulars know one another. Service is friendly, although the greeting at the door is a bit cold.

PERISTYLE			
Nouvelle French/Eclectic	★★★★★	Expensive	**QUALITY** 98
1041 Dumaine Street 593-9535	Zone 1, French Quarter		**VALUE** B

Customers: Gourmets; couples; mostly locals
Reservations: Required
When to go: Early evenings
Entree range: $14–21
Payment: MC, VISA
Service rating: ★★★★★
Friendliness rating: ★★
Parking: Curbside, in a mildly unsavory neighborhood, and very difficult to come by; the best idea is to take a cab.
Bar: Full bar
Wine selection: Modest list of offbeat, well-chosen wines that match the food well; mostly French, quite a few from Provence
Dress: Jacket recommended but not required
Disabled access: Limited

Lunch: Friday, 11:30 A.M.–2 P.M.
Dinner: Tuesday–Saturday, 6–10 P.M.

Setting & atmosphere: The place has a sort of Art Nouveau, Storyville feel, a remnant of a previous tenant. The current management has toned it down to a cool, romantic setting.

Recommended dishes: The menu changes thoroughly several times a year, but these are relatively stable items: foie gras terrine; celery root rémoulade; gratin of oysters and artichokes; duck confit; beet-and-crabmeat salad; pork chop with squash gnocchi; roasted tuna with pine nuts and celeriac gratin; pan-seared squab with rice dressing and Port reduction; grilled duck with lentils. Dessert specials.

Summary & comments: Although the brilliant founder of this very appealing small restaurant passed away in 1994, the transition to the next chef/owner was seamless. Peristyle's food remains marvelously exact and polished. The menu changes with some frequency, but a semi-French nouvelle–cuisine style persists, which relies less on sauces than classic French cooking. The presentations are beautiful without being fussy; much of their beauty derives from the stunning quality of the raw materials. (You'll never see a lettuce leaf with a spot of yellow or a hint of wilt here.) The dining room staff is well-orchestrated in its unpretentious activities. And the wine list is selected with care and verve.

RIB ROOM			
			QUALITY
Nouvelle Creole	★★★★	Very Expensive	91
			VALUE
621 St. Louis Street 529-7045	Zone 1, French Quarter		D

Customers: Businessmen at lunch; hotel guests at dinner

Reservations: Recommended

When to go: Anytime; Friday lunch is usually a full house.

Entree range: $15–26

Payment: All major credit cards

Service rating: ★★★

Friendliness rating: ★★

Parking: Validated (free) in Omni Royal Orleans Hotel garage

Bar: Full bar

Wine selection: Substantial list, good international balance; 20 by-the-glass selections

Dress: Jacket recommended but not required

Disabled access: Limited

Brunch: Sunday, 11 A.M.–3 P.M.
Lunch: Every day, 11:30 A.M.–3 P.M.
Dinner: Every day, 6–10:30 P.M.

Setting & atmosphere: A large room with lofty ceilings, brick walls, big windows affording a view of the passing parade on Royal Street, and big, cushy seats. A power center at lunch, a romantic spot for dinner.

Recommended dishes: Spit-roasted shrimp with Creole mustard sauce; crab cake; crab bisque; Rib Room salad; roasted salmon; any special involving crawfish as a main ingredient; veal Tanet (large panéed slice of veal atop a romaine salad); rotisserie chicken; mixed grill; prime rib; rack of lamb. Dessert pastries; chocolate mousse.

Summary & comments: The Rib Room didn't start out as the flagship dining room of the top-class Royal Orleans Hotel, but it soon became that. In the center rear of this expansive room is the station where the namesake prime ribs of roast beef are carved to order. While still as good as any others around, these are now the least interesting of the offerings. Better is what's behind the carving board: a wall of rotisseries with all sorts of meat, poultry, and seafood roasting. The rest of the menu has a distinctly Louisiana flavor with a touch of continental polish. The specials, at both lunch and dinner, are usually the best eating here. Service here has never been as gracious as one might like; much of the staff has been here a little too long.

RISTORANTE CARMELO

Northern Italian	★★★	Moderate	QUALITY
			79

541 Decatur Street 586-1414	Zone 1, French Quarter	VALUE
		C

Customers: Mix
Reservations: Recommended
When to go: Anytime
Entree range: $8–16
Payment: All major credit cards
  except Discover
Service rating: ★★★
Friendliness rating: ★★★

Parking: Pay lot nearby
Bar: Full bar
Wine selection: Decent list, mostly
  Italian; a few very unusual Italian
  wines
Dress: Dressy casual
Disabled access: Full

Lunch & Dinner: Every day, 11:30 A.M.–10:30 P.M.

Setting & atmosphere: A casual trattoria, with a breezy dining room dominated by a luscious display of antipasto on the first floor, and a more formal dining room lined with wine racks on the second floor.

Recommended dishes: Antipasto Freddo (a combination plate with antipasto, prosciutto, Genoa salami, mortadella, capicola, cheeses, vegetables, etc.); bruschetta with tomatoes, fresh basil, and olive oil; zuppa della casa; risotto with mushrooms; pasta aglio e olio with broccoli; penne Calabrese arrabbiata (homemade penne pasta sautéed in spicy tomato sauce); pappardelle pasta with prosciutto and peas; grilled swordfish; salmon with capers and asparagus; veal Marsala with porcini (mushrooms); manicotti of eggplant. Cannoli; tiramisu.

Summary & comments: After creating the best chain of pizza stands New Orleans has ever tasted, Carmelo Chirico decided to present some real Italian food, and here it is. Parts of its menu reach the heights, mostly in the Northern Italian idiom. The seafood dishes are especially good. The wine list offers one of the most comprehensive and interesting assortments of Italian bottles hereabouts.

RUTH'S CHRIS STEAK HOUSE

			QUALITY
Steak	★★★★	Very Expensive	**90**

	VALUE
	D

711 N. Broad Street 486-0810   Zone 6, Mid-City/Gentilly
3633 Veterans Boulevard 888-3600
   Zone 10, Metairie above Causeway/Kenner/Jefferson Hwy.

Customers: Politicians; media figures; businessmen; couples at dinner
Reservations: Accepted
When to go: Anytime
Entree range: $16–26
Payment: All major credit cards
Service rating: ★★★★
Friendliness rating: ★★★★
Parking: Valet (free)

Bar: Full bar
Wine selection: Substantial list, heavily tilted toward the red end of the spectrum, from all over the world; nothing extraordinary, though, which is just as well because they don't handle wine very well here
Dress: Dressy casual
Disabled access: Full

Lunch & Dinner: Every day, 11:30 A.M.–11:30 P.M.

Setting & atmosphere: Both locations have a simple, masculine, but very comfortable layout. There are many booths to hide out in, and many tables from which to see or be seen. Power and celebrity crackle in the air.

Recommended dishes: Shrimp rémoulade; stuffed mushrooms; house salad with Creole French dressing; filet mignon; New York strip; porterhouse for two; lamb chops; veal chops; pork chop (lunch only); salmon fillet; boiled lobster; Lyonnaise potatoes; french fries in any of four shapes; baked potato. Bread pudding; cheesecakes.

Summary & comments: The leading chain of premium steak houses in America started on Broad Street six decades ago. Ruth Fertel, now the world's most successful female restaurateur, took it over in the sixties and has kept it moving upward ever since. The essence of Ruth's Chris is the very simple preparation—in a superheated broiler, followed by a dousing with sizzling butter—of top-class steaks and chops. In the case of the beef, it's dry-aged USDA prime. Also here is big lobster and thick flanks of salmon. Side dishes are nothing especially original but prepared very well. The a la carte prices are quite high; you can really drop a bundle here at dinner. Lunches are more affordable. Service is effective and without ceremony.

SAL & JUDY'S

			QUALITY
Creole Italian	★★★★	Expensive	86

		VALUE
US 190, Lacombe (504) 882-9443	Zone 12, North Shore	B

Customers: North Shore people; families
Reservations: Not accepted
When to go: Weeknights
Entree range: $10–19
Payment: MC, VISA
Service rating: ★★

Friendliness rating: ★★
Parking: Free lot adjacent
Bar: Full bar
Wine selection: Limited list of Italian wines
Dress: Casual
Disabled access: Limited

Lunch & Dinner: Sunday, noon–10 P.M.
Dinner: Wednesday–Saturday, 5–10 P.M.

Setting & atmosphere: The pink, frilly curtains notwithstanding, this looks like a minimal roadhouse both inside and out. But then we *are* out on the road, in a small rural village.

Recommended dishes: Fettuccine Alfredo; stuffed artichoke (with bread crumbs and garlic); fried calamari; baked oysters Cinisi (mushrooms and Italian sausage); trout Jimmy (with artichokes and lemon); soft-shell crabs; spaghetti aglio e olio with Italian sausage and roasted peppers; spaghetti with oysters. Cheesecake; gelato.

Summary & comments: It's one of the best and most popular restaurants on the North Shore, drawing from both the Slidell and Mandeville/Covington areas. Sal Impastato came here from Sicily many years ago; he's picked up as many good Creole moves as Italian. The printed menu here looks unimpressive, but among the specials you will find a great deal of very good eating, mostly in the veal and seafood departments. Everything is surprisingly inexpensive given the goodness and quantity; the corners are cut on the frills. At any normal dining hour you're likely to wait for a table.

SCLAFANI'S

			QUALITY
Nouvelle Creole	★★★★	Moderate	91

		VALUE
301 Dauphine Street 524-5475	Zone 1, French Quarter	A

Customers: A small hard core of locals, plus hotel guests
Reservations: Accepted
When to go: Anytime
Entree range: $6–16

Payment: All major credit cards
Service rating: ★★★
Friendliness rating: ★★★
Parking: Free lot adjacent
Bar: Full bar

Sclafani's (continued)

Wine selection: Decent list, mostly California

Dress: Casual
Disabled access: Limited

Breakfast: Every day, 6–10 A.M.
Brunch: Sunday, 11 A.M.–2:30 P.M.
Lunch: Every day, 11:30 A.M.–2:30 P.M.
Dinner: Every day, 5–10 P.M.

Setting & atmosphere: An old-fashioned and slightly worn elegance, with a view to a courtyard.

Recommended dishes: Louisiana crab cake; shrimp rémoulade; stuffed eggplant soup; Sclafani salad with shrimp; pasta with shrimp and sun-dried tomatoes; stuffed shrimp; eggplant Belle Rose (topped with crabmeat, mushrooms, and hollandaise); panéed veal with fettuccine; chicken Barataria (stuffed with oyster dressing); roasted venison tenderloin. Tiramisu; white chocolate bread pudding.

Summary & comments: This is the restaurant of the Chateau LeMoyne Hotel, but it's a completely independent operation. Peter Sclafani III, grandson of a famous New Orleans Italian chef, is an inventive soul who shops the markets for interesting ingredients and then turns them into specialties with a distinctively New Orleans flavor—which is to say, a bit on the rich side and rather intense in other ways. This is the place to go when all the famous Quarter restaurants are full: The food will be just as good and you'll actually get a table.

SHALIMAR			
Indian	★★★	Moderate	QUALITY 82
535 Wilkinson Row 523-0099 Zone 1, French Quarter			VALUE C

Customers: A mix of locals and tourists
Reservations: Accepted
When to go: Anytime
Entree range: $8–15
Payment: AMEX, MC, VISA
Service rating: ★★★

Friendliness rating: ★★★
Parking: Jackson Brewery pay lot, one block
Bar: Full bar
Wine selection: A few house wines
Dress: Casual
Disabled access: Full

Brunch: Sunday, 11 A.M.–3 P.M.
Lunch: Every day, 11:30 A.M.–2:30 P.M.
Dinner: Every day, 6–10 P.M.

Shalimar (continued)

Setting & atmosphere: A pretty room replete with as many Indian artifacts as can be crammed in, and Indian music playing in the background.
Recommended dishes: Mulligatawny soup; lamb samosas; vegetable pakoras; lamb-stuffed mushrooms; shrimp in a white sauce with peanuts, cashews, and almonds; marinated, grilled tuna steak with moghlai sauce; tandoori chicken or lamb sausage; biryanis (mostly-rice dishes with various meats, seafoods, and vegetables); lamb with tomato-and-raisin curry; Madras-style lamb with spicy curry sauce; chicken or lamb saagwala (with creamed spinach). Rice pudding; mango mousse; fruit cup.
Summary & comments: Around back of the Upper Pontalba is the latest and loveliest Indian restaurant from Anila and Har Keswani, who pioneered the cuisine locally and have managed to keep feeding it to us even in the face of disaster (their first two attempts bit the dust). As in their other extant place (Taj Mahal), the focus is on the tandoor, a superheated claypot oven where marinated meats and seafoods, along with fresh breads, are roasted to a dry intensity. The menu also does fine things with biryanis ("Indian jambalaya," they call it, not inaccurately), curries in a wide range of pepper levels, and vegetarian dishes. Not good enough to satisfy a Brit, but great in New Orleans.

SHOGUN				
Japanese/Sushi Bar	★★★★	Moderate	**QUALITY**	**86**
2325 Veterans Boulevard 833-7477			**VALUE**	**C**
Zone 9, Metairie below Causeway				

Customers: Locals; singles; families at the teppanyaki tables
Reservations: Not accepted
When to go: Anytime
Entree range: $8–20
Payment: AMEX, MC, VISA
Service rating: ★★★

Friendliness rating: ★★
Parking: Free lot adjacent
Bar: Full bar
Wine selection: A few house wines
Dress: Casual
Disabled access: Full

Lunch: Monday–Friday, 11:30 A.M.–2 P.M.
Lunch & Dinner: Saturday and Sunday, noon–10 P.M.
Dinner: Monday–Friday, 5–10 P.M.

Setting & atmosphere: In this big restaurant are three distinct areas. The sushi bar is the city's largest. The standard tables are utilitarian and quick-turning. But the most popular part of the restaurant is a recent addition: They bought the teppanyaki tables from the local Benihana when it closed, and now that showy steak grilling takes up half the place. (Impressive for kids; otherwise, once will last you a lifetime.)

Recommended dishes: Baked seafood appetizer; gyoza; red miso soup; any form of sushi; sashimi. Teishoku (box) dinners; shabu shabu (thinly sliced beef quickly boiled at the table); seafood nabe.

Summary & comments: Shogun was the first restaurant to make a commercial success in New Orleans with a sushi bar. It remains the definitive local sushi restaurant (although adherents of other places will loudly contest that), while at the same time offering a vast range of other Japanese eating styles. At the tables, they serve a dizzying assortment of teriyaki, tempura, noodle, Japanese barbecue, and sukiyaki-style dishes, all arranged into complicated complete dinners. But the best food here will always be the work of the sushi chefs.

SIAMESE			
Thai	★★★	Moderate	**QUALITY** 84
6601 Veterans Boulevard 454-8752			**VALUE** C
Zone 10, Metairie above Causeway/Kenner/Jefferson Hwy.			

Customers: Locals
Reservations: Accepted
When to go: Anytime
Entree range: $7–14
Payment: All major credit cards
Service rating: ★★
Friendliness rating: ★★

Parking: Free lot adjacent
Bar: Full bar
Wine selection: A few house wines
Dress: Casual
Disabled access: Full

Lunch: Tuesday–Sunday, 11 A.M.–2:30 P.M.
Dinner: Tuesday–Sunday, 5–10 P.M.

Setting & atmosphere: Way in the back of a confusing strip mall is this storefront Thai restaurant, which looks like it could be turned into a convenience store in a matter of hours. A bit stark, but not unpleasant.

Recommended dishes: Satay of beef, chicken, or pork (on skewers with peanut sauce); mee krob (crisp-fried noodles with shrimp and chicken); golden wings (stuffed mid-section of chicken wings); spicy and sour shrimp soup; coconut chicken soup; squid or shrimp salad with lemongrass; pad Thai; chicken with eggplant and mint leaves; roasted duck with red curry

Siamese (continued)

and pineapple; pla soong kruenng (fried pompano with curry paste); red bean curry; steamed mussels.

Summary & comments: Your education in Thai cooking is facilitated by a book of photographs illustrating most of the menu's 78 entries. It's good that's around, because making contact with either the printed menu or the service staff is a bit difficult. But don't worry about it, because the only complaint you're likely to have about the food (assuming you like the distinctive Thai flavor palette) is that they don't give you quite enough of it here. And, given the prices, that might not bother you either.

SID-MAR'S			
			QUALITY
Seafood	★★★	Moderate	83
			VALUE
1824 Orpheum Avenue 831-9541			A
Zone 9, Metairie below Causeway			

Customers: Locals; families	Friendliness rating: ★★★
Reservations: Not accepted	Parking: Free lot adjacent
When to go: Weekdays; Fridays and	Bar: Full bar
Saturdays are incredibly busy here.	Wine selection: A few house wines
Entree range: $4–16	Dress: Anything goes
Payment: All major credit cards	Disabled access: Limited
Service rating: ★★	

Lunch & Dinner: Tuesday–Sunday, 11 A.M.–10:30 P.M.

Setting & atmosphere: On a spit of land between the 17th Street Canal and the lake is the working part of Bucktown, an old fishing community now mostly absorbed by the suburbs. Here you find docked the boats that fetch all those crabs and shrimp we eat, their owners probably cursing to themselves. Also here is Sid-Mar's, an equally fine relic of another era. The delightfully stark interior dining room is surrounded by more tables on a screened porch.

Recommended dishes: Oyster soup; seafood gumbo; boiled crabs; boiled shrimp; boiled crawfish; Wop salad (sorry, that's what they call it—a common name in New Orleans); roast beef poorboy; oyster or shrimp poorboy; fried seafood platters; grilled fish; fried chicken; daily specials. Bread pudding.

Summary & comments: Most of the time every seat is occupied by somebody eating a pile of boiled crustaceans, a fried seafood platter, or a homely special. Sid-Mar's suddenly got better in 1992 when the second generation took over, bought the building, and fixed it up—but not too much.

TAVERN ON THE PARK

			QUALITY
Steak/Creole	★★★	Expensive	**80**

			VALUE
900 City Park Avenue 486-3333	Zone 6, Mid-City/Gentilly		**C**

Customers: Locals; businessmen at lunch
Reservations: Recommended
When to go: Anytime
Entree range: $12–24
Payment: All major credit cards
Service rating: ★★★★
Friendliness rating: ★

Parking: Curbside
Bar: Full bar
Wine selection: Decent list, good international balance
Dress: Jacket recommended but not required
Disabled access: Full

Lunch: Tuesday–Friday, 11:30 A.M.–2:30 P.M.
Dinner: Tuesday–Saturday, 6–10 P.M.

Setting & atmosphere: The Tavern is an extraordinarily handsome marble-and-glass restaurant in a historic building. It's across from the entrance to City Park, which affords a lovely view—particularly from the second-floor balcony, which they don't use enough.

Recommended dishes: Fried onion rings; shrimp rémoulade; baked oysters 3&3 (Rockefeller and Bienville); tomato blossom salad (with feta and Vidalia onions); turtle soup; stuffed soft-shell crab Creolaise (hollandaise with Creole mustard); Asian-Cajun duck with pepper jelly; rack of lamb; filet mignon; veal chop. Bread pudding with rum raisin ice cream; chocolate cake; pecan snowball with chocolate sauce.

Summary & comments: It started as a premium steak house but evolved into a general-menu Creole cafe, with an emphasis on straightforward, traditional dishes. The food here is pretty good, and at times it rises to extraordinary. The latter is more likely in the introductory courses, which are full of nice surprises. The quality of your entree we wouldn't hazard to predict, regardless of what you order. The service staff is unusually effective and gracious. That makes the main problem here perplexing: On rare occasion, the management has been so inhospitable that a few diners have told us they'll never return.

TREY YUEN

			QUALITY
Chinese	★★★★	Expensive	85

			VALUE
600 Causeway Boulevard, Mandeville (504) 626-4476			D

600 Causeway Boulevard, Mandeville (504) 626-4476
   Zone 12, North Shore

Customers: North Shore people;
   families
Reservations: Not accepted
When to go: Weeknights
Entree range: $8–20 (median: $12)
Payment: All major credit cards
Service rating: ★★

Friendliness rating: ★★
Parking: Free lot adjacent
Bar: Full bar
Wine selection: Decent list,
   emphasis on California
Dress: Casual
Disabled access: Full

Lunch: Wednesday–Friday, 11:30 A.M.–2:30 P.M.
Lunch & Dinner: Sunday, noon–10 P.M.
Dinner: Monday–Saturday, 6–10 P.M.

Setting & atmosphere: A sort of rotunda in a Chinese style, the main dining room was built using many antique Chinese pieces and well-designed modern accents. The restaurant is surrounded by ponds, waterfalls, and gardens.

Recommended dishes: Spring rolls; potstickers; hot and sour soup. Tong cho anything, but especially oysters, soft-shell crab, and wor shu op (Mandarin duck); satay squid; shrimp in a cloud; lobster with black bean sauce; scallops imperial; presidential chicken; spicy lemon chicken; steak kew. Lotus banana; ice cream.

Summary & comments: A major breakthrough: When this Asian palace opened in 1981, it was the first time that an area Chinese restaurant offered beautiful surroundings, good service, and unusual food using first-class ingredients. Trey Yuen remains one of the best and most popular Chinese restaurants around, with a menu that essays many styles of Chinese cooking. Seafood is a particular strength here, but they cook everything well, even some of the tired old fake-Cantonese standards that people insist on ordering. There's a far better list of wines and desserts than in a typical Chinese place. Service is unceremonious but good, except when the place is very busy—which it often is. Another Trey Yuen of equal goodness is in Hammond.

TUJAGUE'S

Creole	★★★★	Expensive	QUALITY
			87

823 Decatur Street 525-8676	Zone 1, French Quarter	VALUE
		C

Customers: Tourists, some locals; quite a few Quarterites at lunch
Reservations: Recommended
When to go: Anytime
Entree range: Table d'hote: $20–29
Payment: All major credit cards
Service rating: ★★★
Friendliness rating: ★★★★

Parking: French Market pay lot, one block
Bar: Full bar
Wine selection: Limited list of inexpensive wines
Dress: Casual
Disabled access: Limited

Lunch: Every day, 11:30 A.M.–3 P.M.
Dinner: Every day, 5–10 P.M.

Setting & atmosphere: Two floors of delightfully unrenovated space in a building that has been a restaurant since before the Civil War. The bar is a magnificent antique. Despite all the history, this is a very casual, easygoing place; even families fit in.

Recommended dishes: Table d'hote dinner menu has entrees that change daily: shrimp rémoulade; crabmeat and spinach soup; boiled brisket of beef with Creole sauce; chicken bonne femme (batterless fried half-chicken with a tremendous amount of garlic, parsley, and fried potatoes); filet mignon. Cranberry bread pudding; pecan pie.

Summary & comments: One of America's oldest restaurants, Tujague's began as a food service to the workers in the French Market and on the French Quarter docks, serving a table d'hote meal of the day. In the late 1800s, this was the base for the city's first superstar chef, Madame Begue, who wrote what may have been the first Creole cookbook. Today, Tujague's serves the traditional five-course homey Creole meal, with five or so choices for the entree. One of the courses is always the restaurant's signature boiled brisket. This is a great place to come on the major holidays; they're open for all of them.

UGLESICH'S

Sandwiches/Seafood	★★★★	Moderate	QUALITY
			86

1238 Baronne Street 523-8571	Zone 3, Uptown below Napoleon	VALUE
		D

Customers: Locals and tourists, most on the young side; restaurant people
Reservations: Not accepted
When to go: Avoid noon hour
Entree range: $6–14
Payment: No credit cards

Service rating: ★★
Friendliness rating: ★★★
Parking: Free lot adjacent
Bar: Beer
Wine selection: None
Dress: Anything goes
Disabled access: Limited

Lunch: Monday–Friday, 11 A.M.–4 P.M.

Setting & atmosphere: After seven decades of slow decay, Uglesich's has given itself a paint job, the less to frighten the many visitors who enter the rough-looking neighborhood in search of the most convincing example of New Orleans culinary funk. The premises remain the shabbiest occupied by a good restaurant, but soak it in. Your clothes will: After a half-hour, you'll smell as if you've been frying seafood all day.

Recommended dishes: Oysters on the half shell; barbecued oysters; crawfish bisque; grilled fish plate; crawfish étouffée; fried oyster poorboy; roast beef poorboy; french fries; blackboard specials.

Summary & comments: Consistently soul-satisfying, with standards a few very expensive restaurants could copy. The oysters on the poorboy, for example, are not only fried but shucked to order. All the sandwiches and platters are great, robust eating; take seriously any advisory that a dish may be spicy. Eating raw oysters at the bar is a great way to kill the long time it takes for your entree to be whipped up, and while waiting for a table. No matter how busy they are, seats will magically appear when it's time.

UPPERLINE

Nouvelle Creole	★★★★	Expensive	QUALITY
			88

1413 Upperline Street 891-9822 Zone 4, Uptown above Napoleon	VALUE
	C

Customers: A mix of locals and tourists; gourmets
Reservations: Recommended
When to go: Anytime; the garlic festival in summer

Entree range: $13–20
Payment: All major credit cards
Service rating: ★★★★
Friendliness rating: ★★★★
Parking: Curbside

Upperline (continued)

Bar: Full bar

Wine selection: Modest list, but
wines well-chosen for the food;
many by-the-glass selections

Dress: Casual

Disabled access: None

Dinner: Wednesday–Monday, 6–10 P.M.; closed Tuesday.

Setting & atmosphere: The place rambles from one building to another, with many tables in odd, intimate corners. The front room gets a little cluttered and frantic at times.

Recommended dishes: Fried green tomatoes with shrimp rémoulade; trout and dill mousse; Creole white bean soup with tasso; duck gumbo; watercress, Stilton, and pecan salad; grilled fish with barbecue shrimp; shrimp curry with rice and Indian condiments; calf's liver à l'orange; rack of lamb with spicy Merlot sauce; filet mignon with spicy garlic mushrooms; duck étouffée with pepper jelly; garlic-stuffed pork tenderloin. Pecan pie; double chocolate amaretto mousse.

Entertainment & amenities: Major folk art collection from local artists throughout restaurant, as well as on building facade.

Summary & comments: One of the first nouvelle Creole bistros, the Upperline's distinctiveness is due not only to its food (always good, occasionally wonderful) but to the delightfully quirky imagination of owner and genuine bohemian JoAnn Clevenger. Her most famous creation is the summer-long garlic menu, but she has also done menus based on the food in the books of Jane Austen, the movie *Babette's Feast,* and the notebooks of Claude Monet. Despite that, she has no hesitation to fill her regular menu with the classic Creole dishes, including a tasting menu of gumbo, beans and rice, etc.

VAQUEROS			
Mexican/Southwestern	★★★	Moderate	QUALITY 90
4938 Prytania Street 891-6441 Zone 4, Uptown above Napoleon			VALUE C

Customers: Uptowners; gourmets;
daters

Reservations: Not accepted

When to go: Anytime

Entree range: $8–19

Payment: All major credit cards
except DC

Service rating: ★★★★

Friendliness rating: ★★★★

Parking: Curbside

Vaqueros (continued)

Bar: Full bar
Wine selection: Modest list, but wines well-chosen for the food; many by-the-glass selections

Dress: Casual
Disabled access: Full

Brunch: Sunday, 11 A.M.–3 P.M.
Lunch: Monday–Friday, 11:30 A.M.–2:30 P.M.
Dinner: Every day, 6–10 P.M.

Setting & atmosphere: Anyone who likes the food and the style of Santa Fe should love all the stucco, tiles, and weathered wood. The rear room is a semi-open patio.

Recommended dishes: Chips and five different salsas; seafood and chicken taquitos; Navajo fry bread; venison black bean chili; corn-fried rock shrimp salad; cheese or chicken enchiladas; Santa Fe salmon cakes; Puerto Rican stuffed sopaipillas with grilled chicken and beans; duck tamales; southwestern grilled pizza; chicken al carbon with red mole sauce; fajitas. Taco galeta (a fruit-filled cookie shell); flan.

Summary & comments: Easily the most ambitious and exciting Mexican restaurant ever to open in these parts, Vaqueros explores all parts of the cuisine with imagination. In the center of the main room is a station where cooks prepare flour tortillas from scratch; these taste as good as they smell. The tortilla chips are served in a gigantic handmade platter surrounded by five different house-made salsas. Live music, interesting drinks, and occasional festivals make the place even more engaging. Tends to be rather busy; you may have to wait for a table.

VINCENT'S ITALIAN CUISINE

Creole Italian	★★★★	Moderate	QUALITY 90
			VALUE A

4411 Chastant Street 885-2984
Zone 10, Metairie above Causeway/Kenner/Jefferson Hwy.

Customers: Locals; couples and foursomes
Reservations: Required
When to go: Weeknights and lunch
Entree range: $9–19
Payment: All major credit cards
Service rating: ★★★★

Friendliness rating: ★★★★
Parking: Free lot adjacent
Bar: Full bar
Wine selection: Decent list, mostly Italian
Dress: Casual
Disabled access: Limited

Vincent's Italian Cuisine (continued)

Lunch: Monday–Friday, 11:30 A.M.–3 P.M.
Dinner: Monday–Saturday, 6–10 P.M.

Setting & atmosphere: A neighborhood cafe in every physical measure.
Recommended dishes: Eggplant sandwich (two panéed rounds with spicy mozzarella and Italian sausage); veal meatballs on garlic toast; corn and crab bisque en croûte; veal cannelloni in a crêpe; soft-shell crab with tomato garlic sauce; panéed fish with crab cream sauce; garlic chicken; bracialoni (top round sliced very thin, rolled and stuffed with bacon, artichoke hearts, hard-boiled eggs, green onions, and bread crumbs, then served with red sauce over angel-hair pasta); veal Florentine; osso buco. Tiramisu; chocolate mousse cake; Torroncino ice cream.
Summary & comments: After a long career as a bartender and waiter, Vincent discovered that he could cook as well as any of the chefs who screamed at him. So he set about serving some of the most impressive food ever sold at prices this low. The style is mostly homestyle New Orleans Italian, but many dishes show what the chef learned at some of those fancy places in his past. He has a particularly skillful hand with seafood, saucing it with great versions of either red or white sauce. A few dishes are not only great eating but highly original. The salad, vegetable, and dessert courses, as well as the wine list, lack something. But everything else could be served in the grandest restaurant in New Orleans.

VIZARD'S

Creole	★★★★	Expensive	QUALITY 88
5538 Magazine Street 895-5000			VALUE B
Zone 4, Uptown above Napoleon			

Customers: Locals; couples and foursomes
Reservations: Required
When to go: Anytime
Entree range: $9–19
Payment: DC, D, MC, VISA
Service rating: ★★★★

Friendliness rating: ★★★★
Parking: Curbside
Bar: Full bar
Wine selection: Decent but short list, mostly California
Dress: Casual
Disabled access: Limited

Dinner: Tuesday–Saturday, 6–10 P.M.

Setting & atmosphere: The place used to be a hangout for bus drivers, and wasn't dramatically reconfigured. The bar dominates the single dining room.

Vizard's (continued)

Recommended dishes: Crabmeat Sycamore; oyster brochette with prosciutto; broiled oysters on shells; crabmeat maison; trout amandine; seared
salmon with spicy orange sauce; Moroccan chicken with couscous; roasted
duck with portobello mushrooms; filet mignon with caramelized onions
and Stilton. Bread pudding with apples; crème brûlée.

Summary & comments: Kevin Vizard (rhymes with "wizard") is as talented a chef as ever fronted a Creole bistro kitchen, but he never stayed in
one restaurant for more than a year or so. This is the first restaurant that
he's owned himself, and from day one (in 1996) its appeal has been infec-
tious. The menu sounds fresh, but at the core of almost every dish is a Creole classic that Vizard enjoyed somewhere else (a fact he cheerfully admits).
In contract with the simplicity of the room, the food here is polished and
satisfying.

WINDSOR COURT GRILL ROOM

Eclectic	★★★★★	Very Expensive	QUALITY
			94

300 Gravier Street 523-6000	Zone 2, Central Business District	VALUE
		F

Customers: A mix of locals, hotel
guests, and tourists; gourmets
Reservations: Required
When to go: Wednesday through
Friday nights
Entree range: $18–34
Payment: All major credit cards
Service rating: ★★★★★
Friendliness rating: ★★★★
Parking: Valet (free)
Bar: Full bar

Wine selection: One of the town's
best wine cellars, with a thick
book of unusual bottles from all
over the world; the large stock of
older French wines was assembled
by buying private collections at
auction
Dress: Jacket recommended but not
required
Disabled access: Full

Breakfast: Every day, 7–10 A.M.
Brunch: Sunday, 11 A.M.–3 P.M.
Lunch: Monday–Saturday, 11:30 A.M.–2:30 P.M.
Dinner: Every day, 6–10 P.M.

Setting & atmosphere: A sybarite's dream dining room: big, heavy tables;
extra-wide, comfortable chairs and banquettes; a couple million dollars'
worth of original art on English themes; a Lalique crystal table; and other
rich furnishings. The best tables are on the "porch," whose windows look
down on the statue of St. George.

Recommended dishes: Menu changes frequently. These dishes may still be around: kumamoto oysters with ginger ice; smoked salmon; seared foie gras with caramelized bananas; turtle soup; Windsor Court salad (a Cobb without chicken); Chinese smoked lobster; grilled tuna Rossini; any grilled fish or red-meat chop; rack of lamb with stir-fried watercress; smoked venison loin with cheese grits cake. Dessert soufflé; crème brûlée tart; chocolate breathless (mousse under hard meringue).

Entertainment & amenities: Live chamber music in lounge.

Summary & comments: An asset that helps the Windsor Court Hotel attract its frequent ten-best-in-the-world ratings is its restaurant. The Grill Room brooks no compromise in its quest for the best of surroundings, service, food, and wine; most of the time, a great meal results. The chefs here have always included in their ever-changing menus a substantial array of unheard-of savories, prepared in original styles that elude category. The safest offerings proceed from the grill; these are ideal for purists. The circa-$100 tasting menu of the night's specials with wines is the ultimate meal here. The wine list was built from private collections and is replete with rare vintages from all over.

Hotel Information Chart

Hotel	Room Star Rating	Zone	Street Address
Ambassador Hotel New Orleans	★★★½	2	535 Tchoupitoulas Street New Orleans, LA 70130
Andrew Jackson	★★	1	919 Royal Street New Orleans, LA 70116
Avenue Plaza Hotel	★★★★	2	211 St. Charles Avenue New Orleans, LA 70130
Best Western Airport All Suite	★★★½	10	2438 Veteran's Memorial Blvd. Kenner, LA 70062
Best Western Inn Airport	★★½	10	1021 Airport Highway Kenner, LA 70062
Best Western Inn Landmark Hotel	★★★	10	2601 Severn Avenue Metairie, LA 70002
Best Western Inn on Bourbon	★★★	1	541 Bourbon Street New Orleans, LA 70130
Best Western Patio Downtown	★★★	6	2820 Tulane Avenue New Orleans, LA 70119
Bienville House	★★★★	1	320 Decatur Street New Orleans, LA 70130
Bourbon Orleans Hotel	★★★	1	717 Orleans Street New Orleans, LA 70116
Chateau Hotel	★★½	1	1001 Chartres Street New Orleans, LA 70116
Chateau LeMoyne French Quarter Holiday Inn	★★★	1	301 Dauphine Street New Orleans, LA 70112
Chateau Sonesta Hotel	★★★★	1	800 Iberville Street New Orleans, LA 70112
The Columns	★★★	3	3811 St. Charles Avenue New Orleans, LA 70115
Comfort Inn Downtown/Superdome	★★½	2	1315 Gravier Street New Orleans, LA 70112
Comfort Suites	★★★	2	346 Baronne Street New Orleans, LA 70112
The Cornstalk Fence	★★★½	1	915 Royal Street New Orleans, LA 70113
Courtyard by Marriott	★★★½	2	124 St. Charles Avenue New Orleans, LA 70130
Crowne Plaza New Orleans	★★★½	2	333 Poydras Street New Orleans, LA 70130

Local Phone	Fax	Toll Free Reservations	Rack Rate	No. of Rooms	On-site Dining	Pool
(504) 527-5271	(504) 527-5270	(888) 527-5271	$$$$ $$$–	75	Yes	No
(504) 561-5881	(504) 596-6769	(800) 654-0224	$$$$$+	22	No	No
(504) 566-1212	(504) 679-7612	(800) 535-9575	$$$ $$$–	250	Yes	Yes
(504) 469-2800	(504) 469-2800	(800) 528-1234	$$$+	78	No	Yes
(504) 464-1644	(504) 469-1193	(800) 333-8278	$$$$+	168	Yes	Yes
(504) 888-9500	(504) 885-8474	(800) 277-7575	$$$$$–	342	Yes	Yes
(504) 524-7611	(504) 568-9427	(800) 535-7891	$$$$$$ $$$$$$–	186	Yes	Yes
(504) 822-0200	(504) 822-2328	(800) 528-1234	$$$$ $$$–	76	Yes	Yes
(504) 529-2345	(504) 525-6079	(800) 535-7836	$$$$ $$$$+	82	No	Yes
(504) 523-2222	(504) 525-8166	(800) 521-5338	$$$$$ $$$$–	211	No	Yes
(504) 524-9636	(504) 525-2989	(800) 828-1822	$$$ $$$–	45	No	Yes
(504) 581-1303	(504) 523-5709	(800) HOLIDAY	$$$$$ $$$$+	171	Yes	Yes
(504) 586-0800	(504) 586-1987	(800) 788-3782	$$$$$ $$$$$	250	Yes	Yes
(504) 899-9308	(504) 899-8170	(800) 445-9308	$$$ $$$–	19	Yes	No
(504) 586-0100	(504) 588-9230	(800) 535-9141	$$$$$–	157	No	Yes
(504) 524-1140	(504) 523-4444	(800) 228-5150	$$$ $$$–	102	No	No
(504) 523-1515	(504) 522-5558	NA	$$$$ $$$$+	14	No	No
(504) 581-9005	(504) 581-6224	(800) 321-2211	$$$$$–	140	Yes	No
(504) 525-9444	(504) 581-7179	(800) 522-6963	$$$$ $$$$+	439	Yes	Yes

Hotel	Room Star Rating	Zone	Street Address
Dauphine Orleans	★★★½	1	415 Dauphine Street New Orleans, LA 70112
Days Inn	★★½	8	5801 Read Boulevard New Orleans, LA 70127
Days Inn Kenner Airport	★★½	10	1300 Veteran's Boulevard Kenner, LA 70062
Days Inn New Orleans/Canal Street	★★½	6	1630 Canal Street New Orleans, LA 70112
DoubleTree Hotel Lakeside New Orleans	★★★★	9	3838 Causeway Boulevard Metairie, LA 70002
DoubleTree Hotel New Orleans	★★★½	1	300 Canal Street New Orleans, LA 70130
Econo Lodge	★★½	8	13552 Chef Menteur Highway New Orleans, LA 70129
Embassy Suites New Orleans	★★★★	2	315 Julia Street New Orleans, LA 70130
Fairmont Hotel	★★★★	2	123 Baronne Street New Orleans, LA 70140
The Frenchmen	★★½	5	417 Frenchmen Street New Orleans, LA 70116
French Quarter Courtyard Hotel	★★½	1	1101 Rampart Street New Orleans, LA 70116
French Quarter Suites	★★★	1	1119 N. Rampart Street New Orleans, LA 70116
Grenoble House	★★★★	1	329 Dauphine Street New Orleans, LA 70112
Hampton Inn and Suites	★★★	10	5150 Mounes Street New Orleans, LA 70123
Hampton Inn Downtown	★★★½	2	226 Carondelet Street New Orleans, LA 70130
Hilton New Orleans Riverside	★★★½	2	2 Poydras Street New Orleans, LA 70140
Hilton New Orleans Airport	★★★½	10	901 Airline Highway Kenner, LA 70062
Historic French Market Inn	★★★	1	501 Decatur Street New Orleans, LA 70130
Holiday Inn Airport	★★★	10	2929 Williams Boulevard Kenner, LA 70062

Local Phone	Fax	Toll Free Reservations	Rack Rate	No. of Rooms	On-site Dining	Pool
(504) 586-1800	(504) 586-1409	(800) 521-7111	$$$ $$$+	112	Yes	Yes
(504) 241-2500	(504) 245-8340	(800) 325-2525	$$$$$–	143	Yes	Yes
(504) 469-2531	(504) 468-4269	(800) 325-2525	$$+	312	Yes	Yes
(504) 586-0110	(504) 581-2253	(800) 232-3297	$$$ $$$+	216	Yes	Yes
(504) 836-5253	(504) 836-5262	(800) 222-TREE	$$$$$–	210	Yes	Yes
(504) 581-1300	(504) 522-4100	(800) 222-TREE	$$$$ $$$$–	367	Yes	No
(504) 254-9140	(504) 254-3789	(800) 553-2666	$$$$+	83	No	Yes
(504) 525-1993	(504) 522-3044	(800) EMBASSY	$$$$ $$$+	226	Yes	Yes
(504) 529-7111	(504) 522-2303	(800) 562-1003	$$$$$ $$$$$–	750	Yes	Yes
(504) 948-2166	(504) 948-2258	(800) 831-1781	$$$$$+	25	No	Yes
(504) 522-7333	(504) 522-3908	(800) 290-4233	$$$$$ $$$$–	51	No	Yes
(504) 524-7725	(504) 522-9716	(800) 457-2253	$$$$$ $$$$$–	17	No	Yes
(504) 522-1331	(504) 524-4968	(800) 722-1834	$$$$$ $$$$–	17	No	Yes
(504) 733-5646	(504) 733-5609	(800) HAMPTON	$$$ $$$–	128	No	Yes
(504) 529-9990	(504) 529-9996	(800) HAMPTON	$$$$ $$$–	186	No	No
(504) 561-0500	(504) 568-1721	(800) HILTONS	$$$$$ $$$$$–	1600	Yes	Yes
(504) 469-5000	(504) 465-1126	(800) HILTONS	$$$$$+	317	Yes	Yes
(504) 561-5621	(504) 566-0160	(800) 827-5621	$$$$$ $$$–	68	No	Yes
(504) 467-5611	(504) 469-4915	(800) HOLIDAY	$$$$$–	303	Yes	Yes

Hotel	Room Star Rating	Zone	Street Address
Holiday Inn Downtown/Superdome	★★★	2	330 Loyola Avenue New Orleans, LA 70112
Holiday Inn French Quarter	★★★	1	124 Royal Street New Orleans, LA 70130
Holiday Inn Metairie	★★½	10	3400 I-10 at Causeway Metairie, LA 70001
Holiday Inn New Orleans I-10	★★★	10	6401 Veteran's Memorial Blvd. Metairie, LA 70003
Holiday Inn New Orleans Westbank	★★½	11	100 Westbank Expressway Gretna, LA 70053
Holiday Inn Select	★★★½	2	881 Convention Center Blvd. New Orleans, LA 70130
Hotel de la Monnaie	★★★★	1	405 Esplanade Avenue New Orleans, LA 70116
Hotel de la Poste	★★★½	1	316 Chartres Street New Orleans, LA 70130
Hotel Inter-Continental New Orleans	★★★★	2	444 St. Charles Avenue New Orleans, LA 70130
Hotel St. Marie	★★★½	1	827 Toulouse Street New Orleans, LA 70112
Hotel St. Pierre	★★	1	911 Burgundy Street New Orleans, LA 70116
Hotel Ste. Helene	★★★★	1	508 Chartres Street New Orleans, LA 70130
Hotel Villa Convento	★★★	1	616 Ursulines Street New Orleans, LA 70116
Hyatt Regency New Orleans at Superdome	★★★½	2	Poydras Street & Loyola Avenue New Orleans, LA 70130
La Quinta Inn	★★★	10	2610 Williams Boulevard Kenner, LA 70062
La Quinta Inn	★★★	10	5900 Veteran's Memorial Blvd. Metairie, LA 70003
La Quinta Inn Bullard	★★★	8	12001 I-10 Service Road New Orleans, LA 70128
La Quinta Inn Causeway	★★★	9	3100 I-10 Service Road Metairie, LA 70001
La Quinta Inn Crowder Road	★★★	10	8400 I-10 Service Road New Orleans, LA 70127

Local Phone	Fax	Toll Free Reservations	Rack Rate	No. of Rooms	On-site Dining	Pool
(504) 581-1600	(504) 586-0833	(800) HOLIDAY	$$$ $$$+	300	Yes	Yes
(504) 529-7211	(504) 566-1127	(800) HOLIDAY	$$$$ $$$$+	252	Yes	Yes
(504) 833-8201	(504) 838-6829	(800) HOLIDAY	$$$$$–	194	Yes	Yes
(504) 885-5700	(504) 454-8294	(800) HOLIDAY	$$$$–	220	Yes	Yes
(504) 366-2361	(504) 362-5814	(800) HOLIDAY	$$$$$–	307	Yes	Yes
(504) 524-1881	(504) 528-1005	(800) HOLIDAY	$$$$ $$$–	170	Yes	No
(504) 947-0009	(504) 945-6841	NA	$$$$ $$$$–	53	No	Yes
(504) 581-1200	(504) 523-2910	(800) 448-4927	$$$$$ $$$$+	100	No	Yes
(504) 525-5566	(504) 523-7310	(800) 327-0200	$$$$$ $$$$–	481	No	Yes
(504) 561-8951	(504) 561-8951	(800) 366-2743	$$$$ $$$$	100	Yes	Yes
(504) 524-4401	(504) 524-6800	(800) 225-4040	$$$$ $$$$+	72	No	Yes
(504) 522-5014	(504) 523-7140	(800) 348-3388	$$$ $$$+	26	No	Yes
(504) 522-1793	(504) 524-1902	(800) 887-2817	$$$$$–	25	No	No
(504) 561-1234	(504) 523-0488	(800) 233-1234	$$$$ $$$	1184	Yes	Yes
(504) 466-1401	(504) 466-0319	(800) NUROOMS	$$$$	187	No	Yes
(504) 456-0003	(504) 885-0863	(800) NUROOMS	$$$$$–	153	No	Yes
(504) 246-3003	(504) 242-5539	(800) NUROOMS	$$$$	130	Yes	Yes
(504) 835-8511	(504) 837-3383	(800) NUROOMS	$$$$$–	101	No	Yes
(504) 246-5800	(504) 242-5091	(800) NUROOMS	$$$$+	105	No	Yes

Hotel	Room Star Rating	Zone	Street Address
La Quinta Inn Westbank	★★½	11	50 Terry Parkway Gretna, LA 70056
Lafayette Hotel	★★★½	2	600 St. Charles Avenue New Orleans, LA 70130
Lafitte Guest House	★★★½	1	1003 Bourbon Street New Orleans, LA 70116
Lamothe House	★★★	1	621 Esplanade Avenue New Orleans, LA 70116
Landmark French Quarter	★★½	1	920 N. Rampart Street New Orleans, LA 70116
Lasalle Hotel	★★	5	1113 Canal Street New Orleans, LA 70112
Le Pavillion Hotel	★★★★	2	833 Poydras Street New Orleans, LA 70140
Le Richelieu in the French Quarter	★★★	1	1234 Chartres Street New Orleans, LA 70116
Maison De Ville	★★★½	1	727 Toulouse Street New Orleans, LA 70130
Maison Dupuy Hotel	★★★★½	1	1001 Toulouse Street New Orleans, LA 70112
Marriott New Orleans	★★★½	1	555 Canal Street New Orleans, LA 70140
The McKendrick-Breaux House	★★★★	3	1474 Magazine Street New Orleans, LA 70130
Meridien Hotel New Orleans	★★★½	1	614 Canal Street New Orleans, LA 70130
The Monteleone	★★★½	1	214 Royal Street New Orleans, LA 70140
New Orleans Guest House	★★★	5	1118 Ursulines Street New Orleans, LA 70116
Olivier House Hotel	★★★	1	828 Toulouse Street New Orleans, LA 70112
Omni Royal Crescent	★★★★½	2	535 Gravier Street New Orleans, LA 70130
Omni Royal Orleans Hotel	★★★★	1	621 St. Louis Street New Orleans, LA 70140
Orleans Courtyard Inn	★★½	10	3800 Hessmer Avenue Metairie, LA 70002

Local Phone	Fax	Toll Free Reservations	Rack Rate	No. of Rooms	On-site Dining	Pool
(504) 368-5600	(504) 362-7430	(800) NUROOMS	$$$$$–	154	No	Yes
(504) 524-4441	(504) 523-7327	(800) 733-4754	$$$$ $$$$–	44	Yes	No
(504) 581-2678	(504) 581-2678	(800) 331-7971	$$$$ $$$$–	14	No	No
(504) 947-1161	(504) 943-6536	(800) 367-5858	$$$$ $$$$–	20	No	No
(504) 524-3333	(504) 522-8044	(800) 535-7862	$$$$ $$$–	100	Yes	No
(504) 523-5831	(504) 525-2531	(800) 521-9450	$$$+	60	No	No
(504) 581-3111	(504) 523-7434	(800) 535-9095	$$$$ $$$$–	222	No	Yes
(504) 529-2492	(504) 524-8179	(800) 535-9653	$$$$ $$$–	88	Yes	Yes
(504) 561-5858	(504) 528-9939	(800) 634-1600	$$$$$ $$$$	23	Yes	No
(504) 586-8000	(504) 525-5334	(800) 535-9177	$$$$$ $$$$$–	198	Yes	Yes
(504) 581-1000	(504) 523-6755	(800) 228-9290	$$$$ $$$$–	1290	Yes	Yes
(504) 586-1700	(504) 522-7138	(888) 570-1700	$$$$$–	8	No	No
(504) 525-6500	(504) 525-8068	(800) 543-4300	$$$$$ $$$$+	494	Yes	Yes
(504) 523-3341	(504) 528-1019	(800) 535-9595	$$$$$ $$$$–	600	No	Yes
(504) 566-1177	NA	(800) 562-1177	$$$$$+	14	No	No
(504) 525-8456	(504) 529-2006	NA	$$$$ $$$–	40	No	Yes
(504) 527-0006	(504) 523-0806	(800) 843-6664	$$$$ $$$$–	98	Yes	No
(504) 529-5333	(504) 529-7089	(800) 843-6664	$$$$$ $$$$+	346	Yes	Yes
(504) 455-6110	(504) 455-0940	(800) 258-2514	$$$+	52	No	Yes

Hotel	Room Star Rating	Zone	Street Address
Pallas Hotel	★★½	6	1732 Canal Street New Orleans, LA 70112
Park Plaza Inn	★★	10	2125 Veteran's Memorial Blvd. Kenner, LA 70062
The Pelham Hotel	★★★½	2	444 Common Street New Orleans, LA 70116
Place D'Armes Hotel	★★★	1	625 St. Ann Street New Orleans, LA 70116
Ponchartrain Hotel	★★★★	3	2031 St. Charles Avenue New Orleans, LA 70140
Prince Conti Hotel	★★★½	1	830 Conti Street New Orleans, LA 70112
Provincial Hotel	★★★½	1	1024 Chartres Street New Orleans, LA 70116
Prytania Park Hotel	★★★	3	1525 Prytania Street New Orleans, LA 70130
Quality Hotel and Conference Center	★★½	9	2261 North Causeway Metairie, LA 70001
Quality Inn Maison Hotel	★★★	3	1319 St. Charles Avenue New Orleans, LA 70130
Quality Inn Midtown	★★½	6	3900 Tulane Avenue New Orleans, LA 70119
Quality Inn Westbank Harvey	★★½	11	3750 Westbank Expressway Harvey, LA 70058
Queen and Crescent Hotel	★★★½	2	344 Camp Street New Orleans, LA 70130
Radisson Hotel New Orleans	★★★	5	1500 Canal Street New Orleans, LA 70112
Radisson Inn Airport	★★½	10	2150 Veteran's Memorial Blvd. Kenner, LA 70062
Ramada Inn Highrise	★★½	8	6324 Chef Menteur Highway New Orleans, LA 70126
Ramada Limited Causeway	★★½	9	2713 North Causeway Blvd. Metairie, LA 70002
Ramada Plaza Hotel	★★★	3	2203 St. Charles Avenue New Orleans, LA 70140
Rathbone Inn	★★★½	5	1227 Esplanade Avenue New Orleans, LA 70116

Local Phone	Fax	Toll Free Reservations	Rack Rate	No. of Rooms	On-site Dining	Pool
(504) 558-0201	(504) 529-1609	NA	$$$$$	1036	No	No
(504) 464-6464	(504) 464-7532	(800) 504-7275	$$$+	128	No	Yes
(504) 522-4444	(504) 558-0580	(800) 659-5621	$$$$ $$$–	60	No	No
(504) 524-4531	(504) 524-4531	(800) 366-2743	$$$$ $$$$–	80	No	Yes
(504) 524-0581	(504) 524-7828	(800) 777-6193	$$$$ $$$$–	104	No	No
(504) 529-4172	(504) 581-3802	(800) 366-2743	$$$$ $$$–	50	Yes	No
(504) 581-4995	(504) 581-1018	(800) 535-7922	$$$$ $$$	100	Yes	Yes
(504) 524-0427	(504) 522-2977	(800) 862-1984	$$$$ $$$+	62	No	No
(504) 833-8211	(504) 833-8213	(800) 228-5151	$$$+	204	Yes	Yes
(504) 522-0187	(504) 525-2218	(800) 831-1783	$$+	130	No	Yes
(504) 486-5541	(504) 488-7440	(800) 827-5542	$$$$$+	105	No	Yes
(504) 348-1262	(504) 348-0624	(800) 221-2222	$$$$–	106	No	Yes
(504) 587-9700	(504) 587-9701	(800) 975-6652	$$$ $$$+	129	No	No
(504) 522-4500	(504) 525-2644	(800) 777-7800	$$$ $$$+	759	Yes	Yes
(504) 467-3111	(504) 469-4634	(800) 333-3333	$$$$	244	Yes	Yes
(504) 241-2900	(504) 241-5697	(800) 228-2828	$$$$–	204	Yes	Yes
(504) 835-4141	(504) 833-6942	(800) 228-3838	$$$$+	128	No	Yes
(504) 566-1200	(504) 581-1352	(800) 443-4675	$$$ $$$–	132	Yes	No
(504) 947-2100	(504) 947-7454	(800) 947-2101	$$$$ $$$$–	15	No	No

Hotel	Room Star Rating	Zone	Street Address
Rodeway Inn Airport	★★½	10	851 Airline Highway Kenner, LA 70062
Rodeway Inn Downtown	★★	6	1725 Tulane Avenue New Orleans, LA 70112
Royal Sonesta Hotel	★★★★½	1	300 Bourbon Street New Orleans, LA 70140
Rue Royal Inn	★★½	1	1006 Royal Street New Orleans, LA 70116
Saint Ann/Marie Antionette	★★★	1	717 Conti Street New Orleans, LA 70130
The Saint Louis	★★★	1	730 Bienville Street New Orleans, LA 70130
Sheraton New Orleans Hotel	★★★½	1	500 Canal Street New Orleans, LA 70130
Shoney's Inn	★★½	10	2421 Clearview Parkway Metairie, LA 70001
The Soniat House	★★★½	1	1133 Chartres Street New Orleans, LA 70116
St. Charles Inn	★★½	3	3636 St. Charles Avenue New Orleans, LA 70115
St. Peter Guest House	★★★	1	1005 St. Peter Street New Orleans, LA 70116
Super 8 New Orleans	★★½	8	6322 Chef Menteur Highway New Orleans, LA 70126
Travelodge	★★	10	5733 Airline Highway Metairie, LA 70003
Travelodge Hotel New Orleans	★★½	11	2200 Westbank Expressway Harvey, LA 70058
Travelodge New Orleans Airport Hotel	★★	10	2240 Veteran's Memorial Blvd. Kenner, LA 70062
The Westin Canal Place	★★★★½	1	100 Iberville Street New Orleans, LA 70130
Windsor Court	★★★★½	2	300 Gravier Street New Orleans, LA 70130
Wyndham Riverfront Hotel	★★★★	2	701 Convention Center Blvd. New Orleans, LA 70130

Local Phone	Fax	Toll Free Reservations	Rack Rate	No. of Rooms	On-site Dining	Pool
(504) 467-1391	(504) 466-9148	(800) 228-2000	$$$–	98	No	Yes
(504) 529-5411	(504) 524-1059	(800) 228-2000	$$$$$–	147	No	Yes
(504) 586-0300	(504) 586-0335	(800) SONESTA	$$$$$ $$$$+	500	Yes	Yes
(504) 524-3900	(504) 588-0566	(800) 776-3901	$$$ $$$+	17	No	No
(504) 525-2300	(504) 524-7825	(800) 535-9111	$$$$ $$$$–	65	Yes	Yes
(504) 581-7300	(504) 524-8925	(800) 535-9111	$$$$ $$$$+	71	Yes	No
(504) 525-2500	(504) 595-5550	(800) 325-3535	$$$$ $$$$+	1127	Yes	Yes
(504) 456-9081	(504) 455-6287	(800) 222-2222	$$$$+	145	Yes	Yes
(504) 522-0570	(504) 522-7208	(800) 544-8808	$$$$ $$$$+	24	No	No
(504) 899-8888	(504) 899-8892	(800) 489-9908	$$$$–	40	Yes	No
(504) 524-9232	(504) 523-5198	(800) 535-7815	$$$ $$$	23	No	No
(504) 241-5650	(504) 241-2178	(800) 800-8000	$$$$$–	96	No	Yes
(504) 733-1550	(504) 734-1554	(800) 578-7878	$$$–	80	No	Yes
(504) 366-5311	(504) 368-2774	(800) 578-7878	$$$$+	212	Yes	Yes
(504) 469-7341	(504) 469-7922	(800) 578-7878	$$$+	196	Yes	Yes
(504) 566-7006	(504) 553-5120	(800) 228-3000	$$$$$ $$$$–	438	Yes	Yes
(504) 523-6000	(504) 596-4513	(800) 262-2662	$$$$$$ $$$$$–	324	Yes	Yes
(504) 524-8200	(504) 681-1018	(800) WYNDHAM	$$$$ $$$+	202	Yes	No

INDEX

1998 *Unofficial Guide* Reader Survey

If you would like to express your opinion about New Orleans or this guidebook, complete the following survey and mail it to:

> 1998 *Unofficial Guide* Reader Survey
> PO Box 43059
> Birmingham AL 35243

Inclusive dates of your visit: _____

*Members of
your party:*   Person 1   Person 2   Person 3   Person 4   Person 5

Gender: M F   M F   M F   M F   M F

Age: _____

How many times have you been to New Orleans? _____

On your most recent trip, where did you stay? _____

Concerning your accommodations, on a scale of 100 as best and 0 as worst, how would you rate:

The quality of your room? _____   The value of your room? ____

The quietness of your room? _____   Check-in/check-out efficiency? ____

Shuttle service to the parks? _____ Swimming pool facilities? _____

Did you rent a car? _____ From whom? _____

Concerning your rental car, on a scale of 100 as best and 0 as worst, how would you rate:

Pick-up processing efficiency? ____ Return processing efficiency? ____

Condition of the car? ____   Cleanliness of the car? ____

Airport shuttle efficiency? ____

Concerning your dining experiences:

Including fast-food, estimate your meals in restaurants per day? _____

Approximately how much did your party spend on meals per day? _____

Favorite restaurants in New Orleans: _____

_____

Did you buy this guide before leaving? ☐ while on your trip? ☐

How did you hear about this guide? (check all that apply)

Loaned or recommended by a friend ☐ Radio or TV ☐

Newspaper or magazine ☐   Bookstore salesperson ☐

Just picked it out on my own ☐   Library ☐

Internet ☐

What other guidebooks did you use on this trip? _____

_____

_____

_____

On a scale of 100 as best and 0 as worst, how would you rate them?

_____

_____

_____

Using the same scale, how would you rate *The Unofficial Guide(s)?*

_____

Are *Unofficial Guides* readily available at bookstores in your area? _____

Have you used other *Unofficial Guides?* _____

Which one(s)? _____

_____

_____

_____

_____

Comments about your New Orleans trip or *The Unofficial Guide(s):*

_____

_____

_____

_____

_____

_____

_____

_____

_____

_____

_____

_____

_____

_____